The Ocean of God

The Ocean of God
On the Transreligious Future of Religions

Roland Faber

ANTHEM PRESS

Anthem Press
An imprint of Wimbledon Publishing Company
www.anthempress.com

This edition first published in UK and USA 2020
by ANTHEM PRESS
75–76 Blackfriars Road, London SE1 8HA, UK
or PO Box 9779, London SW19 7ZG, UK
and
244 Madison Ave #116, New York, NY 10016, USA

First published in the UK and USA by Anthem Press 2019

Copyright © Roland Faber 2020

The author asserts the moral right to be identified as the author of this work.

All rights reserved. Without limiting the rights under copyright reserved above,
no part of this publication may be reproduced, stored or introduced into
a retrieval system, or transmitted, in any form or by any means
(electronic, mechanical, photocopying, recording or otherwise),
without the prior written permission of both the copyright
owner and the above publisher of this book.

British Library Cataloguing-in-Publication Data
A catalogue record for this book is available from the British Library.

Library of Congress Control Number: 2020944560

ISBN-13: 978-1-78527-573-9 (Pbk)
ISBN-10: 1-78527-573-9 (Pbk)

This title is also available as an e-book.

And so does the spirit become separated from

The greater spirit to move in the world of matter

And pass as a cloud over the mountain of sorrow

And the plains of joy to meet the breeze of death

And return whence it come.

To the ocean of Love and Beauty [...] and God.
—Khalil Gibran, *A Tear and a Smile*

CONTENTS

Introduction — 1

Part I   Paradigms of Unity and Plurality

Chapter One — Unity or Plurality of Religions? — 13

Chapter Two — The Healing and Poisonous Fruits of the Unity of Religions — 21

Chapter Three — The Synthesis and Aporia of Religious Pluralism — 29

Chapter Four — The Promise of Mysticism — 43

Chapter Five — Polyphilic Pluralism — 53

Part II   Negotiations of Multiplicity

Chapter Six — Convergences and Divergences: Juncture or Bifurcation? — 69

Chapter Seven — Pluralism of Pluralisms? — 81

Chapter Eight — Horizontal and Vertical Pluralism — 93

Chapter Nine — An Experiment in Incompatibilities: Green Acre — 103

Chapter Ten — The Mystery of Distinction and Unity — 111

Part III   Transreligious Horizons

Chapter Eleven — The Transreligious Discourse — 125

Chapter Twelve — Other Religions: From Coinherence to Coinhabitation — 137

Chapter Thirteen — The Earth and Other Worlds: A Story of Cosmic Magnitude — 153

| Chapter Fourteen | The Future of Religions | 169 |
| Chapter Fifteen | One with All Religions | 189 |

Glossary — 201

References — 217

Index — 245

INTRODUCTION

Would ye hasten towards a mere pond, whilst the Most Great Ocean is stretched out before your eyes?[1]
—Bahá'u'lláh

To ask, in the current global context, the question whether and how religions could relate peacefully to one another and to humanity as a whole and, even more, by spiritually enriching our common humanity, is inevitable, but not new. What is new in the current situation is the fact that without the ability to answer this question (or rather the complex of related questions) in an amicable way, the world is in danger of undergoing a regression into states of warfare that, if not initiated or at least fueled by religious fanaticism and strife, mutual condemnation and collective aggression, might bring the seed of its antagonistic instinct to ultimate fruition, in its outcome indistinguishable from ecological death, atomic destruction or any other extinction-level event—at least for humanity.[2] Yet the motivation for asking questions of religious (and nonreligious) mutuality in a sympathetic and constructive, and neither only tolerant or merely critical, nor solely academic or cunningly apologetic, way is deeper than dispelling fear. It is about the very nature and essence of human existence, the identity of humanity as a whole on this planet Earth and in a potentially infinite cosmos. It is about the meaning of human existence and its very destiny.

As the quests of religions are ultimately about the human appearance in the world and its ultimate meaning as well as the meaning of existence as such, we need not wonder

---

1. Bahá'u'lláh, *Days*, #43:5.
2. Even if we don't view war as an inevitable state of the human nature, to which I am willing to concur with in this book, the transformation of warfare from material-based conflicts to information-based destruction (the viruses of the future), information-based economy and social and political processes, although they cannot be conquered like gold mines or land for some ideological or other reasons, is based on ideologies that are themselves proliferative of information-production and -conflict (fake facts) not mitigating warfare, as Yuval Harari (ch. 1) rightly reasons. The real calming force against the wars of the future is not the information-based or science-based society, but the mind that creates, holds and distributes information colored by the (religious) ideologies and powerful myths that drive its movements, only to be overruled by the disappearance of the human mind itself. If mind is not driving, but is based on, algorithms, however, as Harari seems to suggest, the ongoing transformation of collective imaginations into powerful artificial intelligence-based algorithms will be the myth that erases mind and humanity altogether. Alternatively, if mind persists, extinction can only be avoided if these imaginations of myths and ideologies, which in their most powerful forms *are* "religions" in Harari's view (ch. 5), find ways to transform themselves into modes of mutuality, of understanding and of a "peace of mind," which is the transreligious quest explored in this book.

that the motley picture that the religious history of humanity displays is bewildering, to say the least. But our global perspective today (and maybe so already for a long time) has made it even more unavoidable to ask how the claim of religious existence to convey universal meaning *and* the obvious inability to embody such a meaning for the whole of humanity (by any of such claims) can be thought together without immediately obliterating either side: that either the messy plurality of religions is not only a sign, but rather a proof of their ultimate meaninglessness (and, hence, the falsity of their claim to meaning altogether), *or* that no such meaning, at least not in anything less than a common human consciousness, has arisen yet but only remains a faint hope.

Two concepts and ways of thinking have countered the potential simplifications of this paradox, seeking a way out of the aporia that lingers in its intricacies: the healing prescription of religious pluralism, on the one hand, and that of the unity of religions, on the other. Both, of course, overlap, and it is in no way already clear that they are different or identical, compatible or incompatible. Both approaches reflect on unity and diversity of religions in sophisticated ways and in the awareness of the necessity to clear the planes of mutual encounters from unreflected presuppositions that, as history abundantly demonstrates, often incline us toward clashes, distrust and feelings of danger. Instead, their discourses want to instill mutual trust while not excluding questions of truth, meaning and the humanization of humanity—viewed in light of a common future of humanity that would not be perpetuating the pitfalls of mutual exclusions of the religious (and nonreligious) other from such a future. What is more, these concepts and agendas want to create spaces of shared meaning, which eventually would appear as an (as of yet hidden) implication of the healing truth of religions themselves.

Such attempts to think and practice a new kind of relationality between religions (and beyond, with humanity as a whole) are not uncontested by both nonreligious and religious worldviews, some of which work with great energy against such harmonizations, but in the name of the good of the future of humanity.[3] Yet it is in the face of the conflicts that have given rise to such contestation, in the first place, that such new ways of discussing religious multiplicity and unity situate themselves differently and in new ways within these dynamics of refusal, retreat or abandonment of religiosity (or even spiritual reality itself) so as to become means for a creative transformation.

The following considerations will also take into account that approaches to religious pluralism and the potential or actual (even if not yet recognized) unity of religions cannot

---

3. Cf. Faber, *Garden*, 1–12. Many of the religious, nonreligious and anti-religious movements in the history of humanity we can still recall have as a common denominator the seeming impossibility of mutuality of religious diversity, instead seeking renewal, renovation or revolution either in the direction of particularity (admitting the failure of the experiment of relativity and relationality of diversity) or of universality (admitting the failure of particularity itself), without, however, ever having been able to create alternative patterns of thought and living that would yield a better outcome for humanity. In this sense, in this giving up on mutuality and relativity, I see a deep communality between conservative apocalyptic reiterations, transcending Enlightenment rationality and diffusing materialistic contestations of the humanity that has given rise to the phenomenon of religion.

escape that which the famous Anglo-American polymath, mathematician and philosopher Alfred North Whitehead has so aptly called "the fallacy of misplaced concreteness."[4] Indeed, if such ideas and discourses only happen in an abstract space beyond concrete life-forms of religious diversity from which these approaches inherit their questions (even if they can be reflected from a philosophical plane that is not identical, but always interfering with religious particularities),[5] they have lost their primary field of meaning for, and relevance to, religious particularity. In order to escape such generalizations, aloof over the religious landscape they engage, I will situate the discussions of this book within concrete philosophical and religious perspectives, yet not by excluding their own interaction with one another and other such regional enterprises.

For two related reasons I have chosen a process approach based on the philosophy of A. N. Whitehead and the religious and intellectual universe of the Bahá'í religion,[6] in conjunction with that of the "Big Five" (Hinduism, Buddhism, Judaism, Christianity and Islam) in which the discussions often have taken recess (with now growing, but still sparse expansions, for instance, by Zoroastrianism, Sikhism or Jainism).[7] First, both the philosophical and the religious example are minority voices that, if pluralism is correct, must be heard in their unique potential to contribute to the field in order to avoid the discursive closure of generalized philosophical and religious sweeps. Second, both universes of discourse have, in their own way, but not unrelated in their heritage, uniquely and substantially contributed to the character of, and alternatives to, the current understanding of religious pluralism and the unity of religions. Whitehead's philosophy, from its inception, generated a multiplicity of pluralistic approaches, reaching from engagements with both kindred and seemingly foreign philosophical patterns, from the ancient process tradition in the wake of Heraclitus to poststructuralism, and to long-standing interreligious dialogues.[8] It has proven itself to be a contact theory that can bridge religious identities, as it has generated arguments for religious pluralism and related questions from the perspective of, and embedded in, a diversity of religious and intellectual traditions. The Bahá'í religion, again, can claim to be one of the newer religious expressions that is unique in the sense that it does not only assert the truth of virtually all religions, but also

---

4. Whitehead, *Science*, 51.
5. Cf. Smart, *World Philosophies*.
6. I am not claiming to speak "for" either of these movements or their diverse organizations. For process thought, I rest on what I have developed over a 20-year period. Regarding Bahá'í thought, I rely only on my own understanding, my reading of Bahá'í writings, scholarly and spiritual elaborations, and many conversations, but without advancing any institutional claim.
7. Regarding the important paradigm on which this classification is based, namely, that of "world religions" and a deconstruction of the arbitrariness of this term that only appeared in the 1870s with the work of Cornelius Petrus Tiele, cf. J. Z. Smith, *Relating Religion*, ch. 7 ("A Matter of Class: Taxonomies of Religions"). It should also, at this point and for all of the following conversations, not be forgotten that none of these named traditions are in any way monolithic in themselves either; rather, they are always only multiplicities simplified as, for instance, "Christianity," "Judaism" or "Buddhism."
8. Cf. Faber, *Poet*, part 1; *Becoming of God*; Griffin, ed., *Pluralism*; McDaniel, *Hope*; Cobb, *Beyond Dialogue*; Lai and von Brück, 227–34.

utters the conviction that this unity of religions is the very reason for its own existence and the center of its mission.⁹

Yet the use of both of these discursive horizons of process thought and the Bahá'í universe for discussing the transreligious implications of the concepts of religious pluralism and the unity of religions, their interaction and impact on the propensities of future manifestations of religiosity is not only meant to inculcate the necessity of concretization and the inevitability of finding and committing to perspective for any realistic accounts of the usefulness of the conceptual realms of unity and multiplicity for the future of religion. Rather, as both of them indicate *sites* of an architecture in and of becoming, these sites also mandate their importance as spheres of mediation of this process. What they mediate will be the content of the corpus of the text of this book. But how these traditions are introduced, namely, as catalyzers of transformation for an ongoing discussion, will, on the one hand, instill the inevitable impulse only released by acknowledging the knowledges harbored by minority voices and, on the other hand, make their insights available as examples of a vaster and more universal movement for which they can stand as new or complementary means to its deeper understanding.¹⁰

Another consideration should, from the outset, clarify the sustained use of the term "religion" in a broad and porous fashion despite the criticism that it has received in more recent scholarship.¹¹ Not only can this concept still convey the coherence of the long-standing academic field of the history of religions and immediately relate to disciplines such as religious studies and philosophy of religion, but it is also by no means so simple that its more recently received criticism can easily evoke other terms, such as faith, belief-system, confession, denomination, spirituality, tradition, rite, cult, wisdoms and many others, with which to exchange it. It strikes me as overly limited to understand "religion" (in postcolonial critiques) as a Eurocentric construction of colonial origin and flavor since it was readily used long before the modern western colonial codification of thought, of which even the field of *Religionswissenschaft* is sometimes seen as only its latest expression.¹² And this assumption again is, in itself, also overstated, because its intention to upset the colonial endeavors of Christianity (as fueling already older western philosophical Enlightenment discourses) has, with the rise of comparative religion as a field, either misjudged its attempt to counter this colonialism or neutralized it under a generalized

---

9. Cf. Stockman, *Bahá'í Faith: A Guide for the Perplexed*, part 1.
10. There are two related ways (both of which I will use) to understand such a revealing novelty of "sites of mediation" of the vision of a different future of religiosity, such as process and Bahá'í thought envisioning multireligious diversity, unity and peace (and as a critical instrument against their contestation), namely, that of Whitehead by means of *creative novelty* (which I will employ throughout the text), and that of Derrida by means of *supplementation*, that is, by the ongoing recovery of suppressed minority voices in the performative resistance of closure in the very act of closure (which will be emerging as an implication of the former strategy).
11. Cf. Masuzawa; Fitzgerald, 1–16; Geaves, 75–90; S. Owen, 253–68.
12. Cf. Nongbri. Contrarily, other cultures, even under political pressure from the outside and the inside, such as the Japanese, have invented "religion" independently; cf. Josephson, *Invention*. One may also contact the criticism of such postcolonialist generalizations as late-modern remnant of orientalism; cf. Eck, "India," 45–48.

transgressing phenomena of "new (inter-)spiritualities" (commonly referred to as akin to, or essentially being an expression of, the New Age) that the category of "religion" has gained new currency as transformed and transformative category for the recognition of a new interlinked spiritual milieu that cannot be reduced to the simplifications and reductionisms implied in stabilized (and stabilizing discourse on) "world religions,"[27] yet can, at the same time, harbor the resistance to such limitations.[28]

It is in this broad and porous sense, but being aware of its complex and problematic nature,[29] that the term "religion(s)" will in the coming considerations express the multiplicity and unity of religions, and will transfer them into a "transreligious" horizon. Maybe it is precisely with the possibility to coherently understand the concept of "religions" as a multiplicity[30] (beyond its reiterated forms and practices, as well its political use) that not only the imperative of current initiatives to use our energy for creating peace within and between religions is made effective, but also that newer transreligious discourses and models can be recognized.

What transreligious discourse is will be essential to the progression of this book. It may suffice, here, to identify its dynamic as a movement and flow (always both) within and between, into and beyond, religions that is not only justified by the myriads of factual creative receptions, borrowings, reformulations, reformations, recalibrations, imitations, repetitions and so on, of conceptualizations, doctrines, teachings, lifestyles, behavioral patterns, rituals, ideas, cultural expressions and social models of different cultures and religious traditions in and between them, which is evident from the slightest glance at the history of religions.[31] Moreover, in the current context, "transreligious" means a prescriptive category of analysis, comparison, transformation and synthesis that restates the very intellectual basis for the claims of religious pluralism and the unity of religions.[32] And, importantly, this discourse views these multireligious flows as expressions of truth

---

27. Theorists of sociology and history of religion have variously referred to the unifying character of the New Age in a diversified "cultic milieu" in which new spiritualities gained the consciousness of some kind of contiguity, if not similarity and mutual resonance with one another, or even continuity with older forms of religion, reconnecting themselves with their diversity, or reclaiming their depth with their history. Cf. Hanegraaff, 12–18.
28. Cf. Sutcliffe and Gilhus, 260–61. In constructive recovery of relevant remarks of Emile Durkheim, Sutcliffe argues against the limitation of the category of "religion" to the world religions model and in favor of widening the definition or field of evidence, observation and experience to *all* phenomena of religion, inside or outside of established categories of religion or world religion, as they represent certain structural limitations and power dynamics that should not distract from the inherent fluent character of religious phenomena, even and especially beyond (but always also within) more defined or ordered religions with their (hierarchical) identity models. This (non-essentialist) model of approaching "religion" can also be seen as contributing to the category of the "transreligious" explored in later chapters of this book.
29. Cf. J. Z. Smith, *Relating Religion*, ch. 8 ("Religion, Religions, Religious").
30. The concept of "multiplicity," as it will later be introduced in this study, does neither indicate a mere plurality nor a counter-category to unity, but rather a field of mutual immanence or foldings, in the sense of Gilles Deleuze; cf. Faber, *Manifold*, ch. 8.
31. Cf. J. Z. Smith, *Relating Religion*, 11–22.
32. See more in Chapter 11.

and ultimate reality itself in its and our co-effort to gain a shared awareness in which the peace of, within and between religious traditions and identities can become a sign for the spiritual maturity of humanity. This transreligious discourse evokes or anticipates a coming universal consciousness in which differences need not trigger antagonisms anymore, but in which diversity can be perceived as a profound expression of the beauty of existence itself.[33] In other words and in stronger terms: It is the thesis of this book that the future of religion(s) will be transreligious, or there will be no future of humanity with religion, or of humanity as such.[34]

The title *The Ocean of God* evokes this transreligious "essence" of religions and indicates their future with an image that has its own long-standing history throughout diverse religions.[35] It appears in mystical discourses as far apart in space and time as John of Damascus's sea of divine essence and Ramakrishna's ocean of immortal consciousness (*satchitananda*). In the first sense it hints at the transcendence of divine Reality beyond any and all categories of limitation; in the second sense it arouses the feeling of the immersion in Reality. While all of existence resides in it, innumerable paths are meant for reaching its shores. Many scriptural writings of the world's religions indulge in the potency of this image; and so do the Bahá'í writings.[36] In countless variations, the unbounded ocean vibrates as that of God's love, grace, mercy, lights and words, always celebrating the overflowing unity and multiplicity of the Mystery. The ocean is vast and spacious. It is always fascinating and attracting, but also unknown and unknowable, unpredictable and dangerous. In it can appear the signs of Leviathan—that of biblical creative chaos, but also of fierce love that, in Bahá'u'lláh's rendering, "swallows the master of reason and destroyeth the lord of knowledge."[37] It poetically pictures the desire for ultimate unification, but it can be forbidding. One may reach its shores, but

---

33. Cf. Faber, *Manifold*, ch. 5; *Freiheit*, ch. 5.
34. This thesis of *The Ocean of God* is, hereby, connected with, but also different from, that of the *Garden of Reality*, insofar as in the *Garden* the thesis unfolds around the relativity of religious truth, while in the *Ocean* it is about the transreligious multiplicity of religiosity. The latter one claims the future of religion(s)—if this future can be underwood as one of religious peace—as a transreligious one; the former one claims the relativity of the truths of religions as the condition for their particular truths to be true; cf. Faber, *Garden*, 1. In both cases, the positive thesis is related to an exclusionary term, namely, that without the unfolding of the pluralistic-relativistic element either will *religion* not necessarily be surviving, as humanity will not be in need of it anymore because of its "inhumanity," or *humanity* will not be around anymore to know the difference, as it might have used this "inhumanity" to facilitate its own disappearance.
35. I have used the metaphor of the "Divine Ocean" before—as a title in the German form of *Gottesmeer*—to indicate the relationship of mystical traditions, poststructuralist and process thought, based on their own language and conceptualization indicating the related implications to be explored in the course of this book; cf. Faber, "Gottesmeer," 64–95; *Manifold*, ch. 12.
36. The image of the "ocean" is too manifold to function as an analytic category, here, and warrants its own study in general (in religious contexts) as well as in the Bahá'í writings. Hence, it will mostly be used as leitmotif. From the wealth of the usage of oceanic metaphoric in the Bahá'í writings, I have selected few thematically related images, heading and enveloping, as it were, each chapter with their imaginative force.
37. Bahá'u'lláh, "The Valley of Love (of the Seven Valleys)," in *Seven Valleys*, 10.

also drown in its depth. We can embark on a journey of radical openness, encompassed only by an infinite horizon, but it cannot be sailed on without preparation. We may be drops of its substance or waves of its movements, but when we drink it, we will die. As divine revelation rains down from the divine clouds, religions may be the rivers seeking consummation in this ocean's confluence only to become transformed again into pregnant clouds.

The coming fifteen chapters display the following progression. Part I, "Paradigms of Unity and Plurality," comprising the first five chapters, will explore different approaches to religious pluralism and to the unity of religions on their own terms, and in view of the process and Bahá'í contributions to matters involving not only descriptive, but prescriptive unity and diversity. The next five chapters, that is, Part II, "Negotiations of Multiplicity," will address the deeper problems awaiting a satisfying coordination of prescriptive unity and plurality of religions with special reference to the inner complications of the Bahá'í position in this regard, potential solutions as to its own inner clarification and the possible interreligious contribution it may inspire. Part III, "Transreligious Horizons," with the last five chapters, will widen the field from conversations around unity and plurality, religious pluralism and unity of religions, to the transreligious discourse in which these differentiations will become less positional, as if they ever have meant self-identical substances, but more porous with regard to a different understanding of religious identity and plurality, carried forward by the already implied and applied event-paradigm of process thought. In widening the horizon beyond religions proper to transreligious spiritual processes in light of the ecological wholeness of the Earth as well as in the cosmic context, the final propositions will issue into restating the agendas of religious pluralism and the unity of religions in light of prospects of possible futures of religions, if they become infused by such transreligious movements, and by taking up the question in what sense the Bahá'í principles of unity and the process principle of becoming-multiplicity[38] may contribute to this future in constructive ways.

It goes without saying that no such engagement with the future of religions will be final, or even so satisfactory that it will not generate new and different directions of thought, or new attacks on the validity of the general discourse on religious pluralism and the unity of religions, or to the here presented transreligious perspectives. The former alternative is appreciated, the latter, however, not feared. Nevertheless, it is hoped that the islands, archipelagoes, lagoons and reefs in the wide, sometime brackish sea of the mystery that religions populate will not become diminished by this present attempt to set sail between them. Following Whitehead's theopoetic insights that every "event on its finer side introduces God into the world"[39] and that every "act leaves the world with a deeper or fainter impress of God,"[40] at least, this book has tried not to leave the world a lesser place.

---

38. Cf. Faber, *Manifold*, Introduction.
39. Whitehead, *Religion*, 155–56.
40. Whitehead, *Religion*, 159.

Part I
PARADIGMS OF UNITY AND PLURALITY

Chapter One

UNITY OR PLURALITY OF RELIGIONS?

The river Jordan is joined to the Most Great Ocean.[1]

—Bahá'u'lláh

Religious plurality is a fact of our world, and has been as long as we can access historical records.[2] Yet neither the fact itself must be taken for granted—we can always ask, why?—nor the potentially underlying assumption that this plurality was the same or of the same kind at any given time in human evolution.[3] It is, however, not necessarily this plurality itself that is problematic—whether it should be affirmed, theoretically or practically, or in any kind of reflections from within or without the diverse religions in their mutual encounter[4]—but the heritage it has left for our common world today and the impact it has had on human existence and evolution in the past. Religious plurality, whenever it comes into focus, and although it also has had its surprising moments of mutual appreciation (but only moments, short phases, blips in the grand scheme), seems much more thoroughly to impress on us images and feelings of a cauldron of dissention, disagreement, violence and mutual destruction.[5] And we cannot exempt our own time. Proponents of humanization—being, well, a process of hominization (a differentiation of Teilhard de Chardin)[6]—always knew about the necessity to overcome these conundrums of plurality and violence in human evolution of mind and consciousness (and the related emergence of human conscience)—if we want to understand it as a process of spiritualization.[7] Yet that, even after the bloody religious wars of past centuries (in

---

1. Bahá'u'lláh, "Lawh-i Aqdas (The Most Holy Tablet)," in *Tablets of Bahá'u'lláh*, 11.
2. Anthony F. C. Wallace estimated in 1966 that the Earth has seen about 100,000 religions; cf. Novak, 333.
3. Cf. Smart, *Religions*, ch. 1.
4. Cf. James. Prehistoric religions, local divinities and religious rites in Near-Eastern religions and Egypt, for instance, were much more fluent, flowing one into the other, one later classical so-called world religions; cf. Assmann, *Price*, ch. 2. Yet the old shamanistic universalism, present around the world, like the "cosmotheism" of later Egyptian-Greek-Roman character, had also harbored an implicit monotheistic, but tolerant and inclusive transreligious tendency; cf. Sharma, *Primal Perspective*, ch. 1.
5. Cf. Sharma, ed., *Religions*, part 1.
6. "Hominization" indicates the evolutionary propensity of developing consciousness with the coinciding emergences of biological complexity, which implies, for Teilhard, a spiritualization; yet this process is by no means a secured development, as violence inherent in this process may always upset it; cf. Teilhard de Chardin, 164, 169n1, 308n1.
7. Cf. Faber, *Garden*, Prologue, section 3 (Via Dolorosa) and ch. 4:5 (The Indistinction of Suffering).

the east and the west) and the two world wars of the twentieth century, the twenty-first century should much more feel and begin to look like the beginning of the twentieth than a new phase of global convergence of cultures and religions is in a sense devastating. This failure, in times of worldwide communication, cannot exempt religions, but rather demonstrates the historical impotence of religions to spiritualize humanity even to the degree that it would restructure social relations in the spirit of mutual understanding and for the common Earth.[8]

Whitehead has asked (us) the remarkable question: "Must 'religion' always remain as a synonym for 'hatred'?"[9] Much like the contemporary discussion on the possibility of peace (meant as the permanent overcoming of violence and war),[10] the question here is whether this perpetual and still perpetuated destructiveness of (and by) religions in every corner of the world is a necessity of human animality or nature or immaturity, designating humankind as an evolutionary failure on this Earth, or whether it is rather a continent fact of history that has had its evolutionary and historical roots, but could in principle and in fact be overcome if humanity just tried to transform its culturally inherited and transmitted, but not "natural" aggressive habits into peaceful ones.[11] Can, so we can ask further, the perpetuation of human destructiveness in relation not only to humanity, but basically everything humanity touches, be overcome with the mediation of religion(s) or will it persist precisely as long as there are religions?[12] And if we believe the former, namely, that religion should not fall into oblivion for humanity to be freed from its inhumanity, we must still ponder whether religion(s), instead of such a dismissal, need not, as the only viable alternative, be conquered by either a new, understood and lived, unity of religions or a new spiritual transformation of their plurality, a new, understood and lived, pluralism of religions, or both.[13]

The unity of religions is, without a doubt, one of *the* markers of the self-identity of a new kind of religions and movements that appeared during the past few centuries.[14] Among them, the Bahá'í religion arose.[15] It embraces and displays a revelation (in the proximate heritage of Abrahamic and Zoroastrian traditions) that may be viewed as one of the most prominent religious events of our times because of no less a reason than the fact that it signifies, ushers in and represents, in its own understanding and given the concurrent religious landscape at the time of its inception in the nineteenth century, a

---

8. Cf. 'Abdu'l-Bahá, *Promulgation*, #82: "The greatest cause of human alienation has been religion because each party has considered the belief of the other as anathema and deprived of the mercy of God." In 'Abdu'l-Bahá's diagnosis, it is under the manipulation of ignorance and fanaticism that religion "turns into blackest night": 'Abdu'l-Bahá, *Secrets*, 80.
9. Whitehead, *Adventures*, 172.
10. Cf. Pinker, ch. 1; Horgan, ch. 1.
11. Cf. 'Abdu'l-Bahá, *Promulgation*, #14; Renard.
12. Cf. Armstrong, *Fields of Blood*.
13. Cf. Knitter, *Earth*.
14. Cf. Smart, *Religion*, ch. 25; Momen, *Religion*, ch. 19; Knitter, "My God," 100–18. One early western witness is William Blake's book *All Religions Are One* from 1795 CE.
15. Cf. P. Smith, *Bábi and Bahá'í Religions*; 'Abdu'l-Bahá, *Promulgation*, #82.

new axial age[16]—a new way to understand religion and the meaning of the diversity of many religions.[17]

The first "axial age," famously so identified by the German existentialist philosopher Karl Jaspers,[18] was, in his rendering of intellectual and spiritual human history, characterized as the global awakening of humanity by a universal consciousness of existence to a world in need of salvific or healing transformation.[19] It comprises the momentous changes of the middle centuries of the last millennium BCE and rallies around the impact of figures such as the Buddha, Isaiah, Socrates or Confucius. In resonance with this insight—whether true in a narrow sense or rather indicating a shifting human self-understanding in a cosmic context—we could say that the new axial age at the centuries around the turn of the second and third millennium CE, the time we live in, has awakened humanity to a different universal consciousness, namely, that of the mutual interrelatedness of humanity and its religious existence in the context of *one* world-conscience and -responsibility.[20] It is in this sense that the unity or unification of religious worldviews was and is consciously proclaimed by several religious movements in the past centuries,[21] among them in significant ways by the emerging Bábí-Bahá'í religions.[22] In fact, in its matured form, the unity of religions has become the central axiom, desire, endeavor and motive force for the existence and activities of the Bahá'í Faith in the current world-situation with its specific global predicaments and an envisioned future of global transformation.[23] Its urgent drive toward the interlocked unities of ultimate reality, humanity and religion(s) is carried by a strong impulse to imagine, work for and await a different world to come, a civilization of the future that will have ushered in a life of peace in one interrelated world, maybe even one indivisible universe.[24]

---

16. Cf. Lambert, 303–33; Armstrong, *Transformation*.
17. Cf. Warburg, Hvithamar and Momen; A. Martin, chs. 6–8.
18. Cf. Jaspers, *Great Philosophers*.
19. Cf. Bellah and Joas.
20. Cf. Faber, *Garden*, ch. 9. For the early use of the "second axial age," cf. Cousins. For an expansion of the event character of axial ages to a more continuous "axiality" as character of the change of religious consciousness over time, cf. Schewel, 24–27.
21. Cf. Schuon, xxii–xxv. For the variety of new "axial" Indian religious movements that claim the unity of religions (and, hence, their respective truth) in a pluralistic way, but which also have had global influence from the late nineteenth century on, such as those of Sri Ramakrishna, Meher Baba, Upasani Maharaj, Shirdi Sai Baba, Sathya Sai Baba, Sri Aurobindo, Mira Richards (The Mother), Rabindranath Tagore and Ramana Maharshi, cf. Bassuk, ch. 2; Srinivas, chs. 2–3, 5; Warren, *Unraveling*, chs. 4–5, 9, 15. For long-standing transreligious transformations in the background of these new movements in the worship of Dattatreya, cf. Rigopoulos, chs. 6–9. Through the Sufi and Zoroastrian background of many of these figures there exist direct and indirect connections with the Bábí-Bahá'í religions, although of all of these movements before and after they had global reach, the latter ones were the oldest.
22. Cf. Chryssides and Geaves, 101–3. Yet the fact that new religions emerge in a new axial age is not by itself sufficient reason for them necessarily to be interested in the concepts such as the unity of religions and religious pluralism, as an overview of many of these New Religious Movements demonstrates; cf. Daschke and Ashcraft; Chryssides.
23. Cf. Hayes; M. L. Perry.
24. Cf. Stockman, *Bahá'í Faith*, part 1.

If this seems to be a pious wish to some detractors, at the very least this idea and ideal holds dear, defends and displays the flame of profound spiritual transformation toward a future civilization of peaceful conviviality on and with the Earth (and maybe beyond) without which hope can only degrade into either apocalyptic nightmares of human impotence and destruction or in a perpetuation of a Darwinian selection of the fittest into a roundabout of deadly competitions, violent conquests and extinctions until the universe, as in one version of current physical cosmology, disappears in eternal blackness, not even sustaining black holes anymore.[25] In the realm of potential, relevant and actionable alternatives, such as these, undecidable through theory, the vision of such a changed spiritual future of humanity seems to me to be the better imagination, because it is a prophetic call to make a difference now, to work in service of a worthy aim, even if it seems to be unattainable, because it gives us, humanity, individually and collectively, a choice, rather than in exhausted submissiveness yielding to a capitulation before uncontrollable forces or simply fate.

Nevertheless, this new axial consciousness harbors several profound tensions. Should it, now, given this new imperative of unity, emphasize the equality of all religions, or does this imperative rather imply an inevitable progression throughout time and history?[26] If the history of religions was one of humanity as a whole all along, that is, *one* history of religious consciousness, although we might only have realized its importance in our own age,[27] why is it warped by those deep differences by which religions perceive themselves even today, and to what avail? And is the proposed unity of religions a *condition* for a fruitful engagement with religious diversity and divergence, striving to establish a multifarious, but mutually amicable community, or is it meant to symbolize an *aim* of current interreligious dialogues, such that they would, instead of a perpetual conversation, be issuing into an all-encompassing conversion either together into one another, creating religion anew as such, or of all religions into the most advanced one, or into the one with the most power of plausibility?[28]

It is but these historical conditions, universal intentions and deeper, aporetic questions that are the matter of religious pluralism.[29] Issuing from the necessities of the new axial age to address the quandaries of universal religious peace, religious pluralism signals an endeavor to encompass religious diversity in one universal framework of the spiritual development of humanity. This pluralism as a maintained enterprise has become fully possible as, and will have a meaningful impact only if, a universal consciousness of unity has already arisen to be extremely desirable. Yet for religious pluralism this unity cannot but be developed by the unfettered valuation of the *plurality* of religions.[30] Their multiplicity and mutuality, although in an as of yet undetermined way, has become the axiom, the desire and the endeavor of the interreligious dialogue of the past centuries.[31] On an

---

25. Davies, ch. 7.
26. Cf. Runzo, *Philosophy*, ch. 2.
27. Cf. W. C. Smith, *Meaning*, ch. 6.
28. Cf. Weisse.
29. Cf. Meister, ch. 2.
30. Cf. Sharma, ed., *Religions*, part 5.
31. Cf. Weisse, 125–317.

explicitly conceptual level, however, we can only in the past decades or so discern that these conversations and their correlative theoretical considerations have developed into a profoundly thought-through, but also hotly discussed, new paradigm, namely, that of religious pluralism.[32]

But what could this paradigm mean since, noticeably, a prescriptive pluralism beyond any descriptive plurality is not without its own internal tensions? Is it meant to facilitate the encounter of religions on an equal playing field and as equals, or should it rather usher in a new phase of the mutual overcoming of parochial thought patterns and mutually exclusive ways of living within the diverse religious and spiritual projects, or maybe even organized religion itself?[33] Further, does this pluralism highlight the differences between religions to such an extent that it may lead to mutual understanding,[34] or rather, in order to better probe the depth of specific religions over others, subsume inferior forms into a new overarching construct, if not that of any current religion[35] so maybe another super-religion[36] or some as of yet unimagined spiritual life beyond (established) religions?[37] And does this pluralism ultimately seek dialogue in order to help animate a future community of religions, or could it rather tend to initiate a great fluctuation between religious traditions and persuasions, amounting to massive individual and collective conversions and hybridizations,[38] or even the emptying and extinguishing of certain traditional molds because they have lost the force of the plausibility to bind human existence as a whole to certain religious instantiations and arguments or ways of living and their fading attractiveness?[39] History is full of these diverse, divergent and even oppositional movements within and between religions, engrained in their cultural interaction. For religious pluralism, these deep fissures and fault lines only reveal that the factuality of complex multi- and interreligious relations is beyond any simple theory. However, as this pluralism wants to seek a meaningful reconciling understanding, its normativity is not only about what ought to be the case if one engages in the pluralistic quest regarding the messy plurality of religious phenomena and disarrays, but about whence and how such aporetic

---

32. Cf. Race, *Christians*, 71–98. For the prehistory of the becoming of religious pluralism, cf. Schmidt-Leukel, *Pluralism*, ch. 8.
33. Cf. Panikkar, *Dialogue*.
34. Cf. Knitter, *Earth*, ch. 3; Hick, *Problems*, 39.
35. Cf. Netland, *Encountering*.
36. Cf. Smart, *Religions*, 581–86.
37. Cf. Toynbee, ch. 19; Ferrer and Sherman, eds., *Turn*, 1–80.
38. Religious "hybridity" is not just a future imagination of a chaotic state of religious flux beyond fixed organizations and neatly held-apart religious identities; it is, in fact, a current progressive phenomenon in a global world of interaction in search for new forms of identity less oriented along traditional boundaries, as they were mostly defined by respective religious professionals who may be more interested in the perpetuation of their own power than the depth of the spiritual reservoir of their respective religious organizations; cf. Cornille, "Dynamics," 1–6; Bidwell. But it may be even closer to reality to acknowledge that hybridization was always a moment of the processuality of religions, their transformation and renewal; cf. Faber, *Garden*, ch. 4.
39. Cf. Swidler.

complexities, while factually happening, can be decided on, emphasized or transformed, justified or judged untenable, regarding their value.

Another way to ask these questions of the unity and plurality of religions is to take a closer look at the second axial age, how it differs from the first axial age and maybe even from any age before or besides. Several authors, in addressing this paradigm shift, come to the conclusion that the now emergent, new axial event is not primarily a religious phenomenon, but a shift in human consciousness in general that is not only of a similar global impact that the first axial age had facilitated but that, especially at a time of global connectivity today, represents a new level of interconnectedness.[40] Instead of a departure from the integrity of the Earth as the ultimate scene of human existence (in flights into other worlds) and search for meaning (in a cyclical becoming and perishing of worlds), the new consciousness reconnects with the Earth and the all of existence, integrating humanity in unprecedented ways: entanglement, embodiment, evolutionary and ecological interdependence, and new social mutuality through (electronic and quantum) connectivity are its keywords.[41] The first axial age detached the human urge for meaning from embodied humanity and the Earth or the cyclical becoming of the cosmos and opened a horizon of transcendence beyond all of their impermanence, seeking salvation, liberation and realization beyond a "state" that began to unravel as a dark secret: that the world is not as it should be; that humanity has straddled from its original destiny; that we must overcome this valley of pain and tears, full of sin and ignorance; that we are strangers in the universe, exiles in existential banishment.[42] The second axial age, conversely, fuses the becoming of the cosmos with that of mind and spirit, not only of humanity, but rather as the movement of cosmic evolution itself; not *away from* the world, but *deeper into* it; not as salvation venturing *beyond* the world (leaving it to oblivion), but as ripening fruit or harvest *of* the world process *itself*.[43]

In the religious context, it is interesting that some authors like Karen Armstrong view the difference between the first and the second axial age to be consistent with the arising of human consciousness and (after the disintegration of the first axial synthesis) the crisis of its limitations and fragmentation, respectively, allowing for the opportunity of new conceptualizations of wholeness transcending the sectarianism of the past.[44] Other thinkers such as John Haught have already given the first axial age the predicates of the second: that it was the event of a magnitude that is only be rivaled by processes such as the coming into existence of the cosmos, the emergence of life and the liberation of life to mind. It is the fourth revolution: religion as the emergence of universal and connective consciousness of deep meaning, neither falling into the trap of materialism (equating meaning with its material causes) nor the trap of escapism, seeking meaning in realms beyond and not impacted by this world. Rather, in the cosmic story and evolution

---

40. Cf. Bohm; Capra, *Tao*; Wilber.
41. Cf. Massumi; Keller, *Cloud*; Lanzetta, *Heart*; Zohar and Marshall.
42. Cf. Jaspers, *Origin*, 19–43; Hick, *Interpretation*, 29–33.
43. Cf. McFague; Daene-Drummond, *EcoTheology*; Edwards, *Ecology*; Overzee.
44. Cf. Armstrong, *Transformation*, ch. 10; Roemischer; similar: Bondarenko; and on the religious hybridity of this second axial age, cf. Prabhu, Talks.

religion becomes an anticipatory reaction to the sacred desire for the spiritual fulfillment of the cosmic movement itself.[45]

In another turn of the axial wheel, again, new realms of virtual reality and artificial intelligence have commended themselves as a very different type of connectivity, one that paradoxically seems all the more connective the further it transforms the physicality of the universe into a virtuality of which designers and players, algorithms and mathematical patters are the new creators and inhabitants.[46] In speculating whether even this physical world is nothing but such a virtual world, the question of infinite levels of worlds or designers of these (and our) worlds become available beyond any classical religious connotation.[47] Instead of emphasizing embodiments, however, this vision harbors a new dissociation from the world: either, with a new secularized form of apocalypticism in expectation of the "singularity,"[48] the cosmos, at least one that has sustained humanity, will fundamentally change when intelligent machines[49] will extinguish humanity as unnecessary hazard of past ages,[50] or humanity will disappear into virtual worlds of algorithmic entities[51]—instead of ever reaching or desiring to reach the Omega Point of Teilhard de Chardin, which was meant to suggest a bodily fermentation of the cosmic process into an ideal divine body.[52]

In all of these cases, however, the decisive characteristic of the "surviving" religiosity of the future is its *relationality*, a pattern of common fate shared with the way humanity goes, and *forms of unification* that in their depth and force of configuring religions surpass any human particularities of cultural difference.[53] The new axial age appears as an overarching paradigm shift in which all religions will share the same destiny: either to reconnect humanity with the Earth in a transreligious ecological community or to share in humanity's transcultural or even transhuman transformation into something unprecedented.[54] Here, the unity of religions is sustained by the respective patterns of human involvement with the "real" cosmic becoming of humanity itself. Variations are only differentiated as far as these overarching patterns find either inspiration in certain religious cosmologies (more than others) or insofar as (some of) these cosmologies can help the process of such a transformation (more than others). I will return to some of the implications of such approaches in a later chapter.

In any case, in their new axial imperative both the unity of religions *and* religious pluralism have certain reasons for their existence and aims, inherently demanding to be reachable and to be reached, in common. At the very least, they want to avoid the past. In

---

45. Cf. Haught, *Story*, ch.1.
46. Cf. Woolley; Young and Whitty.
47. Cf. Kurzweil, *Age*; Steinhart; Rothblatt.
48. Cf. Kurzweil, *Singularity*.
49. Cf. Brockman.
50. Cf. Bostrom; Geraci; Ashkenazi, 92–94; Stonier, "Machine Intelligence," 133–39.
51. Cf. Tipler, ch. 9; Ward, *Fire*, ch. 16; *Defense*, ch. 7.
52. Cf. Grumett, chs. 1, 7.
53. Cf. Harari, part 3; Toffler.
54. Cf. Cole-Turner.

this sense, they have already judged and not justified the past. Their projects have already decided that they want to migrate away from, or overturn, the history of religions with regard to its record as one of conflict and mutual exclusion, its widespread and historically thoroughgoing display of misuses of religions for power struggles and the justification of mutual extinction, even genocide, by employing the most primitive instincts and emotions of the human animal.[55] The common aim of religious pluralism and the idea of the unity of religions has already determined, or at least seems necessarily to include, the establishment of religious peace as an inevitable condition for, and expression of, a general peace in and with this world, materially and spiritually, politically and individually, culturally and in light of our common humanity, and for its meaningful survival (or posthuman transformation) in the coming changes (of understanding or real mutation) of the cosmic reality in which we seem to (or will) live.[56] They want to contribute to a future harmony of the "one" humanity and to remind it constantly of its own humanization.[57] They want to find alternative ways of conviviality, of "living together" without physical, mental and spiritual violence in a mutual embrace of differences and modes of unification as the new defining characteristics of any interreligious and interhuman encounter.[58] In their own way, both of these projects want to establish a community of spiritual pathways open for any seeker (or group of seekers) to engage in unobstructed and unrestricted ways divine or ultimate reality for the good of humanity and the world.[59]

---

55. Cf. Sharma and Dugan.
56. Cf. Küng.
57. Cf. Knitter, *Earth*, ch. 5.
58. Cf. Faber and Slabodsky; Schmidt-Leukel, *Pluralism*, 7–16.
59. Cf. Fazel, "Dialogue," 137–52; Ferrer and Sherman, eds., *Turn*, 29–33.

Chapter Two

THE HEALING AND POISONOUS FRUITS OF THE UNITY OF RELIGIONS

Be as one spirit, one soul, leaves of one tree, flowers of one garden, waves of one ocean.[1]
—'Abdu'l-Bahá

Unity is the keyword of the Bahá'í story. Yet what is the meaning of "unity" in the phrase "unity of religions"?[2] In Bahá'í thought and in the reflection on its sources, the vast sea of Bahá'í scriptures, scholars have found several meanings implied in the proposition of "unity."[3] In summary, one can detect three pervasive motifs. One motif arises from the conviction of scriptural Bahá'í literatures right away, namely, that all religions are emanating from the same divine or ultimate source.[4] They are manifestations, revelations, self-communications of Reality itself, of the apophatic Beyond that is undefined,[5] but mirrors its Self in the multiplicity of revelations constituting the essence of diverse religions—as this self-manifesting process of Reality is also the mirroring of its infinity in an infinity of things, events, organisms, societies and universes, emanating from this source as its creation.[6] This motif is, of course, no stranger to many traditions, insofar as they understand themselves constituted not only by human impulses, but also by an active presence of God or ultimate Reality itself.[7] What is new and exciting, here, is that the mirror of divine self-manifestation is not exclusively contained in one occurrence or a restricted chain of occurrences (of revelations and religions), but fundamentally distributed as through a prism into a multiplicity of appearances (of revelations and religions).[8] This resonates with the assumption that, although apophatically transcendent, this source is immediately connected with the diversity of world phenomena and not in need of symbolic walls securing its unity from dissipation into the infinite variability of the world.[9] While both the infinite variability of phenomena as divine mirrors and the direct immanence of the One in the many was not unknown to earlier traditions—for instance, in

---

1. 'Abdu'l-Bahá, *Promulgation*, #10.
2. Cf. Bowers, 157–58.
3. Cf. Fazel, "Pluralism," 42–49; May, 1–36.
4. Cf. Bahá'u'lláh, *Gleanings*, #22.
5. Cf. Bahá'u'lláh, *Gleanings*, #21.
6. Cf. Bahá'u'lláh, *Iqan*, part 1, which in its opening sections is devoted to making this point.
7. Cf. Smart, *Phenomenon*.
8. Cf. Bahá'u'lláh, *Iqan*, part 1.
9. Cf. Bahá'u'lláh, *Prayers*, #178.

eastern monisms such as Advaita and Dharmic nondualism[10] and western theological speculations on the decentered universe as in Nikolas of Cusa[11]—the "emanation" into diverse religions with equally valid truth claims was often not understood as an immediate implication of this metaphysical and cosmological trajectory.[12]

Another motif that appears prominently in the Bahá'í writings does not define itself by discussions of the metaphysical dimension of ultimate reality, but refers to the universal characteristics of all religions to transform the character of humanity in a world moved by spiritual evolution.[13] Unfortunately, as history demonstrates, even if earlier ages have produced religious encounters that yielded the insight that the religious Other was also interested in valid spiritual transformation, this insight has seldom issued in a thoroughgoing acceptance of these "other" religious life-forms as legitimate expressions of a common movement, or even as an opportunity for synergies of mutual support in these encounters.[14] Among the many examples that could be cited here, I will only refer to one that has over centuries determined the relationship of the two involved religions as one of suspicion, mutual denigration and war. While Islamic sources knew of the imperative of compassion for such a spiritual transformation as prescribed by Buddhism, this has generally not led to the acknowledgment of resonances with the central Qur'anic epithet of Allah as the All-Compassionate, because Islam perceived Buddhism fundamentally under the paradigm of "idolatry," the worst enemy of God's wrath.[15] That contemporary conversations between these religions have found the contrary insight, that is, the compatibility between *caruna* and *al-rahman al-rahim*, much more "natural,"[16] is but a sign of the new axial consciousness that this kind of "unity" addresses.

Yet another motif can be discerned in contours that would allow us to speak of common aims of religions, such as the education of humanity toward peace and harmony[17]; the realization of all divine attributes and virtues, especially love and compassion, justice and equality[18]; and the salvation from the human propensity to follow all kinds of disrupting and often violent limitations, such as appear in the tendency to take recourse to lower, narrower or more egocentric goods instead of aspiring to the Good of all of humanity and the world as a whole.[19] This understanding of the "unity" of religions has gained much prominence as more recent interreligious dialogues reveal when they progressed to a point at which the doctrinal investigations seem not to yield

---

10. Cf. Sharma, *Philosophy*, chs. 5, 10.
11. Cf. Bond, 19–35.
12. Cf. R. Steward.
13. Cf. Bahá'u'lláh, *Iqan*, §270.
14. Cf. Prothero, *God*.
15. Cf. Elverskog, ch. 3.
16. Cf. Dalai Lama, 79; Shah-Kazemi, 7.
17. Cf. 'Abdu'l-Bahá, *Paris Talks*, #40; 'Abdu'l-Bahá, *Promulgation*, #99.
18. Cf. Bahá'u'lláh, "Lawh-i Dunya (Tablet of the World)," in *Tablets*, 91–92; *Days*, #22:9; 'Abdu'l-Bahá, *Promulgation*, #63; *Paris Talks*, #24. It is interesting to note that the Second Parliament of Religions in Chicago in 1993 has taken up this imperative of global ethical coinherence of religious traditions in much the same manner; cf. Küng and Kuschel, 15–16.
19. Cf. 'Abdu'l-Bahá, *Paris Talks*, ##9, 18.

satisfying conclusions, but at which the global predicaments of our time have opened the door for working together in addressing changes to the better in a common effort.[20]

Given these meanings of "unity," it seems that the function of the unity of religions in the process of spiritual evolution, according to Bahá'í revelatory texts, is maybe best described as a collective pool of mutually related presuppositions, motifs, agendas and prescriptions: of the overcoming of prejudices and the violence based on them[21]; of movements of harmonizations and expectations of universal peace[22]; of the unity of humanity over against any parochial limitation such as ethnicity, race, sex and gender, class and status, hierarchies of power and so on[23]; of the unity of ultimate reality as a basis for the unity of creation in its infinite diversity and in the creative unfolding of the world[24]; of the equality of all religions such that none should be preferred because of subjective attractiveness or contingencies of birth, or dogmatic limitations, intellectual restrictions and the lack of spiritual universality[25]; of the plenitude of reality, which can harbor a plurality of phenomena, individual and collective differences, and complex diversities as propelling enriching forces that drive the spiritual evolution of humanity, and maybe even beyond.[26] All of these functions are *in process*.[27] They are not

---

20. Cf. Knitter, *Earth*, chs. 5–7; Fazel, "Dialogue," 10.
21. Cf. 'Abdu'l-Bahá, *Promulgation*, #103.
22. Cf. 'Abdu'l-Bahá, *Selections*, #221.
23. Cf. Bahá'u'lláh, *Gleanings*, #7; 'Abdu'l-Bahá, *Paris Talks*, #32, 34, 40; *Promulgation*, #44. It is interesting that the sociological study of religion does also not exclude any religion from consideration, not for their truth, but as a human phenomenon. Yet this anthropological standard does in some profound way already presuppose the truth of the unity of humanity in order to be a coherent area of study; cf. Durkheim, 22.
24. Cf. The Báb, *Selections*, 207; Bahá'u'lláh, *Prayers*, ##97, 178; *Gleanings*, #94; 'Abdu'l-Bahá, *Paris Talks*, #42; *Promulgation*, #74.
25. Cf. Bahá'u'lláh, *Gleanings*, #24; 'Abdu'l-Bahá, *Promulgation*, ##41–42, 130–32; *Paris Talks*, #44.
26. Cf. Bahá'u'lláh, *Gleanings*, ##80, 93, 129; 'Abdu'l-Bahá, *Selections*, ##14, 33, 42.
27. This "inclusiveness" of the concept of the unity of "religions," that is, its highly differentiated meaning and connotation, also expresses itself in the fact that the classical discussion about whether the Bahá'í Faith is a "World Religion" (given similarities with other classical religions, such as founder, scripture, organization) or a "New Religious Movement" (which still is identified or self-identified from within this classical paradigm) is still based on a restricted model of religion that the transreligious approach, as we will see later, wants to overcome or not presuppose, in the first place; cf. Fazel, "Is the Bahá'í Faith," 1–16. Fazel is aware of the criticism of the term World Religion, but understands it at least in an heuristic sense to undermine the oppressive restrictions imposed on the Bahá'ís in diverse cultural and religious contexts as long as it is perceived as a "sect" (of another religion) or "movement," which can, therefore, be ignored. Nevertheless, a relevant field of research would, henceforth, be opened (or should be sustained) by not only comparing religious similar structures embodied by the Bahá'í Faith as an organized religion with so-called World Religions (as is often happening in relation to the "Big Five" as paradigm) or with New Religious Movements, but with the religious milieu in and beyond which it developed right from the beginning: organized and unorganized Sufism and diverse other "heterodox" movements in the radius of Shi'ism, such as the Ahl-al Haqq in the mountains of Kurdistan, or the intimate interactions it developed with the Druze communities around Akko, near Haifa (the final residence of Bahá'u'lláh, and the main stage of 'Abdu'l-Bahá's activities in Ottoman Syria). And we would also have to take into consideration

just "there" as facts; they must be established and creatively maintained, heightened and reinvigorated, time and again, in order not to sink back into the limited instantiations of the past, or to stagnate on a certain level of development.[28]

If we stop for a moment and reflect what can be gathered from this short survey of the function of "unity" in the Bahá'í writings (as recognized by Bahá'í scholars) right away, it is that unity does indicate neither sameness nor any defined sense of overarching monotheism, which we might suspect of a tradition arising in an Abrahamic context. It is maybe one of the prevailing misunderstandings of the concept of unity, when it is related to the plurality of religions, that it ought to imply some simple notion of identity, be it of essence or attribution.[29] Yet to claim the equality of the truth of religions is not identical with some kind of essentialism that necessitates the view that anything that is one must essentially be the same thing. This view is often, if it is not just an unreflected accusation with its own biases, brought into discussion from a certain kind of categorization, a philosophical mindset, that prefers substantialism to process thinking.[30] We are warned not to presuppose in any unqualified way, for instance, Aristotelian categories for the Bahá'í writings (although they use them in certain contexts),[31] especially because the immediate philosophical tradition from which the original Bahá'í-Bahá'í discipleship arose, namely, the Shaykhi movement (within Twelver Shi'ism) of Shaykh Ahmad al-Ahsa'i of Bahrain,[32] used process categories instead, which, without any dependency, were maybe closest to the western twin, namely, Whitehead's philosophy of process[33]—but more of that later. Further, the gathered aspects of unity, although they are formulated from within a monotheistic, religious milieu are, at this stage of differentiation, not yet pointing at the way they want to be interpreted, for example, in theistic or monistic fashion.[34] A sign of this reservation can be witnessed by the fact that the one source from which all religions according to Bahá'í scriptures spring is not identified with any appearance of divine attribution, but is strictly of apophatic nature, evading simple identifications[35]—this insight will also play out in important ways later.

Nevertheless, given this processual unity we must now also immediately interrogate the other side of this process: What is the relevance of difference? The Bahá'í writings address this question by referring to the following elements. Revelation, or better, a multiplicity of revelations, is intelligible if we take the temporality of the world into account.[36] With the world being in process, "every age requireth a fresh measure of the light of

---

    the early reception of the Bahá'í teachings before and through the travels of 'Abdu'l-Bahá to the west (Europe and North America) in diverse "heterodox" or "non-orthodox" communities, such as Transcendentalism and Theosophy, among several others.
28. Cf. Momen, "Thinking," 243–70.
29. Cf. Cobb, *Transforming*, 66.
30. Cf. Farmer, ch. 6.
31. Cf. Kluge, "Substratum," 17–68; "Explorations," 163–200.
32. Cf. W. C. Smith, *Religion*, 8–13.
33. Cf. Hamid; Cole, "World," 145–63.
34. Cf. Momen, "God," 1–9.
35. Cf. Lambden, "Background," 37–78.
36. Cf. Esslemont, ch. 8.

God."[37] Hence, differences will arise in relation to historical and local (for instance, climactic, continental and so on) characters of societies in which religions arise, or which they develop beyond themselves.[38] Further, such revelations or religions (not dwelling on the potential differences between these terms at this point)[39] will be as different as there are divergences of the spiritual situations, horizons or formations in specific societies and cultures.[40] The Bahá'í writings also mention differences to be inevitable because of the multiplicity of human aspirations,[41] horizons of imagination[42] and emphases in the realization of virtues, which can differ vastly in different societies, cultures and individuals.[43] As a more metaphysical reason for differentiation, the Bahá'í writings also mention that specific appearances of divine engagements, issuing in diverse religions, will carry different assignments, related to the aforementioned limitations of time and place, history and aspirations.[44] Finally, we may also discern differences on the highest level of religious origination in the divine Reality itself, as its human appearances—for Bahá'ís often visualized in the different religious founders, the Manifestations of the Self of Reality/God[45]—have had different personalities,[46] the emulation of which always leads to different habits and ritualizations in diverse internal and external expansions of their spirit over time, such as the modes of spiritual exercises and forms of organization.[47]

Again pausing for a moment, the conveyed variety of forms of differences among religions (and within their diverse streams) is by no means presenting us with a picture in which multiplicity appears as a subordinated category, at any point supplanted by unity. Additionally, diversity is not just a matter of a lack of unity. While imperfections may lead to antagonisms, differentiations as such (and in the many forms mentioned) are not hindering, distorting or destructing unity, but they provide humanity with the wealth of religious life and insight as well as underscore the deep valuation of the unfathomable divine mystery emanating (into) these differences.[48] Further, religious differences are embodiments of space and time, mirroring the diversification of geography and climate,

---

37. Bahá'u'lláh, *Gleanings*, #34.
38. Cf. 'Abdu'l-Bahá, *Promulgation*, ##41, 112; May, 10–12.
39. In the Bahá'í view, "revelation" connotes the original "enlightenment" of a religious movement by its source, the founders or Manifestations of God, such as the Buddha or Jesus; "religion" is the embodiment of this "light" over time and space. While the developing "religion" might decline and even fall into a winter of absence, as is witnessed, for instance, by Buddhist texts on the future disappearance of the Dharma, the "light" of its origin is never in question regarding its enduring truth and invigorating force. Cf. Bahá'u'lláh, *Iqan*, 44–45; Kourosh, 205–14, 242–57.
40. Cf. Bahá'u'lláh, *Gleanings*, #33; 'Abdu'l-Bahá, *Questions*, #81; *Promulgation*, #50.
41. Cf. Bahá'u'lláh, *Gleanings*, #106; 'Abdu'l-Bahá, *Paris Talks*, #23.
42. Cf. 'Abdu'l-Bahá, *Questions*, ##32, 56, 71, 81; *Promulgation*, ##73, 99.
43. Cf. 'Abdu'l-Bahá, *Questions*, #38; *Paris Talk*, ##7, 28; *Promulgation*, ##38, 45; *Selections*, #159; Momen, "Relativism," 202–3.
44. Cf. Bahá'u'lláh, *Gleanings*, #22.
45. Cf. Cole, "Concept."
46. Cf. Bahá'u'lláh, *Gleanings*, #22; 'Abdu'l-Bahá, *Questions*, #31.
47. Cf. 'Abdu'l-Bahá, *Questions*, #7; *Promulgation*, #55.
48. Cf. Bahá'u'lláh, *Gleanings*, #93.

and allow for processes of becoming beyond any given state of affairs, spiritually and socially. Whether in a local or global context, diversification appears by no means as a uniform, but as a multifarious process of spiritualization—for humanity to recognize its humanness in the most noble sense—in which different spiritual states as well as ways and speed of progression (or degeneration) are not a sign of imperfection, but of infinite divine emanation of (and into) the world as a creative transformation into ever new states, ways and speeds of processes of (toward) perfection.[49] In a profound sense, unity and diversity in the Bahá'í writings indicate different perspective of one process. Rather than being caught up in an antagonism of mutual diminution, they appear and increase together.

Yet the complex dialectic of unity and difference is fragile. It has (as history teaches) many ways and forms of disintegration into either uniformity (suppression of plurality) or fragmentation (loss of unity).[50] So, while the Bahá'í effort toward the unity of religions has its sophisticated delicacy, we can now also begin to see why and under what conditions this concentration on "unity" might create, and has created, problems or even negative effects for the whole divine process of human evolution ever more (or in the first place) to become human.[51] If religions lose their living spiritual initiation and begin to settle on accretions such as dogmatic fixations, doctrinal orthodoxies and constraint formulations of their beliefs, they will become divisive, internally and externally corrupting the very motivation for unification and peaceful differentiation alike—and issue into the feared fragmentations these limited, but false unifications wanted to avoid. If unity becomes a substitute for uniqueness, it will become dictatorial and oppressive and will, finally, empty itself of all evidence of its original healing spirit. If developments in religious communities forget or forgo the inevitable (and in some sense "natural") diversities of spiritual stations (individually within a religion and collectively between religions), then, instead of equality the internally motivated paths of spiritual evolution will degenerate into group-think and mindless identifications with some external opinion, the one with the most social or orthodox power to prevail.[52] Further, as religions can never without remainder uniformly be transported from one culture, climate, geography, history, cultural character and societal spirit into another, such local and temporal limitations of human existence will easily transform into roadblocks for mutual understanding and initiatives of unification.[53] Hence, we must accept these differences as foundational for any unity of religions, even within any one religion in its transpositions into different

---

49. Cf. Hatcher, *Purpose*, 88–93. This will have important implications for the plurality of parallel spiritual developments and their "spiritual velocity" (a term Fazel suggest from a personal conversation with Joan Cole, cf. Fazel, "Understanding," 263). For evolutionary implications, cf. Chapter 13; for implications regarding the future plurality of religious forms of existence, cf. Chapter 14.
50. Cf. Saiedi, *Gate*, 1–14, situates the Báb's message as transcending solution to the impasse of the historic dialectic of the time, namely, between traditionalism and modernism, or fundamentalism and postmodern fragmentation.
51. Cf. Faber, *Manifold*, ch. 2.
52. Cf. Faber, "Sense," 36–56.
53. Cf. Assmann, "Translating," 25–36.

corners of time and place of a changing world.⁵⁴ Unity, by virtue of such limitations, is always in danger of degenerating into monotony; and the religious spirit of a religious community (and the individuals in it) will only be relevant as long as it can be stronger than these processes of disintegration into conformity. In fact, unity is a pale concept as long as it underestimates, and is not brought into conversation with, the multifariousness of a world in becoming in which novelty should not be seen as chaotic nuisance, but as a means of the Spirit to renew life.⁵⁵

Given this reflection on the character and status of the unity of religions, we may realize that we are caught in a series of dilemmas in which unity and multiplicity appear as poles that will always be perceived underdetermined as to their right balance and emphases of realization: *Unity or difference*—which one has or should have preference? *Continuity or novelty*—which one should be considered primary? *Equality or progression*—which one has priority? *Form or content*—must they always remain the same for reasons of identity or can they change, as a matter of staying alive? *Identity or community*—which defines which? *Achievement or process*—can they be harmonized? There may, in fact, be different ways to solve these dilemmas in ever-new harmonizations, and different religions, or phases in the development of a specific religion or of a spiritual path may emphasize one over the other or find genuine contrasts in which to balance either side.⁵⁶ Yet in this polar uncertainty, there remain certain realizations that should be singled out as untenable, as breaking the circle of mutual harmonization, and that, hence, always will tend to lead to opposition and violence. These are the poisonous fruits of unity—of which the related Bahá'í discourse is readily aware.⁵⁷

We can categorize these deformations of unity within five coordinates.⁵⁸ The first is the poisonous fruit of *superiority*: my religion is superior, because it is later, newer, older, wiser, more universal, less limited, more limited to the pure ones, more salvific, only salvific, the only true one. Intimately related is the poisonous fruit of *supersession*: my religion follows, integrates or overcomes yours so that your religion is no longer needed and has become irrelevant. A third poisonous fruit, often lurking behind (and sustaining) the first two, is the claim of *finality*: my religion is final; all others are imperfect or imposturous imitations, "old hats" and, in the best case, only preparatory suggestions for the fullness of time, which appears in my religion. A particularly nasty form of poisoning is the impulse toward *denigration*: your religion is nothing but a fantasy of your mind or a limited perspective or a matter of ignorance while mine is the pure truth; everything you represent is false and probably either bad or even evil and, hence, will issue in (eternal)

---

54. Cf. Kondrath.
55. Cf. Bahá'u'lláh, *Prayers*, #178; Faber, "On the Unique Origin of Revelation," 273–89.
56. Cf. Panikkar, *Experience*. I will explicate the importance of these dilemmas for the understanding of the paradoxes of religious unity and plurality in Chapter 10.
57. Cf. Fazel, "Approaches," 41–53.
58. Cf. Faber, "Must 'Religion' Always," 167–82. Most of these poisonous fruits were in self-critical deconstruction detected from within the pre-pluralistic limitations as espoused by the radical pluralistic transfigurations that began with early iconic statements of the new pluralistic access, such as the articles collected in Hick and Knitter, passim.

self-destruction. Finally, there is the poison of *substitution*: since my religion is perfect, it can do all that yours can and more; it may concede some truth to your religion, but all of that is already and in most perfect ways integrated in my religion.

Since these poisonous fruits of unity, individually or collectively, capture the reasons and motivations for religious persecution, violence, oppression and destruction, we should remain aware of their danger and to the utmost try to avoid them wherever they appear—even if only indirectly, structurally, tacitly or, of course, outright—in the further discussion of the unity of religions.[59] However, these negative markers have also, by themselves, already set the tone for any further fruitful conceptualization of the healing power of unity: indicating *equality* instead of superiority; *remembrance* instead of supersession; *evolution* instead of finality; *appreciation* instead of denigration; and *integration* instead of substitution.

---

59. Cf. Faber, *Becoming of God*, 99; and "Explorations," 13.

Chapter Three

THE SYNTHESIS AND APORIA OF RELIGIOUS PLURALISM

Gather all people beneath the shadow of Thy bounty and cause them to unite in harmony, so that they may become as the rays of one sun, as the waves of one ocean, and as the fruit of one tree. May they drink from the same fountain.[1]

—'Abdu'l-Bahá

The contemporary endeavor to address the questions, dilemmas and conundrums of unity and diversity of religions is called religious pluralism.[2] The primordial fact to be reckoned with here is, of course, that there is a plurality of religions. The question is: should this diversity be considered a norm, too?[3] Religious pluralism answers with a resounding, but qualified, yes! As it is precisely the function of a normative pluralism to mitigate violence prepared and instigated by the inevitable differences between religions, religious pluralism's mission contains the imperative to further mutual understanding and a peaceful cooperation.[4] The simple view of unity as uniformity, the misguided dream of the oneness of only one religion (at which all others have to arrive) or the assumption of the sameness of all religions without recognition of the vast differences of religious identities is considered by religious pluralism as a veritable reason for the perpetuation of the war between and in manipulation of religions.[5] However, the other limit to be avoided is any view of pluralism that stipulates just the integral identity of a given religion combined with mere external tolerance as basis for coexistence with others. This view would leave all wounds not only in play, but would always and any time allow for their activation in the arena of violence and oppression, manipulation and religious xenophobia.[6] From the perspective of religious pluralism, the main reason fueling the religious disharmonies is the claim of (absolute) religious Truth of any religion over all others.[7] So, in a profound sense, religious pluralism is about the investigation into modes of community that will affirmatively, consciously and in a practical and intellectually satisfying way demonstrate that the central issue and the nucleus for the healing process

---

1. 'Abdu'l-Bahá, *Promulgation*, #46.
2. Cf. Mullan; Schmidt-Leukel, *Pluralism*, 1–7.
3. Cf. Eck, *America*.
4. Cf. Knitter, *Earth*, ch. 2.
5. Cf. Weisse, 21–124.
6. Cf. Netland, *Encountering*, ch. 8; Knitter, *No Other Name*.
7. Cf. Hick and Knitter.

that religions in aiming at peace must rediscover is that of the *relativity* of religious truths[8] as their mutual dependence[9]—a claim that is, of course, central to the Bahá'í writings and reflections, too.[10]

In short, against the backdrop of indisposing religious habits of violence, philosophers and religious scholars of religious pluralism engaged in interreligious discourse are now in agreement that there are three typological positions that religions, in their own theological reflections or that of their doctrinal orthodoxies, are able to take and will lean toward in order to address the question whether or not religious truth can and should be relative: exclusivism, inclusivism and pluralism.[11] These alternatives are to be understood as the pivot around which the future of religions will (have to) be decided. Exclusivism is the typological view that only my religion has (the) Truth; all others are wrong or evil. Salvation or liberation or realization comes *only* through my religious path.[12] Inclusivism is the typological view that maintains that while my religion is perfect, all others can eventually reach salvation through the Truth of my religion. Salvation is possible for all religions, or better, members of other religion despite the falsity or limited value of their religion. Contrary to both, pluralism claims that not only is there (the) Truth in all religions, but all religions are their own paths of/to Truth and salvation.[13]

Naturally, as all of these positions can be held within one and the same religious community, it will generally present itself as a composition of these positions. The degrees of their acceptance or nonacceptance will form different bodies of self-reference by which these religions (or sections within religions) find their identity and define themselves with or against other religions (or sects). Additionally, these positions are typological in nature, that is, in practice they can overlap and have complex relationships to one another in the mind of religious thinkers, leaders and practitioners that defy simple antagonisms.[14] Yet the general triad of positions is in itself coherent insofar as no position to the question of the relativity or absoluteness of religious truth and salvation will fall outside of this complex. Although it may not be as clear whether one's view will be exclusively in one or the other corner or a combination of some or all of them regarding certain aspects of the question, the triadic complex is logically exhaustive.[15] This has the interesting effect that no degree of resistance to these alternatives will escape this classification, and that the general model is, therefore, already a mode of communication of these alternatives of truth claims with one another. Regardless of whether one accepts one or the other (or any combination) of the alternatives as true (or false), one must accept the whole field

---

8. Cf. Panikkar, *Dialogue*, ch. 1; Runzo, *Reason*; Connolly, ch. 2.
9. Cf. Knitter, *No Other Name*, 9; "My God Is Bigger Than Your God," 100.
10. Cf. Shoghi Effendi, *Day*, 139; *World Order*, 57–60; Momen, "Relativism: A Basis," 367–97; Schaefer, *Beyond*, 60–63.
11. Cf. Netland, *Encountering*, ch. 5; *Voices*.
12. Cf. Nash, *Jesus*, ch. 11.
13. Cf. Griffin, "Religious Pluralism," 3.
14. Cf. McKim, *Diversity*; Schmidt-Leukel, *Pluralism*, 17–18.
15. Cf. Schmidt-Leukel, "Exclusivism," 13–27; *Pluralism*, 3–4.

of alternatives as true in order to be coherently able to accept one's own position as true alternative, and the others as wrong.[16]

The deeper implication of this insight will become obvious if we realize that—despite the presupposition of the whole field as the true statement of exhausted logical alternatives by which the identity of one's own position is defined as true (or false)—the communication between the alternatives will be significantly altered if one, in this common arena, defines oneself by one or the other perspective on truth. Only if one actually accepts the pluralist position can one communicate truth claims between religions in any meaningful way, while the other positions, although they must accept the field as true, cannot relate to the truth claims of other religions in an affirming way that (for them) will be worthy of any meaningful communication.[17] What can two exclusivists of different traditions communicate about? How can two inclusivists of different traditions ever see eye to eye?[18] Only two pluralists of different traditions can both affirmatively communicate and see eye to eye, including the content of the truth claims of (both of) their exclusivists and inclusivists.[19] In my emphasis on the fact that any position taken within the field of exclusivism, inclusivism and pluralism has already presupposed the whole field as true for taking any of these positions now yields also to the (maybe unexpected) insight that it can only be the pluralist who coextensively may correlate the affirmation of the whole field with the mutual definition of the truth of the three perspectives on truth *as* true. So, from the pluralist perspective the content of the truth of all three alternatives may now not be considered as a combination of true and false oppositions (this is how the field will look like from the exclusivist and inclusivist perspective), but as three differently expanded horizons of affirmations of more or less limited true positions. Now, oppositions have become alternatives (in one field) and alternatives have become variations (of one field). This is an important feature to be discussed later again in terms of transreligious transformations.[20]

Nor is religious pluralism a monolithic position in itself. It is a body of reflections that has developed its own host of literature and has gone through alterations, alternatives and complex discussions on different levels of religious and philosophical engagement—such

---

16. This is similar to the assumption of truth presupposed in the acceptance of the logical square of opposition, traceable back to antiquity, probably Aristotle, combining all universal and particular affirmative and negative judgment regarding any matter: (all) S a (are) P, (no) S e (is) P, (some) S i (are) P, S o (are not) P; cf. Parsons. Whatever the position taken regarding a matter, the logical square is affirmed as true in order to make any further judgment. The impasse of current theologies of religions as sharply diagnosed among others by Kenneth Rose (*Pluralism*, ch. 1), reducing pluralism to some sort of new exclusivism and, hence, affirming particularistic exclusivism instead, is upset by the logical implication expressed here: the universalist affirmation of the field for the particularist denial of its validity.
17. It is the work of Schmidt-Leukel, *Pluralism*, 110–12 (and related articles) that has demonstrated this implication with virtually inescapable clarity.
18. Cf. Nash, *Jesus*.
19. Cf. Race, *Thinking*, chs. 2–3.
20. This argument will be taken up in Chapter 7 regarding a pluralism of pluralisms and in Chapter 11 regarding the implications for a transreligious discourse on religion(s).

as theologies of specific religions, religious philosophies, philosophical theologies, philosophies of religion, theologies of religions, pluralistic philosophies and philosophies of pluralism[21]—and correlated political and ideological agendas,[22] each of them adding their own methodological perspectives and limitations to the theme. Most of the proponents of pluralistic positions come from thinkers of Christian provenience, as the whole movement has had a long history within Christianity of initiating interreligious discourses[23]—except for the fact that the equally important, but earlier Neo-Vedanta tradition of Sri Ramakrishna and Swami Vivekananda adds its own nondual approach to pluralism to the western discourse, as we will see later.[24]

Broadly speaking, pluralistic positions fall into four different modes of articulating the nature and value of religious pluralism and its potential limitations. The following fourfold of religious pluralisms is not structured along historical lines of appearance and chains of influence, which would be complicated to reconstruct in clear causal terms.[25] Yet if one seeks a criterion for choosing these fourfold, it can be constructed from a matrix constituted by the two polar dimensions of monocentric-polycentric and differential-relational pluralization of the field along an apophatic-cataphatic oscillation. The four possible combinations of this double polarity are presented roughly reaching from the monocentric-differential (apophatic) to the polycentric-differential (cataphatic) and from the monocentric-relational (apophatic) to the polycentric-relational (cataphatic) position.[26] While the meaning and context of these terms will become available as the

---

21. Cf. Phan and Ray; Harris, Hedges and Hettiarachchi; Heim, ed., *Grounds*; Tracy; Abdullah.
22. Cf. Prothero, ed., *Nation*; Kurtz; Mislin; Goodman; Hatchison; Nash, *Religious Pluralism*; Esack; Chatterjee
23. Cf. K. Rose, *Pluralism*, ch. 1; Heim, *Salvations*, part 1; Mortensen, part 3; Schmidt-Leukel, *Pluralism*, ch. 2.
24. Cf. Part II of this book, especially Chapters 9–10. The main proponent from this Indian tradition in the western academic pluralism debate is Jeffrey D. Long who is also connected to position 4, the position of process philosophy; cf. Long, "Putting Pieces Together," 151–70.
25. The reason for the following presentation of the history of the establishment and development of religious pluralism in recent discussions with four positions is not to rehearse or reduce the complexity of its becoming, and it does not have a pedagogical intention either, but wants to conceptually allow *paradigmatic* views to come to the fore that have appeared to sufficiently present the field. Knitter (position 1) develops the pluralistic thesis of Hick (position 3) probably further than most, even into hybrid religious identities and mutuality, like the process position (position 4), thereby resembling the polycentric implication of Heim (position 2), although Heim develops his position as revisionist inclusivism; and so on. However, despite the fact that some progress through the thought process of the fourfold may seem to be implied, it is rather meant to be understood as a synchronic field of mutual relations.
26. The further here implied assumption that the apophatic positions will always tend to be monocentric while the cataphatic positions emphasize a polycentric character will become clearer later in the text. This assumption is based on the arguable fact that the language and conceptuality of "one" ultimate reality is only viable as long as it is not reiterated, that is apophatically negated or unsaid; but as soon as it was to be concretized or embodied, it must be pluralized into a multiplicity in order not to lose its character of ultimacy; cf. Faber, *Garden*, ch. 6:1 ("The Nameless Name"). The dialectic between cataphatic pluralization and apophatic unification will be the theme of the next two chapters (Chapters 4–5).

positions are delineated presently, the classification remains fragile since none of the four positions or the polar terms to identify them are in themselves stable, but can rather ambivalently and luxuriantly (by purpose, criticism or sheer play) move into one another.

The first pluralist position, posited, for instance, by the Catholic scholar Paul Knitter, himself intently engaged in interreligious dialogue and questions of transreligious identities,[27] differentiates between two possible outcomes of a normative religious pluralism, both upsetting exclusivist dreams of the replacement of one religion by another or an anticipated fulfillment of all religions in only one, namely: either the permanent mutuality or the persistent acceptance of otherness of religions.[28] Acceptance of the mutuality of religious diversity means that religions remain within their different identities of origination, heritage and history, forms and organizations, but will engage in indefinite dialogue, not only aiming at a deeper understanding of the accepted truth of many religions, but toward the insight of the mutuality of these truth as emphasized differently in different religions. The other alternative, instead, accepts the unbridgeable differences of the many religions not only as one of factual inevitability, but one of the incommensurable truths of and within these religions; its aim would not be mutuality, but diversity.

The problems inherent in these two views of religious pluralism may be the following: How can we decide between these two views, and by what criteria would one be preferred over the other—that is, mutuality over incommensurability and vice versa?[29] And has not *that* view, namely, that of either form of pluralism, trending toward unity (mutuality) or difference (acceptance), respectively, become a more ultimate view of religion than, and already as one to be presupposed by, the religions themselves engaged in such a process of unification or diversification?[30] In any case, it was with utmost clarity that Knitter understood that universality is not finality, and that to view religions as a community is a basis for the community of humanity[31]—a clear categorical crossing to the intention of the conception of the unity of religions.[32]

Another perspective, proposed by the Protestant scholar Mark Heim, suggests that we may look at different religions not only as different paths toward salvation, but also as having genuinely different aims[33]: that *nirvana* is not heaven; that God is not the *dharmakaya*; that *brahman* is not the Buddha nature and so on. One would find salvation by

---

27. Cf. Knitter, *Buddha*; Knitter and Haight.
28. Cf. Knitter, *Introducing*, parts 3–4. Paul Knitter, together with John Hick, may be seen as one of the originators of the current field of religious pluralism in the western/Christian context since the 1970s; cf. Knitter, *No Other Name?*; Hick and Knitter; K. Rose, *Pluralism*, 27–30.
29. Cf. Kirkham, ch. 1.
30. The question seems to be mitigated in this case, as a "theology of religions" takes its cues from a certain religion, in this case, Christianity, and explores the implications for other religions, that is, could counter that it is still embedded in this religion and informed by its specific experience and doctrine; cf. Dupuis, *Toward*. However, then, another problem arises, namely, that such a claim would itself be based on inclusivism instead of pluralism.
31. Cf. Knitter, "Can Christian Theology," 89, 99–100.
32. For the motives and conceptual transgressions between religious pluralism and the unity of religions: cf. Chapters 2 and 6.
33. Cf. Heim, *Salvations*, ch. 5; *Depth*, ch. 1.

affirming the truth of a specific path and would somehow wind up in the respective final state projected by her respective tradition. However, not escaping the question of unity, he also envisions a relational relativity of these paths and aims by introducing some kind of trinitarian mutuality: that they relate to one another like the three persons in the one divinity of orthodox Christianity, that is, that they remain in permanent difference, but are always already relationally united.[34]

The critical points of this proposal are apparent: If there are different aims, and all aims are real for the ones believing in them, isn't the fabric of connectivity, of the web of existence, torn apart? In its most radical form, there seems to lurk a quixotic absurdity in the shadows of this divergence: not only would such a divergent anticipation of different, but separate ultimate realities and final states of salvation be caught in the possible worlds problem (and would look more like the splitting multiverse of Hugh Everett III or Davis Lewis[35]), it would also dispose the relation between them to the point of negation.[36] Is one who believes in a Christian eschaton ending up in it, and the one who hopes for *nirvana* awakening to it? What happens to the ones who do not commit to either or any such aim? How about the fact that many religionists share a pattern of some kind of hybridity, mixed beliefs of the idiosyncratic or multi-orthodox kind?[37] Are they obliterated, or are the unfit parts being ripped from them, or will they "create" their own eternal space?[38] And, even more problematic, if one needs a trinitarian framework of unity to establish relationality between these aims, hasn't, then, one religion holding such a doctrine again become superior over all others, as it would have assumed the unique power to propose the universal framework in which all others must come to rest?[39]

---

34. Cf. Heim, *Salvations*, ch. 6; *Depth*, part 3; K. Johnson.
35. Cf. Faber, *Manifold*, ch. 7.
36. This radical "pluralism" of soteriological aims is partly understandable on the background of Heim's opposition to John Hick's pluralism, which he understands (with many critics, but not necessarily correctly) as a monocentric quasi-substantialization of "one" ultimate reality; similar Griffin, ed., *Pluralism*, chs. 1–2. But this radical polycentrism of ultimate ends turns into a new inclusivism with the use of trinitarian terms; cf. Heim, *Depth*.
37. And the fact, already mentioned (Introduction), that religious identities are generated through the interaction and combination of as of yet unrealized potentials in the confluence of inherited religious traditions; cf. Leopold and Jensen.
38. Such a solution would only work if we assume that we are cocreators of our destiny after death, as all "views" would be constructions (formed by our life's decisions and cultural and social embeddedness as well as the expectations with which we live our lives) influencing our perceptions. This is an option gleaned, for instance, from Hindu and Buddhist sources relating to the pluripotent Akasha field and the Clear Mind, respectively. But then, the question of the "unity" of this universal consciousness would arise again, as these constructions, if they are to be overcome, would not be unrelated to the Reality from which their diversity arises or disappears into again; cf. Chopra, chs. 1–7, especially pp. 87–106.
39. Heim's "pluralism" almost strikes one as ironic given the fact that he opposes "liberal" pluralism as just another form of hegemonic exclusivism, just without the mandate of a specific religion. Hence, he can justify his trinitarian pluralism by rejecting pluralism if it is not based on specific tradition's claim of truth, working inclusively instead of pluralistically; Heim, *Depth*, 17. The trinitarian matrix is also used by the probably most outspoken "exclusivist inclusivist" (i.e., denying pluralism anything but the status of a new form of exclusivism, which he denies),

Yet another proposition comes from the Anglican scholar John Hick who should be understood as one of the most important figures of the whole movement, as he originally and prominently explored the differentiation of religious pluralism from exclusivism and inclusivism.[40] Hick's most iconic statement refining religious pluralism is probably this one:

> That the great world faiths embody different perceptions and conceptions of, and correspondingly different responses to, the Real from within the major variant ways of being human; and that within each of them the transformation of human existence from self-centeredness to Reality-centeredness is taking place. These traditions are accordingly to be regarded as alternative soteriological 'spaces' within which, or 'ways' along which, men and women can find salvation/liberation/ultimate fulfillment.[41]

Most of the literature exploring the implications of religious pluralism has been devised in the wake of, and often in differentiation from, opposition to, critique and refinement of Hick's influential thought.[42] What is more, his view has become a particularly noticeable inspiration for Bahá'í scholars.[43] Hick observes that many religious traditions agree that ultimate reality, as conceived in their own way, is inaccessible, inexplicable, hidden and unknown. That is, ultimacy is of an apophatic nature.[44] Yet its perception creates the main hiatus between religions, which can be grouped together because of this hiatus: inaccessible ultimate reality is either imagined in personal or nonpersonal terms; related religions are either monistic or theistic.[45] While both views can arise within a particular religion, not all streams of that religion may accept Reality as *both* a personal God, under different "names" like Allah, Shiva, Yahweh and the like, *and* a transpersonal Reality, like *dharma*, Buddha nature, *brahman*, *dao*, the One (*hen*) and so on.[46] Yet while claiming that all religions, by concluding ultimate reality to be either personal or transpersonal, or in some way both in some emphasis, harbor equally valid truth, all must then be transcended into a vision for which Reality is both and beyond both, their unification and denial. Ultimacy must be divested of all epithets and deemed as utterly apophatic regarding such manifestations or appearances to our experience, mind, spiritualities and ways of acting based on them. In this sense, all religions are not only limited by their

---

    Gavin D'Costa, who uses it not only to demonstrate the superiority of Christianity, but the universality of its pattern as foundational for religion per se; cf. D'Costa, "Preface."
40. Cf. Hick, *Interpretation*.
41. Hick, *Interpretation*, 240.
42. D'Costa, *Uniqueness*; Hewitt, *Problems*; Quinn and Meeker, *Challenge*.
43. Cf. May, 20–24; Fazel, "Dialogue," 12; "Pluralism," 42; Momen, "Relativism: A Basis," 208; Cole, "'I am,'" 447–76.
44. Cf. Hick, "Ineffability," 35–46.
45. Cf. Hick, *Interpretation*, chs. 15–16.
46. Cf. Hick, *Interpretation*, chs. 15–16. The ability to allow for this differentiation, which ordinarily is conceived as opposition or alternative (one cannot embrace at the same time), has been accepted by many theorists of religious pluralism as a primary matter of concern for the success of such a model; cf. Kaplan, 202.

own emphases of the conceptualization in which they mold their perception of ultimate reality, but they are also false to the extent that they fixate on either of them, or both, for that matter, since the Reality of them is beyond any kind of utterance and expressible conceptual limitation.[47]

The critique of Hick's pluralism over the past decades has gone into every aspect of his proposal.[48] I will only mention a few of the objections. First, Hick's pluralism is built on some of the philosophical conceptions of Immanuel Kant,[49] one of the most influential philosophers of the western tradition, which undermine any knowledge of reality, as knowing is not connective to reality, but isolating the subject of knowledge from the object of knowledge, the sensible from the intelligible world, the phenomenal from the noumenal, such that we cannot know anything, not even any natural phenomenon in itself, in its inner essence, and, even more so, not any spiritual reality per se—except one is of such reality (such as the human mind), but then cannot know the essence of any phenomenon.[50] While the applications of Kant's view has become the basis for the stark juxtaposition between scientific knowledge (empiricism) and philosophical insight (metaphysics), the physical world and spiritual reality (in the wake even to the point of negating the spiritual reality altogether), it allows Hick to postulate the utter unknowability of Reality in itself (the noumenal) with the drawback that Reality seems not to be engaged in anything (the phenomenal), and all seeming engagements are not "its."[51] Second, his system of pluralism favors transpersonal over personal ultimacy since, on the one hand, *personae* and *impersonae* are equally valid perceptions of Reality, but Reality is, on the other hand, ultimately beyond either of them and, hence, transpersonal "by nature," thereby inherently favoring traditions that tend to emphasize the transpersonal.[52] Third, if no religion is true, because the Ultimate is beyond such limitations, all religions are more equally false than true (although Hick was setting out to instill a pluralism of the equal truth of all religions).[53] Fourth, doesn't Hick's system of pluralism, being itself not a religion or presumably taken from any religion, but a philosophical conception, claim superiority for such a philosophical conception over all prima facie religions?[54] How come that Hick knows ultimate truth, but no religion does?[55]

---

47. Cf. Hick, *Interpretation*, ch. 14.
48. Cf. Nah.
49. Cf. Hick, *Interpretation*, 241–46.
50. Cf. Shaviro, *Criteria*, chs. 1–2.
51. Cf. Griffin, *Reenchantment*, 275–77. However, what is easily overlooked is that Hick *does*, in fact (although only in a weak affirmation), sense the necessity to reconnect apophatic Reality with the phenomenal world and, hence, does not totally isolate one from the other. Hick, therefore, speaks of the religious imaginations of Reality not as a fantasy, but as "responses to" Reality *and* as "manifestations" of the Real; cf. Hick, *Interpretation*, 240, 248–49.
52. Cf. Netland, *Pluralism*, ch. 7.
53. Cf. Heim, *Salvations*, 35–43.
54. Cf. Griffin, "Pluralism," 31–35. However, Hick *does* state that Religious Pluralism must be developed from *within* the diverse religions; cf. Hick, *Interpretation*, 377–78.
55. One cannot escape this dilemma by claiming to create a religion(s)-"neutral" philosophical theology as in Robert Neville's attempt of a religion-critical, controlling philosophical approach; cf. Neville, *Ultimates*, 1–24. This philosophical superiority not only falls under

A fourth conception comes from the universe of process thought, which is based on the work of Alfred North Whitehead.[56] As espoused by the Methodist scholar and prominent long-time inspiratory facilitator of the Christian-Buddhist interreligious dialogue John B. Cobb, Jr. and his long-term collaborator at Claremont, California, David Ray Griffin, this proposal promises to overcome the difficulties of the other three attempts by suggesting a "deep" religious pluralism where the others either fail to be deep enough (not being really pluralistic) or too limited to the inspiration by one religion (as such proposals haven't inspired a really interreligious reception), or by being confined by a pluralism that fails in light of a quest of knowledge to finding some kind of unity, harmony or coherence.[57] It is my own tradition of thinking[58] although I do not submit to this proposal as it stands. Instead, I have developed a different understanding of Whitehead's philosophical universe and have envisioned process thought in yet another flavor, which will become clearer as my considerations will develop beyond this point.[59]

Whitehead's "misplaced concreteness," namely, the acceptance of the most high abstraction as the most real reality, namely, *ultimate* reality; cf. Whitehead, *Science*, 51; *Religion*, 50, 149. Moreover, while such a philosophical system of all religions, that is, of "religion" per se (philosophically defined), may still try to be empirically open, as it could allow diverse realms of religious experience and thought to influence its formulation and development (as Neville admits), nevertheless, the philosophical system stays in control as their criterion for access (truth) or access denied—while for Whitehead religious thought becomes the highest expression of such a universal philosophy, which, hence, has no control over the criteria regarding what to accept as authentic religion, as in Neville, but rather co-insists in mutual immanence with the religious movements in their unabridged multiplicity; cf. Whitehead, *Religion*, 32. The controlling, highly abstract methodological monism of Neville, based in his ontological monism of the *ex nihilo* self-creation of creation, which is Neville's ultimate reality, can only accomplish this set task if it also circumvents religious pluralism. And, indeed, this is what Neville suggests, viewing it (with its detractors, exclusivism and inclusivism) only as "a phantom play with abstractions from real engagement" (*Ultimates*, 7), based on a misunderstanding of pluralism as method of identity-politics. However, what is relevant in the current context of the philosophical control of criteria of authentic religion is this: that Neville's own ontological monism (the apophatic *ex nihilo* self-creative act of determination of creation) is not the only philosophical model of discourse on ultimate reality that could figure as the controlling instance (or, as in Whitehead, denying such a control mechanism) and, hence, is itself confronted with a situation in which it has to decide whether to assume an exclusivist or inclusivist position of superiority and supersessionism, as Neville's position, in fact, does with the degradation of religious thought patterns of philosophical magnitude, coming from diverse religions (1–2), to the secondary position. *Or* the philosophical ultimate of such a philosophy will need to engage in mutual relevant discussions with other philosophical models of the same claim to universality, such as the ones related in this chapter and the next ones, thereby necessarily becoming part of a religious pluralism again. But one should also not forget that the whole line of argumentation is brought into play by declared antipluralists, such as D'Costa ("Impossibility," 223–32), not as a valid argument against the identification of religion and philosophy, but as justification of an exclusivist viewpoint.

56. Cf. Faber, *Poet*, §2; *Becoming of God*, Sphere I.
57. Cf. Griffin, "Complementary Pluralism," 1–38.
58. Cf. Faber, *Prozeßtheologie*.
59. Cf. Faber, *Poet*, §40; *Manifold*, part 1; *Becoming of God*, Explorations 7–10.

Without being able, here, to get into details of how and why process thought makes such claims, let me just try to get to the essential propositions of "deep" religious pluralism.[60] Cobb and Griffin propose, with Whitehead, that there is not just one ultimate Reality, but an interrelated manifold and mutually integrating multiplicity of ultimates. Depending on the phase of Whitehead's work, we will, indeed, find twofold,[61] threefold,[62] fourfold[63] or even more differentiations to this effect,[64] and diverse process thinkers have taken up these cues and developed their own understanding of this ultimate manifold.[65] In typological form, Cobb and Griffin prefer differentiating between three ultimate realities. They are ultimate in the sense that they cannot be reduced to either one reality without loss; but they cannot be had without the others.[66] In this view, *God* is the moral and religious ultimate, the divine process of valuating all possibilities for, and the actualizations of them by, creatures; the *World* is the embodied ultimate in which all realizations, actualizations and valuations assume form and concreteness, history and evolution; and *Creativity* is the metaphysical ultimate, the principle by which not only God, but all creatures have the ability and power to their own creativity, valuation of, responsibility to and influence on, the world process and God.[67] Now, Cobb and Griffin state that, given this complexity of ultimacy, neither are all religions based on only one of these ultimates alone, such that we could ever assume only many unrelated paths and aims, nor are they the same, as if there was only one path. Rather, different religions may emphasize many different of these paths in some combination of the three: Abrahamic traditions may emphasize God; Dharmic and Daoic religions may base their religious existence on the principle of Creativity (which is universal relationality, but not a person); and indigenous religions may emphasize the sacredness of the World.[68] Since neither of these ultimates can be reduced to (the) One, this pluralism claims, against Hick and others based on his proposal, to be truly pluralistic, as it does not construct another One beyond all of them. In Cobb's original "complementary" pluralism, relating the two ultimates of God and Creativity, the difference between personal and transpersonal views of the ultimate disappears, not because of unification, but because of distribution.

> One of these, corresponding with what Whitehead calls "creativity," has been called "Emptiness" ("Sunyata") or "Dharmakaya" by Buddhists, "Nirguna Brahman" by Advaita

---

60. Cf. Griffin, "Pluralism," 39–66.
61. Cf. Whitehead, *Process*, 7, 20–22; Faber, *Poet*, §§28, 32, 35; Griffin, *Reenchantment*, ch. 7.
62. Cf. Whitehead, *Process*, 346–48; Faber, *Poet*, §§33–34.
63. Cf. Whitehead, *Religion*, 89–94; Faber, *Becoming of God*, Exploration 7.
64. Cf. Whitehead, *Adventures*, 134, 295; Faber, *Becoming of God*, Exploration 3.
65. Cf. McDaniel, *Hope*, ch. 1.
66. Cf. Cobb, *Transforming*, 123, 185; Griffin, *Panentheism*, ch. 8; *Process Theology*, ch. 4.
67. In this typological form the tripartite differentiation of ultimates has also become the basis for process speculations of their interrelationship as an expression of the Christian doctrine of the Trinity, which has the advantage that the ultimates become modes of unity, but the disadvantage that they may become limited to a Christian understanding of this unity; cf. Faber, *Poet*, §§33–34.
68. Cf. Griffin, "Complementary Pluralism," 45–51; McDaniel, *Hope*, ch. 3; Cobb, ed., *Religions*.

Vedantists, "the Godhead" by Meister Eckhart, and "Being Itself" by Heidegger and Tillich (among others). It is the *formless* ultimate reality. The other ultimate, corresponding with what Whitehead calls "God," is not Being Itself but the *Supreme* Being. It is in-form and the source of forms (such as truth, beauty, and justice). It has been called "Amida Buddha," "Sambhogakaya," "Saguna Brahman," "Ishvara," "Yahweh," "Christ," and "Allah."[69]

Further, "deep" pluralism is not based on absolute unknowability (of the One), but on relationality (of the three), such that neither of the ultimates is without self-reference within and from the other ultimates. This solves the problem how there can be any true knowledge and existential salvation, as there are inherent connections between the ultimate and the phenomenal world.[70] However, different from other polycentric solutions (such as Heim's) their mutuality becomes not caught up in local religious doctrines such as that of the trinity.[71] Finally, this pluralism does not decide between the truth claims of different traditions in their spiritual perception and intellectual rendering of ultimacy, yet not because all are false in their conceptions; rather because perception is rightly different in emphasizing different elements of the mixture of these ultimates.[72]

Naturally, this proposal is also not without difficulties. Are many ultimates (polycentrism) really more intelligible than one (monocentrism)?[73] Who decides how

---

69. Griffin, "Complementary Pluralism," 47; emphases in the original.
70. Cf. Whitehead, *Process*, 49–51, 71–72, 88; Faber, *Poet*, §§10–11, 13–14; Hartshorne, "Concept," 103–13.
71. Cf. Whitehead, *Religion*, 74–75; Cobb, "Assumptions," 259–64; "Relativization," 1–22; Suchocki, *Divinity*. Yet compare with universalist emancipations from this local bondage: Whitehead, *Adventures*, 265–268; Faber, *Poet*, §33; Faber, "Trinity," 147–72.
72. Cf. Cobb, *Beyond Dialog*, 145–50; Faber, *Poet*, §32.
73. Cf. Faber, *Poet*, §28; Neville, *Creativity*; Ford, 79–84. The discussion between Ford and Neville, which could also roughly be viewed as the contrasting opposition between a Whiteheadian polycentric process approach and a Tillich-influenced monocentric approach, is by no means a matter of the past, but cannot be discussed within the boundaries of this book; cf. Faber, *Prozeßtheologie*, §§2, 31, 35; *Manifold*, ch. 6; Neville, *Ultimates*, passim. I may only hint, here, to the similarity of the apophatic approach to ultimacy of Neville (the act of creation "out of nothing") to the self-creative act of creation of (or into) the Primal Will of God (*mashiyyat*, and, by extension, the Mind of God, '*aql*, or the Word of God, *kalimat*, and the Primal Manifestation, *mazhar*) in the Bab's apophatic-theophanic vision, as the "creator" leaving the apophatic Godhead's essence (*dhat*) in apophatic inaccessibility. However, this self-creative act of the creation-creator's nondifference (of the Primal Will) is closer to Whitehead's similarly apophatic-theophanic creative act than to Neville's *ex nihilo*, as this is not a transeunt act of determination (as is presumed in Neville), but a receptive act *ad intra*, unifying a multiplicity that, in the same act, becomes relational multiplicity, in the first place—thereby, equally embracing indeterminacy and determinacy. This is true for the Primordial and Consequent Natures of God in Whitehead and regarding (the similar difference between) Actual Matter and Potential Forms in the Primordial Will in the Bab's understanding, thereby (in both cases), in a specific sense, but universally, embracing the act itself in itself; cf. Saiedi, *Gate*, ch. 7; Faber, "Mystical Whitehead," 213–34; *Poet*, §§25, 35. In my understanding, this is a process not of determination (as in Neville), but of "indetermination" and "in/differentiation"; cf. *Poet*, §40; "Sense of Peace," 41–45; *Manifold*, ch. 4 (Indetermination); *Becoming of God*, 26 and Sphere 5; *Garden*, ch. 1:6.

many ultimates there are, as process thought could allow for more or less than the three mentioned here?[74] And if religions become identified with certain of these ultimates, as some proposals have been tempted to assume, although only in a typological fashion, are we not creating the error of essentialism,[75] that is, binding breathing phenomena of life, the respective complex bodies of religions, to lifeless and fixed ultimates?[76] Since in some versions of this proposal these ultimates are, in fact, many, one wonders what the status of their relation actually is[77]—in my view, the weakest point over against which I have emphasized that "mutual immanence" is the "one" ultimate of all.[78] And if these ultimates are interrelated, what does this say about a specific religion in its insistence that the truth lies in their alternative, not their combination? Can a Buddhist, for instance, really accept that she has to assume God as the missing ultimate besides the *dharma* or the *dharmakaya*?[79] Finally, one objection to all of these pluralistic systems comes also back haunting this proposal: How can a philosophy decide to know more than the religions from or against, without or in reference to which, it was developed?[80]

In summary, even if we are convinced that religious pluralism is to be preferred over exclusivism and inclusivism, we are left with a plethora of sometimes related, sometimes alternative or even opposite understandings of the inner workings and effectiveness of its pluralistic assumption. In this sense—and we will discover further forms of this phenomenon later—religious pluralism is presenting itself in pluralistic form, that is, its field of potential assumptions, positions and solutions cannot be reduced to one without loss (like the ultimate and salvific realities on which it reflects). There is no contradiction in this insight; rather it is to be expected that communication always needs some kind of polyphone relationality of differences since otherwise, that is, if multiplicity could be reduced to unity, it would not ultimately be multiplicity. This is troubling to many religious thinkers, teachers and practitioners, because the implication seems to force us to accept that the unity that fully supports multiplicity, and the multiplicity that need not give way to unity, is in itself profoundly non-foundational: without one fundament and anchor.[81] We seem to have opened the door to relativism, for many the evil twin of

---

74. Cf. Sharma, "Along a Path," 198–202; Knitter, "Can Christian Theology," 83–102. In fact, thoroughly thought through in its relativistic implications, the mutual contextualization of ultimates will lead to an infinite regress of ultimates; cf. Faber, *Manifold*, Intermezzo I.
75. Cf. Faber, *Manifold*, chs. 2, 6.
76. Cf. Fletcher, *Monopoly*, ch. 4; McDaniel, *Hope*, ch. 3.
77. Cf. Schmidt-Leukel, *Pluralism*, 29; Kaplan, ch. 5.
78. Cf. Faber, "Immanence," 91–110; *Prozeßtheologie*, §21; *Manifold*, Intermezzo 1; *Becoming of God*, Exploration 10; *Garden*, chs. 2–4.
79. Cf. Knitter and Haight, ch. 5; Knitter, *Buddha*, chs. 1–2; Cobb and Ives, *Emptying God*. Kaplan's holographic model accepts this possibility for the expression of different ultimates for different people and religions, thereby implying their necessary interrelatedness as the Truth beyond their limitations; cf. Kaplan, *Paths*, 40–43, 152.
80. But again, as for Hick, Cobb and Griffin, on the Whiteheadian basis, gather proposals of "deep" pluralism developed *from within* different religious traditions; cf. Griffin, ed., *Pluralism*, part 2.
81. Cf. Thiel; van Huyssteen, *Essays*.

truth.[82] Yet this is a premature fear. In fact, no pluralistic position, however far it may lean toward the limit of plurality over that of unity, can consistently claim ultimate diversification without some kind of relationality in between or a horizon above and beyond.[83] It suffices, at this point, to register that the pluralistic limit and the limit of oneness in the diverse religious pluralisms are neither simple opponents nor easy partners. While the emphasis on plurality in religious truth claims seems unavoidable, the sustained interest of the sort of pluralism intended here always remains to be able to state some kind of parity between religions regarding their truth claims.[84] Herein, paradoxically lies the unity of their plurality.

---

82. Cf. Margolis.
83. Cf. Keller, "Introduction: The Process of Difference," 1–30; Faber, *Poet*, §§13, 26.
84. Cf. Griffin, "Religious Pluralism," 3.

Chapter Four

THE PROMISE OF MYSTICISM

Your souls are as waves on the sea of the spirit; although each individual is a distinct wave, the ocean is one, all are united in God.[1]

—'Abdu'l-Bahá

After having identified the problems of both religious unity and religious pluralism to be that of the relativity of religious truth, we can now, after surveying different proposals, also ask the question: Are there ways to state the unity and plurality of religions, not by either seeking saving unity or difference, but rather by demonstrating the interference of both unity and multiplicity, on a level that, simultaneously, does avoid their possible opposition?[2] In fact, not only have many of the spiritual compositions of the new axial age and the diverse current philosophical renditions of the problem, but also the religions of the first axial age, left us with rich resources, which to this effect either register in their own histories or are recognized by current reflections on them.[3] One common element in all of these projects is their appeal to mysticism[4]—either as an obvious or hidden stream in their own development or as critical corrective to the overly oppositional thinking of their respective orthodoxies.[5] And so, the appeal to mysticism has been right at the center of many current propositions of religious pluralism as well.[6]

The definition of mysticism is less important here, as it changes with the perspective by which it is engaged.[7] Rather, we can filter the important characteristics that concern a selection of influential enterprises of formulating the contribution of mysticism(s) to our questions. For our purposes, then, we can identify mysticism with experiential, experimental and cognitive exercises and their impact on respective religious and philosophical worldviews that begin or end in, or always in all other approaches and expressions of a religion or philosophy eventually refer to, ultimate reality as being *apophatically* unavailable, that is, beyond any categorization, perception or experiential grasp, while also in some way *cataphatically* being apparent, immanent or revealing itself in this world of

---

1. 'Abdu'l-Bahá, *Paris Talks*, #28.
2. Cf. Ramadan, ch. 2.
3. Cf. Knitter, ed., *Myth*, parts 2–6.
4. Cf. Brodd, 11.
5. Cf. Reat and Perry.
6. Cf. K. Rose, *Pluralism*; Schmidt-Leukel, *Pluralism*, 24–26, 40, 48–53, 69, 86, 94; Cornille, *Im-Possibility*, 213.
7. Cf. Kessler and Sheppard.

physical and spiritual embodiments.⁸ Religions in their mystical streams also often either presuppose in their history, or consciously in their formation, some kind of mutual influence and what can be called *transreligious* movements through different religious spheres and communities, even between east and west, of their central tenets. Despite or against their orthodox denials and efforts to suppress such a common story of the spiritual evolution, they have established themselves as an underlying heritage of humanity as a whole⁹—and the Bahá'í writings are also no stranger to the recognition of the mystical core of all religions and the sensitivity to this common heritage of humanity.¹⁰

Here are three outstanding classical examples. One of the extraordinary representatives of a whole (religious) philosophy being built on these characteristics of mysticism in the west, or better, in a complex exchange between east and west, is Plotinus.¹¹ In his *Enneads*, he proposes ultimate reality to being ultimate precisely because it is beyond all categories. Customarily, it can be named the One, God or the Good—in order not to lose contact with the actual religious and philosophical language choices of spiritual paths—but it is really beyond all of those categorizations inaccessible and unknowable.¹² "It" cannot be named, and even with the almost blind epithet "the One" Plotinus uses just a placeholder in language for the inexpressible. What is more, in this apophaticism of the abnegation of any position or coordinate system for positioning (and, hence, any positive assumption), "it" is to be "posited" beyond being and nothingness and, hence, resides beyond all dualities utilized to differentiate "it" from anything and everything.¹³ However, it is the ultimate reality *of* the world and its innumerable differentiations and multiplicities. "It" emanates (into) the world, its differentiations and multiplicities, in a cascading flow of levels or stations of expansion: from the One manifested in Mind (*nous*), the beginning of reflection, consciousness and composition, to (the Mind manifested in) the World Soul (*psyche*), as the embracing living unity of all world phenomena, which feels and knows of them, to the exhaustion of the whole movement in Matter (*hyle*), the realm of particles and blind encounters. It is in the emanation process of these three *hypostases*—One, Mind and Soul—that the world appears from,¹⁴ and is, simultaneously, moving backward into, the One,¹⁵ like exhaling and inhaling, both spanning time in a transtemporal movement, a parallel movement of eternity and temporality, and vertically between them. One of the most intriguing implications of this mystical philosophy, which has become embedded in many spiritual renderings of the Abrahamic traditions, is the insight that the One *is* all things *and* none of them.¹⁶ It is this insight that connects

---

8. Cf. Brainard, chs. 3, 8; Ellwood, ch. 2.
9. Cf. Teasdale.
10. Cf. Bahá'u'lláh, *Seven Valleys*, 1–4 and passim; *Hidden Words*; Savi, *Summit*; "Baha'i Faith," 5–22; Lawson, "Globalization," 35–54; Shoghi Effendi, *Directives*, #223.
11. Cf. Gregorios.
12. Cf. Roy, ch. 4.
13. Cf. Sells, "Apophasis," 47–65; *Languages*, ch. 1.
14. Cf. Majumdar.
15. Cf. Hines.
16. Cf. Plotinus, *Enneads*, V.2.1; Faber, *Poet*, §40.

Plotinus with eastern and western forms of nondualism,[17] that is, the proposition that Reality is not only beyond all differences, but also that this *is* its difference from everything.[18] In this sense, "it" is different by being neither identical with nor different from anything and, hence, is in a profound sense non-different from anything.[19]

Plotinus's analysis and insight has had enormous influence on the development of ancient and medieval western thinkers and mystics such as Pseudo-Dionysius the Areopagite, who introduced the term "mystical theology" in the religious vocabulary of Christianity,[20] as well as the overarching figures of Meister Eckhart and Nicolas of Cusa.[21] In their rendering of ultimate divine Reality as "being" beyond any differences attributed to and within creation, the apophatic Godhead became differentiated from "God" in (relation to) creation, who is the only God in differentiation from the world, but non-different from creation in Godself.[22] Moreover, we may also trace influences to other forms of Abrahamic mystical non-difference, such as the mutually resonant Jewish Kabbalah[23] and the intercultural, intercontinental and interreligious spiritual complex of Sufism,[24] especially as it survived in the Persian philosophers and poets such as Suhrawardi, Mulla Sadra, Rumi and Hafez,[25] among others, and with the Bahá'í writings.[26]

In the wake of this insight of non-difference, the next example has had direct relevance for Bahá'u'lláh's meditations on ultimate reality, mediated through the great Sufi philosopher Ibn 'Arabi and his school.[27] While often misunderstood as pantheism, the teaching that God and the world are the same or coextensive, Ibn 'Arabi developed a version of this non-difference, which later became known as the Sufi doctrine of *wahdat al-wujud* (often heavily opposed by Islamic orthodoxies),[28] which brought the profound relativity of religious truth in differential relations to light and into pluralistic focus. In a radical twist, he formulates the underlying insight of the relation of ultimate reality (the oneness of God) with the multiplicity of religions by claiming that, since God cannot be known by anyone, not the least by any religion, every religious conceptualization of God is but a reflection of one's religion's own limited imaginations and projections.[29]

---

17. Cf. Kloetzli, "Nous," 140–77.
18. It is interesting to note here that Karl Rahner, the great "orthodox" Catholic theologian of the twentieth century, has indicated this very insight of nondualism to be the differentiating marker of true Christian theism that is neither dualistic nor pantheistic (monistic); cf. Rahner, 62.
19. Cf. Faber, *Becoming of God*, Exploration 15; *Poet*, §§32, 40; *Manifold*, ch. 13; *Garden*, ch. 6.
20. Cf. Golitzin, 8–37.
21. Cf. Flasch, *Metaphysik*.
22. Cf. McGinn, "God beyond God," 1–19.
23. Cf. Scholem, ch. 1; Matt, 24–25; Hallamish, 191.
24. Cf. Toshihiko Izutsu, part 1, chs. 2, 9, 11; Schimmel, *Dimensions*, chs. 3, 5.
25. Cf. Schimmel, *Islam*, chs. 6–7; Walbridge, *Wisdom*.
26. Cf. Faber, "Bahá'u'lláh," 55; Kluge, "Neoplatonism I," 149–202; "Neoplatonism II," 105–93; Hazini.
27. Cf. Bahá'u'lláh, *Lawh Basít al-Haqíqa*, 203–21; Faber, "Bahá'u'lláh," 80–85.
28. Cf. Toshihiko Izutsu, part 1, ch. 5; Savi, *Summit*, ch. 2.
29. Cf. Chittick; Sells, *Languages*, ch. 4; Momen, *Religion*, 196.

Here, Sufi thought, Bahá'í writings and Whitehead's philosophy coincide in one profound sentence: *that it is as true to say that God creates the world as it is to say that the world creates God.*[30] While this sentence is understood differently in these religious and philosophical renderings (as we will see later), they capture the important relativity that undermines all dogmatic reiterations of God or ultimate reality in principle: while we may be created in God's image, it is us, the image, that always recreates God in its own limited image.[31] Divine imagination is, therefore, always multiple, differentiated and divergent. Yet because of this insight, if it is taken seriously, we don't have to make such limited reflections become the reason for strife, opposition and religious wars either, as we are all, as it were, in the same boat.[32] Bahá'í writings have taken up this relativistic approach and—as we will see shortly—wrapped it into their understanding of divine immanence and revelation itself.[33]

One of the most radical proponents of this nondualism is a saint and sage (philosopher) of Buddhist origin, Nagarjuna, to whom the Madhyamika school of Buddhism traces its origin and identity.[34] In his work, the *Mulamadhyamikakarika*,[35] he exerts the utmost effort demonstrating that any conceptualization whatsoever will fail to reach ultimate reality, because it is necessarily built on differentiations that create oppositional fields of tension. If I say one thing, I must exclude another; if I confirm one element, I must negate another and so on. Hence, all "views" are not only limited, but really false. They must be exposed as such and overcome. Only in leaving all views behind will ultimate reality be realized. This would be enlightenment.[36] In reflection and as spiritual beings, we must end in silence.[37] However, Nagarjuna does not conclude that all realities that we encounter and know in our everyday life are mere illusions.[38] On the contrary, they are also "real" and, hence, exhibit their own truth on their own level of existence. Like Ibn 'Arabi and the Bahá'í writings,[39] ordinary reality has its reality and truth, but its site is of a lower level; it is of less intensity than Reality itself (the unspeakable Beyond, that is, Reality and Truth itself), which is the ultimately "real." His teaching is captured

---

30. Cf. Momen, "God," 14; Whitehead, *Process*, 348; Faber, "God in the Making," 179–200. The formulation is Whitehead's and it will later be quoted in the text.
31. Cf. Corbin, 195–200; Sells, *Languages*, 97–100.
32. Cf. Schmidt-Leukel, *Pluralism*, chs. 8–9; Momen, "Relativism," 367–97; Faber, *Manifold*, ch. 2; *Garden*, chs. 3–4.
33. Cf. 'Abdu'l-Bahá, *Questions*, #37.
34. Cf. McCagney.
35. Cf. Garfield, 342–60.
36. Cf. Williams and Tribe, 140–52. The fourfold logic of position, negation, both position and negation, neither position nor negation, that Nagarjuna uses as means to overcome any position, leading to the experience of Enlightenment and the nonduality of *nirvana* and *samsara*, can also be found in the reflections of Nicolas of Cusa on the unknowability of God; cf. Baier, "Reality," 92–97, 107–11. But they also appear in the mystical path as elaborated by Bahá'u'lláh in the *Seven Valleys*.
37. Cf. Lopez, 24–33.
38. Cf. Harvey, *Buddhism*, 197.
39. Cf. Bahá'u'lláh, *Gleanings*, #148; 'Abdu'l-Bahá, *Questions*, #37.

with the theory of "two truths"[40]—one of them ordinary, the other ultimate.[41] What is true on one level is not so on the other, but we live in both worlds.[42]

Three examples from recent and current discussions will round out the landscape of this mystical approach. To begin with, perennialism is the view that all religious traditions harbor a mystical core, which, despite different cultural contexts, languages and terminologies, refers to the same experiences of ultimate reality.[43] As instantiated, for example, by the work of the Methodist thinker Huston Smith,[44] the Sufi master and scholar Frithjof Schuon[45] and the writer and mystical theorist Aldous Huxley,[46] the perennial truth of all religions comes to light when we realize that the common inner traditions of mysticism, harbored in all religious traditions in some way, are closer to one another than they are not only to any orthodoxy, but to the external identities of their own traditions that house them. The core spiritual insight of this inner life of religions is the oneness of God or ultimate reality with our experience of "it." This *unio mystica* is not (necessarily) based on pantheistic identity (and undue identification of a substantial Reality or "sameness"),[47] but on the transreligious realization of nondual insights in all traditions, a common pattern, as it were, of experience, spiritual life and thought.[48]

---

40. Cf. Newland, ch. 6.
41. Cf. R. Jones, *Nagarjuna*, 135–58, 180; Abe, *Zen*, ch. 4.
42. Cf. Bahá'u'lláh, *Gleanings*, #37; 'Abdu'l-Bahá, *Selections*, #92; A comparison between this twofold existence in Nagarjuna and the Sufi doctrine of living "in two worlds," as well as its Bahá'í affirmation, with an additional reference to a similar approach in Whitehead must be left for future reflections; cf. Savi, *Summit*, 282–84; Whitehead, *Process*, 350; Faber, *Becoming of God*, 117, 125–26; *Garden*, ch. 8. Yet it is interesting that such a resonance exists at all given the vastly different philosophical and terminological backgrounds of their respective thought patterns.
43. Cf. Lings and Minnaar, part 5; Versluis.
44. Cf. H. Smith, *Truth*.
45. Cf. Schuon.
46. Cf. Huxley.
47. It is, in my view, an unfortunate simplification to think that perennialism is nothing but a way to identify sameness as the central message of all religions. This seems to be rather the counterpropaganda of exclusivists who want to save the uniqueness of their religion in the concert of religions, or rather the falseness of all religions except their own, mostly in terms of fundamentalist Christian self-affirmation. This strategy of identifying similarities in transreligious encounters as "from the devil" has a long tradition in Christian apologetics, reaching back to the early Church fathers, but is still met with despise when one reminds orthodox exceptionalism of such transreligious fluency; cf. Riley, *River*. One should have been warned already by the assumption of perennialists that the "unity" of religions can be found not in any positive orthodoxy, but in the apophatic unsaying of such particularities that they do not intend to substitute one particularity (or a plethora of those) with another.
48. If we resist the simplification of identifying this oneness with sameness, the transreligious pattern that perennialism perceives in different religions might less be a matter of discovering the same or any "reality," but one of patterns of mutual relatedness that is closer to the newer idea of a "holographic pattern" of oneness, as in Kaplan (ch. 4), or a "fractal pattern" of difference, as in Schmidt-Leukel (*Pluralism*, ch. 14). Contrary to Haught (*Story*, ch. 1), we must, to say it again, always be cautious and forgo identifying perennial intentions with sedimentations of this mystical core, as it is of apophatic nature and, in this sense, not "analogical" (just

One of the most outstanding contributions to nondual thought comes from the Catholic theologian and theological consultant to the Second Vatican Council, Raymond Panikkar. Of Spanish and Indian descent, he became, himself heavily engaged in interreligious dialogue and discourse, a prototype of a transreligious personality.[49] He became famous for saying that he was a Christian, went to India, became a Hindu and returned to the west a Buddhist without having renounced being a Christian.[50] Panikkar insists that religious truth is neither one nor many, but plural. This is a hard concept to fathom for many, but essential in order to understand the whole project of his religious pluralism. On this view, one and many are ultimately abstractions from the inaccessible Truth that cannot be formulated in one coherent intellectual system. Hence, as is factually exhibited by religions, we must normatively *embrace* difference, variety, pluriformity, radical diversity, perspectivism, relativity and incommensurability in all of our systematic endeavors to create formulations of ultimate value.[51] As Truth/Reality/God is beyond any "system"—beyond the Logos of Christianity, beyond manifest Brahman of Hinduism (*saguna brahman*) and beyond the Mind (*nous*) of Plotinus—it is the perennial Mystery. As such "it" mirrors itself only in a multiplicity of reflections and is the inspiration of all of them.[52] Hence, we must neither fear incommensurabilities between the different religions in addressing this mystery nor posit the reiterated identity of their formulations as necessary asset for grasping the mystery. Rather, we must necessarily engage the relativity of all of these attempts *as* the revelation of the mystery itself, namely, to be beyond any fixations within thought and experience, orthodox or otherwise, but revealed in them in their multiplicity *as* mystery.[53]

Finally, the so-called Participatory Turn of the scholar of transpersonal psychology, Jorge Ferrer, is worth mentioning in this context, as it also comes close to my own understanding of the matter (although, in my case, developing from a different basis, namely, process thought).[54] Ferrer suggests that the future of religion will not be bound by dogmatic identities locked in mutual strife and exclusion, but will be freed by the insight that the global society of today demands that we develop the ability to make peace with difference through the mutual sensitivity to, and participation in, one mystical landscape arising from the diverse religions and spiritual movements. This may be necessitated by the global pressure of mutual dependence in life and thought, the search for solutions to current human predicaments and the salvation from mutual destruction.[55] He envisions several future paths to which such a situation can lead us.[56] It can either issue into a

---

imitating eternity in time), but "anticipatory," that is, always lacking a final fulfillment of the apophatic promises in time or even eternity.
49. Cf. Prabhu, ed., *Challenge*.
50. Cf. *The New York Times*, September 6, 2010, A20.
51. Cf. Panikkar, "Pluralism," 7–16.
52. Cf. Panikkar, *Experience*.
53. Cf. Panikkar, *Silence*, ch. 9.
54. Cf. Ferrer and Sherman, "Participatory Turn," 1–78.
55. Cf. Ferrer, *Revisioning*, part 2.
56. Cf. Ferrer, "Future," 14–16, 63–64. In the original article, Ferrer had assumed for the Bahá'í Faith to be implementing a simple notion of "unity" as sameness; in a later publication,

new consciousness of mutual transformation in the encounter of the diverse religious traditions, an enrichment that does not necessarily demand abstaining from remaining differences of heritage and religious identity. Or the future could hold a new level of spiritual formation in which a less defined inter-spiritual movement may glean wisdom from different traditions, but will be engaged in a global ethic and an ecological responsibility for the world beyond their (organizational and doctrinal) limits. A third path could lead into a transformation of religions as such into a global spirituality that is no longer in need of any religious organization, such as is already effective in movements such as New Age and postmodern spirituality. Or, as a fourth path, we could end up with a renouncement of the utility of religion with its supernatural realities as such and venture in a new time of spiritual naturalism, devoid of any doctrines of salvation that try to overcome the cosmos in which we live. All of these visions of the future of religions are based on the mystical insight of the incommensurable transcendence of Reality beyond simple religious identities.[57] Yet it is central to Ferrer's conceptualization that these different forms *are* participations in the mystery and are cocreative of the meaning of Reality in a relational web of shifting multiplicities and coherences.[58] In resonance with Ferrer, I will take up the projections of the spiritual future religion on the basis of my constructive proposal of the pluralistic, mystical and transreligious rendering of both unity and plurality of religions in the third part of the book.

Here, I want to highlight one counterintuitive insight that we may gain with this review of the mystical source of religious pluralism. Mysticism as an intellectual endeavor (reflecting on or even being part of mystical experiences) is in its sophisticated versions not a monistic stream or a pantheistic resistance to Abrahamic theism, or, contrarily, a mere "negative theology" of the disappearance in apophatic silence, or maybe (for the Abrahamic "realms") a Trojan horse of "heretical" adaptations of eastern religions, undermining and destroying the cataphatic emphases of western traditions on revelation and divine activity in nature and history.[59] Instead, this transreligious river of traditions is about apophatic non-difference, which paradoxically means most intense immanence.[60] I have named this signification of ultimate Reality its "absolute transcendence" (not to satisfy non-pantheism, but) in order to indicate that this whole project is not about the relativity *between* apophatic transcendence and infinite forms of immanence,[61] but about the non-difference *of* both transcendence and immanence in an "absolute" way.[62] Absolute and relative are not opposite or polar adjective attributions that can be somehow distributed or are somehow limiting one another—which may be the misunderstanding that feeds the fear of mysticism's inherent relativism.[63] Rather, they are beyond being

---

however, after our email exchanges, he has at least partially corrected this view; cf. *Participation*, 306n4. For implications regarding hopes and fears for the future of religions, cf. Chapter 14.
57. Cf. Ferrer, *Participation*, ch. 10.
58. Cf. Ferrer, *Participation*, 219.
59. Cf. Underhill, *Mysticism*, part 1, ch. 5.
60. Cf. Faber, "Bodies," 200–26.
61. Cf. McLean, "Prolegomena," 37–44.
62. Cf. Faber, *Prozeßtheologie*, §31.
63. Cf. R. Jones, *Mysticism*, 73–78.

different and identical and, hence, mutually affirmative in their non-difference of unity and multiplicity.[64]

Certain consequences follow from this insight. For one, it makes the perennial assumption feasible that mystical streams can communicate beyond the boundaries of their externally defined orthodoxies and religious organizations, cultural integrities and categorical systematizations of different religious spheres all over the world, but without also assuming that this communication is based on sameness.[65] Furthermore, mysticism does not necessitate either a restriction of truth to specific expressions of the mystery over that of the religious other, or the contrary move, to deny the orthodox traditions in which it was formulated.[66] This explains why many mystics have, despite all of their radical unorthodox formulations of the mystery,[67] not tried to corrupt their religious traditions and the external beliefs held by their respective communities;[68] but it explains also why they were not necessarily limited by their affirmation so as not also to be able to engage other faith's belief systems without fear of animosity.[69] It would be a misunderstanding to attribute such patterns of irenic yielding merely to their orthodox suppression or personal fear not to be branded as heretics—although many performatively resisted orthodox closure and died as martyrs of this insight anyway.[70] Finally, sophisticated mystical discourses know of their most cherished insights as still finite and impermanent in the great scheme of things. Such discourses display not only endless variations in their expressions to uninitiated seekers to which the writings of mystics are often directed, but they are in themselves infinitely regressive by always "negating" all positions as merely finite (and never final) states of achievement in the infinite/indefinite endeavor to understand the mystery of Reality/God.[71] This most certainly characterizes eastern strategies of reasoning (generally more than western) with their complex paradoxical expressions of truth not as either (true) or (false), but as both (affirmation) and (negation), and neither of them.[72] This plurality in approximating truth becomes the appropriate movement of thought needed to overcome limitations of simple alternatives or oppositions at any given point.[73] However, the

---

64. Cf. Faber, *Poet*, §40; *Manifold*, chs. 1–2, 8; *Garden*, ch. 6:2.
65. Cf. Waldenfels. Senzaki details the encounter between Inayat Khan and Nyogen Zenzaki. On the fluency between Meister Eckhart and mystics from diverse eastern and western religious traditions, cf. Fox.
66. Both purposes can be witnessed, for instance, by Ibn 'Arabi's "God in all Faiths" and Nicolas of Cusa's heavenly gathering of all religions in *De Pace Fidei*, referred to at other places in this book.
67. One might immediately think of the outrageous formulations of Meister Eckhart—of "being" God, of the Godhead beyond God, of losing God for God's sake and the like—that led to a condemnation of many of them by a papal bull from 1329 CE; cf. Woods, ch. 1.
68. Cf. McIntosh.
69. Cf. Ma'sumian, "Mysticism," 12–17.
70. Cf. Janzten, chs. 1–2; Lanzetta, *Wisdom*, ch. 8.
71. Cf. Franke, *On What Cannot Be*; R. Jones, *Mysticism*, ch. 4.
72. Cf. Faber, *Manifold*, ch. 13; Stcherbatsky, *Logic*; *Conception*, 62; Abe, *Zen*, ch. 5.
73. Cf. Faber, *Manifold*, Intermezzo 1.

implication is not that a "negative dialectic" has necessarily the final word regarding mysticism[74]; rather, this movement could also be spun as a radically pluralistic affirmation of the plurality of such expressions. This is the figure of thought to which I will now turn.

---

74. Cf. Knepper, *Negation*.

Chapter Five

POLYPHILIC PLURALISM

The Most Great Ocean overflowed with gleaming and life-giving waters.[1]

—Bahá'u'lláh

While the appeal to mysticism and mystical thought patterns might bring us closer to a mutual resonance of the impulses of non-oppressive unity as highlighted by the Bahá'í writings and of new nonviolent differentiation as highlighted by religious pluralism, the "mystical explanation" as regards this inquiry has its own problems. First of all, if mystical silence beyond all categories of understanding has the last word or, as it were, remains always beyond any word, the world of religions with its perceptions and experiences, experiments and conceptions, of ultimate reality will easily deflate into a relativism for which any differentiation between religious truths and values, any valuations and emphases, any measure of approximation and remoteness, even any limitation and exclusion of problematic valuations and emphases will be indistinguishable from illusion.[2] The multireligious patience for the limitations of any positive expression of mystical truth in specific religious teachings and some common horizon for moral judgments as well as the transreligious independence from the constraints of any religious tradition will easily be mistaken for, or lowered to, a passivity of egalitarian indifference that quickly can lose any impulse for the importance of embodiments of life and distinctions of consequence. Essential characteristics of oneness, ecstasy and ineffability[3] of mystical experience can, out of a feeling of self-involved silence, easily degenerate into indifference, aloofness and inconsequential lassitude. The Bahá'í writings know of this situation,[4] as do many mystical discourses.[5] Hence, they don't force us to remain in silence, but refer to, or in many cases even insist on, the intrinsic *noetic* character of the mystical discourse by which radical relativity can be distinguished from mere relativism.[6] With these noetic negotiations, mystical discourses will situate themselves right on the boundary of, or in probing the boundary between, silence and utterance, unknowability and insight, mystery and its embodied variegations.[7] The process

---

1. Bahá'u'lláh, "Lawh-i Hikmat (Tablet of Wisdom)," in *Tablets*, 146.
2. Cf. Berger, chs. 1, 4.
3. Cf. Stace, 79.
4. Cf. Momen, "God," 14–17.
5. Cf. Momen, *Religion*, 41–43, 195–99.
6. Cf. Forman, 705–38; Teasdale, 23–25; Happold, 45; R. Jones, *Mysticism*, ch. 3.
7. Cf. Keller, *Mystery*, 18–19; Underhill, *Mysticism*, 72.

of mystical insight is one of "unknowing," but not one of becoming unconscious or insentient.[8]

In fact, mystical discourse avoids irrationality and incommunicability, but embraces some kind of intimate and felt (not only reasoned) "surrationality,"[9] a rationality that is empowered by its own self-emptying into and out of its own limitations from a horizon beyond, but neither without expressive affirmation nor without imaginative creativity.[10] Herein lies also the promise of mysticism to circumvent the postmodern "traditionalism," the evasion of rationality as such (which is given its dramatic and totalitarian failure in the aftermath of the era of western Enlightenment), which not only falls into a relativism of a plurality of "traditions," but also a "rationalism" that finds closure in itself.[11] Hence, in all serious mystical traditions (or religions, as their core is mystical), both the reliance on tradition and on reason as (secure access to) "reality" is disavowed. For Buddhism, enlightenment reaches beyond both into the experience of Reality itself.[12] For the Bahá'í writings, one should neither rely on tradition (the beliefs of the ancestors or the opinion of its official interpreters) nor reason (*'aql*), but experience and mystical insight (*'irfan*), which is considered the purpose of spiritual life, but without denying its expansion into both tradition (continuity) and reason (coherence).[13]

Related to this primary appraisal, a few other unfortunate side effects of "mere" mysticism must be taken into account. For one, the mystical movement into silence, that is, the overcoming of all categories as too little, too small, too late, too involved and even too imperially grasping, could be issuing into the construction of a new characterization, that is, limitation, of (the accessibility of) the unfathomable Beyond, namely, that of utter insouciance by which Reality itself disappears not only into disinterested silence, but also into unconcerning passiveness regarding, and irrelevance for, the world process and our responsibility in it.[14] Further, enunciations of the process of mystical unknowing can easily be mistaken to inherently impel the preference for a monistic position regarding

---

8. Cf. Sells, *Languages*, 1–13; Faber, *Manifold*, ch. 12; Keller, *Cloud*, ch. 2.
9. Cf. Faber, *Manifold*, ch. 3.
10. Cf. R. Jones, *Mysticism*, ch. 1; Corbin, 190–95.
11. Cf. Saiedi, *Gate*, 11–14.
12. Cf. Trungpa, Introduction, chs. 1, 3. Reason can become a self-justification (rationalization) of the ego and its desire over against Reality; as can be the expectations regarding a religious or spiritual leader (guru) to guaranty one's path (falling into traditionalism).
13. This "surrationality" is, as a daily regimen, stated in the Short Bahá'í Obligatory Prayer, cf. Bahá'u'lláh, *Prayers*, #181; and as *'irfan-i haqq* (insight into Reality) it is remembered as the reason for the mystical core of religion, cf. Bahá'u'lláh, *Gleanings*, #29; Savi, "Bahá'í Faith," 6. Reason alone tends to measure everything from its own inherent coherence that might just be ignorance or the closure of a limited horizon, which again would feed into a traditionalism in which reason would be embedded through continuity, thereby shielding against novelty; Bahá'u'lláh, *Aqdas*, ¶99; 'Abdu'l-Bahá, *Questions*, #83; 'Abdu'l-Bahá, *Bahá'í World Faith*, 369. While reason (*'aql*) has a high importance in the Bahá'í writings—as a special divine gift to humanity (cf. 'Abdu'l-Bahá, *Paris Talks*, #19; *Promulgation*, ##97, 113)—and, hence, is meant to counter any traditionalism, it is only accessing the Mystery if it is, like a polished mirror, enlightened by the sun/spirit; 'Abdu'l-Bahá, *Questions*, #55.
14. Cf. Faber, "God in the Making," 191–95.

ultimate reality, that is, instead of recognizing a somehow personal reality indulging in a nonpersonal field of energy or consciousness.[15] By that preference, however, the degrading of personal relationships and manifestations of personal characteristics will also demean the essential affirmations and the immanent accessibility of Reality (both as subject and object) as voiced by compassion and love to secondary images or to mere means for meeting the monistic aim of dissolution in ultimate reality.[16] And finally, by ultimately taking refuge in silence and muted detachment, such seclusion is prone to spiritual or secular skepticism, in its negative dialectic easily becoming a last resort for justifications of anti-mystical naturalism, deism and atheism. Indeed, mystical reticence regarding the "reality" of Reality can become indistinguishable from (its) mere construction, the disappearance of which would leave us with nothing, without meaning or only with a religion of our own making from our material make-up.[17]

These dangers are the reason that great mystics and mystical thinkers of all religions and ages, as well as the religions that recognize their mystical streams, have found mere seclusion from the world as ultimately futile and immaterial to the mystical process.[18] Instead, they have acquired ways to recover from taciturnity new modes of utterance, with creativeness[19] venturing into a world now seen in new ways. Mysticism must not segregate us from the world, but, to the contrary, make us more susceptible to its predicament: its suffering, violence, evil, sin, individually, but also collectively with regard to social evil and environmental destruction, racial and gender prejudices, and power inflicted hierarchical justifications of oppression.[20] Only then will mysticism not (be misled and misinterpreted to) make a case for the separation of Reality from all realities, highlighting either their or "its" mere illusion, but rather for its intimate propinquity to all realities. Only then will mystical insight also motivate our impulses to become declarations of "its" closeness, which must be performed, for instance, through practices of loving kindness, compassion, the relief from suffering and the infusion of enjoyment.[21] It is perhaps because of this, on occasion, perceived lack of the motivation of mystical accounts to reenter to realities from Reality that many new spiritual movements within and without established religions today favor practical compassion and liberating

---

15. Cf. Chopra, 129–30.
16. Cf. Sharma, *Philosophy*, ch. 1.
17. Cf. Berger, 66; Rue. Religion is maybe only a fantasia of not yet perfected or disturbed algorithms at the heart of evolution and humanity as part of this process, becoming irrelevant in a time (as ours) of the genetic transformation and artificial cybernetic reconstruction of humanity; Harari, part 3.
18. Cf. Faber, *Poet*, §40. In an iconic way, this is presented by the "temptation" of the Buddha not to preach the *dharma*, the fulfillment of which finally became one of the major Mahayana transformations of the Buddha wheel, in the ideal not of the *arhat* who strives for personal enlightenment, but the *bodhisattva* who cannot become enlightened as long as any sentient being is still suffering (which is exactly why s/he *is* enlightened and the Mahabodhisattva equals a Buddha); cf. Akira, 27–32; Krishan, 199–232.
19. Cf. Keller, *Face*, ch. 10.
20. Cf. Boesel and. Keller, *Bodies*; McGinn, *Thought*, ch. 1.
21. Cf. Hick, *Interpretation*, 377–78; Ferrer, *Participation*, 231–33; Lanzetta, *Wisdom*, ch. 11.

activeness over against mere insight and doctrinal unity or any theoretical explanation of the problem of religious unity and diversity[22]—an insight also not unfamiliar to Bahá'í discourse and practice.[23]

Nonetheless, in light of the inescapable challenge to inculcate coherence between theory and practice we ought not to give up on thought, insight, consciousness and the effort to apprehend the world we live in—as this is the intent of religions, wisdoms and philosophies alike—but, instead, we ought to try adopting the movements of mystical insight into the mystery and back into a changed world-consciousness for a meaningful clarification of the problem at hand: how to be pluralistic without losing the mystery that enables us to do so; how to welcome unity without dissolving the plurality of religions in their value and diversified contribution to human evolution, and maybe even beyond?

One of the promising ways of reframing the recognition of the apophatic core of all religious traditions, but not by being bound to its misunderstanding as a movement of simple retreat from cataphatic plurality into mere relativism (and in this move similar to Ferrer's participatory approach), is Kenneth Rose's "apophatic pluralism."[24] It stipulates that no cataphatic language, categorization, symbolism or doctrinal content can ever become identical with the apophatic mystery that is always differentiated (note the passive voice here!) from any approach that tries to approximate or appropriate it. Rose's approach also affirms that a mystical core of many religious traditions must express itself in some kind of soteriological symbolizations of (mutually recognizable) saintliness, avoiding the poisons of a merely intellectual hegemony of unity or inclusivist reductionism, or even the virtual danger of violence by or for its embodiments, as well as the irrelevance of mere historical relativism—thereby building on the pluralistic thesis of Hick and Knitter.[25] Instead of remaining merely restrained by apophatic negation as the necessary limitation for any positive fulfillment—as a pluralism motivated by the perpetual process of natural and historical change, relentlessly pluralizing cultures and languages in which religions appear and are transformed into ever new successors, would affirm (as does Rose)—this apophatic pluralism allows these inevitable pluralizations to be understood as diverse modes of access to a spiritual reality of deathlessness that cannot simply be reduced to imaginative projections or naturalistic processes. In this sense, religious plurality is always "in becoming" as/because spiritual reality "itself" always *appears* under temporal and historical conditions of limitation and change. However, in the way this *apophasis* is conceptualized, the ambivalence remains whether the affirmation of the truth of the pleroma of expressions of spiritual reality is itself a new inclusivism in which case the apophatic openness itself becomes the truth of the matter,[26] or whether

---

22. Cf. Knitter, *Earth*, chs. 4–9; Teasdale, ch. 7.
23. Cf. Momen, "Mysticism," 107–20.
24. Cf. K. Rose, *Pluralism*, Introduction and ch. 8. For a similar position, but extrapolated from a Christian and theistic universe of symbolism, cf. Haight, *Future*, 158.
25. Cf. Chapter 3; Hick, *Interpretation*, ch. 17:2; K. Rose, *Pluralism*, ch. 1. On the analysis of Hick's position to combine epistemic relativism with the soteriological criterion of saintliness in order to be able to differentiate the relative value of religions, cf. K. Rose, *Knowing the Real*.
26. This follows from Rose's criticism of, or contestation of, the limitation of the Neo-Vedanta–based position of Jeffrey Long to be inclusivist because of his affirmation of the *truth* in the

such apophatic distancing from any cataphatic particularity in which the truth of Reality appears (and there is no other way) does not again substitute these pleromatic expressions with mere negation.[27] In other words, in what sense can any appreciation of apophatic "reality" be understood as "divine" *activity*, or as activity of ultimate reality "itself"? Or must "it" be understood as another modality of spiritual imagination in the play of multiplicity devoid of access to reality?[28]

In my own view, which developed over the past two decades,[29] the most promising approach to this matter comes from process thought.[30] It has its own history of intricacies, which I cannot introduce here.[31] Instead, the following remarks will suffice to make the case for the innovative import of the Whiteheadian project respecting the difficulties of mystical explanations of unity and multiplicity (of Reality and with regard to religions). And then, since it was this engagement with Whitehead's philosophy of process and

---

plurality of religious expressions of Reality; cf. K. Rose, *Pluralism*, 34–35. Another example of such an inclusivist pluralism is Roger Haight's Spirit-Christology that, against John Hick's presumed apophatic passivity of the Real, accepts other religions (beyond Christianity) not as participation in Christian salvation, but as expression of the salvific *activity* of the divine Spirit in all religions *on their own terms*. Yet this approach would also remain in the dialectic between pluralist universalism and inclusivist contextuality, as the Christian conceptuality of the Holy Spirit could be seen as the limitation of its pluralist opening; cf. Haight, *Jesus*, ch. 15; Fredericks, 8–10, 23–25; K. Rose, *Pluralism*, 32–33; Faber, *Garden*, ch. 8:3.

27. Cf. K. Rose, *Pluralism*, 12–13; chs. 5–6. If the *apophasis* of this second-order grammar of negation is impressed on religious traditions, however, as Rose indicates, for instance, with Buddhism, Hinduism and Jainism (cf. 3, 90, 98–101), and as witnessed in the use of concepts such as *sunyata*, *nirguna brahman* and *anekantavada*, that is, if they are taken to be exemplifications of this grammar, in this interaction, apophatic pluralism becomes virtually indistinguishable from a new inclusivism; cf. Chapter 7 regarding Hinduism; regarding the inclusivism of Jainism, cf. Faber, *Garden*, ch. 8:5.

28. As K. Rose (*Pluralism*, 56–57, 100) seems to build his case for an apophatic pluralism on the absence of the accessibility of ultimate Reality in a world of becoming (in which no universal agreement can be reached and all religious positivity will be swept away by new transformations of the contingencies of history), he seems to have abandoned *divine* activity in favor of the necessities of the *absence* of any cataphatic expression of such activity (if it is accepted at all) and, hence, his apophatic pluralism may become indistinguishable from a simple non-existence of the spiritual realm the sui generis reality of which Rose is otherwise affirming for his position. This is where my "polyphilic" pluralism may differ from apophaticism as the basis for pluralism, as it understands *apophatic indetermination* as historic (salvific) *activity* of Reality "itself"; cf. Faber, *Garden*, ch. 1:5. However, Rose is aware of the dialectic of a negation of negation in eastern (Upanishads) and western (The Areopagite) mysticism that can be seen as the "logical" approximation of *polyphilia*; *Pluralism*, 98.

29. Beginning with my publications since the start of the twenty-first century, cf. Faber, *Prozeßtheologie*, passim; "Gottesmeer," passim; and "De-Ontologizing God," passim.

30. Although I see certain synergies with Jorge Ferrer's turn "beyond" mysticism of his "participatory religious pluralism," which he developed from transpersonal psychology and philosophy; but he also recognizes "deep" process pluralism; cf. Ferrer, *Participation*, 226–27, Postscript; Faber, *Garden*, ch. 8.

31. Cf. Faber, *Poet*, passim; *Becoming of God*, passim; Cobb and Griffin; Cobb, *Christian Natural Theology*.

relationality that led me to new shores, I can explore the alternative approach to the merely apophatic aspirations toward mystical unity and multiplicity that I have called polyphilic pluralism.[32]

Process thought understands the process of becoming as fundamental to all existence, more fundamental than the categories of being and nothingness, mind and matter, subject and object, epistemology and ontology and so on.[33] Against all such dualisms, which always come already too late onto the scene, it posits the process of becoming as one in and for which these categorizations are abstractions from the concrete process in which all becoming of events, organisms and even universes are one in mutual immanence and in their mutual movement into one another. Such mutually limiting categories, then, are only conceptually explicated divisions or constructions by which we try to identify and differentiate elements being engaged in concrete processes.[34] In other words, such analyses are necessary noetic landscapes for grasping "becoming" as movements of synthesis. And so are simple juxtapositions of God and the world also mere abstractions from their mutual process of becoming, noetic stabilizations (if not fixations) of a concrete cycle of universal mutuality.[35] Every happening, be it divine or mundane, for process thought is one of relationality and creativity, that is, one in which novelty (such as that of ever-new events, new times and localities, histories, salvations and so on) in the ongoing process arises as a gathering of its interrelated past, but without necessarily being a mere repetition of that past. In this ingathering (as the becoming concrete of the concrete reality of becoming), novelty is a creative realization of new possibilities that are as of yet unrealized, but hidden in these relations or unknown to them.[36] God is the locution that indicates the primordial expression and primary realization of this process: the primary remembrance of all that happens and the creative source of a novelty that God infuses in any and every happening in the world in order to lure it to its best self at any given moment.[37] This creative nature of God—Whitehead calls it the Primordial Nature of God as it harbors all possibilities and potential worlds in divine valuation—names and infuses the beauty and creativity of the world; and the receptive nature of God—Whitehead calls it the Consequent Nature of divine remembrance and experience of all actualizations, events, organisms and worlds—names and evinces divine love and compassion in the world.[38] God and the world live together in a mutual coinhabitation, mutually immanent to, and caught up with, one another in a mutual

---

32. Cf. Faber, *Poet*, 325; *Manifold*, Intermezzo 2; *Becoming of God*, Exploration 14; *Garden*, ch. 6:6; Faber and Keller, "Polyphilic Pluralism," 58–81.
33. Cf. P. Rose, *On Whitehead*.
34. Cf. Faber, *Poet*, part 2.
35. Cf. Faber, *Poet*, §§27–29; Faber, "De-Ontologizing God," 209–234; "Infinite Movement," 171–99.
36. Cf. Hosinski, part 1; Kraus, chs. 4–5; Faber, *Poet*, part 3.
37. Cf. Hosinski, part 2.
38. Cf. Whitehead, *Process*, part 5; Cobb, *Theology*, 92–106; Faber, *Poet*, part 4; *Becoming of God*, Sphere 3; Dombrowski, ch. 4; Griffin, *Reenchantment*, ch. 4.

adventure of relationality and creativity, compassion and beauty, love and surprise—a dance I have named the cycle of love.[39]

This creative-responsive movement of mutual love[40] has important implications: God does never act by coercion, but ever by persuasion,[41] as all events exercise their own creativity, in degrees of freedom acting on divine infusions of their best possible trajectories into their future (or to refuse or alter them in their own actualization).[42] By offering ever-new healing possibilities and, thereby, inducing an ever-wider connectivity into a broken web of relationships (compassion, forgiveness, creative transformation), ever-new peaceful realizations on individual and collective levels are made available.[43] The divine process wants to lead organisms to a life without violence, to peace without the tragedy of their past that follows them like a demon,[44] to a beauty that overcomes destruction and to a wisdom that avoids oppositions by transforming all tensions into contrasts of togetherness[45]—and, hence, also into a new religious conviviality.[46] God, in Whitehead's words, is not the creator of the world out of nothing, like an emperor decreeing existence (and then controlling it),[47] but "the poet of the world,"[48] saving it by luring it with Truth, Goodness and Beauty toward unity and differentiation, complexity and mutuality, peace and diversity, or, better, into the realization of *this* divine character.[49] A few quotations from Whitehead will demonstrate this vision:

> The depths of [God's] existence lie beyond the vulgarities of praise or of power. He gives to suffering its swift insight into values which can issue from it. He is the ideal companion who transmutes what has been lost into a living fact within his own nature. He is the mirror which discloses to every creature its own greatness.[50]

> Every event on its finer side introduces God into the world.[51]

> It is as true to say that God creates the World, as that the World creates God. God and the World are the contrasted opposites in terms of which Creativity achieves its supreme task of transforming disjoined multiplicity, with its diversities in opposition, into concrescent unity, with its diversities in contrast.[52]

---

39. Cf. Faber, *Poet*, §30; *Manifold*, ch. 13; *Becoming of God*, Exploration 9; *Garden*, ch. 4:4.
40. Cf. Cobb and Griffin, ch. 3.
41. Cf. Whitehead, *Adventures*, 265–69; Griffin, *Reenchantment*, 143–44; Faber, *Poet*, §35.
42. Cf. Cobb, *Theology*, ch. 3.
43. Cf. Suchocki, *God*, part 1.
44. Cf. Whitehead, *Adventures*, 286.
45. Cf. Faber, *Poet*, §37.
46. Cf. Faber, "Must 'Religion,'" 167–82.
47. Cf. Whitehead, *Adventures*, 165–69; Faber, *Manifold*, ch. 6.
48. Whitehead, *Process*, 236.
49. Cf. Faber, *Poet*, §35; *Becoming of God*, Sphere 5; "Sense of Peace," 36–56; Cobb and Griffin, chs. 3–4.
50. Whitehead, *Religion*, 154–55.
51. Whitehead, *Religion*, 155–56.
52. Whitehead, *Process*, 348.

The second quotation, which was already mentioned in the Introduction, lays bare, in the shortest possible form, that divine presence is meant to indicate a process; a process whereby every event always already fulfills a divine potential beyond its powers and horizons, but never without its own actualization of this potential.[53] The first quotation, conversely, indicates this process as one of value and valuation[54] already embraced by the cycle of love, the oscillation between divine perception and creative instigation interested in the greatest potential of fulfillment in the sense of beauty and motivated by the greatest compassion not only for the restitution, redemption and liberation from the process of becoming, but the transformation of its losses into real occasions for new infusions of love and realizations of beauty into the world process.[55] The third quotation, also already hinted at earlier,[56] then, names the inner workings of the process of sympathic synthesis by which every event, and exemplary and in infinite greatness the divine event, performs this creative-relational task, namely, by the conversion of states of opposition (not only arising from alternative possibilities, but even more from hardened dualisms) into the ever-fluent malleability of contrasts.[57]

It is, then, in this context that the experiential and experimental togetherness of divergences in such contrasted unifications, even only for a time and always remaining in process of venturing out again in the pursuit of new shores, will mark the importance of, and the need to be manifested in, the processes of unity and diversity of religions.[58] The transreligious process of contrasting unifications will not only introduce God/Reality on its finer side, a kind of translucency of divine presence,[59] but also contribute to ever-new realities of religious diversifications since any unification will become part of the process of a new multiplicity of such unifications that it has enriched and diversified.[60] Here, the processes of unification and diversification of religions become "the ought" for the introduction of Reality into the world, or of its diminuendo if it is opposed. This processual togetherness of unity and multiplicity of religions, then, is not only the relativistic criterion for the truth and worth of any of its individual claims,[61] but the very essence of a divine poetics that constitutes the creative and liberating relationality of Reality with the universe in general and with religions in particular (if we assume them to be the perceptual expressions of and spiritual reactions to this process).[62]

---

53. Cf. Faber, *God as Poet*, §§17–18; Keller, *Face*, ch. 10.
54. Cf. P. Rose, *On Whitehead*, chs. 1–2; Leue.
55. Cf. Faber, *Poet*, §31; *Becoming of God*, Exploration 9; *Garden*, ch.5:3.
56. Cf. Chapter 4 on the mutual creativity of God and the world.
57. Cf. Faber, *Becoming of God*, Sphere 1; Hosinski, *Fact*, part 2.
58. Cf. Corbin, *Alone*, ch. 3; Faber, *Manifold*, ch. 5; *Garden*, ch. 3:5; McDaniel, *Hope*, chs. 1–2; Suchocki, *Divinity*, ch. 3.
59. Cf. Faber, *Manifold*, 464–69. This is close to the Bahá'í writings' understanding of a spiritual transformation as an "enlightenment" in which this translucency becomes experiential; cf. Bahá'u'lláh, *Gleanings*, #52; Abdu'l-Bahá, *Tablets*, 705–6.
60. Cf. Faber, *Becoming of God*, Sphere 5.
61. Cf. Faber, *Garden*, 1.
62. Cf. Faber, *Poet*, parts 3–4.

This "theopoetics"[63] brings me to the notion of *"polyphilia,"* the love of the manifold.[64] As God unifies (neither by division nor by fusion, neither by isolation not by uniformity, but) by the transformation of opposites into contrast of mutual immanence, God *loves the manifold* in "unison" with, and as a unified (but developing), multiplicity of ever-creative manifestations of remembrance and novelty.[65] Hence, in distinction from mystical "solutions" of the unity and multiplicity of religions, the polyphilic approach means to point out that religious pluralism is not established and perpetuated by "negation" (negative theology, apophaticism) whereby God is always viewed as ultimately suspending presence by an absence in silence and remaining essentially an aloof or passive mystery for which religions are mere illusions.[66] Rather, *polyphilia* announces that God/Reality, in the turn from silence, is ultimately the manifest and responsive Reality of relationality and creativity for and in their becoming.[67] Not silence, but the Word is, as it were, the aim of divine existence; not unknowability, but participation is the satisfaction of the divine process. Like the self-exuding nature of the Good in Platonic thought (and from there on), Reality wants to be realized in the infinite variation of the process of becoming.[68] As in the mystical explanations, the Mystery is "indifferent" (not to, but) *from* the world in nondual non-difference.[69] But as "it" lives equally beyond (categories of) existence and nonexistence, which makes them "abstractions" (only penultimate ontological categories) from this Life, the Mystery "in-sists" *in* the manifold that "it" loves.[70] That the Mystery does not "exist," but "in-sist" in the process of becoming—as a matter of the processual form of the unity and diversity of existence—is a concept that, I think, deeply resonates with the Bahá'í concept of the infinite and indefinite (never ending) diffusion of creative grace *(fayḍ)*[71] and with the "in-sistence" of the Mystery in divine Manifestations—of which I will say more later.[72]

---

63. Cf. Faber, *Becoming of God*, Sphere 5; *Poet*, 14–15; *Manifold*, part 1; Keller, *God*, 149–52; "Theopoetics," 179–94; *Intercarnations*, ch. 6.
64. Cf. Faber, *Poet*, Postscript; *Becoming of God*, Exploration 14; *Manifold*, Meditation.
65. Cf. Whitehead, *Process*, 345; Faber, Manifold, *Manifold*, part 2.
66. While I agree with the "apophatic pluralism" espoused by Kenneth Rose (*Pluralism*, 2–5, and ch. 8) on the implication of apophatic inaccessibility of absolute Truth regarding any religious doctrine to create the unavoidable space for a plurality of changing positions and accesses, I differ from his assessment as I emphasize that this relativity is the expression of Reality "itself," as the text will explain presently. Yet I concur with Rose's later claim (ch. 8) that his position is not just a second-order criticism of any cataphatic positioning of and within religions, that is, merely of a scientific, philosophical or cultural mode of thinking, but *religious* in nature, as it indicates the spiritual nature of human desire and the search of religion(s) of that spiritual realm (of deathlessness).
67. Cf. Faber, "Intermezzo," 212–38.
68. Cf. Faber, *Poet*, 102, 137, 149, 224; *Garden*, ch. 6.
69. Cf. Faber, *Poet*, §40; *Becoming of God*, Sphere 5.
70. Cf. Faber, "De-Ontologizing God," 218-114; *Poet*, §40; *Manifold*, ch. 8; *Becoming of God*, Exploration 14;
71. This indefinite and infinite "outpouring" *(fayḍ)* resembles Plato's *bonum diffusivum sui*; cf. Bahá'u'lláh, *Iqan*, 141. I want to thank Moojan Momen for highlighting this connection (personal communication, December 2017).
72. Cf. 'Abdu'l-Bahá, *Questions*, #37; Momen, "God," 17–20; Lambden, "Background," 77–78.

In this divine "in-sistence" lies the difference of the polyphilic pluralism proposed here from apophatic pluralism. While both conceptions embrace the *mystical* dynamics of *apophasis* and pluralism (both conditioning one another), *polyphilic* pluralism differentiates itself from *apophatic* pluralism in several important ways. Apophatic pluralism is based on the "neutral" (second order) presupposition that in a world of permanent becoming, which it shares with process thought and the Bahá'í understanding of cosmic becoming,[73] no utopic state of permanence can be reached in which any religion would ever be able to embrace the whole of the world of humanity or convince all human beings of its particular, contingent and permanently changing truth. This again implies that the nature of ultimate reality is its inaccessibility that never allows any cataphatic embodiment (of orthodoxy) to capture ultimate truth so that religious truth can always only be accessed pluralistically.[74] However, while apophatic pluralism may presuppose that there "is" such an ultimate reality, which apophatically necessitates pluralistic and successive religious embodiments,[75] *whether or not* such a spiritual reality is *real* may become indistinguishable from human projection or imagination because the apophatic "movement" is not necessarily understood as *divine* activity or of the ultimate nature of any existence.[76] Besides remaining caught in the cycle of suspicion of mere projection (of the human mind or imagination or desire), this "neutrality" ultimately does not even *allow* the polyphilic implication of divine in-sistence to inform the reality of the pluralism of religions as *divinely inspired* multiplicity, as *operation of spiritual reality* "itself" (not just as its appropriation *per negativum*, as argument from its absence), because any assertion of truth/reality may already entail the "overstated" claim to a particular truth that would undermine the pluralism of *apophasis* and be suspect to a new form of non-pluralism (be it of inclusivism or exclusivism).[77] In my understanding, however, the

---

73. As will be further explained in Chapter 13, the Bahá'í universe recons with an infinite universal cycle of becoming and obliteration of worlds, fundamentally characterized by inescapable change; cf. Taylor, 112.
74. Cf. K. Rose, *Pluralism*, 2–3, 7, 10, 29–30, 50, 56–57. In philosophical, cosmological and ontological terms, I have elaborated on this inevitable pluralism of becoming as "in/finite becoming"; cf. Faber, *Manifold*, ch. 8. Later in the text, in Chapter 13, it will, on a cosmic scale, reappear as the basis for a similar argument made by a polyphilic pluralism that understands divine activity as always expressed with an infinity of worlds, such as the Bahá'í universe presupposes, for the establishment of an *inevitable* plurality of religions even in the context of a view of progressive revelation.
75. Cf. K. Rose, *Pluralism*, 9–10, 14–15 and ch. 8.
76. This is a central tenet of Whitehead's differentiation between God (the Primordial Nature of possibilities, ideas and virtualities) and Creativity, the ultimate metaphysical principle of activity of any actuality, be it God or any other event or organic integration of events; cf. Whitehead, *Process*, 346; Bracken, *Matrix*, 4; Faber, *God as Poet*, part 4.
77. Cf. K. Rose, *Pluralism*, 34–35, 56–57. As already mentioned, Rose seems to understand *all* claims of the truth of particular religious manifestations as inclusivist clauses over against the radical pluralistic thesis of noncommitment to any such truth claims, defending the latter claim of apophatic relativity not as a new truth claim of the first order (competing with other cataphatic truth claims), but a critical criterion of the second order; cf. 27–28. However, in avoidance of the suspicion that this may just be another abstract claim without religious relevance, he modulates this second-order category into first-order assumptions of the sacred texts

apophatic move is one of Reality that/whom religions seek and mediate for experience, that is, one of the Divine Manifold "itself," *revealing* "its" apophatic Self precisely in polyphilic form.[78]

Since I have explored these considerations elsewhere in detail,[79] I will refer here only to the most obvious implications for our question of the unity of religions and the truth of religious pluralism in the form of a polyphilic pluralism of the loving "in-sistence" of the Mystery in an infinite world of becoming. The divine mystery is not just hidden, but wills and affirms an infinite and infinitely varied world. But the world is a creation of mutual immanence, of mutual coinherence in movements of relationality and creativity.[80] While God does not exist, but in-sist, still, God takes on existence as "ex-sistence" (from the other) in compassion by mutuality (in compassionate recognition vis-à-vis the world).[81] It follows, then, that neither any expression of creaturely recognition of divine immanence nor any creative divine reception of, and reaction to, creaturely imaginations is refused by God or isolated from one another.[82] Rather, as *in* God's "in-sistence" everything only "ex-sists" *from* one another,[83] it is the nature of all existents to mutually be transformed into ever new, ever more contrasting infusions of the divine loving presence into an ongoing "spiritual" process toward a cosmic realization of peace.[84] Such spiritual peace, again, is the widest horizon for the realization in consciousness and action of both the unity of

---

of Hinduism and Christianity (chs. 5–6), thereby, by his own admission, rendering them inclusivist affirmations of a particular (albeit extremely vast) truths.

78. It is, of course, clear, as was stated often in any given debate on religious pluralism and the possibility or impossibility of interreligious dialogue, that there cannot be any agreement between different traditions in doctrinal issues, but also between factions holding to either exclusivist, inclusivist or pluralist interpretations of the same doctrinal questions, or between denominations or sects of a particular religious universe. In the *apophatic* mode of pluralism, this would allow for discussions that discover the necessity of the "unsaying" of all doctrinal, literal meanings into the mystery, without, in the best scenario, giving up the meaningfulness of the doctrinal formations of experiences of certain religious contexts; cf. K. Rose, *Pluralism*, chs. 7–8. In the *polyphilic* mode, however, these differences would not only be mediated through apophatic negation of negation back into some kind of cataphatic universals or pointers toward common issues, such as deathlessness and beatitude. Instead, we could affirm the different doctrines as viable ways of addressing the apophatic truth in such a way that they can neither be stripped of their specificity without losing the interesting accent in which they speak the mystery, nor be held up only because of our limited mind, as a lack. They would rather, in their incommensurability, be expressions of the apophatic affirmation of their differences that would not be in need for any further coherence, as long as their mutual co*in*herence can be detected, for instance, in their mutual incompleteness or processuality toward novelty. It is their mutual indetermination that would be of interest here; cf. Faber, *Garden*, ch. 1: 5.

79. Cf. Faber, "De-Ontologizing God," 218–24; *Poet*, §40; *Manifold*, chs. 12, 15; *Becoming of God*, Exploration 14; *Garden*, ch. 6.

80. Cf. Whitehead, *Adventures*, 134; Faber, *Prozeßtheologie*, §21; *God as Poet*, part 3; *Manifold*, part 1; *Becoming of God*, Exploration 10; "Immanence," 91–110.

81. Cf. Faber, *Manifold*, chs. 14–15; *Garden*, ch. 15.

82. Cf. Faber, "God in the Making," 195–200; *Manifold*, ch. 7.

83. Cf. Faber, *Manifold*, chs. 3, 7 and 8.

84. Cf. Faber, "God in the Making," 195–200; Faber, "Process," 6–20.

contrasts of most beautiful diversity, intensity and harmony, and of a manifold of such realizations in mutual diversity, intensity and harmony.[85]

Yet against all suppositions of a mere relativism or the mere apophatic indiscernibility between mystery and human projection, it is precisely in such an "subtractive affirmation" of "in-sistence" that Reality does not "disappear" in the manifold of "its" polyphilic expressions (although it is also veiled in them), but becomes revealed *as* apophatic in nature.[86] In the polyphilic Whiteheadian context, this is expressed with the difference between God, with the unique ability of divine valuation, and Creativity, with its indifference of realization in all existents,[87] but also the identification of God with a "principle of concretization," which limits all possibilities to the most valuable ones at any given moment, thereby avoiding both indifference of realization and the limitation to reductive sedimentations of orthodoxy, and giving any creative process a spiritual direction without hindering an infinite process of ever-new such formations and evolutions.[88] In the Bahá'í context, this subtractive, but affirmative attraction is uniquely expressed by the divine Manifestations (plural), which in their uniqueness polyphilically *name* the apophatic Mystery not only with regard to "its" inexpressibility, but also with regard to "its" inimitable in-sistence. They avoid the dissolution into relativism by differentiating themselves against all possible idolatry since not *all* possible "names" with which religious identities may refer to divinity would be beyond the danger of losing the power and justification to mediate the polyphilic in-sistence of God/Reality. Precisely in the names of the Manifestations,[89] which indicate in their relativity to one another the unique ineffability of God/Reality, would religions be manifestations of divine *polyphilia* of the apophatic Mystery.[90]

---

85. Cf. Faber, "Theopoetic Justice," 160–78; "Ecotheology," 212–38; *Manifold*, ch. 14.
86. Cf. Faber. *Manifold*, 69–70 and ch. 3. In the Lin-chi sect of (the "Five Houses" of) Zen Buddhism, we can discover a form of the "fourfold logic," which we can also find in modulation in the work of Nagarjuna and Nicolas of Cusa as well as in Bahá'u'lláh's *Seven Valleys*, as the movement toward such an affirmation instead of an apophatic negation or a dialectic of negation. Over against the states of negation of either subject or object or both of them (seeking apophatic "unity"), complete unity lies in the *complete affirmation of both* in perfect mutual immanence; cf. Dumoulin, 119–21.
87. Cf. Whitehead, *Process*, 31–32; Faber, *Poet*, §28.
88. Cf. Whitehead, *Science*, 178–79; *Process*, 31; Faber, *Poet*, §27; *Manifold*, ch. 4. This "limitation" is, of course, in a Whiteheadian context, not one of reduction per power (effective causality), but of seduction per attraction (final causality); cf. Whitehead, *Adventures*, 165–66, 198.
89. Cf. Bahá'u'lláh, *Gleanings*, ##21, 81; 'Abdu'l-Bahá, *Questions*, ##40, 59.
90. The polyphilic "divine *act*" of the apophatic "presence" in the diverse revelations, contrasting the potential apophatic indistinguishability of the divine *apophasis* from the mere relativism of human projection into "nothing" (or at least into an incommensurable and incommunicable *Deus absconditus* of absolute silence), can also be expressed with the difference introduced by divine self-naming, with the "I am (will be) that/who I am (will be)" of Exodus 3:14, on the one hand, and with the unpronounceable proper name YHWH of Exodus 3:15, on the other. While "the God that is Being" of the former verse (to which interpretation of this verse traditionally amounted to) is apophatically unknowable and, hence, relatively (in) everything (indistinguishable from/beyond its multiplicity), the divine name of the latter verse is so unique that it cannot be expressed even in any fixed semantic coordinate system, and traditionally

Religions would, on this view, be formations of the realization of such a divine polyphilic movement within the world with which Reality in-sists in unison. They would, in fact, not just be the strange historical appearance of a phase of a developing human consciousness that is afraid of the world it does not understand (as many theories of religion particularly in the nineteenth century have proposed), but axial events expressive of a becoming, unifying and unified cosmic Poetic Mind in the Spirit of and toward peace.[91] Their plurality, then, is also divinely inspired (by) *polyphilia!* In their mutuality, they would seem to be other than in their isolation, opposition, supersession, denigration, superiority or substitution—the poisonous fruit of unity—poetically realizing, manifesting, revealing, embodying divine or ultimate Reality, which/who is in-sisting in the world's and religion's manifold as the reflection of the divine love of the world *as manifold.*[92]

The consequence of such a polyphilic nature of the in-sisting Mystery and a correlative religious pluralism would, then, appear to necessitate the following propositions: First, there must always be *many* religions as there are always many unique experiences and societies characterized by such ever-new experiences of divine infusion (revelation) and compassion (remembrance) involved in the poetic of their actualization.[93] Second, there must always be *new* religions, as the world process is creative and infinite, and neither God's creative engagement with the world nor the ways of experiencing God ever exhaust themselves. Third, there must be an unending *history* of religion(s) as God's

---

is not named either; cf. Soulen, chs. 3–5. While the whole question of the implications for the Abrahamic understanding of God is beyond the horizon of this book, these renderings of the unique proper name of God reappear in the Bahá'í context with the "hidden name" of God and its relation to the Sinai revelation, on the one hand, and the affirmation of the Tetragrammaton in mutuality with *bahá'* (BHA'), also the Tetragrammaton, on the other hand; cf. Faber, *Garden*, chs. 6:1 (The Nameless Name) and 6:6 (Polyphilic Pluralism). Not only does Bahá'u'lláh connect both of them intimately (like the Glory/*kabod* of YHWH in the Book of Exodus, but also as the *kyrios* of the New Testament) in the mutually inclusive and interchangeable YHWH-BHA' that/who appears as the Speaker in the bush addressing Moses. Bahá'u'lláh also insists on the *inexhaustible uniqueness* of both names as *unexchangeable* for any other name, that is, not simply to be overcome by "progressive" revelation of divine names— *counter* to the mere relativistic assumption of the many names for the nameless nature of God/ Reality; cf. Lambden, "Word," 19–42; "Sinaitic Mysteries," 65–184; Bahá'u'lláh/Lambden, "Mysteries of the Call," 33–78; Shoghi Effendi, *World Order*, 104. Beyond the Abrahamic context, however, that is, here, in the polyphilic versus an apophatic pluralistic discussion, this means: Not *any* affirmation of religions is per se a divine manifestation or expressive of ultimate reality, because the plurality of divine names is *constrained by an apophatic subtraction that expresses itself in unexchangeable unique namings* over against which all other "names" are nothing but idolatrous. Hence, the polyphilic plurality of affirmations of religions through apophatic subtractions (relating to such divine/ultimate names) is indicated by highlighting *precisely the names that express the uniqueness of these revelations*, namely, *in the names of the divine Manifestations themselves*, like the Buddha, Jesus, Krishna and Bahá'u'lláh; Shoghi Effendi, *God*, ch. 6.

91. Cf. Faber, *Becoming of God*, Exploration 6.
92. Cf. Faber, *Manifold*, Intermezzo 2; Faber, "Multiplicity," 187–206; "Mystical Whitehead," 213–34; Faber and Keller, "Taste for Multiplicity," 180–207.
93. Here, novelty and uniqueness converge on the infinity of different experiences; cf. Mellert, 32.

polyphilia always loves our responses and transforms the past manifestations of religions into new potentials for an unprecedented future. Fourth, this history must be connected by a divine/ultimate *activity* in the name of unique figures of "its" manifestation in which the multiplicity of religions is not a mere projection of an indifferent Mystery, avoiding *both* the irrelevance inherent in the affirmation of all possible appearances of religious identity formation *and* idolatrous exclusivist limitations of orthodoxy by (internally and externally) naming the unnamable uniquely, but admitting to mutually coinhering relationality.

Any diminution of this fourfold multiplicity would equal a denial or denigration of the divine poetic process of polyphilic in-sistence and, hence, not only be illusionary compared with the multiplicity of religious appearances as the very sign of the presence of Reality. It would also indicate nothing less but the innuendo that to introduce less than Reality on the finer side of every decision and relationship in the practice of religions is to be preferred over polyphilic satisfaction and theopoetic intimacy with the Mystery. On the positive side, what this fourfold multiplicity could teach us regarding interreligious relations is that the *mutuality* of religious reactions to the divine or ultimate Mystery is the criterion for the unique truth claims of each religion *individually* to be valid.[94] In this polyphilic pluralism, the mutual "ex-sistence" of religions reveals the unity of the "in-sistence" of Reality, as "unison" with/within them.

---

94. This is the thesis elaborated in my book *The Garden of Reality* (cf. its Introduction).

Part II
NEGOTIATIONS OF MULTIPLICITY

Chapter Six

CONVERGENCES AND DIVERGENCES: JUNCTURE OR BIFURCATION?

The waves rising from this Ocean are apparent before the eyes of the peoples of the world and the effusions of the Pen of wisdom and utterance are manifest everywhere.[1]

—Bahá'u'lláh

So far, we have had a look at the alternatives of current ways to engage with the unity and plurality of religions throughout a field of diverse traditions and schools of thought, of which the Bahá'í Faith was highlighted as current apt religious enunciation. We have traced their adoption of diverse systems of thought and spirituality and their respective solutions to problems involving not only religious diversity, but also opposition, warfare and strife—especially in developing pluralist models countering those problems with a deep appreciation for this manifold. Now, we will ask how the mediation of these conceptualizations of unity and plurality of religions (as proposed here) through the unique synthesis of its elements in the Bahá'í universe of discourse will contribute to a clarification of their inner problematic and to potential directions their contemporary understanding could and should take the discourse. So, how have Bahá'í authors found themselves involved with, and been challenged by, these discussions—especially with their emphasis on the unity of religions? In general, we find evidence for the following intentions of, and correlations in, a Bahá'í dialogue with religious pluralism.

Regarding the threefold matrix of alternatives responding to religious diversity, namely, exclusivism, inclusivism, pluralism, we can, first, observe that most Bahá'í scholars interested and engaged in this discourse have accepted the importance of refuting religious exclusivism as foreign to the Bahá'í writings.[2] To the contrary, they would affirm that the Bahá'í writings unequivocally insist on the truth of a plurality of religions and, hence, they understand many religions as true expressions of the divine engagement with the world.[3] What is more, they even denounce exclusivism as the most incriminating reason for the generation and persistence of religious violence.[4] Second,

---

1. Bahá'u'lláh, "Tarazat (Ornaments)," in *Tablets*, 40.
2. Cf. Fazel, "Understanding," 239–82; "Pluralism," 42; May, 1–3.
3. Cf. Sours, *Station*, chs. 3–5; *Syllable*, chs. 1–3; Stockman, *Bahá'í Faith*, 35–43; Schaefer, "Unity Paradigm."
4. Cf. 'Abdu'l-Bahá, *Paris Talks*, #13; Fazel, "Understanding," 240–41.

we can also observe that most Bahá'í voices in this field affirm that religious inclusivism, although it might not be easily avoided,[5] can only be of a very limited relevance.[6] As there are not only many true religions, the Bahá'í writings, on the one hand, affirm the unrestricted truth of the many religions, that is, that other religions (messengers, revelations, scriptures) do not present a mixture of falsity and truth (as the inclusivist position would imply),[7] and, on the other hand, even affirm the finality (and limitations) of its own revelation. So, contrary to typological inclusivism there are and will be true religions beyond the Bahá'í Faith.[8] Third, these Bahá'í voices in this area have, as a consequence, affirmed the validity of religious pluralism as the alternative to exclusivism and inclusivism. That is, not only does the assertion of the truth of all religions fall squarely into the pluralistic camp (whether or not one assumes a pluralistic position),[9] but Bahá'í authors have also realized the compatibility of the Bahá'í writings with the pluralistic project as being much closer to, and more congenial with, the different streams of the vast ocean of utterances in their scripters than the other projects if they seek a balance between unity and plurality of religions in relation to God or ultimate reality at all.[10] This balance may be expressed in different forms, such as unity in diversity or as temporal evolution, as contrasting resonances or as progression beyond any fixed status of finality, as multireligious community of loving engagement or as mystery beyond any grasping.

In any case, neither unity nor plurality of religions undermines the truth of both unity and plurality. The main arguments employed among Bahá'í voices that converge with diverse forms of pluralism, but also, although unknown to them, it would seem, with its polyphilic variant,[11] are these: First, since God is inaccessible, the mystery must manifest

---

5. Cf. Phillip Smith, "Bahá'í Faith"; Grant Martin, "Why," 179–201.
6. Cf. May, 19–24. In the sense that in temporal progression later revelations embrace the earlier ones, a kind of inclusiveness will naturally flow from later syntheses; cf. Bahá'u'lláh, *Iqan*, §40.
7. Cf. Bahá'u'lláh, *Gleanings*, #24; Schmidt-Leukel, *Pluralism*, ch. 9; Sours, *Syllable*, ch. 1.
8. Cf. Bahá'u'lláh, *Gleanings*, ##13, 22; 'Abdu'l-Bahá, *Paris Talks*, #41; Fazel, "Pluralism," 42–43; "Approaches," 43–44. For K. Rose (*Pluralism*, 95), this insight of non-finality and self-transcendence is the most important sign for a *strong* version of apophatic pluralism. Yet the Bahá'í view differs from this pluralism in that it *also* (although undiminished accepting the former) insists on the importance of the recognition the new religion of the time into which all other naturally would issue, which is a strong sign of inclusivism. How (especially in relation to polyphilic pluralism) to constructively understand and conciliatorily solve this unique tension in the Bahá'í constellation of the relation of religions, which is also registered by Ferrer (*Theory*, 306n4), but stands unresolved, will be the theme of this second part of the book.
9. The document *To the World's Religious Leaders* (2002) of the governing body of the worldwide Bahá'í community, the Universal House of Justice, has taken up the most radical formulation of religious pluralism (over against limitations of exclusivism and inclusivism) as it is known from John Hick and process thought (cf. Chapter 3), namely, "that all of the world's great religions are equally valid in nature and origin"; Haifa (2002), section 1: https://www.bahai.org/library/authoritative-texts/the-universal-house-of-justice/messages/20020401_001/1#195254150; see also Chapter 12 in this volume.
10. Cf. Savi, "Pluralism," 25–41; May, 15–29; Fazel, "Pluralism," 43–49; Chew, "Pluralism," 27–44; McLean, "Prolegomena," 25–67.
11. Cf. Faber, *Garden*, ch. 7.

itself in infinite and infinitely different forms. The "oneness" of God cannot be reified.[12] "Oneness" is—as in Plotinus—only a placeholder for an unnamable Beyond since the divine "essence" (*dhat*) is not only beyond any naming, but also—as in Nagarjuna— beyond any unnaming.[13] However, since the divine "aim" is not a disappearance into super-conceptual experiences as a final state, in distinction from Nagarjuna, ultimate Reality is seeking to infinitely manifest "itself," "its" Self (*nafs*), in an infinite manifold.[14] Second, since the unity of religions is not meant to imply uniformity, but rather an infinite movement from and toward the source of their existence, the creative transformation of humanity cannot consist in a uniform realization of divine aims either. Hence, the different "aims" of religions are to be understood not to be in competition with, but they contrast, one another.[15] Third, unity in diversity is a process, not a state; a process that always seeks novel forms and, by being receptive to minority expressions in the development and progression, does avoid "otherness" to be reiterated, suppressed or forgotten.[16] Fourth, given these arguments, religious truth is not relative because we could find all religions to say the same thing, or be about the same appearance of reality, but because they develop in a relational manner for which absoluteness is apophatically hidden from any dogmatic fixation or final scheme of understanding and religious expression.[17] Fifth, the pluralism employed in the Bahá'í writing is not only radically perspectival (which is close to a relativism based in mysticism),[18] but mirrors the responsiveness to, and the diversity of, the engagement of the mystery that is God *itself* in history.[19] In other words, as in polyphilic pluralism and in accord with Whitehead's Consequent Nature, God in the Bahá'í writings appears not only as mystery that no spiritual projection can reach,[20] but even more as the in-sisting infusion (*fayd*) within such different projections, which are therefore the Mystery's own affirmed divine expressions.[21] The following admonition of Bahá'u'lláh will make this point tangible.

---

12. Cf. Momen, "God," passim; Faber, *Garden*, chs. 1, 6.
13. Cf. Bahá'u'lláh, *Epistle*, 108–10; 'Abdu'l-Bahá, *Selections*, #24; Lambden, "Background," passim.
14. Cf. Bahá'u'lláh, *Tablets*, (#12) 187; 'Abdu'l-Bahá, *Promulgation*, #93. Herein lies also a genuine approximation between the Self of Reality (*nafs*) and the apophatic essence of Reality (*dhat*) as employed in the scriptural Bahá'í writings with the Hindu differentiation between *saguna* and *nirguna brahman*, or between *brahman* and *atman* (Self), or between monism (*tat tvam asi*) and theism (*purisha*), or between the (apophatic) realm of *hahut* and the (polyphilic) *lahut* in Sufi terms, or Godhead and God in the Christian mysticism of Meister Eckhart. In a Whiteheadian context, it can be understood by the difference between God (actuality) and Creativity (activity). Cf. Chapter 3; Momen, "God," 23–25; Faber, *Poet*, §40; Bracken, *Matrix*, ch. 4.
15. Cf. 'Abdu'l-Bahá, *Paris Talks*, #15; Shoghi Effendi, *World Order*, 41–42.
16. Cf. 'Abdu'l-Bahá, *Questions*, #47; *Promulgation*, #18; Shoghi Effendi, *Advent*, 36–37.
17. Cf. 'Abdu'l-Bahá, *Paris Talk*, #41; McLean, "Prolegomena," 37–46; Faber, *Garden*, ch. 1.
18. Cf. Bahá'u'lláh, *Gleanings*, #26; May, 23–24; Momen, "Relativism: A Basis," 204–6.
19. Cf. Bahá'u'lláh, *Gleanings*, 106; 'Abdu'l-Bahá, *Questions*, 20:4; May, 23–24.
20. Cf. Bahá'u'lláh, *Gleanings*, #1; Momen, "Relativism: A Basis," 206–7.
21. Cf. Bahá'u'lláh, *Gleanings*, #148; Faber, "God in the Making," 195–200.

All that the sages and mystics have said or written have never exceeded, nor can they ever hope to exceed, the limitations to which man's finite mind hath been strictly subjected. To whatever heights the mind of the most exalted of men may soar, however great the depths which the detached and understanding heart can penetrate, such mind and heart can never transcend that which is the creature of their own conceptions and the product of their own thoughts. The meditations of the profoundest thinker, the devotions of the holiest of saints, the highest expressions of praise from either human pen or tongue, are but a reflection of that which hath been created within themselves, through the revelation of the Lord, their God.[22]

The first part of the quotation elaborates on the limitation of the human heart and mind to penetrate the Mystery and binds enlightenment to the consciousness of such limitations, namely, that our multiple reactions to the Mystery are and remain contingent constructions.[23] The second part of the quotations, however, counters the potentially illusionary and utterly relativistic character of this insight with the assurance that these creations of the creature are intimately related to the revelations of the Mystery itself.[24] In this sense, the Mystery in-sists *in* these spiritual imaginations and becomes the basis for their transformation into expressions of divine in-sistence *on* multiplicity.[25] *Polyphilia!*

However, this "divine relativism" is not without its own criteria of differentiation between religions and revelations. While religions are the bodies of lived reaction to, and activation of, the Mystery, they are not identical or coextensive with the divine activity that always not only allows for the multiplicity to be valid, but generates a measure of its validity, namely, by the ability in the unfolding of their tradition and history to recover, in anamnetic remembrance, the event of their constitution.[26] In the Bahá'í context, it is then in the origination in, or catalysis through, the founding figures of religions, the events of the Manifestation of God, such as the Buddha, Muhammad, Jesus or Zoroaster, that religions can find their multiplicity to be established and critiqued.[27] It is

---

22. Bahá'u'lláh, *Gleanings*, #148.
23. Cf. Bahá'u'lláh, *Gleanings*, #83; Momen, "God," 14. Momen makes a strong argument from Bahá'í scriptural texts for the epistemological standpoint relativity of religious truth to be bound to the inevitability of cultural and linguistic relativism, but even more so to originate by the finality of the human mind. His proposition of a Bahá'í relativism and a religious pluralism based on it is, therefore, as strong as that of the pluralistic revolution of John Hick and Paul Knitter, as indicated by Kenneth Rose, and addressed in about the same timeframe of the 1980s; cf. Momen, "Learning"; "God"; "Relativism"; "Relativism: A Basis."
24. Cf. Faber, *Garden*, ch. 8.
25. Cf. Faber, *Manifold*, Pre/Face, chs. 2–3.
26. Cf. Faber, *Manifold*, ch. 9, Epilogue (On Chapter 15). For this "anamnetic" character of "presence" or "re"-presentation of the event in its trajectory, of the founding event in the becoming of a religion as that which differentiates religion (the whole arc of becoming) from revelation (event), cf. Metz, §5. As the ritual remembrance of the Exodus, for Jewish consciousness at Pesach, means an *immediacy* of being in this original situation, so recognize the Bahá'í writings this immediacy of remembrance of the divine-human covenant, for instance, with Moses, or any dispensation, for that matter; cf. Bahá'u'lláh, *Hidden Words: Persian*, #19; 'Abdu'l-Bahá, *Selections*, #181.
27. Cf. Bahá'u'lláh, *Iqan*, §§31–32; 'Abdu'l-Bahá, *Questions*, ##37, 59; Promulgation #96. This is the critical difference between "revelation" and "religion" to which I have referred earlier.

inherent in such a criterion that divergences *from* (the) Truth in and among religions may appear—the relativity of which is not primarily or exclusively one of equality, or pluralistic indistinction,[28] but, on the one hand, of the nature of sedimentations of religious imaginations over against the pure infusions of divine revelations that trigger and sustain them[29] and, on the other hand, of the nature of irrelevant expressions vis-à-vis the magnitude of such pure revelations (like the sun blinding the stars in her presence).[30] In other words, revelations are the events from which religions issue and in which they remain genuine—events that cannot be reduced to syncretic combinations, as they are genuine novelties in their synthesis; however, the embodiments of these events in religions can lose or veil or suppress or exhaust or hide or depart from or forget the event in which their life is destined to remain relevant or to disappear. Novelty is inherently the implication of this differentiation between revelation and religion.[31]

With regard to the different categorizations of ultimate reality in which religious teachings find their stabilization over against one another, such as that of personal or transpersonal (or impersonal) images for ultimate reality (remaining aware of the implications that such choices drive for the engagement with the world in ethical, social, political and ecological ways), the Bahá'í writings offer the following insights compatible with religious pluralism: First, personal and transpersonal images of God or ultimate reality are equally acceptable and, at the same time, limited reflections of our finite mind.[32] Further, monism (or pantheism/panentheism) and dualism (or theism)[33] are forms of penultimate truth, (the) Truth being beyond either of them.[34] However, our mental limitations, intimating more monistic or theistic reactions, do not isolate us from ultimate Reality, as if, reminded of a critique of Hick's apophatic pluralism, all religions were ultimately as true as they are false and, hence, in some deep sense irrelevant.[35] As the Mystery is

---

28. Cf. Bahá'u'lláh, *Iqan*, §§29, 30. See also Chapter 5 on the "limitation" of the polyphilic manifold.
29. Cf. Bahá'u'lláh, *Iqan*, §28.
30. Cf. Bahá'u'lláh, *Iqan*, §§31, 35, 36, 42.
31. Cf. Abdu'l-Bahá, Questions, #40. Against any essentialism, it is, therefore, not inherent to any religion that it was to be the last one, that is, the only one that will remain independent from this movements of impermanence and renewal. Furthermore (and for the same reason), it is misleading to assume that any religion that has disappeared was a false religion, or that any perpetuation of a religion per se establishes its truth (to its revelatory event).
32. Cf. Momen, "Relativism: A Basis," 196–212; "God," 8–29.
33. Both groups of terms, the connections among them as well as the contrasts between them are, of course, enmeshed in highly complex implications, the energy of which long-standing philosophical and theological discussion have not exhausted yet. Whether monism equals pantheism or rather panentheism, whether dualism equals theism or rather conforms to nondual theism, whether panentheism equals more theism or non-theism—these are all open question so that the here projected simplification between these contrasting opposites is more meant as a directionality of thought patterns for orientation; cf. Panikkar, *Silence*, ch. 2; Faber, *Divine Manifold*, ch. 13; *Becoming of God*, Exploration 11; *Garden*, chs. 6, 7:5.
34. Cf. Bahá'u'lláh, *Gleanings*, #93; May, 14–15; Momen, *Religion*, 41–43; Faber, *Garden*, ch. 6.
35. Although in the Bahá'í writings this—that all religions are imaginations and, hence, in this sense not representative of Reality—is a true statement, it is the second half of the same statement (just quoted in the body if the text), relating the in-sistence of reality in its Manifestations and

itself, with "its" Self, immanent in the world as a whole and in us, in-sisting as the Will, Mind, Spirit or Word of God,[36] as Wisdom or Compassion,[37] but especially as Love,[38] and insofar as "they" (this divine manifold) embody or, better, mirror this Reality accordingly, religions are true expression of the Mystery in the diverse infusions of these forms of divine in-sistence. These primal Manifestations of Reality are the great embodiments of Truth (*al-haqq*): not only are they themselves revealing a multiplicity in which the unity of religions unfolds, but they embody in relation to themselves the mutual immanence of "ex-sistence" and a unity that cannot be reduced to only one expression of "its" Self.[39]

Regarding the implications of the fourfold modes of becoming that polyphilic pluralism for the future constellations of religions suggests (always new, always many, religions in one multifaceted history, as activity of the Mystery), the Bahá'í writings would seem to approximate all four of these theses.[40] First, religious history is one of many religions, but one history[41]; differences are not in principle incommensurable, but time-related expressions of Reality that will not undermine the truth of the diverse religions.[42] Second, this creative process (generating new religions) cannot produce a final expression or end (no eschaton in any classical sense) and, hence, will always be renewed or issue in new religious manifestations.[43] Third, the *one* religious history of humanity demonstrates a multiplicity of *unique* religious experiences that resonate with the therapeutic renewal of divine responsiveness to different times, places and stages of human development, but also, as a whole, reveals the infinite novelty with which the mystery engages a world of perpetual becoming.[44] Fourth, what in religious identity formation denies religions idolatrous orthodoxies and mere projections is, in light of the apophatic-polyphilic in/

---

being the source of these imaginations (not in their limitation, but in their potential), by which such irrelevance and its underlying relativism is avoided; cf. 'Abdu'l-Bahá, *Questions*, #37.
36. Cf. 'Abdu'l-Bahá, *Questions*, #37; Faber, *Garden*, ch. 7; "Bahá'u'lláh," passim.
37. Cf. Bahá'u'lláh, *Prayers*, #94.
38. Cf. 'Abdu'l-Bahá, *Paris Talks*, #27; Faber, *Garden*, ch. 8.
39. Cf. Saiedi, *Gate*, chs. 10–12. In this "divine manifold" of apophatic-polyphilic expressions of ultimate Reality lies also a strong anti-inclusivist and pro-pluralist assumption for any transreligious engagement, namely, that we are not bound by any language game, be it, for instance, Abrahamic (Will, Mind, Spirit, Word, Wisdom, Glory, Word and so on) or Dharmic (*dharmakaya, brahman, atman, purusha* and so on) or Daoic (*dao, tai ji, wu ji* and so on) or of any other denomination or nomenclature. While these language matrices may not mix without some violation of the rules of their native engagement in their religious, spiritual and scriptural contexts, they can, in light of the exchangeability of the procedures of unnaming and the in-sistence of the Mystery in the diversity (beyond any logical reduction to one scheme), be followed into their own depth, and still will be yielding the apophatic source from which they receive their life and relevance. I understand this, and not any reiterated essence, to be the meaning of 'Abdu'l-Bahá's often repeated statement that the (independent) investigation of Truth/Reality will yield the One Truth (*al-haqq*); cf. *Paris Talks*, #41.
40. Cf. the last section of Chapter 5.
41. Cf. Bahá'u'lláh, *Gleanings*, #132;
42. Cf. Bahá'u'lláh, *Tabernacle*, #2:45.
43. Cf. Bahá'u'lláh, *Gems*, §54; Bahá'u'lláh, *Gleanings*, ##14, 24, 26.
44. Cf. Bahá'u'lláh, *Gleanings*, #95; *Tabernacle*, #1:14; 'Abdu'l-Bahá, *Paris Talks*, #3.

difference and in-sistence of the Mystery, the *attraction* to the Manifestations of God/Reality that/who in their unique, but coinherent names order, limit and direct all possibilities into a *history of spiritual maturation* without hindering the multiplicity and cyclical indefiniteness of this process.[45]

Nevertheless, despite these resonances of philosophical conceptions of religious pluralism and the religious intuition of the Bahá'í revelation, interesting differences between them remain in their respective perception of the status of the unity of religions. Gleaned from the teachings of the Bahá'í writings as devised by multiple Bahá'í voices (whether affirmative or even skeptical of this pluralistic engagement) and the diverse demands of religious pluralism, divergences will become obvious when we ask how, beyond the acceptance of many true religions (as the basic assumption of the pluralistic thesis), it is through the relativity of their religious truth that aims like universal peace and human spiritual unification can be achieved.[46] From the outset, however, it must be noted that the mutual interrogation of Bahá'í revelation and religious pluralism has not had a long and deep history on its own, that is, neither have many Bahá'í voices tried to understand the pluralistic approaches in diverse religions and diverse related philosophical discourses—although the ones that have, made great and deep contributions—nor have decades of interreligious dialogue and theorizing about religious pluralism taken sufficient notice of the innovative and complex Bahá'í voices and contributions that the resources of the Bahá'í writings for religious pluralism will be able to provide.[47]

Given this basic question and the developing, but still insufficiently explicated context of the discussion, we might find the following divergences worthy of further investigation and consideration: First, the factual and sacred history of religions, understood as divine engagements and human responses, is a complex process of improvements and misses. It is not a linear development, but rather a multilayered and sometimes parallel or asynchronistic movement of different directions, speeds and formations.[48] In other words, neither the preaxial religions nor the axial religions, nor even the post- and new axial religions, show any linear appearance in relation to one another or constitute only one series of replacements. Rather, in complex processes religions not only arise from one another, but also constitute their identity mutually in the face of others, be they dependent or independent from their own history, in the first place, often over considerable amounts of time of their existence.[49]

---

45. Cf. Bahá'u'lláh, *Gleanings*, ##21, 81–82, 115; 'Abdu'l-Bahá, *Promulgation*, #37; *Questions*, #3.
46. Cf. Velasco, 95–134.
47. While Hick has at least let himself reflect his pluralistic thesis in a Bahá'í context (cf. Hick, "Can There Be," 1–6) the *failure* of the selecting criterion for inviting mutual thought patterns of religions to be discussed, e.g., in Schmidt-Leukel, *Pluralism*, 145—namely, that he is only including the three religions with universal scope, which hold that "their fundamental beliefs are true and as such universally valid" (Buddhism, Christianity and Islam)—to include the Bahá'í Faith demonstrates the lack of visibility and recognition of the innovative patterns that Bahá'í thought does, in fact, supply for the problems discussed.
48. Cf. Foltz.
49. Cf. H. Smith, *Religions*, ch. 10; Armstrong, *History*; Plate.

Further, different religions, from the same series or milieu or from different series and milieus, can become phases of one another, can survive in foreign traditions and can create new integrated movements, which eventually become new religions.[50] So the question arises: Is the diversity of religions, in time (diachronic differences) *and* space (synchronic differences) normative to the process, or should it be overcome, that is, should there always have been, and will finally be, always only one (organized) true religion (at a time), even if it will remain one in an unending series?[51] Not only practically, in the Bahá'í consciousness, but also with respect to several scriptural witnesses, the affirmation of the latter answer to the question seems not always to be perceived as the simplification of a more complex scenario.[52] Yet such a linear answer would contradict the worth of the permanent multiplicity from the perspective of (most) religious pluralisms.[53]

Second, does universal peace among humankind demand the permanent diversity of religions, or is its condition their overcoming? I will address this question in later chapters again, but it suffices here to say that the disenchantment with religions was historically, at least in the west, massively bound to the inability of societies to cope with a warring multiplicity of religious factions, which led to the conclusion that the contradictory nature of religions cannot be helped by any harmonization, but only by the fall of the human activity called religion itself into oblivion.[54] However, the trust of the age of Enlightenment in reason instead has only proven that one warring multiplicity was replaced with another one, namely, that of totalitarian ideologies. So far, the Bahá'í vision and that of religious pluralism, of peace, seem to face the same conundrum, as no endeavor of harmonization has ever altered the fact that new multiplicities will eventually escape such harmonics by erecting counter-realities to them. But while the vision of religious pluralism generally trusts the harmonization process to finally succeed, the Bahá'í vision may allow for a more radical move, namely, the replacements of all religions through the one that would be most fitting to the material and spiritual state of humanity, especially in a global age. Not only scattered Bahá'í contributions and publications,[55] but also several scriptural passages, indeed, suggest the latter instead of

---

50. Cf. Boyarin.
51. Cf. Lundberg, "Bedrock," 53–67; P. Smith, *Encyclopedia*, 276–77; Fazel, "Approaches," 42–43; Stockman, "Progressive Revelation."
52. Cf. May, xx; Hatcher and Martin, *Bahá'í Faith*, ch. 6.
53. For the complexity of the understanding of the Bahá'í writings on the matter of the mutual relationship of religions and the "progression" of revelation, cf. Faber, "Laozi," section 10. The contrary assumption, namely, that progressiveness of revelation is a merely linear process is, therefore, that is, given the facts of religious history and the complexity of the reception of this history in the Bahá'í writings, a grave simplification and should, despite its heuristic value in apologetic contexts, be avoided.
54. This was already the thesis of the "natural history" of religions devised by the Scottish philosopher David Hume, and more recently and aggressively by the "New Atheism"; cf. Stenger, 342–43.
55. Cf. Smith, "Bahá'í Faith," passim.

the former,⁵⁶ which again would be in contradiction to the findings of religious pluralism in many of its forms.⁵⁷

Third, are these and maybe other less global divergences between religious pluralism and a Bahá'í understanding of the unity of religions, if they arise, a matter of perspective, which can be contrasted (like the undecidability, but also irrelevance, of the interpretation of half a glass of water as either half full or half empty),⁵⁸ or are they alternatives one must decide on? The problem in answering this question (that somehow includes the first two) comes entangled with yet another complication, namely, that religious pluralism, although it may have been housed by one tradition more than others, has developed into a truly multireligious engagement, while the considerations and visions of the Bahá'í religion are conducted from within *one* tradition and must, from the perspective of the pluralism of voices, be considered as one *among* others. However, if the mission of the Bahá'í religion is the unification of all religions, its perspective is, from its own understanding, *overarching* all religions. Hence, while most Bahá'í voices, engaged in contemporary religious pluralism, seem to embrace the former pluralistic position, others side with the latter inclusivist assumption, thereby preferring a permanent divergence between religious pluralism and Bahá'í intentions regarding the unity of religions.⁵⁹ However, if we come to such a conclusion favoring a bifurcation, which is by no means more than a possibility in a field of divergent voices, we must also ask at what given intensity and pronunciation which side would have become guilty of perpetuating or reinstating the poisonous fruits of false unifications in the discourse,⁶⁰ thereby also perpetuating the very antagonisms between religions that they set forth to overcome.⁶¹

Nor can religious pluralism and the vision of certain of its forms be declared exempt from those problems and conundrums. As we have already seen, the many versions of the understanding of normative plurality project a vision of the future that is by no means one of permanent competitive entities, which we might perceive religions to be constituted today. Some of these visions would allow for an overarching scheme, for instance, using a trinitarian formulary, thereby elevating a specific perspective over others (as is natural to the process of valuation), or emphasizing only a future worth imagining if it leads to a diffusion of religious identities into as of yet unprecedented forms of spiritual unity or multiplicity, or the disappearance of this difference itself.⁶² In these cases

---

56. Cf. 'Abdu'l-Bahá, *Selections*, 469.
57. Yet that the scriptural situation is much more complex and interesting, as it reflects on the equality of religions and their renewal, that is, that religions, in their ongoing reformation, are not necessarily deprived of their life-blood if new religions arise, will be central to the further discussions in the coming chapters; cf. 'Abdu'l-Bahá, *Paris Talks*, #29.
58. Cf. May, 27–29.
59. Cf. Martin, "Bahá'í Faith," 197–99.
60. Cf. Faber, "In the Wake."
61. Not only subsuming unity, but also subsuming pluralism can become oppressive if in this subsumption diverse voices become subdued and invisible—more in the next chapter. Compare, conversely, Bahá'u'lláh's avoidance of subsumption, but instead announcing a "condensation" of all religions in his revelation to the effect that it begins to mirror the multiplicity of religions *as they begin therein to mirror themselves*; cf. Bahá'u'lláh, *Iqan*, 237.
62. Cf. Teasdale, ch. 9–10.

the three question just asked for the Bahá'í religion will also apply to those pluralisms and their future expectations. Besides, we must not forget that no religious perspective, if it is in any way pluralistic, as the Bahá'í view certainly is, can escape the site from which it is projected, because this makes the unique perspectives of its pluralistic impulse existentially warranted, while second-level generalizations, with which philosophical schemes of religious pluralism are often blamed, can only hide their particularities partially. It is precisely their singularity that makes them universal—an important point to be revisited later.[63]

At this juncture, then, the best conclusion we can draw from these conversations is that we should not yet draw a conclusion. No pluralistic position is uninfected by one or the other of those conundrums, nor can any of them easily escape their hidden persistence and effects.[64] The situation, whether it should be more adequately symbolized with the image of a juncture or of a bifurcation, is at best ambivalent. We are caught in a dilemma in which whatever side one takes the other cannot be erased, because it seems in a profound sense to be already inherent in the conditions that allow its own affirmation.[65] There is no stranger and "other" anymore that would not be already part of one's own reasoning.

A quotation from Bahá'u'lláh will adduce this ambivalence. It derives from an interview that the only western scholar of religion, the Cambridge orientalist Edward G. Browne, was admitted to conduct with Bahá'u'lláh, in 1891, a year before his passing.[66] In it, Bahá'u'lláh addresses Browne and explains the vision of his mission for which he and many of his companions were accepting severe sufferings and even death over most of the stretch of that century since the Bábi-Bahá'í religions' inception.[67] We can hear of, and feel, the trust, and the divine destiny implied, in the ushering in of a future in which at least nothing of the classical dealings of religions will stay the same—issuing into an unprecedented chapter for humanity at peace.[68] Yet, as it is a vision of spiritual liberation that hints at the unprecedented, it also leaves for human minds, which are always limited in their imaginations, room for different and occasional less radical interpretations.

---

63. Cf. Deleuze, *Difference*, ch. 1; Faber, *Manifold*, ch. 1 (cf. the introduction of this chapter with its Whitehead-related understanding of uniqueness and universality); Faber, "Origin," 273–89.
64. This can be readily witnessed by the oscillation between inclusivism and pluralism in the work of many pluralistic thinkers; cf. K. Rose, *Pluralism*, chs. 1–2.
65. Even arguably most decidedly pluralistic thinkers like John Hick or John Cobb can be understood both ways: either by recognizing their respective philosophical scheme, coming from Kant and Whitehead, respectively, as the limiting inclusivist factor (that always distorts the plurality of other potentials toward their own overarching inclusiveness or even finality), or by their western situatedness in which the Christian vocabulary will remain a limiting factor of this kind. In other words, no apophatic or cataphatic pluralism, be it mono- or polycentric, can be exempt from this oscillation or, on occasion, indistinguishability between the pluralist and the inclusivist perspective.
66. Cf. Esslemont, 45–47, 55.
67. Cf. Momen, ed., *Bábi and Bahá'í Religions*, sections 2–3; Momen, "Persecution," 471–85; Walbridge, "Bábi Uprising," 339–62; Balyuzi, *Bahá'u'lláh*, chs. 17, 33.
68. Cf. the excellent compilation in Hayes.

Praise be to God that thou hast attained! [...] Thou hast come to see a prisoner and an exile [...] We desire but the good of the world and happiness of the nations; yet they deem us a stirrer up of strife and sedition worthy of bondage and banishment [...] That all nations should become one in faith and all men as brothers; that the bonds of affection and unity between the sons of men should be strengthened; that diversity of religion should cease, and differences of race be annulled—what harm is there in this? [...] Yet so it shall be; these fruitless strifes, these ruinous wars shall pass away, and the "Most Great Peace" shall come.[69]

Pluralism or inclusivism? Yet it should have become clear that from the perspective of a polyphilic pluralism—over against any reductionism to either oneness or difference, to either apophaticism or mystical essentialism, or to any of the poisonous fruits of oneness—the solution to this ambivalence in coherently relating unity and pluralism, religious commitment and relativism of truth claims, as well as apophaticism and cataphatic positivity, in both postaxial religious consciousness as well as in any related contemporary philosophical awareness, will have to take into account the divine diversification of insistence in the world of humanity and as a whole[70] in such a way that *any* relaxation of the tension this ambivalence forcefully both hides and presents us with would be a concession of defeat. Instead of giving in to the forces that seem to demand a renewal of more limited (inclusivist) forms of pluralism, relativism and perspectivism, what the polyphilic approach seems to demand, instead, is that we *can* learn to avoid those conundrums (mentioned above) by pushing the meaning of unity of religions *and* religious pluralism even further to the point that the ambivalence these conundrums exhibit and that live from the desire for simplification can be transcended *by completely embracing the processual mutuality and coextensive togetherness of unity and multiplicity*[71]—as the way forward for the comprehensive conviviality of religious minds and hearts and in a future universal society operating from the presumption of the inviolability of religious peace and polyphilic grace. This endeavor will be the task of the following chapters.

---

69. E. G. Browne, from his pen portrait of Bahá'u'lláh, in Esslemont, 46. While this statement, as it is, cannot be considered Bahá'í scripture, the fact that it was in reference and verbatim often cited by 'Abdu'l-Bahá and Shoghi Effendi has made it an authoritative statement; cf. Shoghi Effendi, *God*, 94. But many other passages from Bahá'u'lláh and 'Abdu'l-Bahá would corroborate its content; cf. Shoghi Effendi. *Promised Day*, 116–17.
70. This correlation will be the theme of Chapter 13.
71. This is the *cantus firmus* of my book *The Divine Manifold*.

Chapter Seven

PLURALISM OF PLURALISMS?

The drop must not estimate its own limited capacity; it must realize the volume and sufficiency of the ocean, which ever glorifieth the drop.[1]

—'Abdu'l-Bahá

As with the viewpoint rising from the supposition of the unity of religions, so also has the concept of religious pluralism received mixed reviews not only from proponents of a more reiterated understanding of this unity,[2] but even more so from worldviews and philosophical advocates of pluralism for whom even the differentiation between monocentric and polycentric pluralism does not go far enough. The main reason for the disappointment of those pluralists, based in methodologies inspired by postcolonialism, poststructuralism and feminist/womanist perspectives,[3] among others, is that all of the above mentioned varieties of "monism" and pluralism presuppose a fundamental agreement on the "unity of reality" that is suspicious to them.[4] For a more perennialist monocentric understanding of unity, "monism" of reality seems to imply that this unity of reality is one that, in the end, will finally overcome, or has already always underpinned, the differences between different culturally, socially and psychologically embedded mindsets; while these differences remain operative on an epistemological level, they do not reach the ontological embeddedness in one Reality.[5] The polycentric approaches, again, invariably seem, in the end, not "deep" enough either, because they will have to admit some kind of communication between their supposed ultimates, which lets them appear as another variant of an assumed metaphysical "monism" of Reality.[6]

---

1. 'Abdu'l-Bahá, *Promulgation*, #124.
2. This would, at this point, not only refer to pluralists of "oneness" approaching "sameness" of religious essence, as certain perennialist views and even some Bahá'í voices might favor, but include also the "oneness" of religions in exclusivist and inclusivist manner since both reiterate oneness to one that is only present in one tradition or only in limited form present in other traditions.
3. Cf. Vanhoozer.
4. Cf. Foucault; Lyotard; Best and Kellner.
5. Cf. Schneider.
6. Cf. Faber, *Manifold*, ch. 2. This is also implied in the position of Steven Katz regarding the radically different experiences allegedly subsumed as one mystical sphere of different religions; cf. Katz; for a critical assessment by Stephen Kaplan based on the inevitable necessity of the articulation of communicable categories, cf. Kaplan, ch. 3.

Instead, postcolonialist and feminist/womanist approaches make the point that all of these "monistic" pluralisms are still "Eurocentric" variations on the theme of power, of staying in control of the discourses and dialogues.[7] As they are presumed to be conducted on the basis of Euro-American thought patterns, not in themselves minority-oriented or -admitting, and, hence, limited by patriarchal, paternalistic and racial/ethnic conundrums, they cannot be *truly* pluralistic, multicultural or transcending gender and race restrictions.[8] The whole discussion on postcolonial "hybridity" targets precisely such limitations, namely, the failure of the idea that anyone could think freely beyond such limitations if we just would allow for colonially suppressed indigenes' cultural and religious experiences to surface and become part of the ongoing multicultural and multireligious discourses. The reason is simple: history cannot be erased; its embodied (colonial/subaltern) categorizations have become such markers of mutual encounter (in and between cultures, but also in and between persons) that no archeology of an older "before" or liberated "beyond" can recover what never has in fact happened.[9]

Poststructuralism and similar philosophical persuasions in a broad sense have attempted to upset the whole variety of schemes of thought that finds need in presupposing unity of any kind (metaphysical, cultural, political and so on) *at all* and, instead, have left us with a thoroughgoing perspectivism that cannot be brought into one coherent assumption of reality, either epistemologically or metaphysically.[10] If we would uproot the deep prejudice of oneness, for many poststructuralists we end up in an infinite regress of the deconstruction of "false unifications" that are merely means of power-inflicted control-mechanisms not only of discourses, but also of the very lives of peoples. Pluralism, in this context, means to never admit to any bottom level or foundation of coherence of Reality underpinning the multiplicity of different perspectives, traditions, cultural differences and religious diversities.[11] This is not a merely relativistic enterprise, however, although it is readily misunderstood in such a way,[12] as it follows a deeply ethical impulse of justice and liberation.[13] Instead, the deconstructive endeavor is meant to always find the obliterated, suppressed and lost voices in any form of unification, be it metaphysical or cultural, ethnic or religious.[14] Yet, as the more recent "green" turn of the poststructuralist discourse demonstrates (and especially highlighted by the engagement of process thought in this context),[15] with these uncovered (oppressed or erased) multiplicities cross-cultural, transcultural and transreligious communication and translatability

---

7. Cf. Masuzawa, chs. 1–3.
8. Cf. Bender and Klassen; Pui-lan, chs. 1, 8.
9. Cf. Kraidy, ch. 7; Young, *Desire*, chs. 1–2; *Postcolonialism*, chs. 1, 4.
10. Cf. Faber, "Introduction: Negotiating Becoming," 1–50; Badiou; Gutting.
11. Cf. Derrida, "Différance," 1–28; Caputo; Faber, "God in the Making," 192; Welsch, 260–75.
12. Cf. Kluge, "Postmodernism"; "Relativism."
13. Cf. Faber, *Garden*, ch. 9:4 (Deconstructions).
14. Cf. Keller, Nausner and Rivera; Keller, *God*, chs. 5–6, 8.
15. Cf. Keller, "Introduction: The Process of Difference," 9–22; Latour.

are *always* inherent potentials of human existence[16]—and necessary for the care of our common Earth.[17]

The profound, liberating, resistant and recovering aspect of divergence and difference in these approaches is of utmost importance for any further discussion of religious pluralism and unison. However, a specific implication of related approaches is problematic: if they are carried by the (metaphysical) assumption that the exclusion of any kind of unity from considerations is unavoidable because of its alleged character as oppressive instrument of power instead of truth.[18] This more or less consistently appearing postmodern theme of power and truth is itself conceived on another presupposition, namely, that difference means a divergence that cannot only never be seen as "one" (which is what every serious pluralism would consider valid), but is (or must always be) resistant to mutuality and relationality as such and in any form.[19] Hence, these non-mutual differences and non-relational or non-lateral versions of alterity must in themselves exhibit the utter strangeness of the "Other" (of the oppressed, or of the oppressor, or the foreign culture), and in consistent strategies further the "essential" incompatibility of perspectives (hermeneutical and epistemological) horizons, social locations and cultures.[20] There are, in other words, no ways by which a certain cultural, ethnic or in such ways religiously embedded view of liberating discourses can be understood from the outside, that is, other perspectives are always already objectifying and oppressive.[21] In the end, such a postmodern emphasis on difference as incompatible divergence is in danger of becoming a substantialist understanding of a plurality of "others among others" in which external multiple entities encounter only strange outside worlds by which they must always be misunderstood and can only be "grasped" if they are occupied in colonial moves of unification.[22] While such a substantializing move ("*sub-stare*," stand under or stand from below) is necessary as means of the recovery of minority identity from displacement and

---

16. Cf. Dean; Budick and Iser, part 2 (207–302); Jones, *Theory*, ch. 6. This understanding of communicability must be seen as a subtle avoidance of an essentialism that can befall postmodern thought patterns if they, especially in postcolonialist discourses, assume that the mutual alienation of cultures and the genuine impossibility to understand another culture is final, as I will argue presently in the text; cf. Faber, *Poet*, part 2 and §33. The affirmation of communicability across cultural entities *also* highlights that the forms of pluralism that prefer difference over relation (cf. Chapter 3) are less viable, at least because they would diminish communication and leave transreligious processes, which are not abstract categories, but factual forces driving human and religious history, unexplained.
17. Cf. Spivak, *Critique*, 380.
18. Cf. Faber, *Manifold*, ch. 2; Conversely, on that basis, liberation would also engage power and remain the substitute of truth; cf. Faber, "God in the Making," 192.
19. Cf. Faber, "Touch," 47–67; "God in the Making," 192; Welsch, 260–75.
20. Cf. Faber, "De-Ontologizing God," 212–14; Davis.
21. Cf. Budick, 1–22; Loomba, ch. 2; Desal and Nair.
22. Cf. Krishna, chs. 3–4. This has also led to the reversal of reasonability into multiple incompatible reasons by the affirmation of which scheme a new path of limiting and excluding self-affirmation becomes possible, the formation of a new exclusivism on the basis of postmodern relativism; cf. Hyman,; Milbank, Pickstock and Ward, 1–20.

diaspora,[23] it is also in danger of submitting to another form of essentialization counterproductive to communication and reconciliation.[24] Against this new dualism of otherness (and the enshrined omnipotent and inescapable dialectic of power),[25] the sensitive and advanced postmodern (poststructuralist/postcolonial) discourse has highlighted the porousness of oppositions, apprehending spaces in between, recovering the interstices and the intermezzo, the fold, the rhizome as the site of life engaged in liberation and reconciliation as well as cultural and ecological reconnection.[26]

Process thought has, against such potential substantializations, insisted on two correctives. On the one hand, it registers the "togetherness" of (past) facts in an experiential (present) event-process in light of new possibilities of realization (anticipation) as ultimate movement of individual and collective creative existence, indicating the profound, but bottomless ultimacy of Creativity in the formation of any kind of organism, culture, society and religion.[27] There is no independent or unbridgeable plurality of divergences, as there is always a becoming of many into the fusion of new realities, impermanent unifications, but to mind, always on the move to ever-new combinations, histories, constructions, deconstructions and recoveries of lost voices.[28] On the other hand, process thought insists—as is also recognized by a key thinker of poststructuralism, namely, Gilles Deleuze[29]—that in this polyphonic sounding together of related perspectives pluralism is, as monism and dualism, only an abstraction from "multiplicity," the many-*fold*-ness in which Reality always appears as divergent and convergent, differential and integral, concrescent (growing together) and transitional (moving beyond itself or any fixed state of being).[30] Multiplicity is neither one nor many, but like origami unbreakable, yet infinitely differentiated.[31]

---

23. Cf. Nayar, ch. 6.
24. Other layers of argumentation for a cross-cultural understanding or even mutuality, allowing for generalizations not to be oppressive, but "natural," thereby supporting an understanding of the unity of religions in profoundly similar way to the Bahá'í understanding based on the unity of humanity, come from the research into genetic restraints of being human and related brain sciences; cf. Boyer, ch. 1. But it also arises from new methodological considerations regarding the rediscovery of the dimension of sacredness and other "cataphatic universals" (such as deathlessness or beatitude) within genuine religious studies (with M. Eliade against W. C. Smith) that cannot be reduced to materialistic (anti-religious) or particularistic (religious, cultural, social) explanations (preferred in critical cultural studies and sociological as well as anthropological reductionisms in religious studies) without also ending in some kind of exclusivism; cf. K. Rose, *Pluralism*, ch. 8. This "universality" need not be framed by the inadequate dichotomy of essentialism versus constructivism, as the constructivist fragmentation is itself substantialist in nature while the alleged (new or renewed) essentialist approach can be understood as relativistic process approach of mutual immanence for which the text will presently argue.
25. Cf. Faber, *Manifold*, ch. 11; "Introduction: Negotiating Becoming," 1–50.
26. Cf. Deleuze and Guattari, ch. 1; Baba; Spivak, *Death*; Faber, *Manifold*, chs. 12, 14; "Intermezzo," 212–35.
27. Cf. Faber, *Poet*, part 2; *Becoming of God*, Exploration 1; Bracken, *One*, ch. 3.
28. Cf. Keller, *Intercarnations*, ch. 10; cf. Keller and Schneider, part 1.
29. Cf. Deleuze, *Fold*, ch. 6.
30. Cf. Faber, *Manifold*, ch. 12; Keller, "Process," 55–72.
31. Cf. Faber, *Manifold*, ch. 8; Keller, *Cloud*, ch. 5.

Two aspects converge with *polyphilia*: One (more spatial) aspect promotes multiplicity to be the ultimate irreducible field of existence spanned by the process of becoming—Whitehead identifies it with Plato's *khora*, the medium of intercommunication that does not impose any form or character on its own.[32] Hence, there is no difference without relation, no divergence without communication and responsibility.[33] The second (more temporal) aspect situates both the one and the many as entangled in a process pulsing in transient unifications and differentiations.[34] This process is not an illusion of evil or a lack, but rather the affirmation of multiplicity by the in-sistence of Reality in this process and on it, neither negating differences nor allowing static unifications to have the last word by which it would become oppressive.[35] Polyphilic pluralism emphatically heightens both aspects to the degree that Reality itself is understood as the process of co-construction and co-deconstruction, the movement of sym-pathy, of mutual receptivity and receptiveness, and a process of the impermanence of ever-new events of togetherness.[36] In this sense, it mirrors the philosophical and religious imperatives (as espoused, for instance, by John Hick) implied in the *metanoia* from self-centeredness to Reality-centeredness,[37] equally identified by monocentric and polycentric pluralisms as perennial spiritual and ethical core and corrective of multireligious unity and conversation[38]—and not in need of a monistic reiteration of ultimate Reality.

The Bahá'í writings share similar perspectives. They do not break the "deep" relativity of monistic or theistic ontological approaches to Reality, exempting "it" from any such limitations.[39] But they also, simultaneously, know of the divine virtues of self-overcoming and -transition into an emptiness in the face of ultimacy as the impulse for religions to fulfill the very reason for their existence: the creation of universal spaces of compassion

---

32. Cf. Whitehead, *Adventures*, 134; Faber, "Khora," 105–26; "Immanence," 91–110; *Poet*, 210, 251, 255–56, 281, Postscript; *Manifold*, ch. 9. It is in the sense of *khora* that "unity" as "mutual immanence" forms the basis for my own understanding of unity in the apophatic-polyphilic sense in relation to the Bahá'í notion of the "unity of God/Reality" (with Sufi thought, a translation of the apophatic *tawhid*) as the origin of reality and all religions that express it indefinitely; cf. *Prozeßtheologie*, §21. It can also be found in the Buddhist rendering of *basho*, the Place, of Nishida Kitaro and the Kyoto School as fundamental "unity of reality" indifferent from the multiplicity of phenomena, empty (*sunya*) and in pleromatic embrace of existence; cf. Carter; Wargo; Nishida, *Enquiry*; Faber, *Manifold*, chs. 4, 9. Regarding the "unity of reality," cf. also Chapter 11.
33. Cf. Keller, "Introduction: The Process of Difference," 1–30.
34. Cf. Whitehead, *Process*, 20–22; *Adventures*, ch. 12.
35. Cf. Faber, *Manifold*, chs. 10.
36. Cf. Faber, *God as Poet*, §32; *Manifold*, ch. 13; "Immanence," 91–110.
37. Cf. Hick, *Interpretation*, 240.
38. The occasional critique of Hick's proposal in this regard, I propose, should not be understood as devastating to the core assumption of this *metanoia*, but as expansion of motives of religious existence, which, however, will hardly upset the assumption itself as experientially and empirically, intellectually and spiritually, satisfying.
39. Cf. Momen, "Relativism: A Basis," 185–217.

and justice, loving-kindness and creative modes of relationality.[40] Such modes of unification drive home the point that any sexist or racist restrictions on the pluralism of voices equals the unattainability of the unity of religions these writings mean human history to attain.[41] Because ethnicities are a matter of the manifold of existence, not disturbances, religions like ethnicities are (social) constructions of diversities, which can degenerate into oppositions (and have obviously often done so). But since they are constructions, these oppositional and warring formations *can* be overcome (deconstructed) since they are not "real" in any ultimate sense.[42] In other words, not the construction of their multiplicity is the problem that ought to be overcome, here, but that such constructions can become religiously toxic by falling into the antagonistic traps of essentialized differences (or rather adversarial opposition) or forced oneness (uniformity). It is here that the very impulse of the Bahá'í principle of unity becomes *deconstructive*, that is, in all areas wants to uncover the mechanisms of misconstruction that disguise themselves as such false unifications over and against the profound beauty of multiplicities that religion is to unfold in unifications of peace.[43]

I will return to these insights later. Yet what is immediately of interest, here, is another implication of these conversations: namely, that we cannot find any "perfect" representations of unity and plurality, that is, multiplicity, neither by adopting multicultural and multireligious perspectives nor by embracing postcolonial and poststructuralist perspectives.[44] Instead, *all* religious universes of discourse and embodiments in concrete individual and collective religious existences only persist in an ongoing process, the cycle of love, but also its deviations, always harboring a multiplicity of unifications and pluralisms, as well as their detractors, despisers and opposed convictions.[45] This means that we must differentiate between different pluralisms: a pluralism of exclusivism, inclusivism and pluralism within and between religions, and a pluralism of different pluralisms nurtured by different cultural and social constructions and deconstructions that provide the variegated categories by which pluralism can be addressed from within different

---

40. Cf. Bahá'u'lláh, *Iqan*, §§1–3; *Gleanings*, #19; *Gems*, #83; 'Abdu'l-Bahá, Promulgation, ##29, 57, 72–73; Naghdy, *Tutorial*, ch. 1; Lepard, *Hope*, ch. 5.
41. Cf. 'Abdu'l-Bahá, *Paris Talks*, ##40, 50; *Promulgation*, #95; P. Smith, *Introduction*, 138–45; Hatcher and Martin, 75; A. Lee; M. L. Perry, chs. 3–4; Stockman, *Faith*, chs. 5, 9; Lepard, *Hope*, ch. 9; Maneck, "Women," 211–28.
42. Cf. 'Abdu'l-Bahá, *Paris Talks*, #45, on the construction and illusion of race; *Promulgation*, ##113, 118, on the construction of gender.
43. Cf. 'Abdu'l-Bahá, *Promulgation*, ##109, 112, 135; *Selections*, ##202, 227; *Paris Talks*, #45.
44. In Whitehead's universe, this is a necessity of the impermanence and becoming of events not only for themselves, but always for a community/society/nexus that will be constituted and changed by the impact of their becoming, which again changes the events rising from this new community/society/nexus; cf. Whitehead, *Process*, 20–22, 105, 113. This is what Deleuze in view of Whitehead (and in repetition of James Joyce) named the "chaosmos"; cf. Deleuze, *Fold*, 79–81; Faber, "Surrationality," 157–77; *Poet*, §§15, 41; *Manifold*, chs. 1–3, 7; Keller, "Process," 55–72.
45. Cf. Whitehead, *Adventures*, chs. 17, 19; Faber, *Poet*, §§15, 32.

traditions, but which becomes communicable because of the universal communicability of pluralisms among themselves (as argued earlier).

Regarding the latter pluralism, as Perry Schmidt-Leukel—a religious scholar of long-standing multireligious and pluralist engagement, especially in the Buddhist-Christian dialogue[46]—has aptly demonstrated, the pluralism of any religious tradition may differ regarding its colored ethnical, cultural, social, psychological and philosophical conditioning under which it appears and develops.[47] But while exclusivism and inclusivism cannot communicate with one another beyond the self-constructed limitations of substantialized traditions (and their restricting truth-claims) without denigrating or lowering other such counter-identified traditions (as already mentioned[48]), religious pluralisms from any such traditional heritages and embedded perspectives *can* and *want* to communicate beyond such (essentialized) boundaries regardless of the specific intra-religious argumentations fostering, and fostered by, their character and flavor.[49] Hence, as Schmidt-Leukel says, we need religion- or tradition-specific pluralisms and a respective interreligious discourse that takes these different modes of argumentation for pluralism from within diverse traditions into account not despite, but because of their embedded divergence. By necessitating a dialogue between these pluralisms, such an interreligious discourse will not issue in irrelevant abstractions, but always communicate from and between the different perspectives of the conversations partners.[50] Herein should also

---

46. For Schmidt-Leukel's situatedness in the German history of Christian-Buddhist dialogues and interreligious discourser, cf. Lai and von Brück, 189–90.
47. Cf. Schmidt-Leukel, *Pluralism*, 124–29.
48. Cf. Chapter 3 for the exposition of this thought on the threefold matrix and the communicability of religions (or lack thereof) from its diverse positions.
49. Cf. Schmidt-Leukel, *Pluralism*, 135–36. The problem of the inevitability of any pluralist theory to create a supermodel for all models to integrate, thereby hindering neutrality and equity between the systems, is used in negation of pluralism by D'Costa ("Impossibility," 225–26) and as problem descriptively raised by Thomas Owen ("Plurality," 200). K. Rose (*Pluralism*, ch. 1), however, argues strongly that this transcendental argument as no merit, as it is based on a false identification of first- and second-level language of apophaticism or pluralism based on it.
50. Cf. Schmidt-Leukel, *Pluralism*, 109–14. It is this profoundly transitional, dialogical and mutually engaging character of such a pluralism of pluralisms in this sense of intercommunication, coming from diverse traditions themselves, not being subsumable to just one abstract term "pluralism," that indicates that it is not quite captured by the alternative terminology of "particularism" (exclusivism, inclusivism) and "nonparticularism" (pluralism) introduced in reflection on Schmidt-Leukel by Kenneth Rose (*Pluralism*, 8–9). Although this alternative terminology has the advantage that it can be subdivided into stronger and weaker forms, making the tripartite classical differentiation more contiguous: a strong pluralism would resemble exclusivism as it would claim one universal religious truth (beyond particular religions) to be final or inevitable, while the weaker form resembles a relativism of equally viable forms of religious expressions in the movement of constant self-overcoming into other forms, virtually eliminating the conversation partners, at least in the long run. The pluralism of pluralisms here affirmed, however, would emphasize the *irreplaceable* experiences mediated by these partners in their conversations and offered for mutual learning and access *that would be true whether or not* a religion or their living exponents would have moved on to, or faded away in, successors. In process terms: events are unique, whether in their becoming or as facts of the past. In fact, they are

lie the justification for the importance not to fall back into the generalizing trap process thought and the postcolonial and poststructuralist deconstructions have made us conscious of, namely, to turn a blind eye to, or to exclude, minority traditions such as the Bahá'í Faith, which despite its immediate relevance to the thematic at hand is virtually not noticed by generalized pluralistic dialogues.[51]

Regarding the former, a pluralism of exclusivism, inclusivism and pluralism, which has been suggested by Arvind Sharma especially to be the arena of religious history of India and in relation to the religious complex of Hinduism,[52] I mean to widen the pluralism of pluralisms in significant ways. While Sharma speculates about the indeterminate truth of either position and promotes a nonexclusive, nondual Vedantic approach (not of either-or, but both-and) based on the factual history of Hindu religious thought- and life-patterns, I propose a similar move on grounds of the necessary affirmation of the truth-value of the whole matrix comprising and relating these positions[53] and the process concept of mutual immanence.[54] In accord with a non-substantialist process understanding of multiplicity and in agreement with the poststructuralist impetus of deconstructing simplified unities, as well as with the postcolonial impulse to uncover the false unifications of prevalent discourses as means of power rather than truth (introduced as valuable impulse to radical plurality at the beginning of this chapter), I propose that this pluralism of a multiplicity of pluralist *and* non-pluralist accesses to, or imaginations of, Reality must itself remain relative to their mutual deconstruction.[55] As far as they (have) become opposing identity markers, they must be deconstructed not despite, but because of their constructive reality and hybrid character within religions, which is based on the *mutuality* of these positions, even and especially when they are seen as contradictory ends of a spectrum.[56] This *is* a pluralism, not just a factual plurality, as it understands the

---

never just lost in the past when memory fades; they may be remembered and revivified beyond physical contiguity; cf. Whitehead, *Adventures*, chs. 11–13.

51. Or the Bahá'í stance is, because of its emphasis on the unity of religions, misjudged as monolithic and uninformative.
52. Cf. Sharma, "Can There Be," 56–61.
53. The necessary affirmation of the whole matrix even when denying certain of its positions, because of the inescapable field-character of the matrix *as* pluralism, has been explicated in Chapter 3.
54. Cf. Faber, *Becoming of God*, Exploration 10.
55. Sharma's proposal builds on the relative truth value of either of the three positions, namely, exclusivism, inclusivism and pluralism, such that each of them *may* be true (or more true than the other) and, hence, opts for a relativity of truth for which either of these positions *may* be false; cf. Sharma, "Can There Be," 60. In my understanding of relativity as relationality, the mutual deconstruction is one of the *affirmation* of the relativity *between* these positions, or their mutual coinherence, that establishes the dynamics of truth: that is, *none* of these positions is false *as long as* they stay and oscillate in the mutuality that establishes their dynamics of differentiation; cf. Faber, *Garden*, ch. 4.
56. The mutual deconstruction of these positions becomes visible in the diverse attempts to reduce some of them to others, namely, the respectively preferred positions: Gavin D'Costa understands pluralism as a new exclusivism; cf. D'Costa, "Impossibility," 223–33. Kenneth Rose understands inclusivism as a cryptic exclusivism or as a failed pluralism, which will always fall apart in either direction; cf. Rose, *Pluralism*, ch. 2. Several Christian theologians want to

divergences of exclusivism, inclusivism and pluralism as mutually counter-constructed identities that, as far as they are opposing one another and become means of religious distrust and violence, are expressions of false unifications—much like mutual identities of religions have often defined themselves in the opposing encounter with one another.[57] It is a *polyphilic* pluralism, as it does not circumvent the inconvenient truth that oppositions in opinion are un-liberated variations of the Mystery, still caught in the process of self-overcoming (the *metanoia* from self to Reality) from disjunctions into contrasts.[58] And it is a polyphilic pluralism *of* pluralisms, as this pluralism will appear in different variations in diverse thought systems and lived settings, inspired by different religious traditions, and must, as every pluralism of pluralisms (considering the sites of pluralistic divergences), be addressed from the perspective of their reality as constructions of different religious identities in these diverse traditions.

It is in the mold of this polyphilic pluralism of pluralisms (of exclusivism, inclusivism and pluralism) that the discrepancies of diverse Bahá'í authors, reflecting on the extent to which the Bahá'í writings, in fact or as aspiration, exhibit exclusivist, inclusivist or pluralist tendencies, must be recognized, discussed and brought into mutual transformative conversation.[59] This would be true for any other religious tradition, of course, and only finds its exemplification in the Bahá'í terrain for reasons of diversification of the discourse from the perspective of the new axial consciousness.[60] There is, however, more to it. What is interesting *specifically* in the Bahá'í context is this: that not the exclusion or inclusion of different religions in its principle of unity is in question (so that to this extent *all* Bahá'í positions will be pluralistic!), but that on this basis the unity of religions

---

reconstruct pluralism as (Christocentric) inclusivism or hold on to it as the more stable form of "pluralism"; cf. Clooney, *Comparative Theology: Deep Learning*, 12; Cracknell, 71; Cornille, ed., *Mansions*, 6; Teasdale, 248; Dupuis, *Theology*, 317. And K. Rose (*Pluralism*, 8–9) creates an interesting scale conveying these three positions in form of mutual inclusion or, at least, serial unfolding of the implications of the respectively other positions (between their weak and strong forms) that indicates that they are only relatively different and rather connected one to the other through a *matrix* of foldings.

57. As can be witnessed, for instance, in the mutual counter-identification and -definition of Rabbinic Judaism and Christianity in the first century CE or between Confucianism and Daoism (and later certain forms of Buddhism) in the China of the centuries between the second centuries BCE and CE.

58. Cf. Whitehead, *Process*, 22, 348. This perspectival integration of exclusivism, inclusivism and pluralism is foreshadowed by the self-critical analysis of pluralism—answering the criticism leveled against pluralism—as in some sense always being exclusivism and/or inclusivism in Kaplan (44–48).

59. Cf. Saiedi, *Logos*, 12–13.

60. Not forgetting that all extant religions can be infected by this new axial spirit and have, in the current global inescapability of the exchange of ideas, in fact been changed in sections by this spirit. The whole discourse on religious pluralism, as it finds increasingly a home in diverse traditions, is the best sign of this sea change. Yet in *paradigmatically* understanding the Bahá'í Faith as a religion born from, into or in generation of this new axial age, its *uniqueness* is that it speaks to the issues in question, here, not from reformation and reflection, but from an *event* of innovation and initiation.

itself can be perceived from these divergent and incompatible perspectives. And since we are warned by Bahá'u'lláh not to become stuck in oppositions—as in such oppositions nothing but error on all sides becomes visible—we must seek to further explain *why* religious pluralism and the unity of religions do not simply converge and *how* we can avoid the oppositional energy they generate, the acceptance of which would not just perpetuate their difference, but their un-truth and un-reality. The transformation of oppositions into contrasts would be the event in which Reality begins to become transparent. Here is Bahá'u'lláh's radical admonition for the deconstruction of all oppositions as condition for religion (or any reality) to reflect the in-sistence of Reality:

> O Jamal! On this Day it is befitting that you should exhibit such love, compassion, humility, detachment and sanctity that none of the servants (of God) may inhale from your words and deeds, the unsavory odor of the words and deeds of past communities who, on hearing merely one word, would immediately anathematize and curse one another, for "We have created souls (al-nufús) to be in diverse states" (Qur'an 71:13[14]). There are those who have attained to the highest levels of spiritual comprehension (a`la marátib-i `irfán) while others are different therefrom […] If however, the supporters of […] two positions should contend and quarrel with one another in their exposition of […] two perspectives, both groups are, and have ever been, rejected […] and both groups shall return to the hellfire despite the fact that they, in their own estimation, soar in the highest horizon of spiritual understanding (bi-a`lá ufuq-i `irfán).[61]

Note that, in this quotation from Bahá'u'lláh's letter to Jamal-i Burujirdi, a learned and prominent, but infamous divine, despite the potentially "greater" reality of different spiritual states, the assumption that some could (in some kind of "hierarchy of truths") be "closer" to the truth regarding the polyphilic pluralism of pluralisms than others is *not* the decisive point.[62] Instead, it is the oppositional, antagonistic and mutually exclusive and derogatory mindset between the different approaches by which they define themselves mutually as exclusivist, inclusivist or pluralist that must be addressed.[63] The remedy is only hinted at here: *that no perspective is by virtue of its truth or spiritual insight and closeness to Reality, in fact, closer to Truth and Reality as long as it is created and sustained in adversarial opposition to other views*—which again is an implication of the Bahá'í relativism for which Reality is removed from the plane of oppositional movements in the world of impermanence[64]—an

---

61. Bahá'u'lláh, *Tablet to Jamal-i-Burujirdí (Lawh-i-Jamál-i-Burujirdí)*, 4–8.
62. Cf. Saiedi, *Gate*, 175–80; Brown, "Abdu'l-Bahá's Response," 1–29.
63. On 'Abdu'l-Bahá's solution to the seeming opposition of divine attributes by way of the noncontradictory contrasting of infinite aspects of divine oneness as mirrored into the world, cf. Saiedi, *Gate*, 179.
64. Cf. Momen, "Relativism: A Basis," 205–6. While the discussion of Momen's relativistic understanding (exemplified on a Tablet of 'Abdu'l-Bahá on the Islamic tradition "I was a Hidden Treasure" (Abdu'l-Bahá, *Commentary*, 4–3)) by Saiedi and Brown tries to establish that 'Abdu'l-Bahá does not think that there is relativistic equality between certain standpoints (such as theism or monism), but a "hierarchy of truths," Bahá'u'lláh, in the present quotation, does rather look at the opposition *itself*, if it is built on such adversarial differentiations, as problematic for the definition of closeness to Reality/Truth.

insight that is also shared by Whitehead's "theopoetic" differentiation of God's actuality from the activity that is the world's creativity.[65] Since these differences *as* contrasts (not as oppositions) are not just imaginations, but polyphilic expressions of ultimate Reality itself, Reality is not outside of them, but in-sists in them as the *movens* of their reconciliation—and their reconciliation is "its" manifestation.[66]

---

65. I have named this insight the "theopoetic difference" (between God and Creativity in Whitehead's work), which references that God as Poet is *not* involved in, or is acting as if God were, a causal activity (among cause activities) that is always (in danger of becoming) oppositional, but instead indicates the Eros for the transformation of all such causal divergences into contrastive unities; cf. Whitehead, *Process*, 346; Faber, *Poet*, 14–15, 144; *Manifold*, chs. 1, 11; "Intermezzo," 227–29. This coinheres with the "character" of ultimate reality as understood in Buddhism (*nirvana*), which is also beyond cause and effect (*samsara*) and, hence, liberating; cf. Trungpa, 4.
66. Cf. Faber, "Must 'Religion,'" 179–81.

Chapter Eight

HORIZONTAL AND VERTICAL PLURALISM

Say: The rivers of divine wisdom and utterance which flowed through the Tablets of God are joined to this Most Great Ocean, could ye but perceive it.[1]

—Bahá'u'lláh

In search for a clearer understanding of the complexities and perplexities arising from negotiation of the ambivalence whether to think of the projects of religious unity and pluralism as juncture or bifurcation in light of the twofold pluralism of pluralisms, I will introduce another differentiation, namely, that of *two kinds* of pluralism in light of any proposed unison (multiplicity) of religions. I define the one *horizontally* as synchronic pluralism and the other *vertically* as diachronic pluralism. In other words, one kind of pluralism, the horizontal one, will not only recognize the factual synchronic parallelism of multiple religions, but also establish its normativity for a healthy and healing conviviality of religions and a future civilization of peace.[2] In its most general form, this synchronicity states that no matter what the future holds for religious reconciliation, it must always begin by recognizing the truth of the concurrent religions, whether or not they are of the same lineage[3]; and it must assume that this multiplicity is not a failure, but a mode of polyphilic wealth of divine outpouring (emanation of the Good, *fayḍ*) and its beauty.[4] The other kind of pluralism, the vertical one, will look at the whole scenery from a temporal perspective and interpret the appearance of new religions, without which there would never be a concurrent multiplicity of religions, as a necessity for the same divine outpouring and beauty to be an infinite pleroma.[5] On this view, there will always be an unending process of generations of new religions.[6]

---

1. Bahá'u'lláh, "Suriy-i Haykal," in *Summons of the Lord of Hosts*, 19 (§33).
2. Cf. Faber, "God in the Making," 197–200; *Garden*, ch. 5:5.
3. Cf. Kaufman, 190–91.
4. Cf. Beyers, ch. 6, on Knitter and Heim claiming such mutuality.
5. Cf. Bahá'u'lláh, *Gleanings*, #19; 'Abdu'l-Bahá, *Selections*, #33. Bahá'u'lláh fundamentally builds his understanding of the intimate relationship of temporality and divinity on the axiom that there was never and will never be a time in which there will not be divine revelation available to creation. In his understanding, one of the major causes for religious violence is the opposite view, as it *either* creates the illusion of the poisonous fruits of unity, especially the finality of revelation, religion and history (cf. *Iqan*, §148) *or* a secularization of religion in which situation only desperation of meaninglessness and directionless competitive struggle can follow (cf. *Iqan*, §29).
6. Cf. Sours, *Station*, 58; Faber, *Garden*, Prologue (sec. 4–5).

It is worth noting at this point that in the process universe these two axes are mirrors of the creative process of becoming itself, whether that of an event or any nexus of events, that is, organizations of life forms and ecologies or cultures and religions.[7] As every becoming is a gathering of a multiplicity to a novel unity, it will transcend the givenness it transforms. But no such novel gathering can avoid also yielding its uniqueness to a new multiplicity of forms, organizations, organisms, fields, species, cultures or religions it has joined.[8] In Whitehead's mantra, "The many become one, and are increased by one,"[9] is enshrined the basic universal constitution and operation of "a world (any world)," be it that of an organism or a universe. The horizontal axis, then, expresses the always moving and increasing multiplicity of a "new world" that is gathered and enriched by the vertical axis, representing every new event of the unification of these "worlds" to a new synthesis. Yet any "world" is also disturbed by the very existence of the novelty, the novel event or organism or religion that transcends the horizon of the preceding multiplicity and its hitherto prevailing unifications, directions and limitations. In fact, as Whitehead so eloquently says in closing his book *Symbolism*: "It is the first step in sociological wisdom, to recognize that the major advances in civilization are processes which all but wreck the societies in which they occur:—like unto an arrow in the hand of a child."[10] In turn, every new religion is an event that, if it presents us with a new horizon of civilization, will wreck the prevailing horizons and, in uncovering their closedness, refigure the whole spectrum of viable options for future directions civilizations can take. In any case, on this view both axes are necessary for the advance of civilization, as the "essence" of civilization is self-transcendence[11]—a basic principle of the Bahá'í understanding of the import and impermanence of religions.[12] Yet these refigurations will already rest on the viability of the multiplicity that was united and, even more importantly, the multiplicity the novel event of a religion creates by becoming one fold among the many it has left, one of the new manifold it creates and leaves behind as a site for a new horizon to come.[13]

The consequences for the interplay of the two axes of religious pluralism may now become obvious: While the horizontal plurality becomes prescriptive by accepting the multiple truths of, and issuing into, processes of reconciliation of the established differences between those religions in an ongoing and open-ended conversation,[14] the vertical plurality establishes these differences, in the first place—by the appearance of novel religions in the landscape of existing religions. Since this novelty does not necessarily make the

---

7. Cf. Faber, *God as Poet*, §§13, 15; Whitehead, *Adventures*, chs. 12–13.
8. Cf. Whitehead, *Process*, 22; Faber, *Manifold*, chs. 5, 15; *Becoming of God*, Explorations 1–2.
9. Whitehead, *Process*, 21.
10. Whitehead, *Symbolism*, 88.
11. Cf. Whitehead, *Adventures*, 295; Faber, *God as Poet*, §46.
12. Cf. Bahá'u'lláh, *Gleanings*, #109; 'Abdu'l-Bahá, *Promulgation*, #42.
13. In the Bahá'í writings, this is the context where its understanding of the "progressiveness" of revelations is situated; cf. Bahá'u'lláh, *Iqan*, §219. As the memory of the transcended multiplicity becomes part of a new multiplicity, enriched by the new event, religion or universe, one could with Laszlo (*Science*, 102), even propose a "cyclical progressive evolution in the Metaverse."
14. Cf. Kaufman, ch. 12; Panikkar, *Dialogue*, chs. 2, 4; Schmidt-Leukel, *Pluralism*, chs. 8–9.

existing plurality of religions a norm of their future, a new religion could in exclusivist manner demand the dissolution of all existing religions into its own novel existence. As many religions have tried to understand themselves in such a manner (at least at some point in their own unfolding), vertical plurality not only creates and expands the horizontal plurality, but also infuses the problem of religious strife with all the poisonous fruits already mentioned: superiority, supersession, finality, denigration and substitution. Prescriptive vertical pluralism, by embracing perpetual novelty in an ongoing process of the creation of religions, would not necessarily deny the truth of other religions, but could make them outworn or even obsolete forerunners of itself, perhaps being their fulfillment and perfection.[15] Nevertheless, vertical pluralism would not necessarily insist on most of the poisons of unity. It could let go of finality by understanding the temporal development of religions as that of equally true expressions of one mystery at different times, as the Bahá'í Faith does,[16] and would, thereby, avoid denigration of earlier forms.[17] But such a vertical appeal to temporal and essential transcendence would still have to clarify whether its inherent process into novelty has substituted the older versions of religion, or would even be superior to them and, hence, supersede them.[18] While Bahá'í writings do not dwell on the superiority of their own revelation over and against all others in the past,[19] we are left with questions regarding substitution and supersession. Only by counterbalancing vertical pluralism with horizontal pluralism, which insists on the validity of all religions in a concurrent landscape of religions, would it avoid these dangers of substitution and supersession.[20] But such a horizontal trajectory could still appear to be insensitive to the fact that every religion in its concurrent field is also already the outcome of a novelty that, as soon as it is introduced, may have lived by the perceived superiority of its new position over the older ones so that many of them may have (in their background or origination) already incorporated forms of (at least) substitution, denigration and supersession, maybe even (motivated by) finality.[21]

It is a fact and a necessary matter of recognition that every new religion will wound other religions to some extent by its novelty,[22] unavoidably demanding some kind of superiority and supersession, but not necessarily finality, denigration and substitution.[23] For

---

15. Cf. Schaefer, *Beyond the Clash*, 45–49.
16. Cf. Fazel, "Approaches," 44; Lundberg, "Adam," 59–82.
17. Cf. Sours, *Station*, chs. 3–4.
18. Cf. Sours, *Station*, chs. 6–7.
19. Cf. Sours, *Station*, ch. 5.
20. Cf. 'Abdu'l-Bahá, *Paris Talks*, #41; *Selections*, #225.
21. Cf. Faber, *Garden*, ch. 4; "Religion," 169–70.
22. Cf. Bahá'u'lláh, *Iqan*, §§66, 81.
23. This insight into the factual "supersession" of religions by new ones through the event of novelty that constitutes the vertical pluralistic axis is importantly different from the triumphalist poisonous fruit of supersessionism, as it indicates not only the factual non-finality of religious evolution, but also the humility of an apophaticism with which it must be embraced in order to release its "religious" value: that of nonattachment, of the dialectic of nothingness and divinity (Saiedi, *Gate*, 164) and of impermanence (Faber, *Garden*, ch. 7:5). It can be understood as means of "purification" (K. Rose, *Pluralism*, ch. 4) or as inevitable correlate to creative novelty

example, if Christ is the fulfillment and (in St. Paul's mind) the overcoming of the Law of Moses, the eternity of the law promised to Moses is substituted.[24] But while Christianity understands itself often as final revelation of eschatological proportions and, hence, as superior and superseding Judaism,[25] St. Paul was not drawn to claim the substitution of the promise of God to the elected people of Israel.[26] Another example is the integration of the Buddha into Hinduism as an *avatar* of Krishna or Vishnu, characterizing it as a divine attempt to test the community with Buddhist illusions and detractions from the right path until the next *avatar* appears.[27] Buddhism, conversely, in its own understanding, supersedes Hinduism and, as it does not accept the Vedas that define the identity of any Hindu religion, as well as any notion of ultimate theism, in some important sense denies it.[28] Religious Daoism (*dao jiao*), after divinizing Laozi as Lord Lao, the Dao "in person," included in a multireligious sweep not only the Buddha as its/his "incarnation," but also the prophet Mani who already saw himself as the confluence of Christ, Zoroaster and the Buddha.[29] Although Sikhism accepts the truth in Islam and Hinduism (and in all religions), it supersedes its scriptures and even substituted them with their own.[30] In other words, every new religion, by virtue of its novelty, will create a wound in the central spiritual identity of the religions it emerges from and, in this sense, supersedes it.

The problem of horizontal pluralism is the wounded heart of this contradictory multiplicity of religions, initiated by the vertical pluralism of essential novelty (even if accepting the truth of the thereby outmoded others) without which there would be no other religions, in the first place. While equally affirming the divine indistinction between

---

(Whitehead, *Process*, 21) as the driving force of spiritual evolution (Faber, *Garden*, Prologue, section 5).

24. Cf. Exodus 12:14, 24; 31:16; Leviticus 16:29–31; 23:21, 31; Deuteronomy 5:29; 11:1; 2 Chronicles 2:4; Matthew 5:17–19; Romans 6:14; 7:1–14; Galatians 2:19–20; 3:10–13, 24–25; 4:21; 5:1, 13; 2 Corinthians 3:7–18. Cf. also 'Abdu'l-Bahá, *Promulgation*, #71 with *Paris Talks*, #33.

25. Cf. Stein, chs. 3–5.

26. Cf. Romans 9–11; Soulen, 9. The hybridity of St. Paul's religion, here, comes to the fore when we understand it as a "failed attempt to universalize Judaism" in the Hellenistic pluralistic context, so that the overcoming of the Law and its substitution with Christ (Romans 7:4) does not erase or simply overcome the heritage from which it arises, but can even embrace it in an eschatological teleology; cf. Theissen, 165. In the Bahá'í context, it is interesting to note that the transformation into a new area naturally, as it were, implies the renewal of any Law related with revelation and faith, and the "heart" of religiosity, that is, it is not meant to substitute the spiritual and revelatory heart of any dispensation; cf. Fazel, "Understanding," 251. The deeper connection that Soulen, 9–14, sees severed in Christian thought and practice over centuries, so as to have even yield to the catastrophe the Shoa, but which can be reestablished by reconnecting the Christian notion of God and the Trinity with the Sinai events of Exodus 3 and the divine name, is, in fact, central to Bahá'u'lláh; cf. Lambden, "Mysteries," 65–184; Faber, *Garden*, ch. 6:1.

27. Cf. Sharma, "Buddhism," 234–40.

28. Cf. Smart, *Religion*, 78–81; Akira, chs. 1–3.

29. Cf. Kohn, 24–28, 39–40; Faber, "Laozi," section 10.

30. Cf. Islam, 101–16.

all revelations,[31] Bahá'u'lláh has provided us with maybe one of the strongest images of such a wounding of novelty when he proclaims the event of unprecedented novelty of a revelation as the sundering of the "heaven" (the horizon) of the religious landscape in which it explodes:

> In like manner, strive thou to comprehend from these lucid, these powerful, conclusive, and unequivocal statements the meaning of the "cleaving of the heaven"—one of the signs that must needs herald the coming of the last Hour, the Day of Resurrection. As He hath said: "When the heaven shall be cloven asunder."[30] By "heaven" is meant the heaven of divine Revelation, which is elevated with every Manifestation, and rent asunder with every subsequent one. By "cloven asunder" is meant that the former Dispensation is superseded and annulled. I swear by God! That this heaven being cloven asunder is, to the discerning, an act mightier than the cleaving of the skies! Ponder a while. That a divine Revelation which for years hath been securely established; beneath whose shadow all who have embraced it have been reared and nurtured; by the light of whose law generations of men have been disciplined; the excellency of whose word men have heard recounted by their fathers; in such wise that human eye hath beheld naught but the pervading influence of its grace, and mortal ear hath heard naught but the resounding majesty of its command—what act is mightier than that such a Revelation should, by the power of God, be "cloven asunder" and be abolished at the appearance of one soul?[32]

With the intersection of vertical and horizontal plurality of the religious landscape in mind, we can now construct a pluralistic matrix, a field of interactions between the horizontal and vertical axes of pluralism. The extreme positions on either side of that field would be, on the one hand, a pure vertical pluralism without horizontal intentions and, on the other, a pure horizontal pluralism without vertical intentions. Between these limits, diverse emphases and interactions between both axes will constitute diverse religious views of pluralism (and pluralism of pluralisms) and the unity of religions. A position closest to the vertical limit would be an "exclusivist" (pluralist) projection that, although there might be true religions in the past, no religion besides the one that supersedes all of them should exist, or it would, in an "inclusivist" (pluralist) manner, accept a plurality of past religions as preparation for itself as their evolution's end.[33] An example of the former would be Buddhism in relation to Vedic religions; of the latter kind is the integration of the Hebrew Bible into the Old Testament of Christianity. Conversely, a religion closest to the horizontal limit would be trying to negate or overcome the wounding differences between diverse religions by transcending their organized hulls themselves and, instead, constituting an eclectic mixture of their teachings fused into more amorphous spiritual movements.[34] Here, the equality of religious truth becomes available in an "exclusivist" relativism of its appearances, and probably, in an attempt to find their unification, in some kind of "inclusivist" essentialization of spiritual truth beyond any religious form of

---

31. Cf. Bahá'u'lláh, *Iqan*, 103–4, 176.
32. Bahá'u'lláh, *Iqan*, §46.
33. Cf. D'Sa, 16–18.
34. Cf. Ferrer, "Future," 14–16, 63–64; Martin, *Religion*, ch. 10.

truth.[35] An example would be nonreligious spiritualities (spiritual, but not religious), spiritualities that despise any organization and organizations that accept all kinds of religious beliefs into their fold (or even unify as spiritual materialists beyond any religious truth claims, such as a "church" of atheists).[36]

However, neither expression close to these limits can totally avoid the recognition of the other axis. An exclusivist or inclusivist vertical pluralism must accept, as its horizontal axis, at least the plurality of its own religious heritage from which it has constituted itself, such as the emergence of Christianity from the synthesis of Judaism and Hellenism.[37] Conversely, a nonreligious spirituality cannot exist without claiming its own novel spiritual unity as superior to older, more organized forms of religions, as its vertical axis, or by selectively denying at least some of their doctrines, such as some spiritual futures envisioned by the participatory turn, the integral movement[38] or the interspiritual movement,[39] or new organizations that embrace highly diverse religious denominations, but, as in the case of Unitarian Universalism, by exclusion of trinitarian views.[40] While a shift to the vertical axis needs the past of a horizontal axis from which it collects itself, in a shift to the horizontal axis the future is embraced as vertical novelty over against the horizontal plurality of the present.

In between these limits, we will encounter intersections of both horizontal and vertical pluralism in their mutual negotiations and diverse harmonizations of these limits and their respective implications of healing and poisonous fruits of unification. In fact, all negotiations of multiplicity and unity within and between religions will fall into this field of tensions, whether pluralistic or not. However, no pluralistic negotiations will escape the engagement with more than only one potential equilibrium between them; in order to remain pluralistic, the *whole* scale of possibilities will have to be addressed in some coherent way. In my view, this is especially true for new axial religions and spiritualities with their emphatically pluralistic intuition to reconcile the multiplicity of religions, and so also for the Bahá'í Faith.[41] Two examples will suffice to substantiate this

---

35. The future of religions proposed by the "apophatic pluralism" of K. Rose (*Pluralism*, 6 and ch. 8), as well as Ferrer (*Participation*, ch. 10), may come close to such a position on the horizontal-vertical pluralism scale, namely, as one of permanent renewal through religious innovations and unabating creativity that remains *religious* in nature (not feeding an anti-religious skepticism), that is, it is not just human projection or mere relativism, but an expression of ultimate reality as the "source" of this process—similar to my claim of polyphilic pluralism; cf. Faber, *Manifold*, Intermezzo 1 and 2.
36. Cf. Hanegraaff, chs. 15–16; Buehrens and Church, *Chosen Faith*, ch. 6.
37. Cf. Hengel.
38. Cf. Wilber, *Spectrum*, ch. 5; Medina, *Faith*, 126–34, 145–47.
39. Cf. Teasdale, chs. 9–10. Although on closer investigation, one will find that such seemingly horizontal forms of pluralism, such as Teasdale's interspirituality, are in fact closer to a local inclusivism (in his case of Catholic color) instead of exhibiting hidden vertical premises of the pluralistic nature discussed here; cf. K. Rose, *Pluralism*, 53–54; Faber, *Garden*, 402–3.
40. Cf. Buehrens and Church, *Chosen Faith*, 121, 171–72, 213–15; Lai and von Brück, *Christianity*, 198–99. William Ellery Channing states in his 1819 manifesto for "Unitarian Christianity" that Trinity is incompatible with the "unity" of God; cf. Peters, *God*, 38.
41. Cf. 'Abdu'l-Bahá, *Paris Talks*, #41; Velasco, "Reconciliation," 95–134.

spectral commitment. Compare the following quotations from the Hindu sage Swami Vivekananda from a Vedanta perspective, on the one hand, and Bahá'u'lláh as well as 'Abdu'l-Bahá from the Bahá'í perspective, on the other—both of their movements making their appearance in America at approximately the same time[42]—for the articulation of the two axes and their intersection.

Asserting the horizontal axis in the first set of quotations, we read how both Vivekananda and Bahá'u'lláh acknowledge the broadest possible horizontal consensus by not only accepting other religions as true, but by not discriminating them regarding their status in relation to God/Reality. Rather, all religions are of divine origin and equally able to remit from the human predicament, further human transformation, instill divine virtues and promote a vision of a future civilization of reconciled peace.[43] Their differences are therefore no justification for opposition; and their unity is an impulse to facilitate reconciliation because of their equal validity.

> Religion believes that there has been, and still is, one religion in the world. There never were two religions. It is the same religion [presenting] different aspects in different places. The task is to conceive the proper understanding of the goal and scope of humanity. This was the great work of Krishna: to clear our eyes and make us look with broader vision upon humanity in its march upward and onward. His was a heart that was large enough to see truth in all, his the lips that uttered beautiful words for each and all.[44]

> That the divers [sic] communions of the earth, and the manifold systems of religious belief, should never be allowed to foster the feelings of animosity among men, is, in this Day, of the essence of the Faith of God and His Religion. These principles and laws, these firmly established and mighty systems, have proceeded from one Source, and are the rays of one Light. That they differ one from another is to be attributed to the varying requirements of the ages in which they were promulgated.[45]

Nevertheless, the horizontal equality also, in both quotations, implies already a vertical element. Neither of these texts assumes an abstract standpoint that is not motivated by the concrete religious site from which the respective horizontal pluralism arises. With Schmidt-Leukel, I have already reasoned that any relevant religious pluralism must also realize itself in the horizon of a pluralism of pluralisms (of localized religious argumentation instead of generalized abstraction). In our quotations, Bahá'u'lláh's new dispensation and that of Krishna are named as the vertical anchor of the validity of their horizontal multiplicity, and as motivation for their reconciliation.[46]

---

42. Vivekananda is the surprise speaker at the World Parliament of Religions at the Expo in Chicago 1893, while the Bahá'í Faith is first mentioned, there, by a Christian pastor. Cf. Seager, *Dawn*, chs. 3 (on the first mentioning of the Baha'i Faith) and ch. 54 (Vivekananda).
43. Passages such as these from the Bahá'í writings evidence the basis for most of the Bahá'í authors involved in a pluralist position.
44. Vivekananda, "Krishna," in *Complete Works I* (April 1, 1900).
45. Bahá'u'lláh, *Gleanings*, #132.
46. And the Bahá'í writings accept Krishna as a Manifestation of God like Christ or the Buddha; cf. 'Abdu'l-Bahá, *Paris Talks*, #9; *Promulgation*, #109.

The next set of quotations rests on the other axis, the vertical appeal to novelty. In both cases, this novelty is now presented in such a way that, without taking away from the truth of the other religions (or other modes of one and the same religious multiplicity) from which they may arise, or even the ones that might come after them (as not every appearance of a religion must count as novelty), the uniqueness of the respective movement becomes the criterion for the validity of the diversity of horizontal truth claims. In other words, the unique "novelty" (or unequaled wisdom) of the respective tradition is able to unite all other religions regarding the unprecedented or not again equaled intensity of the presentation of truth.

> I quite agree with you that only the Advaita philosophy can save mankind, whether in East or West, from "devil worship" and kindred superstitions, giving tone and strength to the very nature of man. India herself requires this, quite as much or even more than the West. Yet it is hard uphill work, for we have first to create a taste, then teach, and lastly proceed to build up the whole fabric.[47]
>
> Verily I say, in this most mighty Revelation, all the Dispensations of the past have attained their highest, their final consummation. Thus counseleth you your Lord, the All-Knowing, the All-Wise. Praise be to God, the Lord of all worlds.[48]

While Bahá'u'lláh argues with fulfillment in a strict sense of the novelty (*bada'*) of the Bahá'í Faith,[49] Vivekananda argues with the opposite figure, the age and completeness of wisdom of Advaita Vedanta, never reached again in the flow of time, to express the fulfillment of the other traditions in their own.[50] Yet in this vertical account, we detect also a vital horizontal element: It is the distributed truth of the many religions that in the new or wisest one comes to fulfillment. That is, by the affirmation of the vertical dimension, the horizontal multiplicity comes into its own. They (in their horizontal multiplicity) are no strangers to the novel or wisest traditions (the vertical unity),[51] but the unifying

---

47. Vivekananda, Epistles, #40, in *Complete Works VIII* (April 24, 1895).
48. Bahá'u'lláh, *Gleanings*, #161.
49. Some Bahá'í authors have envisioned such quotations from the Bahá'í writings as justification for a non-pluralist position, rather resembling an inclusivist supersession of all (or specific) religions; cf. Martin, "Bahá'í Faith," 197–99; Fananapazir, *Islam*, part 2.
50. The reference backward into the "eternity" of Hindu scriptures, the eternal *sanatana dharma* (which, in this sense, is even beyond the limitations of historical Hinduism) or the at least ancient synthesis of Advaita Vedanta in the argumentation of Vivekananda over and against new religious appearances, harbors also an important element of vertical rediscovery, binding this approach back to the understanding of sacred space beyond time in primal religions; cf. Sharma, *Primal Perspective*, 38–39. This reversed verticality, not oriented toward novelty, but toward paradigmatic archetypes, will be taken up in Chapters 12 and 14 again.
51. According to Mbiti (96–97), the past-orientation of African religious time, which is in a paradigmatic sense mythic, ancestral, primordial time into which all current time flows, reaches a cul-de-sac as it remains tribal and nationalistic; primal religions, he feels, can only become universally relevant if they would also embrace the "third" time (besides present time that flees, and past time that gathers together), namely, the future, the event of novelty, the potential of renewal embedded in the seeking of salvation for which the axial religions became the historical expression. It is in this tension between the paradigmatic nature of the eternal past

traditions are an essential affirmation of the very essence of the multiplicity of their truth. Now, the last set of quotations consciously negotiates both axes.

> A real Vedantist must sympathise with all. Monism, or absolute oneness is the very soul of Vedanta. Dualists naturally tend to become intolerant, to think theirs as the only way. The Vaishnavas in India, who are dualists, are a most intolerant sect.[52]
>
> In like manner truth is one, although its manifestations may be very different. Some men have eyes and see. These worship the sun, no matter from which point on the horizon it may dawn; and when the sun has left the winter sky to appear in the summer one, they know how to find it again. Others there are who worship only the spot from which the sun arose, and when it arises in its glory from another place they remain in contemplation before the spot of its former rising. Alas! these men are deprived of the blessings of the sun. Those who in truth adore the sun itself will recognize it from whatsoever dawning-place it may appear, and will straightway turn their faces towards its radiance.[53]

Both texts are aware of, and don't avoid, the inconsistencies that arise from the harmonizations of both pluralistic axes.[54] However, they also represent two different modes of contrasting their obvious incompatibilities. Vivekananda immediately short-circuits them almost without mediation. While Vedanta is all-sympathetic to anyone's tradition—which it can allow itself to postulate as it is their truth that it expresses on the most profound level—it is also different from those because their emphasis on the theistic articulation of *brahman-atman*, such as enveloped by Vishnu and Krishna, reveals them to be less universalistic, since this personalism seems to imply, in Vivekananda's analysis, mutual exclusiveness and competition of sects and, by extension, religions.[55] If we admit the Abrahamic display of exactly this mutual exclusivism and competition of their "same" God, the monistic alternative seems to have a point.[56] It is, in this case, "absolute oneness" (in an apophatic sense, but even in the sense of material causality) that secures multiplicity not to become warring. Again, multiplicity is not the problem, here, but competition generated from mutual limitation. Conversely, 'Abdu'l-Bahá's statement has a different angle; it is about refinement. It favors a sophisticated mediation between

---

    to which all gravitate and the release of novelty from the future that the texts of Vivekananda and 'Abdu'l-Bahá span the vertical dimension of pluralism.
52. Vivekananda, Inspired Talks, in *Complete Works VII* (July 3, 1895).
53. 'Abdu'l-Bahá, *Paris Talks*, #40.
54. Which is also the reason that neither axis individually can claim to represent a complete position in the respective tradition, confirming the pluralism of pluralisms (of exclusivism, inclusivism and pluralism) as a matter of mutual negotiation; cf. Fazel, *Pluralism*, 42–43.
55. This again demonstrates the reason for the preference of the transpersonal view of Advaita: because it is unifying while theistic Hindu religions are viewed as competitive and adversarial—and by extension all theistic renderings of ultimate reality. Bahá'u'lláh, on the other hand, does not prefer the monistic view because of the implied transcendent unity, but respects the plurality of such positions (regarding theism and monism) as *equally* valid, yet *penultimate*, as the opposition between monism and theism also includes adversarial tensions to be overcome; cf. Bahá'u'lláh, *Uncompounded Reality*, 203–21; Faber, "Bahá'u'lláh," 83–85.
56. Cf. Prothero, ed., *Religions*, 1–24.

both axes of the pluralistic truth of all religions or within all religions through different modes of the articulation of spiritual states (*maqam*)⁵⁷—some more monistic, others more theistic, others again more materialistic than spiritual. That is, while horizontally these spiritual states are all true in their own way and sphere,⁵⁸ they also reside in a vertical cascade of layers on which they differ regarding closeness and remoteness from (the) Truth itself.⁵⁹ Yet none of them is totally deprived of the Sun of Truth.

The twist in the second half of the quotation of 'Abdu'l-Bahá, however, indicates another solution to the productive interference of both axes insofar as, here, more than in any other "solution," bifurcation becomes transformed into juncture. The paradoxical mutuality of the two axes clears, in 'Abdu'l-Bahá's mind, if we begin to (spiritually) see them as "the same" process! Only differentiated by a more space-like and a more time-like movement, *from a divine viewpoint (the Sun of Truth) they are not different at all*.⁶⁰ Rather, the movements of both axes are as non-different as ultimate reality is "indifferent" from space-time (created multiplicity), and divine life from impermanence. If one accepts the horizontal truth wherever, whenever, it arises, one has already accepted the vertical process of renewal and vice versa.⁶¹ Herein, I propose, rests a hidden remedy for the process of reconciliation through the negotiations of religious multiplicity. Yet in the "real" world of historical contingencies, this non-difference of the pluralistic axes seems always to appear in, and to display, mutual incompatibilities, hiding their reconciliation in a different (kind of) future, as we will encounter next.⁶²

---

57. Cf. Savi, *Summit*, 61–62, 403, 456, 475.
58. This is one of the central theses of Momen's relativism, that it is primarily about a standpoint epistemology, that is, the relativity of a truth perceived or recognized in relation to the perspective from which it is projected, which is not implying the necessity of that truth from any other such standpoint or perspective; cf. Fazel, *Dialogue*, 147.
59. This is the position taken by Saiedi and Brown referenced earlier with regards to 'Abdu'l-Bahá's *Commentary on the Islamic tradition*: "*I was a Hidden Treasure*."
60. It is one of the foundational epistemological spiritual truths of the Bahá'í writings that the knowledge of God—not the reasoning, but the mystical insight ('*irfan*)—is only achievable if the seeker or wayfarer or inquirer is granted, by his own effort, but ultimately by grace, a view *from* the perspective of God, that is, God's Manifestations, to see things "with God's eye"; cf. Bahá'u'lláh, *Iqan*, §16; *Gleanings*, #127; *Prayers*, #176; Bahá'u'lláh in Shoghi Effendi, *Advent*, 77; Kourosh, 103–6; This goes back to the Islamic Tradition *Hadith an-Navafil*, which states that God will become the eye and ear of the servant of God; cf. Schimmel, *As through a Veil*, 273, 329.
61. Cf. 'Abdu'l-Bahá, *Paris Talks*, #40.
62. Cf. Faber, *Poet*, 85, 102, 126–27, 132, 159 and §32, regarding the "reconciled non-difference" of God from the world.

Chapter Nine

AN EXPERIMENT IN INCOMPATIBILITIES: GREEN ACRE

We must not consider the separate waves alone, but the entire sea. We should rise from the individual to the whole. The spirit is as one great ocean and the waves thereof are the souls of men.[1]

—'Abdu'l-Bahá

Swami Vivekananda and Bahá'u'lláh, as well as 'Abdu'l-Bahá, are in interesting ways entangled through the story of the first World's Parliament of Religions, held at the Columbian Exhibition, Chicago, 1893,[2] and its consequences, namely, a series of meetings in the wake of the Parliament over several decades at Green Acre in Maine. The central figure of these extraordinary multireligious encounters was Sarah Farmer, who presided over their development.[3] She is the center of a tragic story in which the tensions between the two axes of pluralism unfolded and, hence, provides us with a concrete example or empirical display of their interaction.

The Parliament itself was an achievement. It was the first time in (at least western) history that a gathering brought together representatives not only from the host country, mostly recruited and organized by Christian denominations and nonconformist spiritual alternative movements, but from diverse instantiations of Buddhism, Hinduism, Daoism, Confucianism, Jainism and many other traditions and movements, such as that of Theosophy.[4] They met in a free arena in a spirit of reconciliation and the desire for religious peace, including in their hope for multireligious conviviality among the whole of humanity.[5] History is replete with attempts of religious conversations, ideas for convivial recognition and conceptualizations of potential interreligious discourses. A few examples may suffice. In fifteen-century Italy, Cardinal, philosopher, mystic and peace-arbitrator Nicolas of Cusa imagined a gathering of religions in amicable conversations regarding their diversity and the truth of their multiplicity in his writing *De Pace Fidei*.[6] He reflected from an apophatic character of the Godhead beyond any affirmations, but all-relationally immanent in the world, on the notion that diverse traditions were not

---

1. 'Abdu'l-Bahá, *Paris Talks*, #28.
2. Cf. Seager, *Parliament of Religions*.
3. Cf. Stockman, *Bahá'í Faith in America*, 142–48, 217–19.
4. Cf. Seager and Eck.
5. Cf. Ziolkowski.
6. Cf. Bond, 8–9; Biechler and Bond. For its Bahá'í reception, cf. Schaefer, *Beyond the Clash*, 110–22.

different as "religions," since there is only one religion of God, but different "rites," meaning, practically (ethnically, culturally) differing ritual modes of worshipping the one true God.[7] Yet his imagination was playing out only in "heaven," an ideal space, the imaginary perfect state (from the perspective of God's perfection), a potential unrealized in this world. His gathering was only theoretical and anticipatory.

Other examples took a more concrete form. In sixteenth-century India, the Mughal King Muhammad Akbar the Great would not only display tolerant politics regarding diverse religions in his realm, invite regularly to interreligious discussions in a designated "temple" (*ibadat khana*, house of worship) for this endeavor, but also create a new religion, the Religion of God, or Divine Religion (*Din al-Ilahi*), to which he invited selective religious sages and scholars of diverse backgrounds and persuasions.[8] Yet, again, neither did his tolerant imperial policy long survive his reign, nor was this "religion" anything more than a token idea that never went beyond a small elite of idealist members.

A last example comes from the vastly multireligious realms along the Silk Road of Northwestern India and Central Asia, spanning the intermediary regions between the Byzantine Empire and Islamic Caliphates in the west and China in the east. Mongol leaders were generally neutral to the different religions in their realms despite their personal leanings to Nestorianism, Manichaeism, Judaism, Islam, Hinduism, Buddhism or Daoism, respectively—after all, economy was about trade. But, at times, they even initiated actual and regular interreligious discussions into their courts to test the diverse arguments and also to lessen the tensions between these religious communities and their interests, sometimes with the contrary effect of heightening their mutual intrigues in their courtship for the attention of the king.[9] Yet the limitations of these gatherings was obvious: the intrusions of politics and economy, mutual intrigue, hostile argumentation, mutual misunderstanding, lacking deeper knowledge of the other traditions, apologetics, victor mentality and so on.[10]

What makes the Chicago meeting special is that it did not happen in any such setting. Although it was initiated by progressive protestant pastors with their own imagination of the superiority of Christianity (or their respective denominations) that would certainly (in their mind) win the day in this display of other religions.[11] And it was a certain economic and political climate that allowed the idea of such a meeting to become actualized. But its spirit was vastly different from the wide variety of multireligious disputes that fill the histories of many regions of multireligious encounters.[12] It was a display of different traditions in their own right, allowing for first-hand encounters and the free flow of information from their own representatives. What is more, the gathering was about a vision

---

7. Cf. Keller, "Unspeakable Conviviality," 149–52.
8. Cf. Schimmel, *Empire*, 38, 109, 116.
9. Cf. Foltz, 106–8; Elverskog, 133–45.
10. Some would also include ninth- to tenth-century Andalusia under Islamic rule, although there are differing opinions on how tolerant this "*la concivencia*" actually was; cf. Keller, "Unspeakable Conviviality," 141–64.
11. Cf. Seager, *Parliament*, 82.
12. Cf. Beneke.

of peace and a sign of the real potential for a future convivial community of religions of the one humankind to be achievable.[13]

It is in this context that Swami Vivekananda, only in his thirties, delivered the opening speech that provided the tenor of conviviality for the whole gathering, but also made the interferences of horizontal and vertical pluralism obvious that burns under the surface of such an encounter. Not only did he address the generally American audience as brothers and sisters (of the west), implying the unity between east and west before any antagonistic divergences (between Indian and western civilization), he also emphasized the perspective of such a unity in the embrace of Hinduism as the Mother of all religions, which has always displayed this spirit of tolerance and invitation to all religions, historically by harboring the remnant of Israel, for instance, and spiritually by affirming the truth of all religions, the unity of religions as that of different paths on their way to the same divine peak.[14] In his speech, the horizontal pluralism of truth is embedded in the vertical pluralism of the oldest and most embracing religion of Hinduism.[15] His vertical pluralism differentiates the conceptualization above, as it functions by virtue of the old age (the eternity of the Vedas) instead of a novelty by which age would become not only "old," but in some way obsolete. In this sense, instead of novelty the forgotten underpinning unity of religions is the vertical anchor that must be rediscovered for his horizontal pluralism to assume a peaceful future.

It was at the same Parliament that the Presbyterian missionary in Syria, Rev. Henry Jessup, just a year after Bahá'u'lláh had died,[16] ended a written speech (read by a Rev. Ford) with the first public mention of the Bahá'í Faith in America:

> In the palace of Behjeh, or Delight, just outside the fortress of Acre on the Syrian coast, there died a few months since a famous Persian sage—the Babi saint, named Beha Allah, the "Glory of God"— the head of that vast reform party of Persian Moslems who accept the New Testament as the word of God, and Christ as the deliverer of man; who regard all natives as one, and all men as brothers. Three years ago he was visited by a Cambridge scholar, and gave utterance to sentiments so noble, so Christ-like that we repeat them as our closing words: "That all nations should become one in faith, and all men as brothers; that the bonds of affection and unity between the sons of men should be strengthened; that diversity of religion should, and differences of race, be annulled; what harm is there in this? Yet so it

---

13. Cf. Lai and von Brück, 195–205.
14. Cf. Vivekananda, *Sisters & Brothers*.
15. It must, at this point, be admitted that especially in relation to Hinduism, which is in itself a plurality of religious identities, moods and ways, the differentiation between inclusivism and pluralism is particularly fuzzy and probably necessarily indicative of a mutuality that a "pluralism of pluralisms" (of exclusivism, inclusivism and pluralism), as conceptualized in Chapter 7, can present as a test case of factual religious complexity cohering with the respective theory; cf. Sharma, "Can There Be," 57. In any case, the vast complexity of Hinduism, on which the Neo-Vedanta view of Vivekananda builds, as well as the related Hindu philosophy of religion, for instance, of Radhakrishnan, should not simply either be attributed to a limited inclusivism or a "neutral" universalistic pluralism; cf. Coward, *Pluralism*, 80; K. Rose, *Pluralism*, 89.
16. Cf. Momen, *Bahá'u'lláh*, ch. 6; Balyuzi, *Bahá'u'lláh*, ch. 42.

shall be. These fruitless strifes, these ruinous wars shall pass away, and the "most great peace" shall come. Do not you in Europe need this also? Let not a man glory in this, that he loves his country; let him rather glory in this that he loves his kind."[17]

In a spirit of true horizontal pluralism, without any apologetic diminution of the foreign religion, the Christian pastor accepted the novelty of the Bahá'í Faith as vertical surprise, but linked it in effect to a Christian renewal, and thereby established the intention of the oneness of religions and a humanity of religious peace.[18] While Vivekananda based the horizontal diversity on vertical universality, the "eternal" religion (*sanatana dharma*), Jessup, in this quotation, embraced the vertical novelty of the Bahá'í religion with his horizontal sentiment of equality and mutual relatedness by offering it as a sign of the continuity of renewal within his own tradition.

It was in Green Acre that this spirit of multireligious engagement was revived under the auspices of Sarah Farmer. In the yearly summer camps on her resort (the former Hotel Eliot), she invited diverse religious representatives and communities in this spirit of peace and mutual listening to present their religious view. It was under her reign that the first peace flag was raised—from the outset a religious symbol.[19] In order to avoid tribalism and apologetic regression, argumentative antagonisms and mutual criticism, she insisted on wise ground rules for these meetings, the most important of which states that it was to be in the spirit of mutual listening that the display of diverse religious perspectives and their truth should be received. Forbidding argumentative criticism, she assumed, appealed to and furthered an intellectual and spiritual maturity in all participants to draw their own conclusions without disputations.[20] It was in the spirit of such amicable gatherings that the diverse voices could be heard and listened to, in the first place, and that first encounters between east and west took some kind of institutional form. Green Acre became a magnet for the international who's who in religion at the time, such as the now famous Hindu sage and teacher in the tradition of Ramakrishna, Vivekananda, the famous Japanese Buddhist scholar and teacher T. D. Suzuki, Transcendentalists, Universalists, reformed Rabbis, Annie Besant of the Theosophists, Sufis, other Indian gurus and representatives of the social gospel and NAACP, George Herron and W. E. B. Du Bois, respectively.[21]

Over time, however, Sarah Farmer's own position shifted. While in the beginning the Green Acre conferences were dominated by the open spiritual search beyond any dogmatic fixations—a position that she shared—her quest became one of finding a spiritual

---

17. Saeger and Eck, 42; cf. Neely; Shoghi Effendi, *God*, 256; *Bahá'í World*, Vol. 2, 169.
18. This is not to say that Jessup was by his own words convinced of the legitimacy of the new revelation; his otherwise rather conventional evangelical (and missionary) habit of understanding his Christianity as superior in other texts seems to indicate rather the opposite.
19. Cf. Ann Gordon Perry.
20. Cf. Schmidt, ch. 5, especially p. 193. Many of the details of Sarah Farmer's story and transformation are rarely available. Schmidt collected unpublished material as well as archival documents regarding Green Acre and Sarah Farmer.
21. Cf. Schmidt, 195.

home. Not that the participants did not often come to this sharing being teachers rather than seekers themselves, being settled within their own traditions, but hoping for an audience of such seekers. Yet what would happen if Sarah Farmer herself would find a spiritual haven? Would that be a betrayal of the whole enterprise? Would it lead to a change of the character of the meetings if she were to claim the same right of her spiritual search to be free in directions not precedented by herself or foreseen by her collaborators, even if it would mean that "open-endedness" was not to be the future defining mark of her search? Sarah Farmer was a religious pluralist, and she had demonstrated the requisite practice of embracing the truth of the various religions over decades of forging conviviality and interreligious peace. Could finding a spiritual home, *as* a pluralist, mean that she was now no pluralist anymore?

Sarah Farmer knew, of course, of the Bahá'í propositions regarding its pluralist implications of and for the unity of religions. In 1900 she was among the first westerners to embark on a sea journey to Acre to meet the living leader of the Bahá'í's, 'Abdu'l-Bahá, the son of Bahá'u'lláh and designated authoritative interpreter of his revelation and scriptural writings.[22] She maintained years of correspondence with him and received many of his letters/tablets and ample encouragements for her endeavors. Finally, Sarah Farmer became a Bahá'í.[23] And symbolically, in a significant sense, she embodied this change by renaming Greenacre, as the estate was spelled until this point in time, Green Acre in memoriam of Acre in Ottoman Syria, the resting place of Bahá'u'lláh, worldwide *kiblah* and place of pilgrimage for Bahá'ís, as well as the residence of 'Abdu'l-Bahá.[24] While she went on to organize the regular multireligious meetings, now, from her perspective, she had found a new lens for doing so: the unity of religions that 'Abdu'l-Bahá so eloquently elucidated to her and the world, and with the encouragement of the pluralistic conviviality that 'Abdu'l-Bahá himself lived and committed himself to in his teachings.[25] While Sarah Farmer did not impose her newly found faith onto the community, and held separate Bahá'í meetings at Green Acre, she received growing resistance from her companions who perceived her transformation as a move in the wrong direction, as a betrayal of the commitment to open-ended spiritual search and as a threat to the very mission of her gatherings.[26] In a letter responding to the criticism reflecting the breach

---

22. Cf. Schmidt, 190.
23. Cf. Peter Smith, "American Bahá'í Community," 162.
24. Cf. Schmidt, 207
25. Cf. 'Abdu'l-Bahá, *Selections*, #13.
26. Cf. Schmidt, 209–10. This discrepancy between the universal multireligious inclusivism of the Transcendentalist and Metaphysical milieu and their reaction to Farmer's commitment, although it was as inclusive or universalist as theirs, is important to recognize as revealing the deeper differences between the often similar spiritual, philosophical and cosmological concepts and schemes at a point, fairly early on in their interaction, when, for a few decades (until the later 1920s), they were hidden under the common interests in a spiritualized future of humanity, hence, recruiting audiences for 'Abdu'l-Bahá in his 1911–13 journey to Europe and America specifically from this milieu (Esoteric, Spiritualist, Metaphysical, Transcendental, Theosophical and so on, spheres). The Farmer controversy would, therefore, be a highly significant event in the study of the differences between nineteenth- and early twentieth-century

that began to form between the Transcendentalist and New Thought companions and her in 1901, Sarah Farmer wrote to Horatio Dresser, of the wing of the metaphysical movement, liberalism and progressivism:

> Thank you dear Brother, for your clear and kind letter, but it shows me that you cannot realize my point of view. My joy in the Persian Revelation is not that it reveals one of the streams flowing to the great Ocean of Life, Light and Love, but that it is a perfect mirror of that Ocean [...] It is a Revelation of Unity such as I had never before found.[27]

One can only witness the heartfelt joy of Sarah Farmer's new perspective on religions and its motivation: the unity of religions in which the vertical axis of novelty has taken preeminence over the horizontal axis, without eliminating it, as all religions are now harbored in the ubiquity of their mutuality. The perception of 'Abdu'l-Bahá in their exchanges became more alarmed as her health deteriorated under the pressure of her peers, and he finally suggested that she gently transform the school into a place for the new revelation instead of giving in to the voices that despised her move and condemned her determination.[28] Over finances and other intrigues with her co-organizers, Sarah Farmer was eventually committed to a sanatorium and, removed from Green Acre, fell into deep depression.

When, in 1912, 'Abdu'l-Bahá visited Europe and America, very publicly participating in peace conferences on the verge of the Great War, which he predicted within the next two years to occur, and very publicly taught the equality and unity of religions as well as the equality of genders and race-amity,[29] it was upon his arrival at Green Acre that Sarah Farmer was released a last time from her new prison to visit the place of her accomplishments. 'Abdu'l-Bahá was convinced that she has not been mentally ill, but was in a spiritual heightened state and should be left alone.[30] In 1916, after she was "liberated" from the sanatorium, she died[31]—in some sense, a martyr of the peace between religions

---

    esotericism, occultism, spiritualism, theosophy and Transcendentalism and its offshoots and more modern "reincarnations" or developments in diverse movements becoming self-conscious as New Age—a study which would be highly desirable, but which has not gone beyond a few historic and systematic prolegomena. In any case, the Farmer event, and also 'Abdu'l-Bahá's reaction to this conflict, would be of great importance for the understanding of the different motivation, pathos, worldview and underlying philosophical pattern between these movements and the Bahá'í Faith in its origins and developments that could easily be overlooked when just operating on a level of potential "correspondences." Cf. Hanegraaff, part 3; Lundberg, "New Age Phenomenon," 69–80; on Annie Besant, cf. *'Abdu'l-Bahá in London*, 27–30, 127.

27. Quoted in Schmidt, 206.
28. Cf. Schmidt, 208; Stockman, *'Abdu'l-Bahá*, 235. In speeches at Green Acre, 'Abdu'l-Bahá particularly was countering the view that novelty (a new revelation and religion) must, per default, be inferior to old religions and their long-standing wisdom. This issue reflects the earlier quotations of Vivekananda's and 'Abdu'l-Bahá's relationship to the synchronic and the diachronic dimensions of pluralism and unity to one another.
29. Cf. Stockman, *'Abdu'l-Bahá*, chs. 4, 6; Hughey, 7–56.
30. Cf. Schmidt, 211.
31. Cf. Schmidt, 212.

and a Bahá'í of extraordinary sensitivity to religious pluralism. Green Acre, the unique place of the experiment in religious pluralism, never achieved before or after, was not to survive without Sarah Farmer. The alliance was broken, and after years of legal battle the estate ended up becoming (and still is today) a Bahá'í school.[32]

In the vision of 'Abdu'l-Bahá, however, Green Acre was, at one time in the future, meant to become a university, a new model of a multireligious and nonreligious learning and of a conviviality that does not discriminate anymore between religions, as it would also obliterate and deconstruct the restrictions on gender and race, ethnicity and class, should it come to be.[33] In the wake of both the changed climate and the influx of the World Parliament and Green Acre, Vivekananda founded the Vedanta society on the east coast (as a branch of the Ramakrishna mission)[34]; the Sufi musician and master Pir-o-Murshid Hazrat Inayat Khan toured the United States and established his Universal Sufism community on the west coast[35]; Suzuki[36] and his wife (who, during their residence in America, had close Bahá'í contacts) returned to Japan[37]; the Theosophists in America and Europe, though not in India, went into decline after Jiddu Krishnamurti under Anne Besant's leadership resisted to function as its Maitreya savior[38]; the Universalists became united with Unitarians and organized themselves as a multidenominational and -religious church with progressive and multireligious purposes[39]; and the Transcendentalists all but disappeared from history while their visions of a common humanity live on.[40] The Parliament of Religions did not meet again until 1993, 100 years after its momentous first meeting and more than 70 years after the pluralistic experiment at Green Acre broke apart over incompatibilities in the tension between different kinds of pluralism and regarding the prospective viability of a unity between religions.

As a study on the interference of diachronic and synchronic pluralism, the story of Green Acre exhibits several important insights. Sarah Farmer began her journey at the horizontal limit of pluralism, hosting a multi-spiritual community of seekers and teachers in the spirit of amicable mutual listening; she moved toward the vertical axis of pluralism when she embraced the Bahá'í religion as a means of integrating religions from the perspective of the novelty of the Persian revelation; and she moved back into a middle position of the "balanced" interference of both axes by allowing her new home to further or inform, instead of to hinder, the open-ended search of the multireligious gatherings. From the perspective of the co-organizers, the situation was different. Sarah Farmer's "balance" was perceived as *her* "unbalance," even "fanaticism."[41] But it also revealed

---

32. Cf. Hatcher and Martin, 57.
33. Cf. 'Abdu'l-Bahá, *Promulgation*, #92; Stockman, *'Abdu'l-Bahá*, 245–46.
34. Cf. Vrajaprana, 36.
35. Cf. Wittenveen, ch. 2–4.
36. Cf. Snodgrass, 12–13.
37. Cf. Tweed, 249–81.
38. Cf. Lutyens; Lavoie, ch. 1.
39. Cf. Buehrens and Parker. Several process thinkers were and are Unitarian Universalists.
40. Cf. Gura.
41. Cf. Schmidt, 206–7, 209–10. One detractor spoke of the Bahá'í religion as "fatal, unbalanced disease" (210).

their own "unbalance" regarding the two axes of pluralism. Her detractors situated themselves at the limit of the horizontal axis, reacting sensitively against the vertical axis as means of inclusivism instead of pluralism. They, thereby, all but excluded novelty as event (a new revelation and religion, dedicated to the common ideal of a united humanity) that they preached as novelty of openness. But what if openness happens, as event?[42] They were, nevertheless, blind to the interference of the vertical axis in their own endeavor since the alleged open-ended spirituality was, in fact, based on their own vertical positions of unorthodox views, mostly of the transcendentalist and universalist kind. The visiting sages, scholars and teachers, finally, came into this horizontal equality of spiritual listening from a strong vertical perspective of their own tradition, performing their verities for a pool of very receptive seekers, and, over time, not only seeking followers, but, as 'Abdu'l-Bahá observed, monetary contributions.[43] And 'Abdu'l-Bahá's position reflects these multiple dynamics. While he encourages the multireligious horizontal listening and learning,[44] he also was clear on the vertical novelty of the revelation of his father, which, in his eyes, made the claims of implicit superiority exhibited by some participants obvious, and the claims to open-endedness by others at Green Acre a drama of the envy of the "old" and the undecidedness of the ones who remain uncommitted to any religious truth in the face of equality and novelty.[45]

That the whole fragile alliance at Green Acre dissolved only demonstrates that the togetherness, or even in-difference, of these axes of pluralism in practice is not solved by syncretistic mixing, but only by *circumvention of the very antagonism that spans the whole field of these axes*—as hinted at in Bahá'u'lláh's admonition to Jamal-i Burujirdi, quoted earlier. But how can an uneasy peace be achieved if the very creation of religions is based on the tension and interference of these incommensurable axes?

---

42. Cf. Faber, *Becoming of God*, Sphere 3; *Garden*, Prologue: sections 4–5.
43. This observation and tendency (or danger) is confirmed by Trungpa, chs. 3, 5.
44. Cf. 'Abdu'l-Bahá, *Selections*, #13.
45. Cf. 'Abdu'l-Bahá, *Promulgation*, #78.

Chapter Ten

THE MYSTERY OF DISTINCTION AND UNITY

Say: Out of this Most Great Ocean there hath branched the Pre-existent Sea; blessed the one that hath attained and found repose upon its shores.[1]

—Bahá'u'lláh

With the productive incompatibilities of the coordinate system of horizontal and vertical, synchronic and diachronic pluralism and the imperative of the two pluralisms of pluralisms, detailed in the preceding chapters, in mind, we can, now, seek to discern the unique contribution of the Bahá'í universe of discourse, paradigmatic for the new axial consciousness of the unity and plurality of religions, for the contemporary global engagement with one humanity and of humanity with the one Earth.[2] This concretization does, of course, not take anything away from other potential exemplars of such a new axial discourse,[3] especially, as we have seen, if they are as resonant as the Neo-Vedanta approach of Swami Vivekananda.[4] Yet the unique position of the Bahá'í religion in this context results from the fact that it is not a philosophy of pluralism[5] or a theology of religions[6] or a hybrid transreligious theology[7] or mystagogy.[8] Nor is it a reform movement of, or denomination within, a religion[9] or a hybrid religious

---

1. Bahá'u'lláh, *Days*, #29:3.
2. These global, ecological and even cosmological implications of the new axial discourse on pluralism will be the theme of the third part of this book, especially Chapters 12–14.
3. The philosophical basis for the necessity to operate from such "concretizations" are the process-poststructuralist assumptions, affirmed in this book on the basis of A. N. Whitehead and Gilles Deleuze, and my understanding of *polyphilia* (cf. Faber, *Manifold*, passim), namely, that no general analysis can be less than abstract (given Whitehead's "ontological principle" that the only reasons are concrete events; cf. Whitehead, *Process*, 19–26); that only reference to singularity harbors universal implications (Deleuze, *Difference*, ch. 1; Faber, "Origin," 273–89); and that only finite "concretizations" are the sites of values (Whitehead, *Science*, 178).
4. Cf. Chapters 8–9. This is the perspective chosen by Jeffrey Long to contribute to the discussion of religious pluralism, which also resonates closely with polyphilic pluralism since Long engages process thought for his synthesis; cf. Long, "Anekanta Vedanta," 130–45.
5. Like, for instance, the contributions of John Hick, John Cobb, Arvind Sharma and Jorge Ferrer.
6. Like, for instance, the contributions of Perry Schmidt-Leukel, Kenneth Rose and Joseph Bracken.
7. Like, for instance, the contributions of Raymond Panikkar and Paul Knitter.
8. Like, for instance, the mystical, hybrid fusions of Thomas Merton.
9. Like, for instance, the Ahmadiyyah Community within Islam or diverse reconstructive churches of nineteenth century's Christianity around and after the Millerites.

community.[10] Rather, it signifies *the event of a new religion of, and in the character of, this new axial age*[11]—something that cannot be substituted by any other category just listed, although they all also contribute their own unique features to the discourses here employed.[12] So, then, if we follow the Bahá'í scriptures in their own negotiations of religious pluralism with their declared aim of establishing the unity of religions,[13] we are prompted to this utterance of Shoghi Effendi, the great-grandson of Bahá'u'lláh and the last authoritative interpreter of these scriptures,[14] reflecting in condensed form the complex play of the two axes of pluralism as it reflects on the relativity and mutuality of religions:

> The Faith standing identified with the name of Bahá'u'lláh disclaims any intention to belittle any of the Prophets gone before Him, to whittle down any of their teachings, to obscure, however slightly, the radiance of their Revelations, to oust them from the hearts of their followers, to abrogate the fundamentals of their doctrines, to discard any of their revealed

---

10. Without any overly narrow definition in mind, we could look at other such events of revelation at a similar time frame to find comparables, such as that of Joseph Smith, Mary Baker Eddy or Nakayama Miki. Yet these movements did not understand themselves as devising pluralism, but rather as recovering an original and later lost revelatory event of the past—instead of affirming other such events as a matter of vertical pluralism. We could assume finding close comparables in several reform movements within Hinduism of the time or slightly later, such as that of Shirdi Sai Baba, Meher Baba or Sathya Sai Baba, all of which affirm religious pluralism and the unity of religions. Yet, while they are all squarely promoting a universal new axial consciousness, their relationship to, or independence from, their Hindu-Sufi-Zoroastrian parent traditions remains ambivalent. Hence, the probably closest comparable event of the new axial age might be Guru Nanak, and this event may be situated at the very edge of its dawning. For more, cf. Chapter 12.
11. Cf. Faber, *Garden*, ch. 9.
12. Cf. Faber, *Garden*, Prologue, section 4 (Event and Horizon) and ch. 4. The insights gained, thereby, are not apologetic in purpose or nature, but aim at the wider contemporary discourse on pluralism, unity and religious peace. However, in my view, this unique Bahá'í perspective can release its gifts best in the conversation with a process approach and polyphilic pluralism.
13. Although these negotiations appear pervasively as a foremost theme in the whole body of scriptural Bahá'í texts, the probably most concentrated presentations of their background, novelty and inevitability in all of Bahá'í scripture can be found in Bahá'u'lláh's *Kitab-i Iqan*. For one of the probably best exegetical and historical introductions to its "shocking" pluralism that became the basis for the event of the Bahá'í revelation, cf. Buck, *Symbol*. Another wealth of directly related discussions, although hitherto only sparsely analyzed, can be found in the tablets of Bahá'u'lláh to the Parsee emissary to the Zoroastrian community in Iran at the time, Manakji Limji Hataria, collected in *The Tabernacle of Unity*, commenting on related questions of multireligious engagement and religious differences, including Jewish, Christian, Islamic, Zoroastrian and Hindu universes of discourse. For an analysis of the interreligious implications of these tablets, cf. Cole, "Introduction."
14. It may be noted, at this point, that another pluralism is implied in this fact (that no one, no institution and no individual can interpret the Bahá'í scripture authoritatively today), namely, that every Bahá'í is free to understand the scriptural texts independently. Yet even more fundamentally, this independence is inscribed as unalienable in the basic charter of Bahá'í principles, pervasively elaborated by the grandfather of Shoghi Effendi, 'Abdu'l-Bahá; cf. *Paris Talks*, ##40–41.

Books, or to suppress the legitimate aspirations of their adherents. Repudiating the claim of any religion to be the final revelation of God to man, disclaiming finality for His own Revelation, Bahá'u'lláh inculcates the basic principle of the relativity of religious truth, the continuity of Divine Revelation, the progressiveness of religious experience. His aim is to widen the basis of all revealed religions and to unravel the mysteries of their scriptures. He insists on the unqualified recognition of the unity of their purpose, restates the eternal verities they enshrine, [and] coordinates their functions.[15]

Later in the book, I will come back to deeper implications of the first half of this quotation, but for now, it will allow us to expose its inherent tensions of the axes of pluralism as they become visible in the form of a series of dilemmas: What can we say regarding the priority or precedence of unity or diversity, continuity or novelty, equality or progression, unison or uniqueness?[16] With respect to the first dilemma of *unity and diversity*, we can ask the following questions: If God/ultimate Reality is apophatically inaccessible, will all manifestations of "it" not also necessarily be manifold? If the manifold of divine appearances or theophanies is the expression of this unity, can we ever be without many religions?[17] If diversity is a necessary corollary of a nondual understanding of unity, should we not want many religious communities to prevail as the plenitude of the mystery of this unity?[18] Regarding the second dilemma of *continuity and novelty*, we may make the following observations: While all religions grow in their history from other religions as the presupposed background, field of connections and place of departure, all religions are, nevertheless, new events, irreducible to these histories. While new religions strike the spiritual core of the religions from which they arise, without their novelty renewal of religion is impossible.[19] Regarding the third dilemma of *equality and superiority*, we may gather the following trajectories: Bahá'í scriptures know of the unity, equality and mutuality of all religions, but they also know of the difference between them in scope, form and impact of their revelation. Bahá'í scriptures also know of a progression of revelation, not based in the nature or value of their revelation itself, but enshrined in the differences of the historical environment in and from which they appear.[20] However, they understand the

---

15. Shoghi Effendi, *Promised Day*, 108. I will come back to the implications of this quotation in the last chapter with the analysis of a comparable quotation from *World Order* (57–58).
16. For the introduction of such dilemmas in the context of the conceptualization of the unity of religions, cf. Chapter 2. Here, I concentrate on the four most iconic ones. All of them can now be understood as different cuts through the interference of the two axes of pluralism capturing different ways in which they inevitably remain coextensive in a process of incompatibility. The emphasis of one side or the other will represent one or the other axis.
17. Cf. Chapter 5. Remember Ibn 'Arabi's claim of the necessity of many religions in the image of their "lord" or the diverse emphases of realized divine attributes in human beings, individually and societally; cf. Chapter 4; Momen, *Religion*, 196.
18. Cf. Daoud, 57.
19. While renewal is part of religious traditions, such as the promise of a new covenant in late prophetic and apocalyptic writings of the Hebrew Bible and intertestamentary writings, in the event of Jesus it obtains a new frame, transcending the projected continuity of the intra-religious renewal; cf. Collins and Collins, chs. 4–7.
20. Bahá'u'lláh, *Gleanings*, #34.

later revelations as imminently more relevant over former ones with regard to the time to which they relate.[21] Finally, as to the fourth dilemma of *unison and uniqueness*, we find that the Bahá'í writings use different terms to express unity either as concordance, unification and inclusive unity (*wahid*), or as exclusive unity, uniqueness and oneness beyond comparison ('*ahad*).[22] The question then arises: Does the uniqueness of the unity of God force the unity of religions to be "one," and if so, in what "form"—as preestablished oneness or as process of unification, as exclusive or inclusive unity, as sameness or as manifold of unique folds? In other words, does the process of the reconciliation of religions, in which religious history appears to be in its healing mode (as Bahá'í scripture insists),[23] necessitate the erasure of the traces of their histories and the futures of their unique impulses?[24]

Two series of quotations from the Bahá'í writings will sufficiently demonstrate the processual indetermination of these dilemmas. First, pressing the vertical axis of pluralism, the diachrony of novelty or renewal appears in these dilemmas as we read in the following three passages from Bahá'u'lláh's writings regarding the transcending character of the new revelation expressed in the form of the unprecedented theophany of its source in a new divine Manifestation (such as, and adding itself to, for instance, Zoroaster, Christ and the Buddha).[25]

> Arise, and proclaim unto the entire creation the tidings that He Who is the All-Merciful hath directed His steps towards the Riḍván and entered it.[26]
>
> It was as though the Ancient King had revealed Himself unto Himself, and then, with undisputed sovereignty, unto His servants and His creatures in the realm of creation.[27]
>
> This is the Day whereon fire and water were joined together as one, and the veils were removed from the face of all mysteries, inasmuch as the Beauty of the Unconstrained came forth arrayed in the raiment of His own Self, the Help in Peril, the Almighty, the Incomparable.[28]

Here, indeed, the new revelation is in its depth a new creation, characterized as all-surpassing event, emphasizing the vertical axis of subsuming oneness, unprecedented novelty, transcending superiority and exclusive unification. Note Bahá'u'lláh's use of the term "the All-Merciful," which for Islamic sensitivities is, in the traditional list of God's 99 most beautiful names and as the beginning of all *surahs* (except one) of the Qur'an, arguably one of the central epithets of Allah,[29] in fact, the divine name par excellence,[30] as specific for the character of this revelation. Hence, Bahá'u'lláh refers to the new

---

21. Cf. Fazel, "Pluralism," 42–43.
22. Cf. Diessner, ch. 1; Savi, *Summit*, 24.
23. Cf. Bahá'u'lláh, *Tablets* (#3), 22; *Gleanings*, #34.
24. Cf. W. C. Smith, ch. 6; Smart, *Religion*, ch. 25.
25. Cf. 'Abdu'l-Bahá, *Promulgation*, #109.
26. Bahá'u'lláh, *Days*, #6.10.
27. Bahá'u'lláh, *Days*, #10.12.
28. Bahá'u'lláh, *Days*, #10.18.
29. Cf. Savi, *Summit*, 17.
30. Cf. Corbin, 168.

revelation not only as one further manifestation of divinity, but as the one that mediates its utmost limit.[31] This is even more emphasized by the use of the image that this revelation is in its innermost nature such that it equals nothing less than God revealing Godself to Godself! In other words, all veils are removed, and as Bahá'u'lláh boldly states in other passages (already quoted), this revelation has rent asunder the heavens of all religions.[32] Again, without disputing the truth of all revelations (in the past), they are now consumed in the gravity of the novelty of this, Bahá'u'lláh's revelation. One could not more radically express the vertical axis in this event of all-consuming novelty!

However, in other passages this verticality is thoroughly countered by the equally important insistence on diversity, continuity, equality and inclusive unison (multiple uniqueness), that is, the horizontal axis of synchronic conviviality, as witnessed in the following citation again referencing the religious figures (Manifestations of God, *mazahir-i ilahi*) from whom religions originate and through whom the unison of value is acclaimed in the highest possible terms.

> Every one of them [= Manifestation] […] connecteth this world with the realms above, and [is] the Standard of His Truth unto every one in the kingdoms of earth and heaven.[33]
>
> Therefore, whosoever, and in whatever Dispensation, hath recognized and attained unto the presence of these glorious, these resplendent and most excellent Luminaries, hath verily attained unto the "Presence of God" Himself, and entered the city of eternal and immortal life.[34]

Here, the vertical axis is profoundly contrasted with, even upset by, the horizontal axis insofar as one cannot from the earlier passages simply reason that the "other" religions (before the current Manifestation) have (after its appearance) necessarily lost their import, their impact and their healing effect on humanity.[35] To the contrary, all religions are mediating the exulting and remedying presence of God in their own way, and a believer, by having embraced them, or one of them, is (still) accessing Reality.

Given the paradox of the two axes of pluralism, the question then arises whether and how, in the Bahá'í writings, they are balanced, or can be harmonized; whether and how they might overlap and interfere; and, if there is to be found any such "superposition" of both axes, whether and how such findings would contribute to the current discussion of the unity of religions and its relation to, as well as impact on, religious pluralism. Or, conversely, we ask: How can religious pluralism be advanced from (or with) such a Bahá'í perspective on the unity of religions?[36] In the search for a suitable reference, the following

---

31. Cf. Bahá'u'lláh, *Days*, ##21, 44: now, Reality is shining with its "naked glory," devoid of all veils.
32. Bahá'u'lláh, *Iqan*, §46; cf. the respective quotation in Chapter 8.
33. Bahá'u'lláh, *Gleanings*, # 21.
34. Bahá'u'lláh, *Iqan*, 151.
35. 'Abdu'l-Bahá makes various scattered comments on the current salvific spirit of past revelations such as Christianity and Shi'ism, even encouraging believers to become more like the Manifestations of those dispensations, thereby fulfilling their essential Bahá'í duty; cf. 'Abdu'l-Bahá, *Tablets I*, 193; *Questions*, #38; *Promulgation*, ##88, 116; *Selections*, #20.
36. Cf. Faber, *Garden*, chs. 5, 8.

one may offer a point of departure as its states such a "superposition" in an interesting manner, namely, as being inherent in the divine Mystery itself in its interaction with the world: as a mystery equally of distinction and unity.

> Conceive accordingly the distinction, variation, and unity characteristic of the various Manifestations of holiness, that thou mayest comprehend the allusions made by the creator of all names and attributes to the mysteries of distinction and unity, and discover the answer to thy question as to why that everlasting Beauty should have, at sundry times, called Himself by different names and titles.[37]

The suggestion here seems to be that the understanding of the mutuality of unity and distinction, which the two axes of pluralism impress on us, is not to be found in any relational scheme of balances, but in a "superposition" that issues from and into a mystery. This mystical signification immediately relates us back to earlier considerations on the importance of mysticism and its nondual thought patterns, which have played an important role in our quests regarding a refined understanding of religious pluralism.[38] Bahá'u'lláh's statement, then, is one in which both sides of the mystery are affirmed, but not simply mediated or explained away as mystery. What is more, this withholding seems to indicate that harmonization cannot be achieved by any theory or system, but must precisely be perceived and practiced *as* mystery. However, this also entails that the meaning of unity and plurality of religions must not be explored by simple elimination of one side or by a simplifying emphasis on one side over the other, as these moves would equally announce undue "rationalizations" or even the elimination of the mystical character of their revealed, experiential and experimental togetherness.[39]

In other contexts, I have called this movement of the mystery beyond differentiations (into unity and diversity) its *subtractive affirmation*: that God/Reality *affirms* the multiplicity of self-manifestations *and* religious responses (*polyphilia*), but always remains beyond these differentiations, that is, *subtracting* "itself" (its Self) from this multiplicity as its creative and responsive source, always perpetuating an infinite theophanic process, but never being "different" from it either (polyphilic pluralism).[40] For this movement to make sense, the intended relativity of religious truth, then, must embrace the processual interaction of three elements: first, *apophasis*—that the One (like in Plotinus, lacking any better placeholder) is beyond unity and plurality, closeness and distance, beyond any attribute and opposition[41]; second, *multiplicity*—that the One must be expressed, or will express "its"

---

37. Bahá'u'lláh, *Iqan*, 21–22; also prominently quoted in Universal House of Justice Letter from October 15, 1992: http://www.bahai.org/library/authoritative-texts/the-universal-house-of-justice/messages/#d=19921015_001&f=f1-20.
38. Related considerations are central to Chapters 4–5. Cf. Momen, "Relativism," in *Lights of Irfan* 12, 370–85.
39. Cf. Faber, "Mysticism,"187–206; Faber, "Surrationality," 157–77.
40. Cf. Faber, *Poet*, Postscript; *Manifold*, ch. 3; *Garden*, ch. 2:5.
41. Cf. Bahá'u'lláh, *Iqan*, §104: God "standeth exalted beyond and above all separation and union, all proximity and remoteness." Cf. 'Abdu'l-Bahá, *Questions*, #27: "The reality of the Divinity

Self, in a multiplicity of infinite appearances and even worlds[42]; and third, *relationality*—that this multiplicity is mutually immanent "in" the One.[43]

With these differentiations in mind, which I have explored in my book *The Garden of Reality*, we can now detect the respective "superpositions" of the two axes of pluralism regarding the four just delineated dilemmas in which their "indifference" presents itself to us as mystery. As to the first dilemma, the Bahá'í writings display the effort to recreate a world in the image of unity *in* diversity:

> Let us look rather at the beauty in diversity, the beauty of harmony, and learn a lesson from the vegetable creation. If you beheld a garden in which all the plants were the same as to form, color and perfume, it would not seem beautiful to you at all, but, rather, monotonous and dull [...] Thus should it be among the children of men! The diversity in the human family should be the cause of love and harmony, as it is in music where many different notes blend together in the making of a perfect chord.[44]

Here, religious multiplicity (as well as any other multiplicity) is not a problem of opposition, antagonism, mutually excluding alternatives, striving for false unifications, that is, simplifications of differences. Rather religious multiplicity, here, is the means for the intensity and harmony of the whole body of religious evolution.[45] It goes without saying that it is by the valid concurrent differences of religions (horizontal axis) that religious evolution (vertical axis) will avoid dullness and monotony; that it would retain the ability to live the fundamental religious and ethical impulses of love and harmony; and that it can continue to express the divine beauty, which may in a profound sense be named the origin and aim of creation. This multiplicity is unified not in poisonous ways, but like a musical cord, as a multiplicity in relation, without elimination, but with mutual affirmation.

Bahá'u'lláh's statement on the mystery of unity and distinction, just quoted earlier in this section, has already spoken to the second dilemma, the togetherness of continuity and novelty, that is, that neither side must overtake or overcome the other, that the mystery is precisely revealing itself in the paradoxical confirmation of continuity *within* (the process of) novelty. Here, multiplicity is relational without simplification or elimination because of the mystery's apophatic subtraction in its affirmations.

As I move on to the third dilemma, in the next two passages the Bahá'í writings propose equality *without* superiority.

> Likewise, when you meet those whose opinions differ from your own, do not turn away your face from them. All are seeking truth, and there are many roads leading thereto. Truth has many aspects, but it remains always and forever one.[46]

---

is sanctified above singleness, then how much more above plurality"; #37: "All the attributes ascribed to the highest degrees of existence are, with regard to this station, mere imagination."
42. Cf. Bahá'u'lláh, *Iqan*, §106.
43. Cf. Bahá'u'lláh, *Iqan*, §103; Faber, *Garden*, ch. 1.
44. 'Abdu'l-Bahá, *Paris Talks*, #15.
45. Cf. Faber, *Poet*, §§12, 15, 27.
46. 'Abdu'l-Bahá, *Paris Talks*, #15.

> Know ye 'that the paths to God are as numerous as the breaths of the creatures' yet there is no soul but one and there is no religion but one, and it is the Cause of God. And our command is a single act.[47]

These two texts establish that the oneness of truth does not hinder its infinite diversity.[48] In the context of the creative and healing movement of subtractive affirmation, the mystery displays the apophatic nature of Truth so that it cannot be reiterated, "one" against another one. Hence, it prevents us from claiming superiority of our understanding over against another, individually, but also collectively, in religious history, pitting one religion against another. This again intimates that we should also avoid any limited assertion of "our" claim to be neutral (objective), and any other claim to be limited (subjective) and, hence, illusionary.[49] Mutual immanence of all aspects of Truth suggests that we all are illusionary if we try to reiterate some truths over against others.[50]

With regard to the fourth dilemma, the Bahá'í writings confirm unity *through* uniqueness. In strongest terms, 'Abdu'l-Bahá does, in the following quotation, make space for a dramatic insight that differences are not only human, all-too human, but profoundly contribute to the religious advancement of humanity in its maturation as spiritual beings. What is more, it is precisely the multiplicity of unique religions that we can now begin to envision as the greatest contributor to harmony, rather than uniformity, reduction to the same, dissipation of the old into the new (and vice versa) or imperial occupation of the respective other. Here, the relativity of religions and their truth claims becomes the very criterion for these claims to *be* true.[51]

> Consider the flowers of a garden: though differing in kind, color, form and shape, yet, inasmuch as they are refreshed by the waters of one spring, revived by the breath of one wind, invigorated by the rays of one sun, this diversity increaseth their charm, and addeth unto their beauty. Thus when that unifying force, the penetrating influence of the Word of God, taketh effect, the difference of customs, manners, habits, ideas, opinions and dispositions embellisheth the world of humanity. This diversity, this difference […] reinforceth harmony, diversity strengtheneth love, and multiplicity is the greatest factor for coordination.[52]

What these negotiations of these four dilemmas may expose is that we should not attempt to somehow "unite" the two axes of pluralism, but to direct our attention to the possibility of answering their mutual incommensurability by breaking through the assumption

---

47. The Báb, *Risalah fi's-Suluk (The Way to God)*, 231.
48. Cf. Faber, *Manifold*, Intermezzo I.
49. Cf. Momen, "Relativism," 374. Such a strategy has lost its innocence; it hides the power dynamics of the master narrative to propagate itself as general, neutral, objective and universally applicable while the minority views, that is, the ones without social, political or cultural power, are, thereby, made invisible, or confined to, idiosyncratic, irrelevant, subjective and parochial phenomena.
50. Cf. Faber, *Becoming of God*, Explorations 10, 15; "Religion," 170.
51. Cf. Faber, *Garden*, Introduction.
52. 'Abdu'l-Bahá, *Selections*, #225.

that their tensions are unavoidably forcing an escape into either synthesis or opposition. Rather, in the face of their functioning on the presupposition of apophatic oneness and polyphilic multiplicity as the *mystery* of distinction and unity, we are pointed toward a spiritual, epistemological and metaphysical, but still tentative, "according" differentiation between *layers of reality* that, as we move through them, can transform oppositions into variations, and variations into indistinctions or indifferences (or in a reverse process degenerate into antagonisms). In other words, such accords and harmonies of the in-sistence of Reality do not deny these differences, but constitute themselves through impermanent and permanently moving differences that only become oppositions and antagonistic aporias if they are reiterated *as* themselves "real." Instead, the diverse forms of multiplicity become something like a "horizontal" (now meaning: immanent) skillful means[53] (all residing in one plane) in light of different "vertical" (now meaning: transcending) levels of apophatic indifferentiation and polyphilic differentiation (moving between these planes). The "superposition" of the two axes, then, is a matter of a discourse that gains the fluidity of a (immanent) *transreligious* movement between and within religions, but is embraced by the (transcendent) *trans*-religious movements of the subtraction of the mystery on any level of affirmation of multiplicity into another apophatic level of indifferentiation.[54] The Bahá'í writings have addressed these infinite vertical levels of apophatic and polyphilic movements of the in-sistence of Reality by adapting the Sufi scheme of the infinity of spiritual worlds that are not only a multiplicity, but rather a cascading manifold of layers of hiddenness and theophany.[55] Like an accord with its many tones, overtones and cocreated resonances, what seems to be an opposition on one expressed level (*zahir*) is united in another (hidden, *batin*) one[56]; what is united in one level is but a distinction from another, more apophatic level.[57]

It may not come as a surprise that, in the Bahá'í writings, this differentiation between more time-like "horizontal" diversity and more space-like "vertical" reconciliation—to which I will return later, again—and their mutual immanence are, as the point of convergence of the mystery of unity and distinction, expressed with the central concept of the *Manifestation(s)* of divine revelations and the body of religions.[58] While divergent

---

53. Cf. Faber, *Manifold*, ch. 4.
54. Cf. Faber, *Becoming of God*, Exploration 16. The differentiation between "transreligious" (between religions) and "trans-religious" (beyond religions), here, already hints at the different modes of being transreligious that Chapter 11 will discuss.
55. Cf. Ma'sumian, "Realms," 11–17; Momen, "God," 22–31; Lambden, "Background," 59–60. This is not a new invention of the Bahá'í writings, however, but seriously embedded in the "ancient wisdom" of many religions, expanding from the Islamic mystical philosophy to ancient Hindu differentiations; ch. Corbin, 164–67; Savi, *Summit*, 31–36; *Mandukya Upanishad*, 203–5; Chopra, 125–30; Faber, *Garden*, chs. 5:2, 7:6.
56. Cf. Saiedi, *Gate*, 59; Savi, *Summit*, 23, 257. "Revelation" means that the hidden mystery (*batin*) becomes manifest (*zahir*) in an infinite series of renewals in which both the diachronic and the transcending "vertical" axes coincide.
57. Cf. Saiedi, *Gate*, chs. 7–8; Momen, "God," 23–26.
58. Cf. Hatcher, *Face*, chs. 4–5. The concept of the Manifestation is one of the concepts without which the Bahá'í universe cannot be understood; cf. Cole, "Concept." In paradigmatic new axial spirit, it approximates complex and age-old discussions within and between diverse

divine Manifestations figure in the temporal world of becoming, that is, on the historical plane, as central to different instantiations of religions, at the same time, in "vertical" (trans-temporal) apophatic abstraction from time and location, that is, in divine non-difference, they are (as) "one soul,"[59] that is, they encompass the synchronic and diachronic axes of pluralism in both the polyphilic "horizontal" (temporal physical) distinction and the apophatic "vertical" (spatial and spiritual) subtraction, in divergence and conciliated convergence in and as their very "Self."[60] It is, then, in this (and through their) multidimensionality, enveloping a layered reality of expression and subtraction, that "we may perceive, with an eye purged from all conflicting elements, the worlds of unity and diversity, of variation and oneness, of limitation and detachment"[61] in mutual non-antagonistic intimation.

Moreover, this coinherence of "horizontal" divergence and "vertical" reconciliation is also exceptionally resonant with Whitehead's intercourse between God's two natures (the primordial and the consequent) and the world of becoming.[62] While in the world of creativity, change means becoming and perishing, divergence and opposition, these oppositions are reconciled in God in two ways. As the Primordial Nature harbors all possible worlds, it unites in itself all oppositions, alternatives and competitive divergences in one divine vision. And in the divine valuation of these potentials as means of creative transformation of the world's processes, the Primordial Nature "incarnates" in the full diversity of the different situations out of which new events and organisms arise.[63] Further, insofar as the Consequent Nature receives all diverse and divergent actualizations in the unity of divine perception, it reconciles them in "soteriological non-difference"[64] beyond any opposition in order to offer this reconciliation again for the advance of the creative processes of the world.[65] What appears as oppositions in the world of becoming, then,

---

religions as well as transreligious processes regarding the human appearance of the apophatic mystery of ultimate reality being, in a sense, an expression of ultimate reality "in person." In this capacity, it relates to both, namely, questions of unmanifest and manifest reality, as expressed with terms of *brahman, dao* or *sunyata* as well as divine predications such as Jahwe, Allah, Logos or Spirit, *and* questions of the presence of these "realities" in religious figures such as the Buddha, Krishna and Christ. A related discussion of the transreligious importance of this concept of the Manifestation will follow in Chapter 12.

59. Cf. Bahá'u'lláh, *Iqan*, §161.
60. Cf. Bahá'u'lláh, *Iqan*, §§170, 196. We find a similar pattern regarding the divine non-difference between "first-ness" and "last-ness," which is also applicable to Manifestations; cf. *Iqan*, 173–74. In fact, what is divergent in the world of becoming (in temporal tension) is united, non-different or even transcended in the realm of divine immediacy. In the realm of the Absolute, these categories become irrelevant and nonexistent; they are neither affirmed nor denied; cf. *Seven Valleys*, 24–25 (Valley of Knowledge), 44 (Valley of Unity). The same implication may be drawn from Qur'an 57:4; Revelation 21:6; Isaiah 48:12.
61. Bahá'u'lláh, *Iqan*, §170.
62. Cf. Whitehead, *Process*, part 5; Hosinski, *Fact*, chs. 7–8; Faber, *Becoming of God*, Sphere 1.
63. Cf. Faber, *God as Poet*, part 3.
64. Cf. Faber, *God as Poet*, 102.
65. Cf. Faber, *God as Poet*, §30; *Manifold*, ch. 1;

is transformed, in divine view, to harmonizations and supplementations.[66] Oppositions become alternatives; alternatives become contrasts; and contrasts, integrated in the unity of divine vision and perception, become one field or landscape or garden or ocean or manifold of reconciled conviviality, in divine *polyphilia* reflected back into the world as potentials of more intense and more harmonious calls to transform divergences into convergent multiplicities.[67]

Nor are such transreligious movements in the temporal "horizontal" world of becoming feats of a syncretistic piracy, of cobbled-together wealth stolen from multireligious insights.[68] To the contrary, as in process thought, the temporal process in which they unfold is sympathetic: it is the whole universe from which every event gathers itself[69]; becoming is an act of compassion and novelty (valuating the past in wisdom).[70] While novelty reconfigures the multiplicity from which it arises, without being reducible to it, it again resides with its uniqueness (of what it has become) in the new multiplicity that it has co-constituted by its emergence.[71] In the creative process, impermanent unity is achieved; and in the transitional process, it is released again into new constellations of the future.[72] That this complex universal movement of religious identities will lean toward alternative interpretations, some seeking self-identity, others searching for interferences of diverse traditions in a diversified world-spirituality, is a natural implication of such a conceptualization. That new events and organisms, such as (new) religions, realize alternative potentials from a continuum of possibilities and, hence, lead to incommensurabilities in their mutual relatedness, is also hardly a surprise. A pluralism of exclusivism, inclusivism and pluralism in such constructions of religious identities is, then, likewise to be expected. But these incommensurabilities, now, appear within a new horizon: Religious pluralism and the unity of religions, as well as their internal and external restraints of alternative views and practices, could, if we are so inclined, be translated into *one confluent transreligious movement* of all of them in a world of becoming in light of the apophatic and polyphilic infusion of Reality that "itself" always transcends all of its achievements without abandoning them. This, it seems to me, is the deeper meaning of the Bahá'í conclusion, that there is only *one* Religion of God,[73] *one polyphilic transreligious presence of Reality in the multiplicity of religions.*[74]

---

66. Cf. Faber, *God as Poet*, §39; Maassen, *Gott*.
67. Cf. Whitehead, *Process*, 351; Faber, *Manifold*, ch. 12; *Becoming of God*, Exploration 16; *Garden*, ch. 7.
68. Cf. Faber and Keller, "Taste," 181–84. For the importance, but also limitation of the paradigm of hybridity and syncretism in our discussion of the event-structure of the becoming of new religions and the pluralism issuing from it, cf. Faber, *Garden*, ch. 4, but also the discussion in the Introduction and Chapters 5–7 of this book.
69. Cf. Whitehead, *Process*, 36, 162.
70. Cf. Whitehead, *Process*, 345–46; Faber, *Poet*, 15, 123; *Becoming of God*, 147, 167, 189.
71. Cf. Faber, *Garden*, ch. 4.
72. Cf. Whitehead, *Process*, 149–50; Faber, *Poet*, 77; *Manifold*, chs. 1, 4, 10.
73. Cf. Esslemont, *Bahá'u'lláh*, 137; Kluge, "The Bahá'í Faith," 44; Fananapazir, *Islam*, ch. 17.
74. Cf. Stockman, *Bahá'í Faith*, 35–43.

Part III

TRANSRELIGIOUS HORIZONS

Chapter Eleven

THE TRANSRELIGIOUS DISCOURSE

Consider the ocean, how serene it lieth, how majestically it reposeth within its bed. Yet the winds of the will of the eternal Beloved cause countless ripples and innumerable swells to appear upon its surface, each wave distinct and divergent from the others.[1]

—Bahá'u'lláh

The analysis of the mystery of distinction and unity and its interpretation from the perspective of polyphilic pluralism in this proposal itself rests on a *transreligious* understanding of religious pluralism and the unity of religions, at this juncture intimating its deeper exploration regarding its presuppositions, implications and consequences, and of some of the vocabulary already used to convey the meaning of the term "transreligious." The word and concept "transreligious" have become more visible in the past years. While some relate "transreligious" to "transgender"[2] or hybrid spirituality, even that in between postmodern attitudes of religious and irreligious postures,[3] others use it more or less indifferent from "interreligious,"[4] or for the fact of fluency between religions.[5] Those are important indications for a new global consciousness with regard to religion—especially at the beginning of a new millennium and in expectation of a human future in it. Yet what are the reasons for such a conversion in terms? That the "trans" in "transreligious" has become relevant today more than ever before, I think, is partly understandable as a reaction to the perceived limitations of interreligious dialogues and multireligious encounters to grapple with the question of truth and practices of mutual amicability (especially in light of unabated violent religious conflicts and the global perspective on the human predicament in its ecological vastness), partly by the urge to seek a new interpretive horizon of our current situation of global interference between all areas of human life from all regions of the world in almost timeless speed.[6] The recognition that, because of this global immediacy, no confessional theological endeavor can, today, only be addressed to the adherents of a specific religion or spiritual persuasion has amounted to the converse insight that all theological reflections, but (in difference from classical *Religionswissenschaft*)

---

1. Bahá'u'lláh, *Days*, #31:11.
2. Cf. Mollenkott.
3. Cf. Nicolescu, 14–18.
4. Cf. Grung, 36, 69 (incl. n37, n39).
5. Cf. Leirvik, 34–35.
6. This simultaneity of reaction time, in form of global mutual current immediacy of local events as well as the universal relevance of past local histories was brilliantly exposed in the 1970s by Toffler (*Shock*, chs. 1–2).

not excluding the question of truth, must be situated in a global religious and pan-human context, being sensitive to the common cultural spaces of multireligious interaction. Today, the religious other is a neighbor who will be impacted by such considerations, but also is immediately able to answer such accounts of other's theological perception of her own tradition. Here, the term "transreligious" indicates the global responsibility implied in any regional statement of religious concern and the impact this responsibility has on the formulation and reflection of any regional tradition for itself. Nevertheless, such "transreligious theology" seems to date still to be an extension of a mostly Christian based, or at least western, discussion of religious pluralism and interreligious dialogue.[7]

It is in this context that Perry Schmidt-Leukel pursues the more radical idea of a pluralism of religion-specific pluralisms, that is, as discussed earlier,[8] a pluralism that is consciously arguing from tradition-specific presuppositions, but in conversation with other pluralisms of different or even (mutually) strange inherent argumentative structures, inalienable from the field of ideas and practices of these specific religions or spiritual movements in their cultural and societal settings.[9] Hence, the universal relevance of such pluralisms will have to be developed in an "interreligious theology" that brings these tradition-constraint pluralisms into conversation across these religious traditions. As its criteria and methods Schmidt-Leukel suggests among others the trust in the truthfulness of the "other" traditions, some kind of religious listening without a hermeneutic of suspicion; multireligious communication instead of single-minded systematizations; and the open-endedness of such a process. In my view, most importantly, he argues for the supposition of the unity of Reality: that whether one belongs to a monocentric or polycentric interpretation of ultimate Reality/Realities, and whether one accepts these discussions to be about constructions of, or addresses from, Reality, both the multireligious pluralistic communication and the fact that one must so communicate in order to avoid mere imaginings presuppose that the one Reality is the ground on which these processes happen, as they would otherwise be meaningless. That, on this view, the respective methods of this interreligious project should be perspectival, imaginative, comparative and constructive is the fruit of long-standing methodological developments of the whole pluralistic movement.[10]

The imperative of the "unity of Reality"[11] brings the assumption of our considerations into focus again, namely, that religious pluralism is intricately and inherently bound up with the unity of religions.[12] But how can this unity be addressed such that

---

7. J. Martin. However, Wesley Wildman, co-operator with the "Open Theology" project, situates it in the space of the secular university; cf. Wildman, xi.
8. Cf. Chapter 7.
9. Cf. Schmidt-Leukel, *Pluralism*, ch. 8.
10. Cf. Schmidt-Leukel, *Pluralism*, ch. 9.
11. Cf. Schmidt-Leukel, *Pluralism*, 133–36.
12. Cf. also Chapter 7. It is at this point that the understanding of "unity" becomes itself a multireligious "reality" and a transreligious trope, as it relates diverse philosophical and religious traditions across the east-west axis to one another: through *tawhid*, *wahid* and *ahat*, we enter the Bahá'í understanding of the unity of God/Reality (as the basis for its understanding of the unity of religions), which again connects with the Whiteheadian "unity" as expressed by,

it does neither insinuate sameness (essentialism) nor become a merely heuristic instrument (non-realism)? Schmidt-Leukel suggests the mathematical model of fractals, that is, the self-recursiveness of patterns and the scale-invariance of such self-imitations, as well as the characteristic of this combination, to allow for the creation of an infinite variability of concrete patterns in their recurrence. Similarity and dissimilarity, here, are not a matter of the patterns themselves, but of the variability of their combination (pluralism) while they still repeat themselves (unity).[13] The promising outcome of this procedure may well be an avoidance of simple, essentialized comparisons of traditions, as if they were mere external others, but also of the undue essentialization of comparative issues regarding familiarity and strangeness between religions or within religions, as if they were fixed entities of undisputed global identity. The same would hold for every level of religious existence and engagement. It would not be enough to just compare a doctrine, a lifestyle, ritual practices, ethical issues, social structures, spiritual types and so on as if they are indivisible unities. This is a truly transreligious procedure, one that addresses plurality and unity on all levels within any form of identity and between them, furthers the porousness within and between traditions, and discovers the "other within," as it were, the accessibility *of* the problems of unity and plurality of religions as recurring within any religion, systematization and even spiritual life, and *from* any of these multiple perspectives.[14]

My own engagement with the notion of a "transreligious discourse" goes further back to the beginning of this century when my friend and colleague Karl Baier[15] and I, after inspiring conversations, decided to use this term and to publish on its relevance; although, as it turned out, we were too early for the reception of its potentials, then. In my related articles at that time—on "transculturalization,"[16] on "transreligious discourse"[17]—the central issue was to avoid essentialism in interreligious comparisons by using a Whiteheadian process model,[18] which does not suppose sameness or similarity

---

and adopted from, Plato's *khora*, that is, as mutual immanence, which again finds its translation, for instance, into Buddhist (Kyoto School) "place of nothingness" (*basho*), which again relates to the Godhead of Meister Eckhart and the apophatic oneness and in/difference it expresses; cf. Whitehead, *Adventures*, 201; Faber, "Gottesmeer"; *Poet*, §40 and Postscript; *Manifold*, chs. 4, 9; "Khora"; "Immanence"; *Becoming of God*, Explorations 10, 15; *Garden*, chs. 1, 6; Momen, "Learning"; Diessner, ch. 1; Wargo; Waldenfels; Nishida, *Enquiry*; Carter, *Nothingness*; Lai and von Brück, 122.

13. Cf. Schmidt-Leukel, *Pluralism*, ch. 14.
14. This communicability is, again, the condition for transreligious processes to be successful; but the factual reality of such processes already demands it against all postmodern fragmentation and assumptions of substantialized cultural incommensurabilities; cf. the discussion of this question in Chapter 6.
15. Cf. Baier, "Transreligious Studies," 372–92; "Transreligiöse Theorie," 65–86; "Kyoto," 85–107.
16. Cf. Faber, "Transkulturaltion, 160–87.
17. Cf. Faber, "Diskurs," 65–94.
18. Cf. Cobb, *Christian Natural Theology*, 201; "Trajectories," 89–98; Hosinski, ch. 6; Faber, "Diskurs," 78–79.

between traditions as basis for mutual understanding.[19] Rather, it is built on "resonances" of the process of "becoming" *before and besides* comparisons.[20] As creative becoming, in this process understanding, is always a many-to-one and one-to-many cycle of organic composition, there are no fixed identities to compare.[21] And, similar to Schmidt-Leukel, interreligious dialogue will as a premise accept the real processual resonances of differences within the multiplicity of the traditions themselves one wants to relate.[22] As these differences not only occur between religions, but recur *in* themselves,[23] resonances of and within multiplicities will allow for the surfacing of webs of interrelationality that emphasize the flow of these multiplicities *within* and *between* them. Such dynamic resonances also have the advantage that we can begin to appreciate these webs, as they are themselves always in creative becoming, not as states of affairs, but movements that always differ within and from themselves in physical, mental and spiritual space and time. It is in this creative process that we can find resonances not only of sameness between traditions, but flows between them, as well as fluid transformations of identities within them.[24] Such resonances are now a matter not of comparison, but of *transformation*,[25] a transformation by which unexpected connections may arise within and between traditions not by systematization, but by *experimentation*.[26] Yet this fluency does not dissolve

---

19. Cf. Faber, "Transkulturation," 160–84.
20. Cf. Faber, "Diskurs," 89–91. Here, I differ from Sutcliffe's adaptation of Durkheim's "elementary forms" of religion, which seem to imply that we could find, across religions, objective (identical?) forms that either have the same function in the respective religions, or objective functions that can be gathered from phenomenologically differing forms, as both methods of comparison have already excluded the non-essentialist presupposition of the transreligious paradigm of "resonating" confluences and divergences; cf. Sutcliffe, 17–20. I differ, here, also from Neville and Wildman (187–210), who understand "comparison" as an elementary "category." While they, in their understanding of the "category" of comparison and, hence, also their understanding of "comparative categories" as the object of comparison, show that they want to situate themselves after Aristotle and Kant, they remain in their tradition, as they have not gone so far as to embrace, or even to reflect on, Whitehead's use of "category" and his "categories, which are markedly different from Aristotle and Kant. Deleuze (*Difference*, 284–85) has clearly seen that Whitehead's categories are pluralistic and empirical, not rationalist and integrative; cf. Faber, *Manifold*, ch. 8. They are not basic, but forms of transformations within actual processes, such that the aim of comparison is not the creation of comparative categories in which to compare objects such as religions, to extract truth as similarity and difference, correctness and falsity. Rather, as modes of affirmation of "feelings" ("sym-pathies" with others) and their transformation, it is now such transformations that ground comparisons and quests for truth; cf. Whitehead, *Process*, 259.
21. Cf. Whitehead, *Process*, 21; Faber, *God as Poet*, §13.
22. Cf. Faber, "Diskurs," 76–81; Schmidt-Leukel, *Pluralism*, 227, 233.
23. Cf. Faber, "Diskurs," 74.
24. Cf. Faber, "Diskurs," 80–81.
25. Cf. Faber, "Diskurs," 70–75.
26. Cf. Faber, "Diskurs," 84; "Transkulturation," 177–78. The epistemological habit of transformation and experimentation fosters, of course, its own dangerous openness: whether one will become different, shifts one's original perspective, embraces in hybridity formally foreign truths of other traditions, or is prone to conversion. This is probably the reason that "comparison" seems the more secure approach, as it in intellectual disinterestedness tries to

into either syncretism or mere perspectivism,[27] denying the function of processes of stabilization and identity, because organic boundaries are as vital to the process of differentiation, intensification and harmonization[28] as the ongoing process of this transreligious transformation itself always reaches for the depth to be sounded through (and beyond) the (conceptually) organized limitations of its insights informing its universe(s) of spiritual life and discourse.[29]

To use another simile, transreligious resonance functions like the sounding of a musical instrument. Neither does an instrument create its own vibrations and resonances (not only every type of instrument differently from others, but any instrument differing itself) nor does it invent its own harmonies in sounding together with other instruments. Rather, any sounding of a specific instrument, if it is brought in proximity to another one, will evoke vibrations in the other instrument that are specific to the uniqueness of both of them, and this resonant oscillation will happen even if the other instrument is only silently "listening."[30] In letting any elements of these fluent webs (instead of fixed identities) "sound" together, two things will happen: first, *we cannot predict* which elements within and between traditions in sounding together will create which resonances before we have experimentally tried out; and second, it is the *proximity*, not the similarity from which those resonances are created. However, such resonance can only be recognized if we are "in tune" with their recognition, that is, if we are *transformed* by the listening for resonances and transform ourselves so as to let this sounding together happen from and with all participants of the transreligious concert.

At the same time and in later years, I have used this approach to find resonances within and between traditions, religious[31] and nonreligious,[32] with sounding webs

---

methodically *avoid* the involvedness that is now, in the transreligious context, considered necessary for even conducting comparisons; cf. Fazel, "Dialogue," 41–42; Faber, "Transkulturation," 163; Cobb, *Beyond Dialogue*; Griffin, ed., *Pluralism*, ch. 2.

27. Cf. Faber, "Transkulturation," 184–85.
28. Cf. Whitehead, *Process*, part 2: chs. 2–3; *Adventures*, ch. 13; Hosinski, *Fact*, ch. 6.
29. Cf. Faber, "Diskurs," 84.
30. With this musical example of the work of "resonance" before any comparison relates to Whitehead's understanding of "sym-pathy," the feeling of feelings in others or of others in one's self-constitution as basic principle of the becoming of events and, hence, as the patterns of processes on the basis of all kinds of existence, as explained in other sections of this book; cf. Whitehead, *Process*, 162. Yet, it also relates to the universal sympathy of all beings in the cosmos in the understanding of Plotinus, who fathomed the relationality of everything with everything, even between physical and mental realms of existence as resonances and envisioned it with the metaphor of a lyra's string's vibration passing on to another lyra; cf. Plotinus, *Enneads*, IV. 4, 41. And, finally, such resonances appear again in 'Abdu'l-Bahá's inclusion of these Neoplatonic resonances in the most profound pattern of relationships between physical and spiritual realms, and the understanding of the mediating sphere as realm of similitudes or resonances, the *'alam-i mithal*; cf. 'Abdu'l-Bahá, *Promulgation*, #99; Savi, *Summit*, 34; Faber, *Garden*, 5:3.
31. Cf. Faber, "Personsein," 189–98; "Nicht-Ich," 42–48; "Baha'u'llah," passim.
32. Cf. Faber, *Prozeßtheologie*; part 3; "De-Ontologizing God," 209–34; "Messianische Zeit," 68–78; "Infinite Movement," 171–99; "Organic or Orgiastic Metaphysics," 203–22; "Introduction: Negotiating Becoming," 1–50; "Touch," 47–67; "Surrationality," 157–77.

created, for instance, by apophaticism,[33] experimenting with multiplicities[34] and relativity.[35] And my book *The Garden of Reality* explores all of these paradigmatic resonances with the meta-call: "Be Transreligious!"[36] Such attempts are, of course, not new; any novelty is constituted by its history of becoming, as, for instance, are multireligious transformations between Buddhism, Hinduism and Christianity, and diverse philosophical traditions from the east and west, in the works of Raymond Panikkar, Paul Knitter, John Cobb, Masao Abe and Kitaro Nishida.[37] I will return to Schmidt-Leukel's triadic engagement of Buddhism, Christianity and Islam in the next chapter by adding Bahá'í resonances.

Instead, here, I shall describe my understanding of transreligious discourse in a somewhat more coherent manner, namely, as (new) horizon for the engagement with religious pluralism and the unity of religions, by differentiating the following coordinates: the meaning of "trans"; the structure of transreligious processes; transreligious strategies; and the purpose of the transreligious discourse.

The "trans" in "transreligious" has four levels of *meaning*, moving from top-down to bottom-up, from the transcendent to the immanent.[38] In one meaning, the "trans" conveys the "transcendence" *beyond* religions, that is, either it insinuates a transcendental meta-historical essence of, or beyond, all religions, or it highlights the horizons in which religions and religious discourses are already always embedded. The first signification may either be denied, as its essentialism does not recognize the processuality of religious realities,[39] or it may be understood in terms of a reference to the perennial character indicating the mystical dimensions of religions.[40] If, however, this transcendent dimension, appealing to Reality, cannot be reiterated and, instead, always exhibits the apophatically unknown, then essentialism disappears. Yet the perhaps most important aspect of this first "trans" may come to light if we understand it as "contextualization" of religion(s), that no religion lives only from its inside world, but always exhibits and exudes an impression of itself to the outside to a wider world (of other religions, but also alternative world

---

33. Cf. Faber, "Gottesmeer," 64–95; "Bodies of the Void," 200–26; "Mystical Whitehead," 213–34.
34. Cf. Faber, "Multiplicity," 187–206; "Immanence," 91–110; *Manifold*, passim.
35. Cf. Faber, "Sense," 36–56; "Khora," 105–26; *Garden*, passim.
36. Cf. Faber, *Garden*, Ch. 5.
37. Cf. Panikkar; *Silence*; Knitter, *Buddha*; Cobb, *Beyond Dialogue*; Abe, *Zen*; Nishida, *Inquiry*; *Logik*.
38. The first three are introduced in Faber ("Inkulturation," 167–68) and restated in *Garden* (ch. 5:1).
39. This would come close to claiming that all religions are basically "the same"—a claim that can be traced not so much to religions themselves, but to the universalization of fundamentalist positions by its detractors (new atheism) or the secular endeavor to discredit or contextualize religion as "one" phenomenon that can be understood from economic, social or psychological conditions and be reduced to them (*Religionskritik*); cf. Pals. But, together with the evolutionary theories of religion up to the nineteenth century in the wake of Hegel and Schelling and Romantic philosophy, these secular reversals of these traditions were still based on the generalization of Christianity as supposedly highest expression of religion.
40. Yet the claim of unity of the perennialists is counterchecked by their understanding of the apophatic character of this unity; cf. Schuon, xii.

views and contexts).⁴¹ The open perception of a multiplicity of views from the outside rescues any religion from triumphalism, as we begin to see "our" religion from other perspectives, not limited to our internal tendencies to smooth over inconsistencies (the tendency of orthodox closures against Reality) and close them off from potential fissures, fault lines and limitations (the tendency to imitate perfection by way of apologetics).⁴²

For the second meaning, we must think of religions as human phenomenon and of humanity in its ecological integration with this Earth.⁴³ Yet we might also think of postcolonial and feminist/womanist as well as liberationist discourses that appeal to the unity of humanity over and against divisions of gender, race, ethnicity, class and power.⁴⁴ The second level of the "trans," then, names the processual "transition" of religious identities and multiplicities between and within religions *into* new events of yet unprecedented gestalt, unfolding from a future of experimentation, ingenuity or revelation.⁴⁵ Alternatively, this understanding allows us to look back into, and gain understanding of, the complex history of the constitution of religions, as they appear as novelty in a history of multiplicities from which they constitute themselves without being reducible to them.⁴⁶

The third level of the "trans" points to the "transformation" that happens *between* and *within* religious traditions, as the flows of worldviews, paradigms, philosophies, wisdoms and material realities (such as economy and political constellations) constantly mutate

---

41. Cf. Kitagawa, ch. 1; Faber, *Garden*, ch. 8. This is not only limited to the religious organization of a worldview, but the conceptuality of such a worldview itself. Hence, even the concept of God (or ultimate reality) will be contextualized in a relativistic recognition of wider horizons of understanding presupposed in the formation of such conceptualizations; cf. Faber, *Manifold*, ch. 5, Intermezzo I.
42. Cf. Albert, chs. 4–5. Albert brilliantly analyses the "tactics of immunization" of untenable positions against argumentation and critique, that is, the epistemological closures built into dogmatic thinking. Whitehead has had the same critique of dogmatism, instead insisting that metaphysical and religious statements are not dogmatizations of the obvious, but tentative statements regarding ultimate realities that are in process—a process that mirrors itself always only in an open process of knowing (knowing as event); cf. Whitehead, *Science*, 178–79; *Process*, 8.
43. Cf. Keller, "Introduction: The Process of Difference," 13–14. Regarding this unity of humanity with the Earth, more will be said in Chapter 13.
44. While this critique of oppressive differentiations within humanity does not presuppose that there is only one kind of oppression, that, in fact, there can be many culture-specific patriarchialism, this does also free from the view that both humanity as an integrated whole and the human self is less than a negotiating and negotiable unit with porous, non-oppressive differentiations as their very processual nature; cf. Butler, "Critique," 201–19. *Gender Trouble*, ch. 2; *Giving an Account*; "On this Occasion…," 3–18; Jones, Feminist Theory, chs. 2, 6; Faber, "Introduction: Negotiating Becoming," 18–27.
45. Cf. Panikkar, *Silence*, ch. 8; Faber, "Advent/ure," 91–112; *Poet*, §39. It is in this (second) sense that the "apophatic pluralism" of K. Rose (*Pluralism*, 3–4, 9–10) as a second-order reflection on the primordial fact of the necessity and unavoidability of change in the world in general and particularly as related to religions—a process that Rose names "departicularization"—is transreligious: it registers and exploits the fact that every religion will be transforming itself or naturally (without any effort really) transitioning into others over time.
46. Cf. Faber, *Garden*, ch. 4; Riley, *River*; Xing.

into new constellations, different worldviews, invariably flowing through religious identities and multiplicities.⁴⁷ This meaning indicates not a mere "translation" of one tradition into another or into a common language, but, as already explained, necessitates an experimentation that cannot remain within standpoints or perspectives that would not themselves immediately be transformed by this very engagement.⁴⁸

On a fourth level, finally, the "trans" indicates the non-difference of the movement of transcending with the movement *into* the depth of immanence: transcending not above, outside or beyond, but below, inside and within.⁴⁹ It is in this sense that experience and understanding of one tradition or better, one of its universes of insight (the web gathered from spiritual and intellectual insights and personal and social practices), will lead *into* the depth of this tradition to the point where it transcends its own categorizations into apophatic unknowing and back into a changed polyphilic landscape of connections within which the tradition is perceived.⁵⁰ Since every method (way) into the mystery has its own flavor, their multiplicity does not amount to monistic reduction to the "same" ultimate (or its perception), but evokes mutual enriching (if treated in their multiplicity) encounters within and between traditions.⁵¹ I will return to this fourfold differentiation and its potential folding into a fifth "trans" in the last chapter.

As to the *structure of transreligious processes*, the most important elements were already named and are utilized throughout the book.⁵² First, the transreligious process is one of *"creative relationality"* of inter- and intra-religious multiplicities. It describes the becoming of stabilized religious identities (and entities) as a becoming from the inheritance of multiple influences and their transition into new forms of life, new worldviews, new constellations of older elements of other religions or alternatives within new traditions. The creativeness of this process values the novelty of the synthesis in which they have gathered. The relationality of this process, again, provides us with the trust that these multiplicities are always connected in some way so that neither can any religious identity be described without the multiple relations beyond itself from which it gathers itself, nor ever be foreclosed from an empathic understanding by which the other is discovered as already inherent in oneself.⁵³

---

47. Cf. Faber, *Garden*, ch. 4:2; Ehrman; Parrinder; Borsch; Borg; Assmann, *Moses*.
48. Cf. Faber, "Transkulturation," 164–65, 179–80; Assmann, "Translating Gods," 25–36.
49. Cf. Faber, "Zeitumkehr," 180–205; "Mystical Whitehead," 213–34; "Advent/ure," 91–112; *Poet*, §§35, 39; *Manifold*, chs. 9–10.
50. Cf. Panikkar, *Silence*, ch. 10. In the *Mandukya Upanishad*, this is the way to the fourth conscious state beyond limitation (and back into the now transformed states of limitation); *Upanishads*, 204; Faber, *Garden*, ch. 7:6. Bahá'u'lláh understands this way "inside" also as falling "into a depth" where every atom reflects divine reality; Bahá'u'lláh, *Gleanings*, #94. And 'Abdu'l-Bahá understands the independent search for Reality/Truth as leading to this "one Reality" although it is in its infinite facets polyphilically complex; cf. 'Abdu'l-Bahá, *Promulgation*, ##16, 63, 96, 128; *Selections*, #227; *Questions*, #82; *Paris Talks*, #40.
51. Cf. Faber, "God in the Making," 200; *Manifold*, ch. 5; *Garden*, ch. 8
52. These three elements appeared already in my original "Discourse," 81–87.
53. Cf. Faber, "Diskurs," 82–84; Faber, *Becoming of God*, Exploration 13; Whitehead, *Adventures*, chs. 12–13; *Religion*, ch. 4; Schmidt-Leukel, *Pluralism*, chs. 10–13; Abe, "Kenotic God," 3–68; Nhat Hanh, *Interbeing*.

Second, the transreligious process is one of "*contrasting*," meaning that the accesses to disjunctive views between or within traditions can never be absolute or prohibitive of mutual transformation into new events of togetherness, as this is the very pattern along and by which religions have developed, and have developed into new religions or worldviews within or beyond (established) religious traditions.[54] Contrasting leads us *either* backward into the creative process that allowed a new religious identity to arise *or* projects into the future the potential alternatives for such developments, but always knows of all traditions as already the outcome of such a contrasting conjunction of (sometimes unimaginably) disjunctive elements.[55]

Third, the transreligious process views the identities of religious multiplicities as indefinite movements of *"open wholeness."* That is, it assumes that such identities have the character of impermanence and creative transformation by which they are never reaching any end-state.[56] Yet these processes are not diverging to the extent that their fluency could be sufficiently analyzed as fragmentations, scatterings into unrelated pieces, or dissolutions, as only their perceived wholeness by which the conjunctive and disjunctive turnabout has a meaningful integrity can, in fact, render them to be experimentally and intellectually perceived as one.[57]

As to the *transreligious strategies* (or methodological restraints) the most important ones applied throughout the current considerations seem to me to be coinherence, resonance and transmutation.[58] "*Coinherence*" means that a transreligious engagement of religious identities and multiplicities always knows of the constitution of any of its elements as also being affected by other traditions or found in different traditions, even if often hidden under simplified assumptions of identity in these traditions.[59] There are no absolutely erratic blocs or unintelligible fragments that would not in some way be connected with, or attached to, complex wholes of, say, specific categories that a certain tradition may find to be unique and inaccessible from any other perspective or tradition.[60]

---

54. No religious figure is "owned" only by the movement or religion it initiates, or one orthodox group within any such movement or religion; cf. Riley, *Jesus*; Faber, *Manifold*, ch. 4; Bahá'u'lláh, *Iqan*, §§19–20.
55. Cf. Faber, "Diskurs," 84–85; *Becoming of God*, Exploration 1; Whitehead, *Process*, 22, 24, 27, 95.
56. Cf. Whitehead, *Process*, 111; Faber, "Apocalypse," 64–96.
57. Cf. Faber, "Diskurs'" 85–87; *Becoming of God*, Exploration 3; Whitehead, *Process*, part 2: ch. 3.
58. These three elements were also already explored in my original "Discourse," 87–94.
59. Originally, I had named this strategy "inclusion," as in "mutual inclusion" or the "conjunction" of different traditions; ch. Faber, "Diskurs," 87–89. Yet I find "coinherence" more adequate to describe the same reality, now, as it does indicate "coherence" by which the identity of one tradition constitutes itself of many elements found in other traditions without being fragmented, instead being uniquely brought to multiple, but internal unifications in divergent traditions, movements, religions or worldviews. Moreover, "coinherence" also indicates the mutual "inherence" of elements sometimes feared to be foreign to one another by orthodox simplifications; cf. Faber, *Becoming of God*, Exploration 8; "Para-doxology," 36–56.
60. This exclusivity of access (strict mystery) is, for instance, claimed by orthodox Christian authors regarding central Christian doctrines, such as the Incarnation and the Trinity, although it can be demonstrated that these doctrines were understood by vastly different religious traditions in their own way; cf. Hick, *Metaphor*, Parrinder, parts 2–3.

"*Resonance*," as already stated, ventures beyond simple comparisons of entities or identities, as it is not clear beforehand which actual experimentation with resounding elements in different traditions or alternative views within traditions will resonate with one another.[61] Instead of comparison seeking identities, similarities or communalities, such resonating will transcend inwardly into the meaningful relations of insights within traditions to the point of a mystical depth that becomes translucent from such points of unknowing so as to allow any element, whether perceived as similar or different, familiar or strange, to function as a potential connection to be explored.[62] From such venture-points of a meaningful universe of insights within one or different traditions, it is not important whether or not elements of different contexts express the same reality or view, but whether their *proximity* enlightens the respective other or whether they enlighten one another mutually in unprecedented ways, thereby deepening the clusters of tradition by such contacts within themselves.[63]

"*Transmutation*" seeks to instill the wonder of the appearance of new or lost patterns and forms of wholeness in the mutual transformation of resonant contrasts.[64] Transmutation allows the creative and constructed nature of all of such unifications to appear; recognizes their importance, as they are the seats of values and depth; but also registers their impermanence, as ever-new alternatives will be found to appear in transmuted oneness of meaning and importance.[65] Such constructedness is not a means for uncovering the unreality of the wholes that are informing and stabilizing within the process, but rather conveys the insight of the apophatic depth they inhabit beyond themselves without which the value of their generation and existence would not exhibit the importance of their particularity and uniqueness.[66] Earlier in this book, I have called this oscillation the "subtractive affirmation" of the apophatic-polyphilic mystery.[67]

Finally, *the purpose of the transreligious discourse* could be summarized with the following dimensions.[68] "*Peace*" becomes the criterion, seeking multiplicity instead of antagonism, reconciliation instead of competition.[69] "*Love over power*" becomes the normative

---

61. Cf. Faber, "Diskurs," 89–91. This can, for instance, be exemplified by the divergent views whether Buddhist nothingness (*sunyata*) should be equated with God or, in a Whiteheadian context, with Creativity, or with Meister Eckhart's Godhead beyond God; Abe, "God," 33–45; Waldenfels, chs. 8–9.
62. Cf. Faber, *Manifold*, 464–469; *Becoming of God*, Sphere 5; Nhat Hanh, *Buddha*.
63. Cf. Faber, "Bahá'u'lláh," 149–202.
64. Cf. Faber, "Diskurs," 91–95; Cobb, *Dialogue*, 48.
65. This impermanence is the basis for the Bahá'í claim that, despite the "eternal" reality of religions being related to "one Reality," new revelations are possible or even necessary in a world of becoming; cf. Bahá'u'lláh, *Iqan*, §§13–16, 23; Momen, *Buddhism*, 39–43.
66. Cf. Whitehead, *Modes*, 1–20.
67. Cf. Chapter 10.
68. I presented these dimensions, and other element of my current understanding of "transreligious discourse," at the conference "Future of Theologies" in the section "Transreligious Theologies" at Claremont School of Theology, California, in February 2017.
69. Cf. Whitehead, *Adventures*, ch. 15; Faber, *Becoming of God*, Exploration 13; "Excess," 6–20. Peace, here, is not an outcome, but already a coextensive presupposition, a spiritual reality, in the process of reconciliation and transformation of competition into coordination. Cf. Karlberg.

perspective by which the discourse dispossesses itself of power-inflictions and confrontational attitudes in conceptuality and practice, as alternatives can always become contrasts.[70] "*Conviviality*" signifies the aim of the discourse, as transreligious processes speak immediately to the survival of humanity and its wider ecological home as the inevitable condition for truth-claims of religions.[71] "*Coinhabitation*" provides the condition by which religions can learn to unlearn the physical restrictions of one thing residing at one place only, and can become the mutual sites of their living together.[72] Finally, transreligious discourse proposes (and always should support) a *universal "minority perspective"* on all matters, that is, not to generalize, but to allow all voices to be heard as if, and because they are in reality, particulars demanding universal recognition.[73] Eventually, as delineated by Gilles Deleuze, a "minoritarian view"[74] becomes the mediator of coinhabitation, as it, in the mutual creative transmutations of the becoming of religions, suggests the means of mutual sensibility and responsiveness of the often lost or suppressed or excluded other who is actually always already a moment of one's own individual and collective existence.[75]

A transreligious discourse of this kind may, indeed, invest into a new future of religious plurality and unity. The impulses of religious pluralism and the unity of religions may now be transmuted into an indefinite process of spiritualization of all religions, humanity and the Earth. A new agenda for religious existence in the future becomes available: *spiritually to become expressions of the apophatic-polyphilic oscillation of Reality in the experience of ever-new forms of creative living together and without the need for antagonisms and mutual exclusions.*[76] If this is desirable, religions ought to be asked to live in a new light, the light that embraces alternatives as part of the freshness of this process and that infuses the trust that it is Reality itself that values these endeavors.[77] Transreligious multiplicity is not an error, to be opposed by some fixed measure of unity, but a God-infusion[78] that offers us the spiritual opportunity to venture into ever-new accords and harmonious constellations of intense, unique forms and expressions of Reality "itself."

---

70. Cf. Faber, *Poet*, §§32, 35. This is the central thesis of the meaning of "theopoetics" in *Manifold*, ch. 11.
71. Cf. Faber, *Garden*, ch. 2:1; Faber and Slabodsky, passim.
72. Cf. Faber, *Garden*, 4:4.
73. Cf. Faber, *Manifold*, ch 2; Shoghi Effendi, *World Order*, 197; *Advent*, 35.
74. Cf. Deleuze and Guattari, 105–6, 496–73; Faber, *Manifold*, ch. 14.
75. Cf. Faber, "Intermezzo," 212–38.
76. Cf. Faber, "Theopoetic Justice," 160–78; *Poet*, §46.
77. Cf. Faber, *Garden*, ch. 8:5; "God in the Making," 195–200; Bahá'u'lláh, *Gleanings*, #148.
78. In other contexts, I have discussed this God-infusion under the heading "divine matrix" and "*perikhora*" (from *perichoresis*); cf. Faber, *Poet*, §32; "Mystical Whitehead," 213–34; "Khora," 105–26; *Manifold*, chs. 9–10, 15; Whitehead, *Adventures*, 167–69.

Chapter Twelve

OTHER RELIGIONS: FROM COINHERENCE TO COINHABITATION

The Sun of Truth, the Word of God, shines upon all mankind; the divine cloud pours down its precious rain; [...] and all humanity is submerged in the ocean of [God's] eternal justice and loving-kindness.[1]

—'Abdu'l-Bahá

One of the perhaps unexpected implications of the transreligious discourse is that the new axial religious pluralism—on the basis of its mystery of distinction and unity and the imperative for pluralisms of pluralisms—cannot be restrained by exceptionalism.[2] The transreligious reach must, therefore, be expanded in at least three directions: deeper into axial (and preaxial) resonances; inward into ecological awareness; and outward into interstellar consciousness. I will address the transreligious resonances with axial (and preaxial) religions, as well as the Bahá'í contribution to their transreligious understanding here,[3] and the ecological and cosmic implications in the next chapter.[4]

The impacts of the new axial age for the development of a transreligious consciousness must never veil the seriousness and creativity of the religions of the first axial age in their contributions to the constitution and development of transreligious consciousness. In fact, we should not even forget the preaxial religious landscape. Primal religions, while they might not have had the same universal horizon and soteriological urge displayed after the axial turn of events, still present us with the habitation of a world that spans wide and dives deep into the human longing for meaning, and today may even help us to recover ecological circularity[5] and interstellar universality.[6] Not only do they present us with questions and operations that still find (in transreligious transferences) their home in many later religious life-forms, such as matters of health, relation to ancestors and the dead, imperatives of good life and good death, the curiosity to develop a relational explanatory cosmology and so on, they also inherently unify the world (including

---

1. 'Abdu'l-Bahá, *Promulgation*, #121.
2. Cf. Bahá'u'lláh, *Gems*, §44; *Gleanings*, ##46, 107; 'Abdu'l-Bahá, *Promulgation*, ##82, 93, 96 110; *Selections*, #29.
3. This chapter relates more to the second to fourth meanings of the "trans" mentioned in the previous chapter.
4. The coming chapter will relate more to the first meaning of the "trans" mentioned in the previous chapter.
5. Cf. Grimm and Tucker, ch. 8; Grimm, 41–54; Selin, chs. 4, 8, 16–17, 20.
6. Cf. Red Star.

humanity) within a transcendent horizon that appears in some profound sense to have been a paradigm of universal unity.[7] That is, without their unifying worldview later monotheisms and monisms of the axial age would not have had arisen; they provided for a sustainable heritage from which axial religions could appear. What is more, primal religions are inherently multireligious, localized and fluent and allow for transreligious processes to happen, probably much more freely than the later axial religions with their competing universal truth claims and divergent salvation standards.

Of the axial religions, Buddhism was historically one of the first religions with a universal claim to salvation or liberation to appear.[8] However, although Buddhism understands itself as advancement on all religions, even in the more exclusivist forms of the earlier Nikaya traditions it could (at least theoretically) accept other religions as true insofar as they realize the Four Noble Truth about suffering and its alleviation, and cannot exclude the appearance of a Buddha independently of *dharma*-teaching (*pratyekabudha*).[9] In Mahayana universalism, the "two truths" understanding by which all religions are in some way immediately related to ultimate Truths, and the assumption of a universal Buddha-nature or -seed (*thatagatagarbha*) by which anyone in any tradition could be awakened to enlightenment, as well as the treatment of all teachings of the Buddha as "skillful means," would allow for a profound transreligious relationality beyond Buddhism's organizational and immediate intellectual boundaries.[10] Daoism, by the integration of preaxial transreligious flows and by virtue of the fluency of the Dao as well as the universal apophatic-polyphilic nature of its movements, is inherently not determined by fixed boundaries of its organizational manifestations.[11] Additionally, one must be amazed by Daoist universalism that, besides its coinherence with Confucianism and Buddhism,[12] already in ancient times developed the notion of universal peace through harmony independent from the religious persuasions and rituals that might differentiate tribes and cultures, ethnicities or regions of the world.[13] And it was the catalytic character of philosophical Daoism that made it a transreligious *movens* in the appearance of newer Mahayana schools of Buddhism such as Chan and Zen.[14]

---

7. Cf. Gill, chs. 4–5; Sharma, *Primal Perspective*, chs. 1–2.
8. Our historical knowledge is, of course, limited not only regarding the appearance of the Buddha, but also the early centuries of the nascent phases of Buddhism. But we know significantly less about the time (eleventh to seventh century BCE) and original message of Zoroaster who would be another axial candidate for the universal declaration of salvation. And the consolidation of Buddhism needed several centuries, probably settling between the fifth century BCE and the first century CE; cf. W. C. Smith, 55–59. This determination of the universalization of salvation could further be interrogated with the Bahá'í view that all Manifestations of God, like Abraham and Moses, would have implicitly or explicitly been addressing all of humanity even if their effect was more or less only local; cf. Bahá'u'lláh, *Iqan*, 11–12.
9. Cf. Kiblinger, ch. 3; Schmidt-Leukel, *Pluralism*, ch. 6; Xing, *Concept*, 50–52.
10. Cf. Faber, *Manifold*, ch. 4; Ingram, 48; Burton, 337–50.
11. Cf. Faber, *Garden*, ch. 3; Hansen; Izutsu, part 2.
12. Cf. Clarke, ch. 2; Cheng, 351–64.
13. Cf. Schmidt-Leukel, *Pluralism*, 74–75; Cheung, 39–40.
14. Cf. Grigg.

The surprising idea of interreligious unity of the Mughal emperor Muhammad Akbar the Great in sixteenth-century India—imagined in an all-embracing construct of one Divine Religion (*Din al-Ilahi*)—has already been mentioned. If nothing else, it demonstrates the urge of the rising new axial age for religious harmony without demanding obliteration of religious difference.[15] The novel apophatic and synthetic approach of Sikhism, again, in the same general timeframe, could be viewed as the very birth of the new axial age. In Kabir's and Guru Nanak's fusion of Hindu and Islamic traditions, and prepared by some Sufi streams of thought, which were themselves often inclined to multireligious identities (although not always), the emergent Sikh religion considered all religions harboring divine truth, understands God as apophatic Reality beyond all categories as well as human salvation as fusion with "it" beyond oppositional identities.[16] Another hybrid identity formed, for instance, half a millennium earlier and under very different religious and geographical conditions, with the Druze religion, which at a certain early point in its history was inclined to consciously integrate Islam with Christianity and diverse other religious traditions,[17] and thereby ventured to reconcile western (Abrahamic) and eastern (Dharmic) sensibilities such as multiple divine theophanies and the transmigration of the soul, which were otherwise only discussed theoretically or excluded in their orthodox parent religions.

Approximate to the Bahá'í time frame, some Hindu sages, over against the traditional insistence on India-Hindu identity, began to agree that the essence of Hinduism (mostly in Vedantic form and variety) could be practiced independently from any situation, time or place in the universe.[18] The Hindu *avatar* Sri Ramakrishna—the teacher of Swami Vivekananda as one of the most prominent exponents of the Vedanta movement in the West[19]—even practiced different religions, such as Christianity and Islam, in order to experience their acclaimed truth. While he remained deeply connected with the Mother Goddess Kali, he accepted all religious as paths to ultimate Reality.[20] And several other acknowledged, declared or self-declared *avatars*, such as Shirdi Sai Baba, Mehar Baba, Sri Aurobindo and the Mother as well as Sathya Sai Baba, combined universal impulses for the unity of all religions with transreligious forms of pluralism, representing their own modes of probing the superposition of the pluralistic axes.[21]

These snapshots are only meant to demonstrate that the new axial age did not appear out of nothing and that Bahá'í Faith is neither alone nor the origin of the new axial consciousness,[22] given that a transreligious horizon was already in the making. However, the event of the Bahá'í religion may indicate the fruit of this emerging horizon in which

---

15. Cf. Smart, *Religions*, 45, 97, 304; Schimmel, *Empire*, 109.
16. Cf. Islam, 92–107, 205–7; McLeod, 302–16.
17. Cf. Hiti, ch. 4.
18. Cf. Long, "Truth," 179–210; *Vision*, ch. 1.
19. Cf. Sister Devamata.
20. Cf. Neufeld, 65–84; Long, "Anekanta Vedanta, 145; *Vision*, chs. 3–4.
21. Cf. Parrinder; Rigopoulos; Bassuk; Srinivas; Warren.
22. In fact, Bahá'u'lláh, states that the new revelation always is "connected with" and reinvigorating "ancient wisdom"; cf. *Iqan*, §5; *Gleanings*, #125.

the ancient and deep transreligious flows throughout the history of religious encounters, issuing in the new axial age, gained, as it were, a critical mass and unique expression.[23] But so did ancient forms of exclusivism, inclusivism and pluralism, which had continuously manifested in the axial and neo-axial religious inheritance, survive in its own appearance. Nevertheless, the Bahá'í religion allowed the ancient and emergent transreligious constellations, the deep flows of religious identities and multiplicities, not to remain hidden or suppressed, but uniquely to come to the surface.[24] And with its distinct insistence on the oneness of all religions, transreligious complexity was spared the fragmenting into syncretic accretions.[25] As I have argued, this coextensiveness of unity and multiplicity is displayed in its own synthesis of a vertical pluralism, insisting on dynamically representing and uniting these transreligious movements in unprecedented ways (as a new event),[26] with the horizontal truth of a multiplicity of religions as the necessary condition for such a synthesis[27] while itself conditioned by the events of revelatory or theophanic or self-manifesting novelty.

The central idea of this Bahá'í synthesis can be recapitulated in the following chain of affirmations: (1) All religions are true.[28] (2) The truth of these religions is relative to one another, to time and cultural restraints, spiritual and material developments, and varying historical conditions. (3) All religions "become," which means that they grow and develop from their inception (beyond their early forms), but also will decline and can die.[29] (4) New religions "have become," that is, they are events of the reformulation of the verities of prior religions in new contexts and under different conditions.[30] (5) While after the inception of a new religion, "older" religions can resist the truth of

---

23. Cf. 'Abdu'l-Bahá, *Questions*, #37; Shoghi Effendi, *God*, 100; Sours, *Station*, chs. 3–6.
24. Cf. Bahá'u'lláh, *Prayers*, #43; *Aqdas*, Note 160; *Gleanings*, #24; 'Abdu'l-Bahá, *Questions*, #40.
25. Cf. 'Abdu'l-Bahá, *Promulgation*, #109.
26. The Báb and Bahá'u'lláh speak of such revelatory events as "momentous happenings" demanding response to their novelty (and eternity); cf. The Báb, *Selections*, 188–89; Bahá'u'lláh, *Gleanings*, #91.
27. As witnessed by the image of the diversity of the garden, which, otherwise, would be uniform and dull; cf. 'Abdu'l-Bahá, *Selections*, #225.
28. That the simplicity of this proposition has, of course, the same complex network of meanings as the expression that all religions are "one," at least in a Bahá'í context, was already indicated in Chapter 2 on the "unity" of religions. This can even be corroborated by the fact that "oneness" and "truth" are both inherent to the term "Reality/God" or *al-haqq*: the "one true God/Reality"; cf. Bahá'u'lláh, *Lawh-i Haqq (The Tablet of the Ultimately Real)*.
29. Cf. Bahá'u'lláh, *Iqan*, §66. Bahá'u'lláh speaks of the eclipse of the teachings of religions (their "suns" and "moons") by the "apocalyptic" event of a new revelation (the appearance of the Sun of Truth); 'Abdu'l-Bahá speaks of the four seasons of religions, implying a winter of religion in which only its outer form and name remain; cf. Bahá'u'lláh, *Iqan*, §42; 'Abdu'l-Bahá, *Promulgation*, #40.
30. Cf. Bahá'u'lláh, *Iqan*, §§20, 270. The process and impact of this intertextuality, especially between Zoroastrian and various Abrahamic traditions, including the Bábi-Bahá'í religions, with its shifting hermeneutical horizons of interpretation (the new event in a process, restructuring its own past and adding itself to a new, changed future, as process categories would see it) is the central thesis of Lambden, *Aspects*.

the new ones, in case of the rejection of the new event they would fail to accept the truth of *all* religions (vertical pluralism).[31] (6) While these religions might (and do) exist on, they have branched from the novelty, as it were, which affirms the continuity of the truth of all religions.[32] Yet these branching religions do not automatically, thereby, lose either their truths or their salvific import, or even their eternal value (horizontal pluralism).[33] (7) In the new universal context (the global connectivity of humanity and its unity as the condition for peace), the Bahá'í religion understands itself as the conscious (divine) event of the universal gathering of all religions in the confirmation of the truth of the religious history as a whole.[34] (8) As the "fulfillment" of all of religious history, it must also exhibit the transreligious unity of *their* truth.[35] (9) Being part of this process of the becoming of religions, the Bahá'í religion is not the final religion to arise; she will

---

31. Cf. Bahá'u'lláh, *Tablet of Ahmad*, 310; *Iqan*, §225; Fazel, "Understanding," 270. It is in the definition of vertical pluralism that it diachronically accepts the plurality of religions, or deviates from their "unity" by effectively denying the *valid plurality* of them.
32. Cf. Bahá'u'lláh, *Tabernacle*, #3:6–8.
33. Cf. Sours, *Syllable*, 8; Lambden, "Dimensions." In contrast to St. Paul's and more current theological undertakings to reconnect the new covenant of the New Testament or of Christianity with the "old" covenant of Sinai, the Thora and Judaism, as mentioned in Chapter 8, Karl Barth understood the Christian "fulfilment" as *preplacement* of the "old" name YHWH-*kyrios* by the new name Jesus-*kyrios*; cf. Soulen, *Name(s)*, 98–101. This is close to one side of Bahá'u'lláh's "replacement" theology in the *Iqan* (17–18), and even with the same argument: as the "elected" people *can see* the new form of God in the Manifestation that they have desired (and prayed for) to become manifest, the "God with us," the Immanuel, in Barth's diction, they *cannot recognize* the new form and, hence, are replaced in their soteriological function; Barth, 318–19. That a new dispensation always includes and superseded the older ones, in the Bahá'í context, goes back to the cosmological and soteriological understanding of the cyclical continuity of revelations that the Báb presented in his *Persian Bayan*, Wahid II, in: Momen, ed., *Selections*, 325–38. But this (vertical) "progression" is fundamentally balanced with the admission of the perpetual (horizontal) "presence" of the Manifestations to the adherents of the dispensations they inaugurated (and beyond, by them coinhabiting all others, too); cf. 'Abdu'l-Bahá, *Promulgation*, #75: for "the memory and glory of Christ continue after nineteen hundred have passed. For His name is eternal and His glory everlasting."
34. Cf. Bahá'u'lláh, *Iqan*, §285; Sours, *Station*, chs. 3–5; *Syllable*, chs. 1–3.
35. Cf. 'Abdu'l-Bahá, *Promulgation*, #135. The *minimal* benchmark for such a view, although in its own *inclusivist* context it was setting a new maximal mark, was post Vatican II formulated in Catholic theology by Jacques Dupuis, who not only accepted the most basic condition for a theology of Manifestation, namely, that the Word of God is not only present in Jesus Christ, but even that such a presence also means that in every diverse religious setting this Word will exhibit novel aspects of its truth that are not already implied in the history of Christian experience; cf. Fredericks, 6–8. Here, already in an inclusivist context, "fulfillment" does not degenerate into substitution or replacement, but elevates all religions by confirmation and accomplishment; Dupuis, *Christianity*, 257. However, any "fulfillment" theology in an inclusivist setting is a distortion of the multiplicity of differences between religions, as it only works by distortion and reduction; cf. Fredericks, 14–23. Here, in a pluralist context, "fulfillment" does mean valuation and elevation of differences. More will be said on this shift of perspective in a pluralist context in Chapter 15.

give way to other revelations, theophanies, manifestations and religions.[36] (10) In order to counter the forces of the enthusiasm that the new event releases, which may border on, or transgress into, quasi-finality (an inclusivism of fulfillment), the Bahá'í religion must affirm the permanent truth of the concurrent multiplicity of branched religion.[37] (11) The new event must be understood as the "fulfillment" of the truth of the ongoing mutual transreligious *coinherence* of all religions.[38] (12) In the case of the Bahá'í religion, the very basis of this coinherence is not just the fragile hope for a transreligious future of conviviality, but a universal divine space (or matrix) that all religions already *coinhabit*.[39] In consequence, the truth of the multiplicity and unity of religion is the awakening to their mutual coinherence; and the coextensiveness of unity and multiplicity is affirmed by mutual coinhabitation of religions in the "one" divine matrix of existence (as an eternal, time-invariant, enfoldment of the horizontal axis)—not only as the hidden ground for coinherence, but as the *manifest* event of their universal "fulfillment" (as the temporal manifestation of the vertical axis).[40] Coinherence and coinhabitation are enfolded in this mutual immanence of eternity and temporality,[41] which again unfolds in the coextensive differentiation of the two axes of pluralism, the processual coordination of which *is* the mystery of unity and distinction.

---

36. The "progressive" character of revelation or religious becoming, which is essential to the Bahá'í understanding of the vertical axis, is complicated by (8) and (9), because, on the one hand, it is meant to relate more than a mere succession of religions, as the new religion(s) are the "fulfillment" of all religions, and, on the other hand, less than a final implication of all religions. It is this mediation of both elements that necessitates the horizontal axis to remain viable in the process of progression—as valid alternatives and a multiplicity that can always be recovered as site for novelty to arise unexpectedly. I will come back to these implications in Chapter 14.
37. Cf. Bahá'u'lláh, *Iqan*, §219; 'Abdu'l-Bahá, *Selections*, #20; *Questions*, #60. Momen ("Learning," 4–6) has made this point with reference to the argument of Bahá'u'lláh in the *Kitab-i Iqan* that the disappearance of the teachings and "presence" of Manifestations after their death in their related religions would be counter to the grace of God; *Iqan*, 57–58. Here, again, the document *To the World's Religious Leaders* (2002), the Universal House of Justice, adds its clear voice: "Unquestionably, the seminal force in the civilizing of human nature has been the influence of the succession of these Manifestations of the Divine that extends back to the dawn of recorded history. This same force, that operated with such effect in ages past, remains an inextinguishable feature of human consciousness. Against all odds, and with little in the way of meaningful encouragement, it continues to sustain the struggle for survival of uncounted millions, and to raise up in all lands heroes and saints whose lives are the most persuasive vindication of the principles contained in the scriptures of their respective faiths"; Haifa, 2002: https://www.bahai.org/library/authoritative-texts/the-universal-house-of-justice/messages/20020401_001/1#392291398.
38. Cf. 'Abdu'l-Bahá, *Promulgation*, #109.
39. Cf. In their divine perspective and soul (their Manifestations), all religions are housed in the same tabernacle; cf. Bahá'u'lláh, *Gleanings*, #22. All religions are embedded in an infinite and indefinite overflow of grace and mercy, and are specializations of the revelation of God in the essence of all things; cf. Bahá'u'lláh, *Iqan*, §14.
40. Cf. Faber, *Poet*, §32; "Mystical Whitehead," 213–34; Bracken, *Matrix*.
41. Cf. 'Abdu'l-Bahá, *Promulgation*, #59.

Bahá'í scriptures have employed several strategies to address transreligious coinherence of religions and the invitation to live their togetherness in a universal horizon of coinhabitation. One strategy plainly insists on the equality of religious origins in the events of their inception, projected on their founders or founding events. None of them is to be treated superior or inferior.[42] Another strategy views the founding figures of religions as recurrence or "return" (*raj'a*) of one spiritual reality[43]—variously named *logos*, mind (*nous*), *dharmakaya, dao, brahman*, Wisdom, Spirit and so on—as the primordial manifestation of the apophatic-polyphilic, dynamic, nondual in-sistence of Reality "itself."[44] Yet another strategy differentiates between eternal verities, divine attributes and virtues, which in their spiritual nature are nontemporal (eternally real), but in their mixture always time-relative (to be realized), on the one hand, and impermanent social and doctrinal verities, which change over time, respective to culture and spiritual maturity, on the other.[45] While the realizations of divine attributes and virtues is dynamic, the social and intellectual constructions of religions change, that is, they will be deconstructed or reconfigured (in new events or dispensations) when the time is ripe.[46] A last strategy to be mentioned, here, affirms both the translatability of, and the undecidability between, the universes of discourse within or between religious and spiritual traditions on the basis of their ultimate non-antagonism.[47] In all of these strategies, we recognize the encouragement to understand the *differences* between and within religions not as oppositions, but as alternatives that enrich rather than diminish the beauty of the world in their realization, which, from the perspective of the ultimate Mystery, is what they ought to manifest. And these strategies employ *unity* in complex ways, not by reducing them to sameness, but rather insisting on the complex resonances of fluent harmonies. Here transreligious processes are evoked as deep and universal mutual coinhabitation of humanity in its manifold spiritual expressions.[48]

One way to test the relevance of this Bahá'í approach to transreligious processes—its innovative, but as of yet unrecognized contribution to it—is to expose it to its ability to do what it seems to say: that for an event to be the "fulfillment" of religious history, it must be able to reveal the transreligious coinherence and coinhabitation of all religions. As a good test object, I will point to the transreligious findings of Schmidt-Leukel in this regard. Focusing on the power to mediate between central theological conceptualizations of the spiritual essence of different axial religions, which seem to be (and, as centuries of quarrels show, were always assumed to be) incommensurable, he asks the question: Can we find coinherence (reciprocal illumination, mutual transformation) between Buddhism, Christianity and Islam in their unique spiritual identities as comprised by the doctrines

---

42. Cf. Bahá'u'lláh, *Gleanings*, #34.
43. Cf. Bahá'u'lláh, *Iqan*, §160; Momen, *Islam*, 109, 128–33.
44. Cf. The Báb, *Selections*, 126; Bahá'u'lláh, *Iqan*, §75; Faber, *Garden*, chs. 7:4; 8:4; Momen, "God," 23–25; Saiedi, *Gate*, ch. 7.
45. Cf. 'Abdu'l-Bahá, *Promulgation*, ##41, 44.
46. Cf. 'Abdu'l-Bahá, *Paris Talks*, ##41, 54; Lample, ch. 1.
47. Cf. 'Abdu'l-Bahá, *Promulgation*, ##16, 121; *Paris Talks*, #41.
48. Cf. 'Abdu'l-Bahá, *Paris Talks*, #15, 42–43.

of the Buddha, the Son of God and the Prophet, respectively?[49] The project in itself is already a sign of the new axial sensitivities of how to relate these great axial religions. But I will not repeat the ways in which he succeeds by rehearsing the history of their mutual intellectual illumination despite their contrary appearance. Rather, I will point to the fact that his primary categorical findings, built on the work of many other scholars and religious authorities of these religions engaged in bilateral or multilateral conversations of this kind, have already a century earlier been advocated by Bahá'u'lláh and 'Abdu'l-Bahá as inherent transreligious truth of a new event (or revelation),[50] that is to say, the Bahá'í scriptures embrace the transreligious coinherence of these religions.[51] Yet it is from the perspective of their primordial coinhabitation to be a revealed truth, rather than a philosophical or theological vision of, and reflection on, a potential coherence between religious universes of discourse and imagination, that their coinherence is affirmed, here, even before they may recognize it as their own reality. What is unique regarding *this* transreligious horizon is that it presents us with a religious *event* of its own magnitude: the shift from philosophical or theological suggestions of transreligious unity to a primary religious insight (revelation), from a reflection of mind to a tenet of the spirit.[52]

In Schmidt-Leukel's summary of three bilateral transreligious conversations, gathered from many different sources (from scholars of these diverse religions), we find (among others) these important arguments. Between Christianity and Islam, the discussion concentrates on the antagonistic interpretation of Jesus as the Son of God (*huos theou*) and Muhammad as the last (*khatam*) prophet (*nabi, rasul*). While (in developed

---

49. Cf. Schmidt-Leukel, *Pluralism*, chs. 10–12.
50. Cf. Momen, *Buddhism*, ch. 3; *Islam*, chs. 3–4; Lepard, *Glory*, chs. 8, 12, 14.
51. Cf. Faber, *Garden*, chs. 7–8; Fazel, "Dialogue," 11–12.
52. Cf. Faber, *Garden*, Prologue: sections 4–5. This shift from philosophical and theological construction in the mode of religious pluralism and the unity of reality to the unconstructed prima facie religious event of the same magnitude and content, from thought to revelation, as it were, is not identical with avoidance or retreat from the "public space" in which religious pluralism and the unity of religions must situate themselves if they want to have any impact on the future of the transformation of humanity to a peaceful coinherence and the realization of coinhabitation. Revelation, here, is not a parochial negation of universality, but it speaks of a universality that only events can constitute, as they are novel compositions of multiplicities, irreplaceable and irreducible in their unique unity. It is *them* that need to be of public interest. In other words, Neville's claim that only theological and philosophical constructions are fit for the public space in a way revelations (first-order religious events) are not, because they do not shy away from "making a case" (*Ultimates*, 9–12), reverts the importance of the originary events with secondary constructions. While he might think that only the abstract constructions of thought can appeal to the only god of public space, namely reason, the critical (Critical Theory) and postmodern critique of reason has shown that it is an illusion to appeal to reason as controlling instance if it is devoid of the processual composition of events, singular universality instead of abstract generality; cf. Faber, "Unique Origin," 273–89; *Manifold*, chs. 3, 7; Deleuze, *Difference*, ch. 1. Besides, in the Bábí-Bahá'í universe, creation, revelation and reason (or intellect) are coextensive and even indicating the same reality, which again changes the meaning of all of them in their mutual relational impact; cf. Abdu'l-Bahá, *Promulgation*, #44; Saiedi, *Gate*, Introduction and ch. 7.

Christian doctrine) the former is "also" divine or of divine nature, the latter (in developed Islamic doctrine) in a line of many Abrahamic and other prophets (Q 33:40) is "only" a human being or of strictly human nature. While Christ is the Word of God "in person" (John 1:1–18; Q 4:171), Muhammad mediates the Word of God, the Qur'an (Q 42:11; 11:4). This aporia was and is perceived as irreconcilable in the common history of these religions' encounters. Yet what might help to overcome the conundrum is the mutual insight that structurally, after similar long-standing doctrinal discussions and deviating views, both traditions elevate the Word of God (Jesus and the Qur'an) to an eternal divine expression. This leads to the transreligious transmutation that it is possible to assume the creative Word of God to be both a person and as a book, without (because of the Christian trinitarian and the Muslim unitarian sensibilities) simply identifying either of them with God/Allah (John 1:1; Q 112:3).[53]

Between Buddhism and Christianity, the doctrinal discrepancy arises around the antagonism of the divinity of Christ and the Buddhahood of the Shakyamuni Buddha. While (in Nikaya Buddhism) Shakyamuni Buddha is "only" a human being (by which similar argumentations would arise as with Muhammad), Buddhahood is in its own (Hindu) context beyond, and set against, claims of divinity. Both would be detrimental to make any sense of the "divinity" of Christ, of course. But at least (without further going into the intricacies of the differentiation between Nikaya Buddhism, Mahayana and Tantra) from a Mahayana perspective, both inadequacies begin to reveal mutual oscillations. It is not "gods" (devas) that resonate with the "divinity" of Christ, but the *dharmakaya*; and like the Logos-infusion of all creation, the Buddha-nature can be announced of all (sentient) beings. The Buddha is also not "merely" a human being, but expands in between, and embraces, the all of existence. According to this Three-Body doctrine, ultimate Reality (*dharmakaya*) becomes "incarnated" in the human being Shakyamuni Buddha (*rupakaya, nirmanakaya*), mediated through the all-cosmic appearance of the Buddha (*sambhokakaya*).[54] Again, as with Christ and the Qur'an, no "identity" between the human Buddha and ultimate Reality is insinuated, but as the three bodies in nondual indifference are mutually empty (*sunyata*), the human appearance is the full presence of ultimate Reality. In this sense, both Jesus Christ and Shakyamuni Buddha are the manifestations of ultimate Reality.[55] Full circle, this understanding can even be traced back to the Nikaya tradition, as the Buddha is not just a human being in it either, but the appearance of nirvana "in

---

53. Cf. Schmidt-Leukel, *Pluralism*, 156.
54. The proposed compatibility, if not direct resonance, between the trinitarian formula of divine economy and the *trikaya* doctrine has its own interesting history and still present relevance; cf. Yagi and Swidler, 54–56; Faber, *Garden*, ch. 7:6.
55. Cf. Schmidt-Leukel, *Pluralism*, 175–76. This approximation between Christ and the Buddha differs from Cobb's and Griffin's model to attach both figures to two different ultimate Realities, God and Creativity, respectively; cf. Griffin, "Complementary Pluralism," 47–48. However, in relation to the relativity of ultimate Reality/God in the appearances of these religious symbolic systems of Christianity and Buddhism it mirrors the differentiation of God from Creativity (ultimate reality) in process thought and correlates with the mystical differentiation between God and Godhead by situating ultimacy in the cycle of love, the mutual immanence and indifference of ultimate reality in all existences, cf. Baier, "Reality," 100–1.

person": it is not bound by the becoming of *samsara*, but timeless and deathless[56]; yet it also infuses itself through the "luminous" or "clear mind" in *samsara* so as to instill the urge for salvation beyond its suffering nature.[57]

Between Buddhism and Islam, throughout history, two doctrinal convergences happened, based on a similar shift: that from the "merely" human figure who mediates the Word of God and the Dharma, respectively, to a divine figure that somehow participates in its ultimate reality. One convergence arises from the Buddhist *dharmakaya* that, as apophatic Reality, resonates with the inaccessible mystery of Allah (the essence of God, *dhat*), which, from the Islamic perspective, also transcends the simple differentiation between personal and transpersonal dimensions. This resonance, again, allows for transreligious transmutation of their respective attributes such as wisdom and compassion (a central Islamic marker of Allah and Buddhist marker of Reality).[58] The other doctrinal convergence was made possible by the inner-Islamic deepening of the notion of the Prophet, as explored by the Sufi tradition following Ibn 'Arabi. As the Face of the inexpressible God, which/who is essentially self-less before Allah (or empty in Buddhist terms) the Prophet becomes, without idolatry, the revelation of all divine perfections "in person" much like the Mahayana Buddha of Buddha-nature. In the highest spiritual reality, the Prophet, like the Buddha, is in "essence" the primary creative manifestation of ultimate Reality, the "Muhammad Reality."[59]

In all three bilateral conversations, Schmidt-Leukel detects the mutual trilateral reverberations of these insights.[60] In our context this refers to the transreligious transference of patterns of differentiation and unity between ultimate Reality and the world such that the founding figures in all three traditions become the immediate and full expression of the apophatic Reality "in person."[61] With their different physical and spiritual and even divine dimensions, their status in these traditions begins to resonate with one another. On the highest level, they relent in selflessness to apophatic Reality (Godhead, Allah's essence, *dharmakaya*),[62] but they also manifest the cataphatic presence of Reality (Logos, Muhammedan Reality, *sambhogakaya*) and its "incarnations" into the physical reality of Jesus, Muhammad and Siddhartha Gautama.

---

56. Cf. Schmidt-Leukel, *Pluralism*, 181.
57. Cf. Schmidt-Leukel, *Pluralism*, 176. The exact nature of this relation between ultimate reality and the "person" in which it appears, such as the Buddha and Christ, is, of course, central to the long-standing discussions between Buddhist and Christian worldviews with their different approaches to duality and nonduality as well as the status of ego and true self. Yet this discourse has demonstrated that the boundaries are much more porous that expected, while the exact emphasis on reciprocity or irreversibility of the divine-human and ultimate-phenomenal reality in this person remains highly disputed; cf. the discussion within the Japanese Buddhist-Christian dialogue especially between Masao Abe and Shin'itchi Hisamatsu, on the one hand side, and Hajime Tanabe and Katsumi Takizawa, on the other; cf. Lei and von Brück, 119–45.
58. Cf. Schmidt-Leukel, *Pluralism*, 195, 197.
59. Cf. Schmidt-Leukel, *Pluralism*, 203.
60. Cf. Schmidt-Leukel, *Pluralism*, 184.
61. Cf. Faber, *Garden*, ch. 7:5.
62. Cf. Bahá'u'lláh, *Gleanings*, #22; 'Abdu'l-Bahá as quoted in Dunbar, 87–88.

Now, it may or may not come as a surprise that this cutting-edge contemporary conclusion of interreligious theology (or the transreligious intellectual efforts of those diverse traditions in seeking mutual coinherence) is already presented by the Bahá'í writings a century earlier![63] Its synthesis is, however, not the fruit of a second-level reflection on a long-standing discourse, still too fragile for a firm prognosis whether or not this mutual coinherence may be mutually acknowledged by all participants. Rather, the Bahá'í synthesis derives from primary religious language (that of revelation) as conveyed by the Bahá'í writings.[64] Bahá'ís think of their founding figure, Bahá'u'lláh, with all other such figures, like the Buddha, Christ and Muhammad, as Manifestations of the apophatic God/Reality (*al-haqq*), as a *mazhar-i ilahi*.[65] While the term has its own Sufi history, in the Bahá'í context it not only embraces the Muhammedan Reality or Light (*nur muhammadiyyah*), but also the divinity of Christ (as in *ho logos tou theou*) and the mediation of the *dharmakaya* in the Shakyamuni Buddha (besides infinitely many other Buddhas), as well as the *brahman-atman* nature of Krishna in his *avataras*, among others—indicating ultimate Reality "in person."[66] All of their spiritual reality is *one* in the (non-different) primordial manifestation (*zuhur, lahut*) of the unmanifest (*batin*) essence of God/ultimate Reality (*hahut*).[67] Two stations and a twofold nature constitute the Manifestations: one divine and spiritual, the other human and physical.[68] In their selflessness, the Manifestations can be

---

63. This statement is factual; it should not be misunderstood as inclusivist claim of superiority. Yet even in the case of such a grave misunderstanding, it should not be forgotten that it is the very ideal and justification of contemporary interreligious or comparative theology precisely to seek out such compatibilities, even on the same basis that the Bahá'í revelation invites us to follow as the reason for such a claim, namely, that of the "unity" of reality; cf. Schmidt-Leukel, *Pluralism*, 133–38.
64. Cf. Momen ("Learning," 4–6), who makes the argument that it is deeply engrained in the writings Bahá'u'lláh and 'Abdu'l-Bahá that no expression of the inexpressible ultimate reality can be formulated without the relativity of cultural and linguistic differentiation so that even gravely different accesses to ultimate reality, such as theistic or non-theistic modes of expression, are only always "true" from their particular cultural standpoint. In our context this means that it would be a Bahá'í "principle" that we should not judge one expression from the perspective of the other, but on its own background.
65. Cf. Sours, *Station*, 30–35; Cole, "Concept," passim. In the context of interreligious discourse, this Bahá'í concept of the Manifestation of Reality/God can, in fact, operate as a bridge concept between different appropriations of forms of divine appearance in human form such as *avatar, trikaya*, incarnation or inspired prophethood, and their mutual play of resemblances and differences that will differ in relation to the respective dialogue partners' mutual approximation of their potential compatibility; cf. Schmidt-Leukel, *Pluralism*, 138. Because of the "negative theology" of the Bahá'í concept of Manifestation—it is neither claiming incarnation (*hulul*) nor mere theophany, neither Docetism nor Arianism, neither *logos-sarx* Christology not Nestorianism—it does not assume any of them, but can, therefore, mitigate their differences as contrastive symbolisms of embodiments of an essentially transcategorial reality.
66. Cf. Faber, *Garden*, ch. 7. Besides the *trikaya* doctrine and the ultimate Divine Personality in the *bhakti* tradition, we might also think of Origen's term *autobasileia*, the indication that Jesus is the soteriological Ultimate (the Kingdom of God) "in person"; cf. Soulen, 234.
67. Cf. Bahá'u'lláh, *Seven Valleys* (Valley of Unity), 40–41; Ma'sumian, "Realms," 11–17.
68. Cf. Bahá'u'lláh, *Gleanings*, #27; *Iqan*, §§79–82, 105–6, 110–12.

called "God," as they mediate ultimate Reality; and in their absolute servitude to divinity (their humanity) they are the mirrors of the apophatic God into the infinite worlds of spiritual and physical constitution.[69] In their "emptiness" toward Reality,[70] Bahá'u'lláh (following the Báb) even addresses the indifferentiation of the personal or semiotic nature of the primal Manifestation of Reality, that is, the undecidability of the Word of God to express itself as a person or as a book[71]—maybe only matched by religious Daoism's equal primordiality of the expression of the mysterious Dao in Lord Lao and the primordial scriptures of pure light.[72] And in the subtractive affirmation of the polyphilic diversification of the universe (or multiverse) in all of its levels of expression, Manifestations unite all opposites without opposition (*coincidentia oppositorum*) and pervade this diversity and divergence as the force of unison and harmonization.[73] They are, in Whitehead's diction, the harmony of harmonies in the dynamic exploration of an infinite (unending) process of ever-new harmonizations.[74]

---

69. Cf. The Báb, *Selections*, 98; Bahá'u'lláh, *Iqan*, §§191–98; *Gems*, §40; *Gleanings*, #22. Indicating an interesting transreligious coinherence between Amitabha Buddhism and Christianity (mediated through process theology), but highlighting an important aspect of the concept of Manifestation in the present Bahá'í context, John Cobb has stipulated that Amida Buddha is not subordinated to Reality (*dharmakaya*), but its *form*; Cobb, "Can a Buddhist," 35–55. Fredericks (148n103) understands that as an interesting note on a Christian rendering of trinitarian modalism instead of subordinationism. In this sense, the Bahá'ís concept of the Manifestation of Reality is not, as it is sometimes misunderstood, an Arian subordinated divinity, but the *form or face* of Reality; cf. Bahá'u'lláh, *Seven Valleys* (Valley of True Poverty and Absolute Nothingness), 60; Faber, *Garden*, ch. 8:6. This would also resonate with the ultimate Reality as "revealed" by the *Heart Sutra*, namely, that *emptiness is form and form is emptiness*, as apophatic absolute Reality (*hahut*/ emptiness) "is (in/different from)" manifest relative Reality (*lahut*/form); cf. Faber, *Garden*, chs. 6:2 and 7:3. This would also reflect the *form of God* for Christ as Manifestation of the invisible God as used in Philippians 2:6 (*morphe theou*) and Colossians 1:15 (*eikon*); cf. Hurtado, 121–22; but also Hebrews 1:3 (*character tes hypostaseos auton*).
70. Cf. Bahá'u'lláh, *Aqdas*, Note 160; *Gleanings*, #22; 'Abdu'l-Bahá as quoted in Dunbar, 87–88; Taherzadeh, *Revelation*, 57–59.
71. Cf. The Báb, *Selections*, 135; Bahá'u'lláh, *Days*, #40:6. In one of his early commentaries on the "preserved book" (the heavenly tablet, the "eternal book" of Quran 85:22), the Báb directly identifies his person with the archetypical Book: "God assuredly made this [person the *Báb*] to be that Book, a supremely great Tablet *(lawh al-akbar)*": Lambden, *Aspects*, 108.
72. Cf. Kohn, ch. 7.
73. Cf. Bahá'u'lláh, *Gleanings*, #85; 'Abdu'l-Bahá, *Tablet to August Forel*, 21–22; *Selections*, #21; Faber, *Poet*, 260; *Manifold*, ch. 13; *Becoming of God*, Exploration 8; *Garden*, ch. 5:2. There is an interesting connection to the Buddhist-Christian discussions on the Buddha and Christ as such figures and how they relate differently or equally to ultimate reality in the sense that they are, at the same time, the inner reality of all existents (*hongaku*), but also express the *becoming* (aware of/enlightened by) this reality (*shigaku*); cf. Lai and von Brück, 138–41. In the Bahá'í context, this difference/non-difference is expressed with the terminology of *hahut*/ *lahut* and *nasut*, the *huwiyyah* of Reality (the Selfhood of the Manifestation) and the primordial Manifestation (the Will of *al-haqq*) as origin of creation and, hence, its human manifestations; Faber, "Bahá'u'lláh"; *Garden*, ch. 7.
74. Cf. Whitehead, *Adventures*, 285, 296.

It is in this sense that the bi- and trilateral arguments of the transreligious approximations that Schmidt-Leukel collects and summarizes have already been made to communicate with one another in the Bahá'í concept of Manifestation. And it is precisely the structurally transreligious nature of this concept that was to be established here, namely, that the claim that the "fulfillment"[75] of all religions in a new Manifestation (not despite, but because of the oneness with all others) must be able to affirm the coinherence of all of these traditions.[76] What is more, vertical and horizontal coextensiveness of the oneness of (the multiplicity of) all Manifestations in the event of the new Manifestation also affirms the transreligious truth of the inalienable mutual cohabitation of their revelations and religions.

This Bahá'í synthesis can be mapped again on the twelve-fold chain of arguments for coinhabitation. (1) All religions are true because their founders are Manifestations of Reality (whether known or unknown, direct or indirect, initiated or under the shadow, originating or converging) or maybe (historically) more carefully: their divine dimension, as represented by, accumulated in, projected on or reverberating out from certain historical and symbolic figures.[77] (2) Such Manifestations (whether historic or symbolic) express a meta-historical and non-different reality in the diversity of becoming.[78] (3) Manifestations,

---

75. Here, "fulfillment" does not indicate the inclusivist tendency to reduce the religious "other" to the same, to a pale version of what one religion possesses anyway already (cf. Fredericks, ch. 1), but the apophatic-polyphilic dynamics of Reality toward *transreligious* universality, which claims the universality of all religions *in* their singularity (not as exchange of universality with regionality), related through a temporally nonlinear (but rather superimposed) teleology of maturation, which can express itself in diverse religious contexts as realization, salvation or liberation, respectively or cumulatively.

76. Cf. Bahá'u'lláh, *Iqan*, §219. Here, Bahá'u'lláh affirms the vertical axis by including all religions based on their revelation as manifestation of a related Manifestation, who always coinheres in all others (cf. *Iqan*, §§170, 196), into the novelty and "fulfillment" of the new revelation/Manifestation: "unto which all the Books of former Dispensations must needs be referred, the Book which standeth amongst them all transcendent and supreme." Yet Bahá'u'lláh immediately counters the vertical with the horizontal axis by adding that all of the revelations/Manifestations—because of their coinherence—are equally education, enlightenment and salvation onto all human beings: "In these cities spiritual sustenance is bountifully provided, and incorruptible delights have been ordained. The food they bestow is the bread of heaven, and the Spirit they impart is God's imperishable blessing."

77. At this point of reflections, it needs not to be decided what exactly the "founding" of a religion and, hence, its "foundation" in a Manifestation of God means or should mean. The simple assumption of this relationship to be like the appearance of a person and the initiation of a community around them is naïve if confronted with the real religious history of humanity. Adam and Noah are etiological constructs of universal human conditions; Abraham is a faint memory; we know virtually nothing of Zoroaster and the Buddha besides centuries of ritualization of narratives; Krishna and Laozi are compound personalities from the histories of different figures; Confucius was not a founder of a religion, but still an initiator of great social change; Jesus did not found Christianity (not more than St. Paul), but wanted to fulfill the Jewish prophesies; other religions do not have any "one" founder, such as Brahmanism and Hinduism; Sikhism has several founders, as does Jainism; and so on; cf. Faber, "Laozi," section 10.

78. Cf. Bahá'u'lláh, *Iqan*, §§161–162, 173–174, 191–198; Faber, "Laozi," section 10.

as they express divinity in the world of becoming, appear in series[79] and across religious boundaries and can be conceptualized with "progressive revelation"[80] and cyclical reappearances because of the changing human, social and cultural conditions and the decline of religions (note, for instance, the expectation for the Buddhist Dharma to disappear).[81] (4) New Manifestations restate the truth of preceding religions, but differ because of the different spiritual and cultural conditions under which they appear.[82] (5) While Manifestations in their higher reality are non-different expressions of one divine Reality, and in their differentiations not only historical (contingent), but meta-historical (purposeful) expressions of this truth, extant religions may not recognize the novel event of another Manifestation so that this negation amounts to a breach of the coinhabitation of all religions (that constitutes them).[83] (6) The branching religions still coinhabit the same divine space, but by mutual opposition diverge into competing branches of one tree.[84] Since Manifestations are eternal epiphanies in contingent situations, the eternal reality[85] of their appearance in these branched religions remains salvific and liberating.[86]

---

79. Cf. Faber, *Garden*, chs. 7:5; 8; "Religion," 170–71; Momen, *Hinduism*, 5–9; *Buddhism*, ch. 3; Parrinder, chs. 2, 3, 8–16; Schmidt-Leukel, *Pluralism*, 190–93.
80. More regarding the term "progressive revelation" will be said in Chapter 15. However, it should be noted that the term would easily be misunderstood if its meaning was to be projected from Darwinian or other nineteenth-century modernist hopes regarding ideals of social, monetary or capitalist progressiveness, which was thoroughly, in theory and practice, defeated by twentieth-century history. It is, therefore, all the more important to know that the term in Bahá'u'lláh's conceptuality as well as his view of human history is often meant to indicate the trust in divine grace, namely, that divine revelation will never end. It is always overflowing, that is, in other words, revelation is *continuous* and not final (personal communication with Stephen Lambden).
81. Cf. Bahá'u'lláh, *Iqan*, §160; Momen, *Buddhism*, 49.
82. Several pluralist thinkers have thought through the implications of assuming that divine presence with a human face must not be reduced to one religious claim to exclusivity. Cf. Hick, *Metaphor*, ch. 9; Macquarrie. Besides multiple "incarnation," Haight (*Jesus*, ch. 14) also allows for different modes of divine (saving) presence, such as scripture (like the Qur'an) or doctrine (like the fourfold truth and the eightfold path of the Buddha).
83. Yet we can also observe reintegrations of new Manifestations in previous religions, such as the Buddha as Hindu Avatar, or Jesus in messianic Judaism, or Muhammad in certain Christian receptions; or they can be shifted into in a new synthesis, such as Zoroaster, Jesus and the Buddha in Manichaeism.
84. Cf. 'Abdu'l-Bahá, *Promulgation*, ##40–41, 82.
85. Cf. Sours, *Syllable*, 128–29; 'Abdu'l-Bahá, *Promulgation*, ##109, 118; *Questions*, #38; *Bahá'í World Faith*, 389; *Tablets I*, 69.
86. Cf. 'Abdu'l-Bahá, *Paris Talks*, #29; 'Abdu'l-Bahá, *'Abdu'l-Bahá in London*, 89, 95; *Foundations*, 74. 'Abdu'l-Bahá says about Christ that "His throne and kingdom were established in human hearts where he reigns with power and authority without end." An extraordinarily clear example of this universal soteriological relevance of a "past" Manifestation" in the "new" horizon of other Manifestation is this: "He who seeketh Christ from the point of view of His body hath, in truth, debased Him and hath gone astray from Him; but he who seeketh Christ from the point of view of His Spirit will grow from day to day in joy, attraction, zeal, proximity, perception and vision. Thou hast then to seek the Spirit of Christ in this marvelous day"; 'Abdu'l-Bahá, *Bahá'í World Faith*, 389. For a more complete collection of important scriptural

(7) Every Manifestation will to the extent that time and spiritual situation allows express the coinhabitation of *all* religions.[87] (8) But a "universal" Manifestation (related to a global consciousness of humanity) makes the transreligious truth of these religions and their unity translucent.[88] (9) However, Bahá'u'lláh does not claim to have ended the series of Manifestations, as this series is as infinite as the creativity, grace, mercy and compassion of God/Reality.[89] (10) In the revelation of transreligious truth of all religions, the Bahá'í writings affirm the truth and salvific relevance of all concurrent religions (limited only by their contingent audiences).[90] (11) The "universal" Manifestation mirrors the coinherence of all religions in their mutual illumination through the concept of the *mazhar-i ilahi*—retrospectively applicable to all founding figures.[91] (12) The basis of this coinherence of religions, enshrined in the concept of the divine Manifestation, does not have to be negotiated, but can be recovered on the basis of the mutual coinhabitation of all Manifestations in their divine unity and cosmic (meta-historical) multiplicity as well as their historical divergences.[92]

In the Bahá'í view, then, this whole stream of transreligious movements toward convergences and coinherences, reciprocal illuminations and mutual transformations, indicates a hidden divine force, an evolving seed, that was initiated from times immemorial and has become prefigured in ever-new forms in the cycle of Manifestations in human history, but it came to some kind of universal fruition in the Manifestation of Bahá'u'lláh[93]—the seed that must become a tree and carry fruits is an often used example not only of the Báb, Bahá'u'lláh and 'Abdu'l-Bahá,[94] but already of the Hebrew Bible

---

    passages indicating the eternal salvific and universal nature of all salvations (although mostly exemplified by only some of them, like Christ, dependent on the addressed audiences) and the diverse aspects this Bahá'í view implies for the negation of superiority as a motivation for salvation or mission cf. Lambden, "Dimensions."

87. Cf. 'Abdu'l-Bahá, *Promulgation*, #44.
88. Cf. Bahá'u'lláh, *Iqan*, §§153, 178–79; 'Abdu'l-Bahá, *Questions*, #30; *Promulgation*, #79; Sours, *Station*, ch. 6; Fazel, "Pluralism," 43. Shoghi Effendi's understanding of the "universal" Manifestation as unprecedented in human history, claimed for Bahá'u'lláh, is based not on the exception of the person of Bahá'u'lláh, as all Manifestations mediate the "Most Great Spirit" (the Primal Will, Mind, Word of God), but the special historical situation of global interconnection that allows, for the first time in human history, for a global transformation of humanity, which is understood as collective process of salvation; cf. Fazel, "Understanding'" 260–64.
89. Cf. Bahá'u'lláh, *Gleanings*, ##13, 14, 27; *Tablets (Tablet of Wisdom)*, #9 (150–151).
90. Cf. 'Abdu'l-Bahá, *Selections*, #13; *Promulgation*, ##41, 45, 47, 108, 110, 132, 135.
91. Cf. Bahá'u'lláh, *Prayers*, #43; *Gleanings*, #43; 'Abdu'l-Bahá, *Promulgation*, ##12, 71, 109, 124, 135.
92. Cf. 'Abdu'l-Bahá, *Promulgation*, #56.
93. Cf. Buck, "Interface, 157–80; Cole, "I am," 447–76.
94. Cf. Bahá'u'lláh, *Gleanings*, ##68, 80; *Prayers*, #106; *Days*, #42:9; 'Abdu'l-Bahá, *Paris Talks*, #31; *Questions*, ##29–30, 33; *Promulgation*, # 139; Woodman, 1–27. Already in the *Persian Bayan*, Vahid 2, ch. 7, the Báb states that "the Day of Resurrection of a thing is not till it reaches the station of perfection. So the Day of Resurrection of the Bayan begins on the Day when He whom God shall manifest shall appear. For today the Bayan is in the state of seed, but in the day when He whom God shall make manifest shall appear, it will have reached its highest

and Jesus for the internal growth of new religious consciousness.[95] Yet in the current multireligious reality, this "fruit" may even more contribute to future mutual transreligious translations, transformations and transmutations when the related Bahá'í universe of discourse does not tempt to be their master,[96] but would follow the Manifestations' nature of selfless service to collective coinhabitation in the spirit of humble conviviality.[97]

---

perfection. So likewise the gathering of the fruit of Islam is naught else than belief and affirmation therein (i.e. in the Bayan)."

95. Cf. Hosea 10:12; Psalm 126: 5–6; Zechariah 8:12; Mathew 13:31–32; 17:20; Mark 4:26–32; John 4:35–40; 1 Peter 1:23.
96. Cf. Bahá'u'lláh, *Gleanings*, #109; 'Abdu'l-Bahá, *Paris Talks*, #24; *Questions*, ##15, 29; *Selections*, #209;
97. Cf. Bahá'u'lláh, *Iqan*, §28; *Prayers*, #97; 'Abdu'l-Bahá, *Promulgation*, ##55, 68, 110.

Chapter Thirteen

THE EARTH AND OTHER WORLDS: A STORY OF COSMIC MAGNITUDE

The billowing ocean of Whose abounding grace hath flooded all creation, in such wise that the waves thereof have cast upon the sands of this visible world their shining pearls.[1]

—'Abdu'l-Bahá

The transreligious mystery of the unity and diversity reveals its true magnitude when we situate the religious universes of discourse into the intriguing horizon of the evolution of humanity on this planet and, beyond Earth, the immensity of universe itself. These are not unrelated expansions. In Whitehead's organismic philosophy, both the ecological and the interstellar horizon for determining the place of humanity in the cosmos and on Earth intersect intensely.[2] As organisms are porous, but stabilized forms of processes of events, they have their becoming and they are interrelated. Every organism is constituted by other organisms, internally or externally, micro- or macrocosmically, ecologically or universally, and is, simultaneously, effecting other organisms. Every existent being is some kind of organism in becoming and in interconnection with others. Every event constitutes itself through temporal relationships to past organisms from which it gathers itself and to the evolution of which it, in its self-transcending future, adds itself; and no organism persists without spatial differentiations of its member processes and environments that have the patience to let them happen.[3] The cosmos is a nested organization of organisms and environments in which every environment harbors the organisms that it can carry and every environment is but another organism within a wider or deeper environment in which it is embedded and by which it is sustained. Since all organisms are in becoming, so also are all environments (as their difference is only a matter of perspective). And since becoming also means transience, change, decline and perishing, ever-new organisms and environments emerge and disappear in infinite rhythms, oscillations and revolutions that, determined by the mutual immanence of these organisms and environments in their creative and destructive moves in resonance with one another, span the space-time fabric of the cosmos, or *a* cosmos.[4] In fact, since this is an infinite and

---

1. 'Abdu'l-Bahá, *Selections*, #19.
2. Cf. Whitehead, *Symbolism*, 79–83; *Function*, ch. 1; *Process*, part 2, ch. 3; *Adventures*, chs. 8, 13; *Modes*, chs. 6, 8.
3. Cf. Kraus, 63–75, 105–6; Hosinski, ch. 6; Cobb and Griffin, chs. 4, 9; Griffin, *Reenchantment*, chs. 5–6; Faber, *Becoming of God*, Sphere 1; *Poet*, part 2; *Manifold*, chs. 7, 14; *Garden*, ch. 5.
4. Cf. Faber, *Becoming of God*, Exploration 2; *Poet*, §§13–16.

indefinite process, Whitehead does not assume any beginning or end of these revolutions and oscillations (in themselves).[5] Rather, we can either expect a series of cosmic epochs, in themselves relatively consistently interrelated, but different from other cosmic epochs of unimaginable patterns of such an organization, or a multiverse of such relatively independent and diverging cosmoi.[6] Throughout this unimaginable immensity of the infinite multiplicity of worlds, there would still be some kind of connectedness; in fact, several kinds of connectivity: that of creative becoming of one from the other[7]; that of the potentials for becoming something[8]; that of a medium of intercommunication of all multiplicities, formless, but pervading like Plato's *khora*[9]; and God, the Primordial Nature, harboring all possibilities and possible worlds,[10] and the Consequent Nature, perceiving, receiving, connecting and transforming all in all (note how the polycentric process model of ultimate reality, mentioned earlier, springs from this manifold of unities).[11] Since these modes of unity and unifications are themselves not a mere plurality (a set of independent entities), but a mutually immanent moving whole of multiplicities,[12] we find ourselves again in the metaphysical proximity to the coextensiveness of unity and multiplicity on the basis of which the question of religious truth can coherently be stated.

Yet we would be wrong if we were to assume that these infinities, complexities and movements of universal unification of sheer unfathomable comic magnitude have not been registered by the human mind since humanity records the history of ideas. In fact, many ancient worldviews and their religious counterparts or homes have had in general a much grander understanding of the universe than we might think. Ancient Greek philosophy already assumed an infinite universe with many places that would bring forth intelligent beings, and would even understand these many "worlds" not as planets, but as universes[13] locked in a cyclical revolution of becoming and aging, destruction and renewal.[14] Small cosmic schemes were the exception, for instance, in Near Eastern models of an earthy disc, swimming in an ocean and limited by a heavenly barrier with water above, all in the shape of a bell or domed plain—of which the old Hebrew cosmology was part.[15] Eastern cosmic models were counting the ages of universes in immensely large quanta of time, in days and lives of gods, in rhythms of creation and conflagration and in unimaginable spaces over spaces and stacked realms over realms.[16] Following an ancient principle of plenitude, this trend was generally sustained until modern times.[17]

---

5. Cf. Whitehead, *Process*, 111; Faber, *Poet*, §35.
6. Cf. Whitehead, *Process*, 35, 84; Faber, *Manifold*, ch. 7.
7. Cf. Whitehead, *Process*, 21.
8. Cf. Whitehead, *Science*, ch. 10.
9. Cf. Whitehead, *Adventures*, 134.
10. Cf. Whitehead, *Process*, 31–32.
11. Cf. Whitehead, *Religion*, 88–93, 98; *Process*, 342–46.
12. Cf. Whitehead, *Religion*, 163; *Process*, 348; *Adventures*, 294–96.
13. Cf. Genta, 5.
14. Cf. Dick, *Plurality*; Kisak; Genta, ch. 1.
15. Cf. Keel, ch. 1.
16. Cf. Sadakata and Nakamura; Dalela, chs. 1, 5.
17. Cf. Weintraub, ch. 1.

While the orthodox Christian universe of the medieval west, having inheriting the small-universe thesis with its linear time frame and a small dome of apocalyptic time, as it were, broke on the Copernican turn to heliocentrism, the philosophical and scientific considerations even during medieval times generally supported large-universe scenarios with boundless worlds and a plenitude of living being as prodigious as planets.[18]

Paradoxically, it was only at the beginning of the twentieth century's physical revolution, set in motion with Einstein's Relativity Theory, that, only for a cosmic blink of an eye, the world seemed (with early big bang theories and a supposedly static universe) to have become smaller again[19] only to explode into even vaster domains later in the same century (with the discovery of an expanding cosmos) with multiverse scenarios to explain the physical facts of and beyond the observable expanding universe.[20] That right before these happenings the ancient and sustained vision of a universe beaming with life seems to have transformed into a graveyard of dead matter, only leaving behind lonely humanity on this forsaken planet, was due to the materialistic implications of the scientific revolution of the past centuries before the discoveries of the new physics.[21] But the counterintuitive implications of the new physics, experimentally widely tested, regained not only traction, but demonstrated the limited value of the old philosophical pattern of materialism from which it sprung. Now, the interrelationality of physical fields renders the substantialism of independent entities obsolete; chaotic processes again leave space for the unprecedented and incomputable; quantum indeterminacy evokes a fresh admittance of creativity and freedom on the most basic levels of physical processes; and observer- and mind-involved theories of physical existence reverse the materialist reductions to a mindless sea of matter.[22] Whitehead was part of this physical revolution process,[23] laying a new metaphysical basis for an intriguing universe beyond the senseless spaces of scientific materialism by welcoming the paradoxes of mind and matter as expressions of the very fabric of the universe itself.[24]

While the discovery of human evolution challenged religious worldviews (especially of the Abrahamic variant) immensely and added another blow to human exceptionalism,[25] it also invigorated, in connection with the other exiting developments, a new effort finding companionship for humanity in the deep expanse transcending Earth.[26] Today, the explorations of the grand mysteries of this vast surrounding space promises again to reveal a living universe, which, more likely than not, feels like an invitation

---

18. Cf. Weintraub, ch. 7; Duhem; Guthke.
19. Cf. Susskind, ch. 2; Willis, 18–20.
20. Cf. Rubinstein.
21. Cf. Whitehead, *Science*, ch. 6; Ward, *Pascal's Fire*, chs. 7–8; *God*, 8–14; ch. 3.
22. Keller, *Cloud*, ch. 4; Penrose.
23. Cf. Wilber, ed., *Questions*; Nagel, *Mind*.
24. Cf. Penrose et al., *The Large*; Laszlo, *Universe*, parts 1–2; Whitehead, *Science*, chs. 6–8; Faber, "Uniting Earth," 61–62; *Poet*, §§9, 43–44.
25. Cf. Haught, *Deeper Than Darwin*; *God After Darwin*; Cobb, *Back to Darwin*; Keith Ward, *God*, chs. 4, 7.
26. Cf. Dick, ed., *Impact*; *Many Worlds*, part 1; Midgley, *Evolution*.

to a multitude of worlds (or even other universes) to initiate and sustain evolutionary processes of life and mind, and maybe religion, too.[27] Recent scientific projects and discoveries have helped to widen our understanding of the universe as a world-process in which biological organisms might not be the exception, but a built-in convergence of evolutionary possibilities.[28] In such an emergent universe, life and mind might not be strangers, but either the ground for its very becoming or its natural fruit.[29] And with the recent discovery of thousands of planets in habitable zones for life (as we know and understand it, not counting other, as of yet unconsidered alternative forms in which life could have developed),[30] exobiology has become a respectable branch of science.[31] Philosophical discussions have reemerged (or continued) that reconsider human evolution in new contexts: of xenology and a multiverse; of multiple evolutions in our universe; of the import of mind in cosmic processes and developments; of the meaning of a multiplicity of intelligent, if not mindful, beings besides humanity; and of maybe even further advanced civilizations,[32] not only in a material sense, such as space-faring species, but (hopefully) in spiritual maturity with penetrating insights in the mysteries of existence.[33]

What would it mean in such an unlimited and evolutionary universe to be religious? How do religions fit, and see themselves fitting, into this cosmic vastness? Many parochial stances and idiosyncrasies of diverse religions will seem too small, too light, too inconsiderate, too static, too prone to human or tribal exceptionalism to be perpetuated in this new horizon. From this vast interstellar and cosmic perspective, much incommensurability between religions could, in this paradigm, diminish to quaint quirks typical for fragile beings such as us.[34] Maybe we will learn to see them as heartfelt asperity by which we recognize the unique beauty of a loved one rather than as naked truths over which it would be worth fighting. Many claims pertaining to religious rightness will be set into perspective, either fall into oblivion or will only be retained in knowledge of

---

27. Cf. Leslie, *Universes*, chs. 4–5; Davies, *Goldilocks Enigma*, chs. 7–9.
28. Cf. Convey Morris, *Solution*; Dick, *Many Worlds*, part 2.
29. Cf. Laszlo, *Science*, chs. 4–6.
30. Cf. Willis, ch. 8; Weintraub, chs. 2–3.
31. Cf. Catling; Vakoch; Genta, ch. 3.
32. Cf. Ashkenazi, passim. While the thesis of biological convergence may be controversial (or even, if accepted, not necessarily implying the inevitability of the development of intelligent life in other regions of the universe), the sociological and psychological implications of certain constraints of the development of intelligence from evolutionary principles (Darwinian or otherwise) seem to allow a stronger theory of convergence regarding similarities of nurturing, communication, memory, learning, social roles and the like (chs. 3–5), but also to limit the variety of potential appearances of civilizations (chs. 9–10).
33. Cf. Genta, chs. 4–5; Wilkinson, ch. 5; Dick, *Biological Universe*; Crow.
34. Iconically, such meditations on earthly antagonisms as irrelevant from a cosmic viewpoint have been heightened ever since humans were able to see the planet Earth from space: these blue Earth photographs have inspired spiritual unity. Recent pictures released by NASA show Earth and Moon a few inches apart, or Earth as a dot in space from the perspective of Mars or through Saturn's rings, or even further away from Voyager I, almost indistinguishable from the special darkness enveloping the whole scene of our local cosmic environment.

their limited value. There is any number of doctrines and stances that in this new world-horizon will not survive without serious changes to their core or only under immediately felt embarrassment. The living cosmos will become the scientific and philosophical criterion for the survival of religious beliefs, the restructuring of identities and a new hermeneutic of religious experience. While outmoded belief-systems can resist the new realms of experience, experimentation and reason only by conspiracy and closure in their own little universe (after all, the Earth could still be flat), the resistance against their mutual relativity with a wider world of humanity, our Earth and beyond, is, of course, self-destructive; they will run themselves down and follow the way of all decaying matters into dissolution.

Even more than in a merely earthly context, the contingencies of religious existence, worldviews and organizations will be felt as irrevocably more limiting from the perspective of this new interstellar consciousness. Christianity, for instance, may ask itself how it can justify central points of its orthodox doctrines, such as creation, sin, Incarnation and eschatology.[35] How can one assume one and only one Incarnation, not only in light of the spatiotemporal landscape of this Earth (as in this case the unity of humanity could still be assumed as its effective and affected sphere), but among a vast multiplicity of non-human spiritual species, without immediately to be caught in devastating conundrums? How can the sin of humanity be effective throughout the cosmos? Did Christ come to the only species that sinned? But if the rest of the cosmos is free from sin, this would upset one of the most cherished Christian doctrines, namely, that of original sin without which the whole salvation story would dramatically change its outlook. Can assuming more than one Incarnation solve this problem? But in what sense: in the sense that all cosmic spiritual species have sinned independently; or, if they haven't, wouldn't the meaning of Incarnation differ from answering sin? Why, if either was the case, does Incarnation not also happen among different cultures on Earth? Conversely, if we may assume many Incarnations, should we really imagine that God incarnates on every planet just in order to die for our misgivings? And how would all of these Incarnations among different species conceptually still be part of the one Trinity? Further, in an infinite multiverse, would we not be hard-pressed not to ask whether we even need God to articulate the origin of creation? And, given the indefinite world-process, can anything resembling linear Christian eschatology (with its originally small-universe linearity view) justifiably survive, as it poses the destruction of this whole universe for a new heaven and a new Earth? And how would such a crude global intervention not destroy the very relationality among creatures that was needed to make a case for original sin and salvation through one death, in the first place? Several sophisticated theological responses—of astro-, cosmo- or exotheology—were crafted around these problems[36]; yet none of them will escape the necessity to challenge the limitation of truth to one's own religion (which should have never been the case, in the first place, given the constitution of Christianity

---

35. Cf. Kraay, chs. 11–12; Weintraub, chs. 8–14; Genta, ch. 30–36; Kisak, chs. 12–13; Vakoch, ch. 18; Wilkinson, *Science*, chs. 9–10.
36. Cf. O'Meara, *Universes*, chs. 3–4, 6–8; T. Peters, *Science*, ch. 6; Genta, 36–40.

by many movements, among them Judaism and Hellenism), but instead to embrace a universal outlook.[37]

Other axial religions, such as Buddhism, fare better in this new paradigm.[38] Neither does Buddhism assume the existence of a creator god[39] nor imagine a global eschatological disaster (as if time was small and linear). Buddhism makes mutual relationality (*pratitya-samutpada*) the very basis of all existence (*samsara*). It shares with Vedic religions the cyclical becoming and perishing of universes and their infinity. It assumes infinitely many Buddhas, Buddha-fields (mutually dependent connectivity) and Buddha-worlds (universes). It knows of the moral character of samsaric relationships, that is, the interference between physics and metaphysics, matter and mind, in the constitution of the universe. Although, as in all axial religions, Buddhism's salvation is transcendence-oriented (*nirvana*) toward liberation from the universe, at least in its later forms it finds an affirmation of the world-process. Despite being the site of the perpetuation of suffering, our impermanent universe is *also* a Buddha-land, the unfolding of the infinite compassion of Bodhisattvas, and expresses the creative aspect of ultimate Reality.[40] This again was the position that (philosophical) Daoism emphasized from its inception: the creative spontaneity of the infinite world-movement as transformation of harmonies between organic stabilizations, but never states of affairs, and without end.[41]

How can we not expect infinite varieties of spiritual beings to evolve in such a vast and unending process? How can any religion really believe that it is the exception; that its adherents are the only chosen ones, the only ones reaching salvation, while the whole multiverse will be dammed? What meaning would the word "god" even have in such a scenario; and wouldn't it be better to forget such a petty specter? (Even if it were true, we would have to fight it like Sisyphus the judgment of the gods in Albert Camus's drama, simply out of decency.) How can we ever again assume one religion to be right and all others to be wrong? How can we ever again justify any meaningful religious truth claim that is not immediately situated in the necessity of an interstellar religious pluralism? In this vast horizon, a pluralism of pluralisms is inevitable, given that communication between religious species, not of common (genetic) ancestry, may carry a great effort for gaining mutual understanding (biologically, linguistically, culturally, socially,

---

37. Cf. Walker and Wickramasinghe, chs. 5–7; Crow, ch. 9; Dick, ed., *Many Worlds*, part 3: chs. 4–5; *Impact*, chs. 10–11, 14; Genta, ch. 2; Stenger, *God*, ch. 16; Vakoch, ch. 19; *Zygon* 52:2 (2016): 405–13, 480–96.
38. Cf. Kisak, chs. 11, 14–15; Dick, ed., *Impact*, ch. 19; Genta, 26–27.
39. This fact does, nevertheless, not take anything away from the complicated transreligious transference of categories either of theistic or non-theistic flavor into or from the Buddhist context, and it does not indicate atheism—as was already demonstrated in Chapter 12; cf. Schmidt-Leukel, *Buddhism*, Introduction; Panikkar, *Silence*, ch. 2; Momen, *Buddhism*, ch. 2; Faber, *Garden*, chs. 6–7.
40. Cf. Weintraub, ch. 17. This is an understanding also shared by the Bahá'í writings in which the higher spiritual realms, such as the Kingdom (*malakut*) as "heaven of justice," are not set apart from the world as external to the series of spiritual realms, but are manifested in the physical world as "heaven of bounty"; cf. Taherzadeh, 59.
41. Cf. Chan, chs. 7, 11, 13, 16.

philosophically) in the first place.⁴² Of course, we cannot exclude a very different scenario when, at first contact, humanity would be confronted with a species that, maybe in algorithmic simplicity, has transcended religion (and maybe philosophy), or would expect a worldwide inclusion of our differences in their worldview, or even would unite humanity against itself with an aggressive exclusivism that disregards any human religious endeavor, or that would (as many earthly princes have done) favor one religion on Earth over all others, or threatens to divide humanity again along the lines of their self-perceived superior truths.

Nor is unity excluded from this multispecies religious pluralism (remember Whitehead's different modes of unification across the universe or multiverse). As long as we assume (given the unity of Reality) that intelligible and spiritual beings will be able to relate and communicate at all without anything more to know right now, we have already granted unity to humanity with the evolution of mind and spirit across the whole of this placeless multiverse without undermining the unimaginable multiplicity its evolution(s) could have produced.⁴³ Yet we cannot expect this multiplicity ever to end or to be overcome by only one comic religion for all potential worlds or even universes. Given the devastating implications or consequences of other form of unification, we will be reminded of, and drawn to, a pluralism of apophatic unity, interrelationality and divergence, a pluralism of pluralisms within an open divine matrix.⁴⁴ With these provisions for a successful transreligious discourse, not exhausted by humanity, but in the hope to find shared resonances in an interstellar consciousness, we would but witness transreligious transfers, transmutations, transformations, creative contrasts and conviviality of unimaginable proportions.

Many religions (on Earth) have developed (or have always already harbored) resources for venturing into this new paradigm so as to be able to embrace it if they so wish.⁴⁵ Generally, the harvesting of cosmic consciousness of religions has taken two directions. In the ancient preaxial and axial belief in spiritual worlds beyond our material existence, elaborated in many complex cosmologies, cosmic consciousness could utilize the mapping of the material worlds unto spiritual ones, engaging the heavenly bodies in the sky as levels of higher heavenly existence.⁴⁶ While in ancient mappings the outer spheres of the space beyond this world signified more perfect layers of movement, themselves embraced by the unmoved divine sphere (as, for instance, in the Aristotelian and many

---

42. Cf. Chiang, 91–145.
43. Cf. Traphagan, ch. 3; Convey Morris, *Life's Solution*, ch. 9; Dick, *Life*, ch. 7; Dick, ed., *Impact*, ch. 6; O'Meara, ch. 1; Wilkinson, *Science*, chs. 3, 7; Willis, *Worlds*, ch. 9.
44. Cf. Faber, *Garden*, ch. 1; *Manifold*, ch. 5, Intermezzo 1.
45. Cf. Weintraub, chs. 6–21.
46. Cf. Crow, *Debate*, 122, chs. 1–3; the exception is Nicolas of Cusa who proposes a "flat" multiplicity of an infinite universe without center and circumference, and infinitely many worlds, only rivaled by Giordano Bruno's similar conception. One example in Bahá'í scriptures, reflecting the Shi'ite audience (Bahá'u'lláh speaking into limited horizons and symbolically), is the mention that traditionally in Islam the ascension of Jesus (after his death on the cross) elevated him to the "fourth heavens" of seven; cf. Bahá'u'lláh, *Iqan*, §98.

neo-platonic cosmological schemes, both philosophical and religious),[47] more modern cosmologies reversed the direction of such mappings and projected the higher beings above in spiritual space onto more advanced beings further away in the physical space.[48] This mutual mapping lays the ground for religions to potentially situate themselves in multiple-world scenarios. Newer religions, whether originating in the east or the west, have, in fact, often made this new paradigm an important part of their cosmology and doctrine: either by believing in the origination of humanity from physical or spiritual space of heavenly or alien beings, or in hoping for a rebirth on other physical or spiritual spheres or planets, or even by becoming involved in the creative production of other and new universes.[49] However, new religious movements of the past centuries are not necessarily subscribing to this universal cosmopolitan shift just by the fact that they arose in the new axial age. Several of these movements have, to the contrary, found their refuge in a complete abandoning of large-universe scenarios—especially in the Abrahamic religious landscape.[50] Yet in the study of the specific resources of axial and new axial religions, we can generally not find any principled aversion against the new paradigmatic interstellar horizon, ready to be activated when evoked by facts and alien encounters.[51] The deeper adventure remains, however, how the religions of this Earth will view their identity and relation to others in this new context if such facts will be established beyond scientific doubt. I will make the wager that only religions with activated interstellar consciousness, mediated through some kind of pluralism of pluralisms and through transreligious communication, will then flourish.[52]

The Bahá'í view is simple: the universe that the Bahá'í writings presuppose and imply is infinite and diversified into infinite worlds.[53] The intricacies of its own view of such

---

47. Cf. Aristotle, *Metaphysics*, 1072b4, 1073b1-1074a13; Hetherington, chs. 1–3.
48. Cf. Hetherington, ch. 8; Crow, *Debate*, parts 2–3; Herrick, *Mythologies*, chs. 3, 9; Genta, *Minds*, ch. 1. A good example of the demythologization of such higher cosmological spheres in the Bahá'í writings is 'Abdu'l-Bahá's explanation of the ascension of Jesus as having spiritual, but not physical meaning since (in accordance with science) the sky is empty space brimming with stars; there is nothing physically to ascend to; cf. 'Abdu'l-Bahá, *Questions*, #23.
49. Cf. Paul; Weintraub, ch. 14.
50. Cf. Weintraub, chs. 12–13.
51. Cf. Weintraub, ch. 21.
52. This wager is only partly depending on the future fact of alien encounter or the actual scientific proof of life in the cosmos other than on Earth. Solving Fermi's paradox is not a necessary condition, but only an imaginary boundary; cf. Wilkinson, *Science*, ch. 7. The reason is that the fact of life and mind on Earth is already an example that does not only imply that they are possible, but actualizations of universal potentials of the cosmic history. There is no rule restraining possibilities to be necessarily only realized once, only contingent reasons of serendipitous coalescence of causes. Whenever such causes or constellations would come together, we can expect such potentials to be realized—again. This is implied in Whitehead's cosmology of multiple worlds (as realization of potentials in constellations), as it is also implied in the birth of every new human being of which we do not expect or fear animals or plants to arise, instead. This is also the argument of 'Abdu'l-Bahá regarding the repetition of cosmic constellations in the actualization of such potentials as life and mind; cf. 'Abdu'l-Bahá, *Questions*, #46; but cf. also *Questions*, ##47, 55; *Promulgation*, #23.
53. Cf. Bahá'u'lláh, *Gleanings*, #79; 'Abdu'l-Bahá, *Questions*, #81; *Promulgation*, #35.

infinite multiplicities lie in the connectivity that this horizon releases when the Baháʾí writings address the seemingly paradoxical diversities between religious traditions from the perspective of their mutual immanence.[54] The Baháʾí worldview fuses the linear historical movement of the Abrahamic religions with the cyclical becoming and perishing of universes of the Dharmic traditions: its universe is large scale, but values the unique events of history.[55] It shares the quasi-illusory character of spirit-deprived material reality,[56] its transitoriness and suffering through unsatisfactoriness, with both diverse eastern and western traditions,[57] but insists with Daoism on the affirmation by Reality of the spontaneity and creativity of the process (*al-badaʿ*) as its very mystery (*xuan*): infinite creativity transforms salvation from world-negation to affirmation of its becoming and even impermanence.[58] It agrees on a world without beginning and end in time, an eternal creation, with some eastern traditions,[59] but without excluding the notion of a creator:[60] yet the creative mystery cannot be defined by either personal or transpersonal limitations of Reality.[61] It embraces infinite spiritual worlds,[62] but also knows of the infinity of physical worlds:[63] life and mind are convergent.[64] It subscribes to the evolution of the cosmos, on earth and anywhere, as being immersed in divine wisdom as the *movens* of becoming: life and mind are divine processes.[65] With process thought, divine immanence in the Baháʾí universe is the motive force of the whole cosmic movement toward spiritualization,[66] that is, the emergence not only of life and mind, but their transcendence into a process of always-new unifications of ultimately religious nature, an anticipatory future of ever-new and ever-vaster fulfillments of this existential and cosmic drive in life-forms of intensifying and harmonizing realizations of divine attributes, such as

---

54. Cf. ʿAbduʾl-Bahá, *Secrets*, 30; *Promulgation*, ##92, 108, 131.
55. Cf. Baháʾuʾlláh, *Gleanings*, ##26, 31; *Aqdas*, Note 172; ʿAbduʾl-Bahá, *Promulgation*, ##52, 79, 114; *Questions*, ##36, 41; *Selections*, ##4, 33, 129.
56. Cf. Baháʾuʾlláh, *Gleanings*, #153; *Days*, #30:7; ʿAbduʾl-Bahá, *Questions*, #79; *Paris Talks*, ##28, 35; *Promulgation*, #9; *Secrets*, 105–106;
57. Cf. Shoghi Effendi, *Promised Day*, 45; *Baháʾí Prayers*, 57; Baháʾuʾlláh, *Gleanings*, ##35, 114, 147; *Days*, #31:13; 27:38; ʿAbduʾl-Bahá, *Paris Talks*, #35; *Promulgation*, #3; *Selections*, #207.
58. Cf. Kohn, 39–40, 53–54; Saiedi, *Gate*, 207–10; Brown, "Response to Darwinism," 68–76, 81–84; the apophatic-polyphilic movement of renewal is sometimes referred to as "the arc of descent and ascent" in the Baháʾí writings; cf. Saiedi, *Gate*, 104, 163, 243, 296, 310–11; *Logos*, ch. 2; Hamid, *Metaphysics*, 413n123, 540.
59. Cf. Baháʾuʾlláh, *Gleanings*, ##26–27, 88; *Tabernacle*, #2:49; ʿAbduʾl-Bahá, *Questions*, ##41, 47, 50, 80; *Promulgation*, ##58, 93; V. Brown, "Beginning," 21–40.
60. Cf. Baháʾuʾlláh, *Gleanings*, ##26, 29, 78; *Gems*, #41; ʿAbduʾl-Bahá, *Questions*, ##47, 53, 80; *Paris Talks*, #15; *Promulgation*, #114, 139, *Selections*, #19.
61. Cf. Momen, "Relativism: A Basis," 207–11; Faber, *Garden*, ch. 6.
62. Cf. ʿAbduʾl-Bahá, *Questions*, #81:12; Faber, *Garden*, ch. 5.
63. Cf. ʿAbduʾl-Bahá, *Questions*, #81:13; *Selections*, #21.
64. Cf. ʿAbduʾl-Bahá, in *Baháʾí World Faith*, 367; *Paris Talks*, #15.
65. As creation, that is, any universe, is motivated to evolve toward spirituality (the spiritual being, sometimes named a perfect human being), so are life and mind initially intended to converge in the emergence of such beings; cf. ʿAbduʾl-Bahá, *Paris Talks*, ##20, 29.
66. Cf. Whitehead, *Religion*, 155, 160; ʿAbduʾl-Bahá, *Selections*, 48–49.

compassion and love, justice and peace, freedom and creativity in the physical, personal and social organizations of the universe(s).

In the context of an infinite physical universe within divine wisdom, then, humanity can hardly be the only species expressing its mind in spirituality and religion. If God is the God of the universe (and being of apophatic nature, but infinitely dispersing grace, ever-creative),[67] we must assume that other cosmic sites would also have been set in motion to developing sentience and life, and Reality-consciousness. Aren't mind and spirit, resonating with the mysteries of existence and God/Reality, themselves infinite and unending processes, maybe even motivations for the creative intention?[68] What, in such a context, can religious pluralism and unity of religions mean? 'Abdu'l-Bahá affirms that "there are other worlds than ours which are inhabited by beings capable of knowing God."[69] An immediate implication would be that there were and always will be other religions *besides* the Bahá'í Faith and any *human* religion. Reflecting back on our small Earth, this immediately also strengthens the argument that we cannot just assume one linear line of religions in which one trumps the other (with the older ones remaining in existence only to be supplanted, or newer ones being only a deviation from original truth). Affirming the spiritual evolution at different interstellar places or even different universes, then, allows us to generate a mind-boggling horizon for multireligious conjectures that is far more pluralistic and complex in its movements and flows of spiritual maturation.[70] 'Abdu'l-Bahá leads us in this direction by making the profound statement that the interstellar process of the generation of spiritual beings, even spanning universes,[71] and, hence, some divine manifestation as well as religious consciousness inhabiting this unending process, will be a *multiplicity* of cyclical evolutions and the renewal of cycles if the extant ones have worn themselves out. While spiritual evolution, that is, the evolution of spiritual beings, will differ in infinite cycles of existence, the aim of the creative and theophanic nature of this evolutionary process would remain the same: the generation of spiritual beings.[72]

> Briefly, there were many universal cycles preceding this one in which we are living. They were consummated, completed and their traces obliterated. The divine and creative purpose in

---

67. Cf. Bahá'u'lláh, *Gleanings*, #19; *Aqdas*, ¶129.
68. Cf. Weintraub, chs. 2, 21; Wilkinson, *Science*, chs. 2, 8; Dick, *Worlds*, part 3; Guthke, ch. 5; Medina, ch. 2.
69. Shoghi Effendi, *Light*, 79.
70. Cf. Lewels; Dick, *Worlds*, part 3.
71. Cf. Faber, *Manifold*, ch. 7; *Becoming of God*, Exploration 6; *Garden*, ch. 5:4. Also implied in this approach is the interesting fact that while in current interdisciplinary discourse between science and religion and with respect of an atheistic approach the multiverse theory is situated in opposition to the thesis of the existence of God—cf. Davies, Goldilocks *Enigma*, chs. 8–9; Kraay, chs. 6–8; Stenger, *God*, chs. 15–16—in 'Abdu'l-Bahá's rendering, however, both multiverse and infinite creative divinity are not only compatible, but inherently connected; 'Abdu'l-Bahá, *Promulgation*, #93.
72. Cf. 'Abdu'l-Bahá, *Questions*, 50:1–5, 64:6; *Paris Talks*, 39; Taylor, chs. 4–5; Troxel, "Extraterrestrial Life"; "Intelligent Life."

them was the evolution of spiritual man, just as it is in this cycle. The circle of existence is the same circle; it returns. The tree of life has ever borne the same heavenly fruit.[73]

There is this interstellar expectation in the Bahá'í writings, fundamentally transforming the most basic assumptions of the meaning of religion(s). Now, the cosmic coextensiveness of divine unison and pluralism of pluralisms emerges as a new baseline for religious existence and truth. This coextensiveness of processual unity and polyphilic multiplicity is even more heightened by the synergy between process thought and Bahá'í account of the universal process as unending and cyclical, but nevertheless directed and historical, that is, without losing the relevance of achievements within these cycles by their cyclical renewal, as this unending process of creative processes evolving life, mind and consciousness of ultimate Reality/God, which is connoted with the essence of religiosity, is not assuming any end-state of fulfillment of, or finality of the process as such to, the infinite cocreativity of divine and mundane becoming—unlike, for instance, in Teilhard de Chardin's expectation of an omega state of convergence to fulfilled cosmic (and religious) unity.[74] While in all of these schemes the in-sistence of God remains in process, for which God is not a past cause, but the attractor from and to a divine future (or in the future) through the cosmic process of which religions become an essential part in fulfilling its spiritual aim,[75] 'Abdu'l-Bahá and Whitehead also concur on "its" infinite and indefinite creative manifestation that does not allow ever final unity to overrule the polyphilic multiplicity of realizations.[76]

Yet implicit in this last quotation, another factor appears equally as important: that different unique experiences of ultimate Reality may express less variations of the same pattern of life or consciousness, but rather unique *forms* of consciousness, only related to one another by happenstances of encounters. In an interstellar context, other spiritual beings would not necessarily even exhibit the same *kind* of consciousness, as they will have developed in very different physical and organic contexts. So, mutually enriching transreligious conviviality will have to bridge these divergent minds.[77]

> The earth has its inhabitants [...] then how is it possible to conceive that these stupendous stellar bodies are not inhabited? Verily, they are peopled, but let it be known that the dwellers accord with the elements of their respective spheres. These living beings do not have states

---

73. 'Abdu'l-Bahá, *Promulgation*, #79.
74. While the concept of a cosmic story of convergence mediated through Teilhard de Chardin, as told by Haught (*Story*, chs. 1–3), agrees with Whitehead on the future of the reality of (cosmic-spiritual) unity, it diverges at this point from the implications of fulfillment if it would be understood as final, which again seems to be an implication of the Christian scheme underlying Teilhard and diverse later Christian theological conceptualizations of eschatological perfection such as that of Moltmann and Pannenberg: cf. Faber, *Poet*, 75–76; *Manifold*, ch. 13; "Adven/ure," 91–112; "Zeitumkehr," 180–205.
75. Cf. Faber, *Poet*, §§35, 39; Bahá'u'lláh, *Prayers*, #165; 'Abdu'l-Bahá, *Paris Talks*, #36; *Questions*, #52.
76. Cf. 'Abdu'l-Bahá, *Promulgation*, ##58, 79; Whitehead, *Process*, 113, 351; *Religion*, 160; Faber, *God as Poet*, §§39–40.
77. Cf. Dick, *Life*, chs. 10-12 18; Willis, chs. 9–10.

of consciousness like unto those who live on the surface of this globe: the power of adaptation and environment moulds their bodies and states of consciousness, just as our bodies and minds are suited to our planet.[78]

There is an expectation of a radical pluralism of consciousness and divergent minds in the Bahá'í writings.[79] And it is this aspect of interstellar religious pluralism that leads us, finally, into the other area of transreligious expansion we must not forget here: the web of evolutionary processes eventually issuing in hominization and the ecological integrity of humanity on this planet Earth.[80] One might think of the divergent consciousness of different kinds of human beings on Earth, such as that of the now lost "other" human branches like the Neanderthals who were religious beings of a different kind.[81] Imagine religious pluralism if more than one kind of humanity had survived today! In any case, the Bahá'í writings do not even assume *human* sameness, much less religious sameness, for transreligious conviviality to arise; yet all of the "fruits of the human tree are exquisite."[82] On the other end of the spectrum, we could also project into the future that, on the tree of spiritual beings on Earth, current humanity might just be the beginning.[83] Here, religious diversity becomes a matter of the manifold of *kinds* of spiritual beings, and their unity remains a mystery of ultimate divine self-communication in which infinitely different ways of the self-presentation of Reality does not hinder diverse vast modes of unity within a divine harmonics of existence.[84]

What is more, this interaction between consciousness and organic embeddedness, just as explained by 'Abdu'l-Bahá, directs our intention also toward evolutionary becoming and ecological embeddedness of any form of mind and spiritual existence in this cosmos and on this world. This intense web of becoming might suggest for other beings on Earth to evolve in the same mold. We know today as a scientific fact of the emerging traits of mental characteristics in certain mammals and even cephalopods, like squid, all of which have been proven to develop highly perceptive and creative forms of consciousness.[85] Without being able to get into any examination of this organic evolutionary inherence of the whole Earth underpinning the human development into spiritual beings, the current discussions on evolutionary convergences might give us a hint that other beings might develop to become conscious and spiritual in the evolutionary matrix of this Earth.[86] The consideration of evolutionary convergence suggests that in any given evolutionary space only certain solutions are sustainable and that the emergence of life and mind is

---

78. 'Abdu'l-Bahá, *Philosophy*, 114–15.
79. For an interesting spectral analysis of infinitely different states of mind of humanity, humanities (other extinct branches of humanity) and animals, corroborating this assumption, cf. Harari, 358–64.
80. Cf. McFague, chs. 2, 4–5.
81. Cf. van Huyssteen.
82. Bahá'u'lláh, *Tablets* (#17), 257.
83. Cf. Dyson, 9; Herrick, *Mythologies*, chs. 5–6.
84. Cf. Bahá'u'lláh, *Gleanings*, #87.
85. Cf. Godfrey-Smith; de Waal, 38–54; Harari, *Homo Deus*, ch. 3.
86. Cf. Conway Morris, *Runes*; 'Abdu'l-Bahá, *Promulgation*, ##81, 99, 123; *Questions*, #47.

in such a sweet spot in the matrix of potential developments. In other words, there is an evolutionary trend toward mind and consciousness.[87] In similar manner, 'Abdu'l-Bahá, embracing one of Rumi's poetic statements,[88] ponders:

> Let us suppose that the human anatomy was primordially different from its present form, that it was gradually transformed from one stage to another until it attained its present likeness, that at one time it was similar to a fish, later an invertebrate and finally human.[89]

'Abdu'l-Bahá's suggestion regarding the appearance of humanity, here, seems to be that the emergence of consciousness and conscience, mind and spirit, is a trend of evolution itself, developing through all earthly evolutionary phases. While it was sometimes misinterpreted to insinuate a parallel evolution,[90] in light of evolutionary convergence this image could, instead, be understood in a different, exciting manner: not as matter of division and opposition between humanity and the rest of evolution on this planet,[91] but as the evolutionary convergence of the rise of spiritual beings at different speeds and in different waves.[92] This would not only resonate with the broad signification of "humanity" with spiritual beings of other worlds and cycles of existence, as just indicated, but also with the complexity of the many speeds and stations we have already encountered as inherent to the "evolution" of and within spiritual realms as understood by the Bahá'í writings.[93]

On the most elementary level, again, we would need to take into account the natural "religiosity" of all existent beings, even elementary particles (as funny as it may sound),[94]

---

87. Cf. Hatcher, *Connections*, chs. 6–10. For the general evolutionary perspective of the development of intelligence independent from Earth, but related to the potential of several such developments, as well as the threshold of symbolism and language for the emerging "identity" of mentality and spiritual beings, human or not: cf. Ashkenazi, chs. 5–6; van Huyssteen, *Alone*, chs. 2–3, 5.
88. Cf. Jalal ad-Din Rumi, *Mathnavi*, verses 3637–46; Arasteh, ch. 3.
89. Cf. 'Abdu'l-Bahá, *Promulgation*, #111.
90. The foreword to the new official translation of 'Abdu'l-Bahá's *Some Answered Questions* specifically denies this view as a viable option for understanding 'Abdu'l-Bahá's comments on human evolution, based on the fundamental principle of the harmony of science and religion; cf. 'Abdu'l-Bahá, *Questions*, xiv.
91. Cf. K. Brown, 1–134; Mehanian and Friberg, 55–93.
92. Cf. 'Abdu'l-Bahá, *Questions*, ##47, 50:1–5. This assumption rests on the view that the same evolution of a material structure will yield spiritual beings. As the emergence of mind is, therefore, enshrined in the basic laws of nature (cf. 'Abdu'l-Bahá, *Questions*, #52) and develops through the emergence of organisms (the animal realm), a multiplicity of such evolutions at different speeds on Earth is, therefore, as possible as the assumption that it develops in different cosmic environments, which is confirmed by the Bahá'í writings; cf. Friberg, 68–70, 72–73.
93. Cf. Bahá'u'lláh, *Iqan*, §§ 266, 272; 'Abdu'l-Bahá, *Promulgation*, ##58, 74, 111; *Questions*, #47; Laszlo, *Science*, ch. 6; Faber, *Manifold*, ch. 7.
94. Cf. Bahá'u'lláh, *Gleanings*, #26; 'Abdu'l-Bahá, *'Abdu'l-Bahá in London*, 95. For process theology, God is present in all events and organisms as their "beginning" from possibility (Primordial Nature) and in God's perception of their actualization (Consequent Nature) as the realization of (ever more) divine potentials; cf. Faber, *Poet*, parts 2–3; *Becoming of God*, Explorations 1–2; Cobb and Griffin, chs. 2, 4.

as in all of them the divine attributes are revealed as their very nature,[95] and as it is these attributes that become the generating agents of life and consciousness, and, thereby, transform themselves into conscientious virtues as well.[96] The ecological implications are glaringly obvious: where divine attributes become virtues, we become responsible for their unfolding, friends and shepherds, healers and mentors of their well-being.[97] While many axial religions have now recovered the ecological situatedness of humanity,[98] and while preaxial religions with their experience of divinity through the gifts of nature seem now much closer to these insights, it is the great potential for new axial consciousness to make these connections a treasure lost and found (this synthesis was already mentioned as paradigmatic for the new axial consciousness). And such considerations are all the more central to the Bahá'í revelation as the divine dimension of all Manifestations, the divine Mind or Will or Spirit, is the very root of the tree of evolution[99]; it permeates everything in such a way that it is the very basis from which the ecological integrity of the Earth evolves.[100]

This also resonates well with Whitehead's "natural religiosity" of all existents.[101] As all events, which constitute and harbor the organization of organisms and environments, are in their inception (their initiation or initial aim) not only defined by their past that they synthesize, but by the space of possibilities by which they can more or less repeat or change their integrity into new directions, it is the inherent divine gift of these potentials from which they arise and are lured to new and more delicate self-realizations.[102] This is all the more the case with evolved organisms in which such divine infusions begin to manifest the signs of life and mind, of new degrees of freedom and horizons of perception, understanding and insight.[103] While such a spiritual nature was always enfolded in the whole process and all of its happenings, as the sensitivity of such beings begins to expand beyond the confines of their immediate organisms and environments to deep perceptions of universal realities, they gain the ability to embody cosmic connectivity, to evermore evolve into mirrors of the divine Spirit (Primordial Nature)[104] of which, in a process understanding, Manifestations of God/Reality are the universal evolutionary

---

95. Cf. Bahá'u'lláh, *Gleanings*, #90; *Prayers*, #178; 'Abdu'l-Bahá, *Promulgation*, #96; *Selections*, #19.
96. Cf. Bahá'u'lláh, *Gleanings*, #82.
97. Cf. Daene-Drummond, *Primer*, ch. 1; McDaniel, *God*.
98. Cf. Tucker and Grimm, passim; Kinsley; Bauman, Bohannon and O'Brian.
99. Bahá'u'lláh understands the Manifestation as the root of the whole tree of life, not only of humanity, and not only of certain religious adherents; cf. Bahá'u'lláh and 'Abdu'l-Bahá, in *Bahá'í World Faith*, 364.
100. Cf. White, 96–112.
101. Cf. Faber, *Poet*, part 3. Whitehead, *Religion*, 105; *Adventures*, 198, 253; *Process*, 67: The "initial phase" of every event "is a direct derivate from God's primordial nature. In this function, as in every other, God is the organ of novelty, aiming at intensification."
102. Cf. Whitehead, *Process*, 244; *Adventures*, 210, 251, 275.
103. Cf. Whitehead, *Process*, 104–5; *Adventures*, 277; Faber, *Becoming of God*, Exploration 3; Hosinski, ch. 6.
104. Cf. Faber, *Poet*, §§38–39. Regarding the creativity of the cosmos in the Bahá'í writings, cf. R. Johnson, 29–60.

motors and ecological fields of integrity,[105] but themselves also the divine actualization of such universal connectivity and creativity "in person."[106]

In the expanded interstellar, evolutionary and ecological horizons, religious pluralism and the unity of religions find truly their nature as inherently *transreligious* processes in all of the four meanings of "transreligious" (as stated earlier): as "transcendence" of religion in a human and transhuman sense, embracing divergent minds and unimaginable evolutions of spiritual beings and their religious expressions in other cosmic contexts; as "transition" of religion into unprecedented encounters by which earthly evolutionary and interstellar developments are always beyond the pale of our limited human imagination, converging to new events in which all that religion could mean might become new; as "transformation" between religions in the interaction of a multiplicity of forms of religions (preaxial, axial, new axial and now evolutionary and interstellar) that can never be reduced to one or the same; and as "transcendence within" by which in the depth of the particularity of one's own conceptual and spiritual field a divine matrix breaks through that spans the vastness of universes and emerges as the true resource for mutual encounters of uniqueness and surprise, of strangeness and difference, but in divine unison against antagonistic closures.[107] One can, at this point, at least legitimately ask: Can anything less than a polyphilic pluralism cover these facts and developments without reducing or ignoring them? And if we embrace the Bahá'í insistence on the coextensiveness of horizontal and vertical pluralism, I ask: Can we expect anything less than a transreligious discourse to uncover this infinite process of religiosity in all existence and the indefinite cycles of ever-new convergences of evolution to spiritual beings, namely, to be the expressions of the universality of ultimate Reality without reinstating parochial limitation and petty exceptionalism?

---

105. Manifestations are the all-permeating "universal power" or spiritual force of creative advance; cf. 'Abdu'l-Bahá, *Selections*, #21.
106. Cf. Faber, *Poet*, § 38; *Becoming of God*, Sphere 3 and Exploration 16. John Cobb explores this connection, infusion and motive force of the Primordial Nature in the processes of cosmic harmonization and complexification within the Christian paradigm with the series of equations of the Primordial Nature (all possible worlds in divine valuation) with the Logos (potentiality as related to the world) and the Logos with Christ (as lure toward harmonization and intensity in the world) and Christ with Jesus, as concrete human manifestation of this divine process of creative transformation; cf. Cobb, *Christ*, ch. 4. Yet there is no inherent reason either in Whitehead's or in Cobb's work why this last identification should be exclusive; cf. Whitehead, *Religion*, 18–20.
107. Cf. Faber, "Ecotheology," 75–115; "Theopoetic Justice," 160–78; "Intermezzo," 212–38; *Manifold*, ch. 14.

Chapter Fourteen

THE FUTURE OF RELIGIONS

The East and West may hold each other's hands and become as lovers. Then will [humanity] be as one nation, one race and kind—as waves of one ocean. Although these waves may differ in form and shape, they are waves of the same sea.[1]

—'Abdu'l-Bahá

In light of the cosmic magnitude and ecological depth of the question of religious unity and religious pluralism, we may ask anew and in new form: In what sense will the future of religions be transreligious, *if* there will be either religion in the future of humanity, or humanity as such, as it will (have to) constitute a society of peace in a world of becoming or be doomed to fade into the evolutionary sinks of becoming? In the context developed in this book, this question of "transreligiosity" can now be specified in the following form: In what sense, given the Bahá'í synthesis of the mystery of diversity and unity, the polyphilic pluralism and the presupposition of a transreligious future of religion(s) to be a matter of "survival"[2] of either religion or humanity, does the horizontal pluralistic axis, the vastness of the multiplicity of religious appearances, point toward novelty, freshness and renewal of religion, thereby integrating with the vertical pluralistic axis, as the infinite spiritual development in *one* universal coextensive horizon? And in what sense (given a Bahá'í and process vision of such an integration proposed in this book) does this universal hermeneutic speak to the problem of the overcoming of religious strife and oppositional antagonisms, as the active impulse underlying religious pluralism and unification?[3] In other words, I ask: What, in light of our considerations, may be the (kinds of) "transreligious" future(s) of religion(s)—maybe even beyond humanity and not only on Earth?[4]

Whitehead had asked this question in similar awareness of the cosmic context of the religiosity of all existence (as just mentioned in the previous chapter),[5] and he answered with the necessity of, and surprising hope in, religion to become (or remain) the basis for more divergent views with regard to the concrete forms this future might take.[6] On

---

1. 'Abdu'l-Bahá, *Promulgation*, #20.
2. In using the concept of "survival," one might not only think of questions of being or nonbeing in a Shakespearian manner, but rather of *sur vivre* in a Derridean manner: living *more* or more *intense*, which would be Whitehead's understanding: to live always means to seek more life, more intensity, the better life; cf. Whitehead, *Function*, 8.
3. Cf. Bahá'u'lláh, *Iqan*, §267; Andrews, chs. 1–3.
4. Cf. Dick, "Cosmotheology," 191–210.
5. Cf. Whitehead, *Process*, 31–32, 207; *Religion*, 94, 98, 155–156; *Adventures*, 198.
6. Cf. Faber and Slabodsky, passim.

the one hand, Whitehead recognizes that because of the "great social ideal for religion [...] it should be the common basis for the unity of civilization" such that it is precisely religion that alone "justifies its insight beyond the transient clash of brute forces."[7] This hope at least potentially enables spiritual beings the overcoming of the antagonistic outlook of the worldviews of the past that might just be a remainder of earlier evolutionary strategies of survival, now obsolete.[8] Whitehead reprimands diverse religious discourses for not recognizing (or developing) the essential link of the inherent (religious) evolution of humanity with non-antagonistic mutuality, and he finds support for this assumption in the philosophical analysis of a divine creative intention to reach such a spiritual peace.[9] Beyond mechanisms of evolutionary competition and aggression, religion(s) of the future will (have to) be the very act of acknowledging the true nature of Reality as creative emanation infusing itself (its Self) into, and, with the emergence of spiritual beings, inherently aiming at, spiritual responses endorsing, embracing and exhibiting coinherence based on coinhabitation.[10] On the other hand, Whitehead finds, enshrined in religious consciousness, the very hope of a new life that is saturated with these implications of the universal depths of religious existence such that it can reconcile itself with the impermanence of an indefinite process of becoming that this "satisfaction" in any given present (as the presence of Reality in a given religion) might assume.[11] In one of the most beautiful statements on the "essence" of religion ever written, Whitehead states:

> Religion is the vision of something which stands beyond, behind, and within, the passing flux of immediate things; something which is real, and yet waiting to be realized; something which is a remote possibility, and yet the greatest of present facts; something that gives meaning to all that passes, and yet eludes apprehension; something whose possession is the final good, and yet is beyond all reach; something which is the ultimate ideal, and the hopeless quest.[12]

With this dynamic at the heart of religiosity, that is, its hope for a spiritual future far beyond our current state of unity and diversity, but also in the awareness never to reach a final state of theophany in which the mystery of unity would supplant the mystery of diversity,[13] we are thrown into an openness that allows for different future scenarios to be

---

7. Whitehead, *Adventures*, 172.
8. Cf. Faber, "Religion," passim; "Process," passim.
9. Cf. Whitehead, *Adventures*, 265–69.
10. Although the terminology is entirely mine, this is what Whitehead is suggesting; cf. Whitehead, *Science*, 111, 204–5; *Religion*, 98–99.
11. Cf. Whitehead, *Adventures*, ch. 15; Faber, *Manifold*, ch. 10. For the explication of this thought with a mystagogy of becoming and perishing, cf. Faber, *Manifold*, ch. 10.
12. Whitehead, *Adventures*, 191–92.
13. This "in/finite becoming," which does never allow the foreclosure of multiplicity for reduction to oneness, is enshrined in the apophatic-polyphilic cycle of love, as it always presupposes infinite becoming not only of beings, but of worlds and universes, an infinite process in which spirituality must mean to always render any finality illusory. That this has immense consequences for any eschatological "satisfaction" was already the theme of Chapter 13; cf. Faber, "God's Advent/ure," 91–112; *Manifold*, 135–41; *Becoming of God*, Explorations 9, 14–15;

imagined.[14] Yet all of these scenarios will be based on this insight and hypothesis: that the future of religion will be *transreligious* or there will not be a *religious* future of religions.[15] This is a consequence of the apophatic-polyphilic pluralism and the resonances and feedback loops of the always moving intersections of the vertical and horizontal pluralistic landscape of religious formations hitherto proposed and explored.

As a first scenario, it is possible to imagine a future state of religions in the prospect of a unified humanity—which has not only survived all modes of war and strife, but also found to some kind of strong mutual immanence of all spiritual paths—that would finally issue into only "one" religion as the expression of the most advanced universal consciousness of humanity on Earth—maybe even evoked by the encounter with other spiritual beings in the vast cosmic expanse.[16] Several Bahá'í authors not only dream of this outcome, but view the Bahá'í Faith as the very inauguration, if not even the very form, of this unity of the one religion of the future[17]—although they generally agree that the Bahá'í writings (and their authoritative interpretations) hesitate to make any more concrete predictions available that would lift the cloud of future possibilities ever more

---

Garden, ch. 6:1; Whitehead, *Process*, 111. It is this shift from any simple apocalyptic expectation of the "meeting with God" (*liqa' Allah*), as in Matthew 24 and Quran 33:44, to that of a process of meeting God in the coming of a new Manifestation that is the central concern of Bahá'u'lláh's *Kitab-i Iqan*; cf. Buck, *Symbol*, ch. 2; Momen, "Apocalyptic Thinking," 243–70.

14. Neither can any actual realization of possibilities exhaust all states of harmony and intensity, nor can an infinite valuation of all potentials, which is the Primordial Nature of God, ever exhaust itself; cf. Whitehead, *Process*, 31–32; *Religion*, 163. This resonates with Bahá'u'lláh's foundational conviction that the mercy and grace of God, that is, God's creative impulse, is likewise infinite and unending, ever newly emanating and always manifesting fresh possibilities for spiritual realization; cf. Bahá'u'lláh, *Gleanings*, ##13, 19, 26; 'Abdu'l-Bahá, *Questions*, #82; *Promulgation*, #93.

15. A "non-religious" future of religions would either be one in which religion is acknowledged as an artifact of the past (that it can be reduced to material, social or cultural functions), or one in which it will have to be abandoned because of the unrelenting preoccupation with the inherent violence of particularistic claims. That the far future in terms of millions of years should always be seen under the imperative of change and substantive transformation we can virtually say nothing about is implied by K. Rose (*Pluralism*, 9–10, 25–26). Yet that there may remain potential restraints on social developments in general, not only on Earth, that would indicate *convergences* to the contrary and, hence, unexpected resonances of such transformations with regards to religious expressions and conceptualities, apophatic and polyphilic insights, is indicated by Ashkenazi (chs. 3–5). This would also be cohering with the longtime expectations of the development of the "unity" of humanity and its religious expressions in the Bahá'í writings; Shoghi Effendi, *World Order* (Dispensation of Bahá'u'lláh), on account of 'Abdu'l-Bahá, speaks of 500,000 years.

16. Cf. Ferrer, "Future," 14–15.

17. Cf. Esslemont, ch. 8. This kind of "inclusivism" was already mentioned earlier; cf. Chapters 2, 7. I add here that, in clear differentiation from simplified "organizational" oneness, it would not necessarily be true to understand this move as simply imagining, and issuing into, a final state, but as an image building on permanent and ongoing multireligious conversation around the "eternal verities" to be found in all religions—much like in the perennialist view—and self-limited by nonfinality; cf. Kluge, "Bahá'í Faith," 37–46.

than providing hints to their most basic structural necessities of integrity (such as the unity of humanity in a scenario of universal peace).[18]

However, by its very nature, this attempt is tantamount to folding the horizontal axis of pluralism into the vertical axis.[19] Even despite any deep fulfillment theology[20] that would speak to this fusion from the perspective of the satisfaction of all religions' intentions in the new mold, this proposal is seriously limited.[21] Not only does this vision assume that unity must issue in some formally unified organization, but it also does not reckon with the possibility that the contingency and finiteness of such a state of affairs may hinder the continuation of this united religious organism right at the moment of the coming of a new religion, revelation or Manifestation, adding a vertical "sundering of the heaven" of this unity. Not only does this vision defy the realistic potential that, as in the past, there will always remain complex and diverse loyalties to many (organized) religious and (unorganized) spiritual paths, based on all kinds of (not yet even imagined) divergent minds and worldviews—which must be valued in the positive way of at least a polyphilic pluralism of pluralisms (of exclusivism, inclusivism and pluralism) in order not to fall into the trap of the poisonous fruits of false unifications.[22] What is more, given our analysis, this vision will find its valid corrective in the profound inexhaustibility of the apophatic nature and theophanic beauty of the appearances of the Mystery in the cosmos, and in the importance of diversity for the expression of this mystery of (and with

---

18. Cf. Shoghi Effendi, *World Order*, 35: "All we can reasonably venture to attempt is to strive to obtain a glimpse of the first streaks of the promised Dawn that must, in the fullness of time, chase away the gloom that has encircled humanity."
19. This consciousness of (vertical) novelty as mode of (horizontal) unification is generally based on the assumption that, first, with this novelty (as related to any new dispensation) other religions have become "old" or are even in decline, and, second, that this novelty is the fulfillment of the prophetic prognostication of these traditions of their own end in a new revelation; cf. *Aqdas*, Note 150; Shoghi Effendi, *God*, 94–99.
20. Some authors have, therefore, understood the present fit of the Bahá'í revelation as a natural issuing of other traditions into it; cf. Fananapazir, "Day of God (*Yawmu'llah*)," 217–38; *Islam*, chs. 1–2; Tai-Seal; Lepard, *Glory*, ch. 14. Others present us with some evidence that this is how the Bahá'í position is perceived, namely, as leaning toward an exclusivist absorption of religions into the one or, in a more moderate sense, here: the absorption of the horizontal axis into the vertical one; cf. Chapter 4 on Ferrer, "Future," 14–15; Fazel, "Understanding," 260.
21. It is the power of apophaticism to set a clear limitation to such a dream. This is explored by Rose's apophatic horizon of any future, reasonable religiosity that any positive assumption will be bracketed by the apophatic unnaming inherent to the becoming of novelty, by sheer temporality and by the inability to convince everyone at any time of "the same" doctrine; cf. K. Rose, *Pluralism*, chs. 1, 8. It is, of course, also the supposition of polyphilic pluralism that such a situation cannot happen, as it would only be possible by avoiding "becoming," which is always multiple, and by avoiding the affirmative part of "affirmative subtraction" (of the activity of reality) which upholds the infinite process as a condition for spiritualization; cf. Faber, *Poet*, §§35, 39; *Manifold*, ch. 8; *Becoming of God*, Explorations, 1–3, 15; *Garden*, ch. 5. This is also the supposition of Bahá'í cosmology; Taylor, 111–12.
22. Cf. 'Abdu'l-Bahá, *Promulgation*, #31: "The differences among the religions of the world are due to the varying types of minds."

regard to) religion.²³ And as an universal cosmic story unfolds, the vastness of the cosmos with its potentially infinite multiplicity of cycles of existence and evolving worlds (besides the infinity of spiritual worlds) as well as the potential future evolutions of "other" spiritual beings on Earth, but at least the progression of future religions beyond the Bahá'í Faith or any religion, will not relieve this attempt of envisioning unity from missing the mark when it does not instill in us the ecological, evolutionary and interstellar awe of divine vastness that defies all attempts to supplant the horizontal multiplicity of religious expressions.²⁴

At this point a second scenario becomes available. With the current trend of interspiritual movements to overcome all such organizational restraints, as inherently carrying the deadly antagonisms of the past into the future, other potentials surface, namely, that of naturalization or interfusion. If we do not find the total naturalization of the human mind a viable alternative²⁵ (although it cannot be excluded from any future scenario and might even become more virulent with speculations on transhumanism, evoked by the potentials to build artificial intelligences),²⁶ the different social organisms living the religious spirit will have to relent to a new religious *life-form* that is not built on, and bound by, the limited organizational structures of the past and present.²⁷ We can imagine a pluralism of pluralisms as a mode of a future conviviality not only constituted from heritages of past religions, but in transreligious transgressions constantly moving between them, thereby creating ever new expressions of religiosity adding themselves to any pool of ideas about, and forms of reverence of, Reality.²⁸ Several passages of the

---

23. Cf. 'Abdu'l-Bahá, *Paris Talks*, #15.
24. This is, of course, all a consequence of the implications of Chapters 12–13.
25. Cf. Nagel, ch. 2. It is also the basic assumption of process thought, based on Whitehead's criticism of the scientific materialism of the nineteenth century, not only in the wake of the revolutions of early twentieth-century physics and it spiritual implications (the basic assumption of mind as force of cosmic import), but also Whitehead's philosophical revolution beyond Kant, who remained stuck in the divide between objectivity and subjectivity, matter and mind, to a new avoidance of such and any dualism, and a processual constitution of duality of mentality and materiality, physicality and conceptuality, as inherent in any existent process, in the sense that this is the basic character of the events-structures and organisms that constitute our universe; cf. Whitehead, *Science*, chs. 6–9; *Process*, part 2, chs. 3, 10; *Modes*, ch. 8; Faber, *Process*, part 2; *Becoming of God*, Sphere 1; Shaviro, *Without Criteria*, chs. 2–3.
26. Cf. Rue, ch. 4; Goodenough; Griffin, *Pantheism*; Vasquez.
27. Cf. Teasdale, ch. 10; Ferrer, *Participation*, ch. 10; A. Martin, chs. 8, 10; Toynbee, chs. 19–20. Generally, such movements are predisposed to religious and spiritual hybridity, that is, the unification of more than one tradition in the practice of persons or communities, but will in any case not be hindered by any fixed identity as basis for religious truth and spiritual practice; cf. Cornille, *Mansions*. In some sense, Sufism has practiced this hyper-identity for centuries and, as some modern developments demonstrate, is even more so bound to become interreligious as the natural place for humanity's spiritualization; cf. Inayat Khan, *The Soul's Journey*.
28. Cf. Sharma, *Religions*, part 7; Unger, ch. 7, makes the case for such a religiosity of "democratic" and "deep" freedom, creativity and flux, unbound by traditional categories of differentiation, as they lead into the oppositional behavior of the past or institutional bindings. Yet his extrapolations are, as many contemporary attempts of future projections, devoid of "Reality"

Bahá'í writings direct us toward such an understanding, namely, that the uniqueness of Bahá'u'lláh's religious renewal was not intended to create yet a new religion, but the overcoming of the whole haunting organizational structure enshrining of religious competitiveness with a new and liberating pattern of spiritual freedom and communion.[29] If we add the Whiteheadian divine matrix not as issuing in structural patterns, but as vibrating by nonorganic Life, that is, a Spirit that always subtracts itself in the affirmation of any structural limitations,[30] we might begin to envision what such an "entirely living nexus"[31] of Reality-infusion might hold for a transformed frame of humanity in transreligious unison with the divine and cosmic manifold.

On this view—given the same elements of the cosmic story of unity and diversity—we may envision this new pattern not to have supplanted or dissolved the horizontal axis, but to have integrated it into new harmonics that is yet beyond our understanding.[32] If it were to become already visible in the endeavors of the interspiritual movements beyond organized religion, such a development seems to reverse the movement of the first alternative, as it may now attempt to dissolve the vertical axis into the horizontal axis.[33] It would retain the vertical drive toward novelty, but dismantle it of its "fulfillment" strategies and imperatives. The new emergent features of religion would be seen as reconfigurations of the horizontal pool of religious ideas and practices, instantly becoming one among the new manifold that it enriches, instead of its overcoming. Their pleroma is the ultimate novelty of this vision.[34] We are, however, warned not to forget that in an essential spiritual transformation of humanity (which the Bahá'í Faith sees itself initiating to realize) ever-new multiplicities may arise that may not only contribute to an ongoing renewal of religiosity, but that could also, in circumstances of degeneration, always fall back onto a plurality of antagonistic movements. While this vision seems to anticipate viable strategies to embrace future evolutionary and interstellar encounters with other forms of life and possibly religiosity, it may also fall short of *their* diversity and divergence if it is held together only by a cauldron of alternatives. These interstellar encounters may be

---

or God, that is, divergent from Whitehead, he is in agreement with an atheistic future of religion as its most mature form; cf. Faber, *Becoming of God*, Exploration 4 and Sphere 4.

29. Cf. Bahá'u'lláh, "Ishráqát (Splendors)," in *Tablets*, #8 (129–30, 132); *Gleanings*, #92; 'Abdu'l-Bahá, *Questions*, #11:35; *Selections*, ##15, 23; *Bahá'í World Faith*, 224–28; Shoghi Effendi, *World Order*, 185; Schaefer, *Beyond the Clash*, 57; Karlberg, *Culture*, chs. 3–4.
30. Cf. Faber, "Mystical Whitehead," 213–34.
31. Cf. Whitehead, *Process*, 104–13. That is, the idea that Life, although harbored by structural supports or organisms, can have a pure expression in the becoming of intensity beyond any organization; cf. Faber, *Process*, part 3 and chs. 32, 39, 42; *Becoming of God*, Exploration 2; *Manifold*, ch. 8.
32. Envisioning such a spiritual society from a Whiteheadian perspective, cf. Faber, *Poet*, §46.
33. Cf. Hanegraaff, chs. 6, 12; Herrick, *Making*, chs. 5–7.
34. Cf. Faber, *Manifold*, chs. 13, 15. This pleroma seems also to be indicated, at least as desirable tendency in some pluralistic, perennial accounts of the future of religion(s), as they are very much being aware of dangers of the poisonous fruits of unity inherent in the first scenario: Toynbee, ch. 18; A. Martin, ch. 10; Smart, *Religion*, ch. 25; Ferrer, "Future," 63–64; *Participation*, ch. 10.

so severe and severely alienating that they may supplant any imagined peaceful religious coinhabitation, forcing old forms of organization to be reinstated or reinvented, on the one hand, in resistance to extinction, and, on the other hand, in order to retreat into a safe haven of security when and while faced with the inability to cope with the new horizons.[35]

In a third scenario, then, in direct reference to the cosmic story, the far future of humanity on this planet (maybe daring to look ahead longer than the past history of human existence on the Earth, maybe half a million years ahead) may issue into a time of either complex ecological developments on Earth (the emergent manifold of spiritual beings on Earth) or interstellar contacts with spiritual beings from far away and of very different kinds, propelling anew all the current questions of unification and religious pluralism to the forefront.[36] Under these conditions, should they ever become actualized, the desire and effort to implement the spiritual value of a *unity* of religions that is meant in the sense of *seeking the harmonies of the vertical with the horizontal axis of religious pluralism*—which the Bahá'í writings in my view imagine to be the healing effect of the new religious life-form on Earth[37]—will, in the best case, have to be elated by, and elevated to, the highest possible expression of, and example for, a civilization in which spiritual transformation has reached transreligious peace.[38] Only in exemplarily practicing such a dynamic state of open spiritual peace, it seems to me, will spiritual maturity in this cosmos appear.[39] Then, maybe, we will have reached the aim that 'Abdu'l-Bahá captures with the image of infinite cycles embraced by the divine intention to create spiritual beings that with their spirit encompass the body of the world and transform it into a divine habitat, the kingdom (of Abrahamic religions), in the translucency of the two worlds, the spiritual and the physical, in the peace between impermanence and eternity.[40] Whitehead allows

---

35. On a "simpler" plane, we can see these exclusivist maneuvers playing out in the militant expressions of religious extremism, especially in the globalized form of post- 9/11 terrorism.
36. Cf. Weintraub, ch. 21; Genta, ch. 2; O'Meara, ch. 8.
37. Cf. 'Abdu'l-Bahá, *Promulgation*, ##69, 108.
38. Similar projections onto potential other star faring civilizations, namely, that they will only succeed in leaving their planetary habitat if they have found such a civilizational unison, tells us more about our own feelings toward such a future, if it may ever occur, to be conditioned by such a presupposition. Hostile encounters cannot be excluded. Yet it might also be possible that we will not encounter any civilization because they have not yet or will never have reached such a state of peaceful unison; cf. Genta, 247–54; Wilkinson, ch. 7. I sense Ferrer (*Participation*, ch. 10) also to direct his attention to such an achievement, as "participation" means the cocreative body of manifestations of ultimate Reality, somehow like a field of immanence or, in the process context, a divine matrix; cf. Faber, *Poet*, §32.
39. On this Bahá'í writings and Whitehead agree firmly, as the whole thrust of mental and spiritual evolution would be driven by the overcoming of antagonistic, Darwinian strategies; cf. Whitehead, *Adventures*, ch. 10; 'Abdu'l-Bahá, *Promulgation*, #14; Brown, "Response," 111–14.
40. Cf. 'Abdu'l-Bahá, *Promulgation*, ## 58, 72, 79; *Questions*, ##52, 67, 69; *Selections*, #21. Several scriptural passages suggest that such a thin interface between this and the next world might yield new sciences and new ways of interaction of material and spiritual realms unimaginable for our time and mind as well as physicality, as we know them; cf. Bahá'u'lláh, *Summons* (*Suriy-i Haykal*), 35–36; *Gleanings*, 5, 80; 'Abdu'l-Bahá, *Promulgation*, #94.

for such a scenario, although only as faint possibility, namely, by assuming that there is no metaphysical necessity that the impermanence of this cosmic epoch is structured such that novelty must imply loss, not only temporally, but by way of not reconcilable antagonistic destructions.[41] Maybe another cosmic epoch would allow for a unison of immediacy and immortality[42]; maybe a transformation of this cosmic epoch, as its natural laws are only habits of the myriads of events, organisms and environments that repeat them, can generate this new coinhabitation of spirit and matter; but maybe such embodiments of a new cosmic life-form are impossible or remain a hope for another (spiritual) realm.[43]

In a fourth scenario, we could imagine that, with a vision harbored by one of the oldest religions on Earth, Jainism, the "ideal time" (*sukham sukham kal*)—the time before and after the predicament of the cycles of degradation—does not have the need for religion at all, as everything becomes translucent in its religiosity, from the particles to organisms, from natural societies to spiritual worlds.[44] In a sense, then, religion may reappear in its most "natural" form, as the free flow of the grace of Reality in all forms of existence.[45] Similar to the six self-less activities (*paramitas*) of the *bodhisattva* in Mahayana Buddhism, and supported by the "natural," but not naturalistic, inherence of the Buddha-nature in all phenomena,[46] to "be religious" would be "natural," that is, would not be based on or act on limited (religious, philosophical, conceptual, investigative) motifs anymore.[47] On this account, even a unification of naturalist and supernaturalist visions of the future of a spiritualized humanity might become achievable[48]—but only if it also is linked with a harmony between science and religion.[49] Like the rays of the sun that are mirrored in all that is or becomes,[50] natural religiosity will appear in as many timelines as there are attributes of the apophatic Mystery.[51] And yet, we would have become what we always already potentially are: "leaves of one tree and the drops of one sea."[52] Here polyphilic

---

41. Cf. Whitehead, *Process*, 340–341; Faber, *Poet*, §39.
42. Cf. Whitehead, *Process*, 351.
43. Cf. Faber, *Manifold*, ch. 7.
44. Cf. von Glasenapp, ch. 5:1; 'Abdu'l-Bahá, *Paris Talks*, #44.
45. Cf. 'Abdu'l-Bahá, *Promulgation*, #58; Compare the interpretation of the "kingdom" within us and beyond (in the world, but not of it) in the Vedantist interpretation of Chopra (63–69) with the Bahá'í vision of its realization "in" this world (without suspending its being beyond) in Beebe, chs. 7–8; 'Abdu'l-Bahá, *Promulgation*, ##2, 81; *Selections*, #188.
46. While non-theistic in certain ways, Buddhism is far from being a "naturalism," as the "naturalness" of ultimate reality, of which in some significant sense everything is an expression, and although it might even be said to be beyond "mind," is still that of the (absolute) transcendence of/beyond "nature" as phenomenal existence; cf. Gowans, 53; Schmidt-Leukel, *Buddhism*, 3.
47. Cf. Trungpa, ch. 12.
48. I have developed such an account philosophically with the notion of "transpantheism," the overcoming of naturalism not by inclusivism (to which panentheism is prone), but by the arising in/difference between multiplicity and divinity ("theoplicity") in the wake of such a pleromatic view of togetherness of Reality and realities; cf. Faber, *Poet*, §40; *Manifold*, ch. 8; *Becoming of God*, Exploration, 11; *Garden*, ch. 6.
49. Cf. 'Abdu'l-Bahá, *Paris Talks*, #40; *Promulgation*, #62; *Selections*, #227.
50. Cf. 'Abdu'l-Bahá, *Selections*, ##35, 45, 207.
51. Cf. 'Abdu'l-Bahá, in *Bahá'í World Faith*, 266; Spong.
52. 'Abdu'l-Bahá, *Promulgation*, #14.

pluralism would have truly advanced a story of cosmic magnitude—and maybe it always is already the unfolding of this story.

One of the paradoxes in the Bahá'í differentiation between essential characteristic, pertaining to divine attributes and their realization in virtues, and the contingent characteristics, such as its social organization, its rites and precepts, doctrines and worldviews,[53] may well be the imagination of the diffusion of religion into a collective spiritualized existence we cannot even imagine yet.[54] This difference has the primary function to explain the oneness of divine intentions and the plurality of realizations, thereby recognizing the horizontal communality of all religions with vertical novelty in their own contingency.[55] Yet, by the same token, it also harbors the paradox that the essence of religiousness does not define religious identity while that which actually restrains matters so as to allow for the formation of religious identities is not essential to religiosity.[56] This does not mean that contingent construction (whether assumed to be a divine remedy for a certain age or human construction) is worthless or unimportant—in Whitehead's rendition, this refers to the insight that only the intersection of infinities with contingencies (finite events, processes, organisms) can actualize values.[57] Rather, their importance is always transient in a wider cosmic context and, hence, will always be transcended into new forms of revelations and the social construction following from their interpretations. If this insight, in a maturated spiritual collective, would be realized coextensively with the essentially ongoing realization of a multiplicity of divine attributes in at least as many intersections as there are beings,[58] we might get a glimpse of a future in which no realization of virtues and divine values would need to be generalized or organized for any group of this spiritual collective (of beings, of religions, of species), but could be lived as corporate organism in which contingency allows for finite actualization

---

53. Cf. Bahá'u'lláh, *Iqan*, §§266–70; 'Abdu'l-Bahá, *Promulgation*, ##41, 50: The new *social* manifestation of virtues would be such that, if it expresses these virtues more than rites and doctrines, will exhibit a new kind of society, a new life-form. This is also one way to find subcurrents of ethical pluralism in inclusivist traditions or renderings of traditions, comparing, for instance, the biblical Christological exclusivism, especially in the Pauline letters, and the theocentric inclusivism of the Synoptic Gospels, with the pluralistic ethicism of (the biblical and intertestamentary Wisdom literature or) New Testament writings such as 1 Timothy and especially James; cf. K. Rose, *Pluralism*, ch. 6. The more Jesus could be seen as Wisdom teacher, the more pluralistic was the outlook attributed to his message; cf. Faber, *Garden*, chs. 7–8; Witherington. We find strong resonances in Bahá'u'lláh's *Tablets* and *Hidden Words* to such a pluralistic Wisdom approach; cf. Lawson, "Globalization," 35–54.
54. Cf. Toynbee, 259–63, ch. 19.
55. Cf. Bahá'u'lláh, *Persian Hidden Words*, #18; 'Abdu'l-Bahá, *Selections*, ##45, 113; *Promulgation*, #94; *Questions*, #14.
56. Cf. 'Abdu'l-Bahá, *Promulgation*, ##31, 49, 60, 62, 121.
57. Cf. Whitehead, "Mathematics," 666–81; "Immortality," 682–700; Faber, "Movement," 185–89.
58. Bahá'u'lláh understands every being as an expression of the uniqueness of God and as a unique fusion of divine attributes; and so does 'Abdu'l-Bahá—both quoted in Brown, "Response," 111; cf. Diessner, 6, 13.

in always infinite variations.⁵⁹ Religion could become as diffused throughout such a collective as is "natural" religiosity.⁶⁰ In a Whiteheadian understanding of a future society of spiritual beings in unison with the divine matrix, we might find such a hope not to be an empty shadow of unfulfilled dreams.⁶¹ In the Bahá'í writings, this immediacy of revelation in all natural phenomena, from every atom to one's own self, would allow "each and every thing, however small," to become or express "a revelation leading him to his Beloved, the Object of his quest."⁶² However, in light of the unprecedented degrees of freedom (the novelty and the reverberating interrelated oscillations of any eventful decision throughout the whole field) that such an excited state of matter and spirit would imply, we may also fear that no final state could be reached that would not again initiate processes of decline.⁶³ Although there is a hope in the Bahá'í writings for a day that is not followed by night,⁶⁴ on a cosmic scale the cycles of spring and winter are never suspended.⁶⁵ And how would natural religiosity have reconciled itself to such a process of disappearance?

As a fifth scenario, closer to our current horizon, but nonetheless of enormous imaginative power, lurk the possibilities of spiritual renewal by as of yet unacknowledged potentials of ancient or suppressed religious traditions, still waiting for their hour to shine. The Bahá'í writings have a great fondness for both the width of spiritual integration without coercion and the deep resources of minorities and oppressed peoples to contribute to the future of the spiritual renewal of humanity.⁶⁶ They speak of the latent energies harbored in revelations or dispensations that do not exhaust themselves with their initiation (like the sun that rises from morning till noon), but need a process of growth, let alone of growth of the ability to fathom its true capacities.⁶⁷ If a concurrent multiplicity of religious speeds and spiritual states is assumed, we must not think of this process to be just one linear progression, but a multilayered and mutually enlivening process.⁶⁸ 'Abdu'l-Bahá gives us hints in both directions. On the one hand, he urges to

---

59. Similar to the attribution of divine uniqueness (*ahadiyyah*) to all creatures, the unity of Reality that exudes infinite variability could express religious organisms in their unison and variability; cf. Lawson, "Epistle," 231: there is only one soul, but infinite paths.
60. Cf. Crockett; Bowman and Crockett; Drees, ch. 5.
61. Cf. Faber, *Poet*, §46.
62. Bahá'u'lláh, *Iqan*, §217 (cf. the wider context of §§116–18).
63. Cf. Whitehead, *Process*, 105, 111; *Symbolism*, 87–88.
64. Cf. Bahá'u'lláh, *Summons*, 34; Shoghi Effendi, *God*, 98. Although interpretation may be tempted to understand this "everlastingness" as a physical prediction concerning this temporal world (*nasut*), it seems to be more fitting to understand it in terms of the unison of the divine Self of all Manifestations (*lahut*): cf. 'Abdu'l-Bahá, *'Abdu'l-Bahá in London*, 31, 79; *Foundations*, 104.
65. Cf. 'Abdu'l-Bahá, *Questions*, ##14, 36, 41; *Promulgation*, ##22, 49.
66. Such oppressions and the inability to listen to, see, recognize and hear minorities of any kind, be it regarding race, class, ethnicity, religion or culture, are due to "prejudices" that, according to the Bahá'í writings, are the mechanism that perpetuate violence; cf. 'Abdu'l-Bahá, *Paris Talks*, ##40, 45; *Selections*, #202; *Promulgation*, ##109, 112, 135; Shoghi Effendi, *Advent*, 35.
67. Cf. 'Abdu'l-Bahá, *Selections*, #16.
68. Cf. Bahá'u'lláh, *Gleanings*, #38; Schaefer, *Beyond the Clash*, 137–38. Such a differentiation of "spiritual speed" would also cohere with the potential evolutionary differentiation of speed

engage the enormous spiritual reservoir of Chinese lands,[69] and on the other, he prophetically envisioned the extraordinary future for the spiritual renewal of humankind resting with the native peoples of America.[70]

There is a certain power to this thought that what seems to be lost in the past has resources that are still waiting to be released, as this assumption strengthens the coextensiveness of both the horizontal and the vertical axis of religious pluralism: While we might be fixated on novelty, which in some sense is always supplanting the concurrent present as (now) "old" reservoir, the appearance from the shadows of this reservoir of spiritual powers supports the necessity to always cherish the horizontal remembrance of the multiplicity of unfulfilled potentials in any novelty. It becomes the ethical imperative of the future to give due respect to the past, which it should give a future, and—as Whitehead recognizes—the more it can do so, the more it highlights the intensity of the harmony this novel future will have achieved.[71]

In light of the process rhythm underlying the "superposition" of the temporal (diachronic) and the "spatial" (synchronic) axis of pluralism, namely, the rhythm between events of novelty as activities of unification of a field of concurrent multiples and the enrichment of this field by this event becoming a constituent of the "spatial" field changed by its appearance,[72] it becomes an epistemological necessity to avoid two reductionisms: On the one hand, we may not (as already employed at several points of this study) fall into the traps of a merely "evolutionary" view of religious progression (away from primal religions, for instance).[73] This temporal reduction of religious change has prevailed in "fulfillment" approaches and has driven early methodological presumptions of religious studies in their (often derogative) attitude toward primal, regional, extinct or "older" (axial) religions. Instead, we must counter this "progressive" dogma through the "spatial" democratization of religious sources regardless of their temporal distribution or relation to axial matters.[74] Yet it may be equally important to avoid the "spatial"

---

in the development of spiritual beings on this or any other planet or comic habitat of life; cf. Chapter 13.
69. Cf. Abdu'l-Bahá, in *Star of the West* 21 (1930): 261; cf. Chew, *Chinese Religion*; "Great Tao," 11–39.
70. Cf. 'Abdu'l-Bahá, *Tablets of the Divine Plan*, 32–33; Buck, "Native Messengers," 97–133.
71. Cf. Faber, *Prozeßtheologie*, §25; Whitehead, *Adventures*, 256–57.
72. Cf. Whitehead, *Process*, 21. This is the central assumption of the "superposition" of the two axes of pluralism in this book.
73. This is the basic assumption that has led to the reconsideration of "other religions" in Chapter 12, namely, neither merely as preparations or as obsolete forerunners of new religions (vertical axis), nor as "fulfillment" of all previous religions—an assumption that can sometimes be felt to motivate simplified interpretations of the concept of Bahá'í Manifestations. Rather, if there can be any "fulfillment" in new axial times—as the concept of Manifestation has been elucidated here—it must, as explored in Chapter 12 and in preparation of Chapter 15, be of the form not only of a *synthesis of*, but of a *sympathy with* the field it fulfills, namely, by releasing its own diversified and often hidden potential.
74. This "correction" of evolutionism is the methodological and epistemological assumption of Sharma in his recovery of primal religions in their importance for contemporary philosophy of Religions; cf. Sharma, *Primal Perspective*, Introduction.

reduction of temporal categories of the religious manifold—a methodological preference of more current accesses to the academic study of religions[75]—because, although this approach allows less prejudice regarding the "evolutionary limited" horizons of past religions to arise (primal religions as "primitive," for instance), the overemphasis on seemingly "democratic" values would have become blind to processuality as such, that is, the event-structure and the rhythms of novelty and reintegration that contract and expand the religious field in more ways than just governing seemingly "timeless" regional, coexisting manifolds; rather, such event-rhythms bind those manifolds to appreciate and receive embodiments of the realization of new potentials. And it is precisely this event-structure that also allows for, and releases, the recovery of unrealized potentials in the "spatial" field and its temporal depth, the forgotten or suppressed past.[76]

Historically, we can follow the mostly peaceful (although never frictionless) contours and integrations of the three religious universes that constituted the unity of the Chinese peoples (throughout all ages of invasions and the many new ethnicities to come into the fold of the diverse Chinese states): Confucianism, Daoism and Buddhism—in all of their diversified internal forms and modes of transgression into one another.[77] The power of Daoism, for instance, was over the centuries not only that of integrating philosophy and religion, preaxial and axial traditions, the religious figures of all three traditions and the many universes of discourse they engendered, into a dynamic wholeness for which transreligious movements were the norm rather than the exception.[78] Laozi and his book, the *Dao De Jing*, became expressions of an ultimate Reality that were able to transmute themselves into the Buddhist ultimate Reality with its three bodies (transcending the Christian-Islamic debate over whether the book or a person is the ultimate expression of Reality)[79]; it could without simplification identify the divinized Laozi (Lord Lao) with the Buddha[80]; and it had no problem expressing indefinite transmutations of Reality into revelations and more localized appearances (manifestations, *avatars*, incarnations) as well as cycles of religious renewal.[81] Is this maybe a model of transreligious unification with creative diversification?

And regarding native peoples of the American continent, 'Abdu'l-Bahá prophetically promised that a time will come when the chains of suppression will be loosened and overcome by education and ethnic revival so that the spiritual future of humanity might be revolutionized by the spiritual potentials of these ancient people.[82] Several authors have followed these prophecies deeper into their future potential, finding already certain prophetic figures (Manifestations) in the indigenous history, for instance, of the Lakota and the

---

75. In our context of the interplay of the two axes of religious pluralism, this would be the adequate "correction" to Sharma's proposal of spatial non-evolutionary methodology.
76. Cf. Whitehead, *Process*, 17, 65–72. Faber, *Poet*, §§12–14, 17–18.
77. Cf. Clarke, 22–28; Chen, ch. 1.
78. Cf. Kohn, part 2; Wong, chs. 1–4.
79. Cf. Kohn, 22n32; Wong, ch. 6.
80. Cf. Kohn, 2.
81. Cf. Kohn, 114–17; Chen, ch. 2.
82. Cf. 'Abdu'l-Bahá, *Tablets*, 32–33.

Iroquois, waiting to be rediscovered.[83] One might also think of native spiritualities to be of great importance for a future of religions envisioned in terms of a more "naturalized" diffusion, because they live "essential" connections with the ecological wholeness of mother Earth instead of following "contingent" features of mutually competing set of laws.[84] In any case, as postcolonialist and subalternity approaches demonstrate, the suppressed minorities might hold a key to the future renewal of religion in a transformed humanity.[85] Yet in both cases displayed here, it seems to be their transreligious abilities (in the recovery of suppressed multiplicity of voices and experiences, if not revelations) of integration, diversification and mutual transformation that will make all the difference.

As a sixth scenario, I will, for a moment (and as introduced at the outset of this book), assume that the current technological abilities of reconstructing humanity (not by hominization, but trans-hominization) is a matter of evolutionary pressure, and allow genetic manipulation and artificial intelligence, the two most prevalent motors of a possible post-human transformation assumed inevitably to be leading into the "singularity," be the context of the future of religions.[86] On the one hand, genetic diversification of humanity and maybe other animals may lead to different forms of minds, as evolution might have done on a cosmic scale already, such that they cannot easily communicate with one another anymore without series of translators of serial proximity.[87] But in such a new world, neither would mind and consciousness, reason and value, ethical and aesthetic impulses and feelings have simply disappeared, but rather only radically diversified, opening venues of unknown multiplicity in need of pluralism and mutuality—for which the transreligious discourses on religious pluralism and the unity of religions may well be the most advanced blueprint. Nor would such a world of increasingly incompatible "ecological niches" and "specializations" (in the double sense of specializing in certain environments and the creation of new species) have overcome the necessity of universal horizons of understanding ("one" reality), but would always, as Whitehead prophesies, be immersed in the creation of new societies of organisms of mutually agreeable environments in need of a process of oscillation between concrete diversification and universal, unifying horizons seeking the coinherence of all (of their specific) "worlds."[88] As long as this will be the case, the transgenetic future of "minds" in such societies of unexplored becoming will not be nonreligious per se, but, as long as they ask questions of existence and meaning, and as they believe or (increasingly) know of the ecological and

---

83. Cf. Buck, "Bahá'í Universalism," 173–201; Horton, 20–62; Cruikshank, 147–67; Addison and Buck, 180–270.
84. Cf. T. Brown; Harkin and Lewis; Grimm and Tucker, ch. 8; Grimm, 41–54; Medina, ch. 6.
85. Cf. 'Abdu'l-Bahá, *Promulgation*, #131; Young, *Postcolonialism*, ch. 1; Beverly, chs. 1–2; Morris, especially part 1: Spivak. This approach to a multiplicity of suppressed and indigenous knowledges has not yet been sufficiently discovered as source of religious recovery of lost "revelations" of ultimate Reality and power-critical religious pluralism, at least in the Bahá'í universe of discourse; cf. Quinn, "End," 168; Amanat, xix.
86. Cf. the discussion of transhumanism in Chapter 1; Harari, chs. 8–10.
87. Cf. Egan, *Diaspora*, chs. 1–3.
88. Cf. Whitehead, *Religion*, part 1; *Symbolism*, part 3.

evolutionary dynamics of mind, consciousness and spiritual awakening to be the motive force of the universe, as ʿAbduʾl-Bahá envisions,[89] it will be in need of the instruments of religious pluralism and vast modes of unification projected in either of the other five scenarios or any of their combination (or still unimaginable other forms yet to come).

Conversely, we may expect a transhuman revolution, by which algorithms practically erase not only the need for humanity, including mind, consciousness, spirituality and religious expressions and symbolisms, but also their very existence, to be a much more radical departure from any future projected for religion(s), that is, their utter uselessness.[90] Yet this presumption is seriously flawed on two counts. First, the projected "dada-religion" of Harari's "homo deus," which presupposes that we are only a bundle of algorithms that will, eventually, give way to a thoroughgoing algorithmic existence (where consciousness, even if it remains a mystery, will becomes irrelevant, practically overturned by the nonconscious intelligence of AIs),[91] would live from the lack of any necessity and urge to uphold the mystery of consciousness, burying it under algorithmic networks as mere fantasies, which have no creative power to transform the world of data-junkies anymore (as we will be totally dependent on such cybernetic networks).[92] But even such a "world" run by powerful algorithms and AIs (being the gods, sovereigns and cooperations of the future) might only indicate the dynamics of a diversifying multiverse of "discourses" in need of "techniques" of pluralism and modes of unification. It is not unimaginable that such algorithms will develop unconscious or conscious futures of diversified symbolisms that might begin to ask the questions that are "natural" and inherent to religious symbolisms: Why is there something at all? What is "our" purpose? Why do "we" do what "we" do, namely, running our programs? Is the mathematical basis for the patterns "we" run through secure, or are there different mathematics, different laws of operation, different universes with different laws and rules of logic and mathematical formation?[93] Why are there different algorithms (identities)? Maybe such algorithms will study the philosophic explorations of these questions and immerse themselves into the religious horizons of their very activity and its contents. There is no reason to believe that all algorithms will unify to one super-algorithm without any space for radical creative diversifications and, perhaps, incompatible divergences.[94] Maybe

---

89. Cf. the discussion of the evolutionary force of mind and spirit in Chapter 13; ʿAbduʾl-Bahá, *Promulgation*, #79.
90. Cf. Harari, chs. 9–10.
91. Cf. Ashkenazi, *What We Know*, 91–92.
92. Cf. Harari, chs. 10–11; Stonier, *Information*, ch. 8.
93. Cf. Maor, *Infinity*, part 1; Chaitin, ch. 6.
94. In Greg Egan's rendering of this diversification of AI programs, developing communities (poleis) and diverse approaches to reality (mathematical, physical, aesthetic and so on) and diversified "personalities" with conscious reactions to the questions posed, here, has, as its outcome, a situation in which two such AIs with different personalities and intentions discover that even millions of universes they have crossed already do not reveal any answer to these questions. Consequently, facing the impossibility to find meaning and reason, understanding and satisfaction, one AI program deletes itself (cyber-suicide) and the other retreats into the inner realm of mathematical patterns with their own infinity (without meaning or as

they will create their own religions and will discover the need for the relativity of their truth-claims inherent in their algorithmic presumptions (as they have not created themselves). If evolution has a trend toward life and consciousness, and spiritual awakening to experiences of (ultimate) Reality, there is no reason to believe that the artificial evolution will mute this very impulse; and if it does, this might only lead to the extinction of *this* line of existence—but what about other worlds and potentially vastly different universes and their lines of evolution?

There is a second reason to be skeptical: There is no reason to believe that humanity *can* be reduced to algorithms.[95] Even if they increasingly restructure our existence into some sort of cyber-humanity, what about the other animals in evolutionary time depths: maybe their minds will replace our AIs and us? What about the fact that no algorithm can replace or explain consciousness, mind (and it various cognitive, ethical and aesthetic functions)—as even Harari admits[96]—and maybe never will: Does this not imply that there will always be a mystical, unrepresentable, unknowable resort resisting in the very presence of the apophatic and the ability to experience anything on its basis—as the mystery always punches deep holes into the closedness of any functionality or closed system?[97] And if we register the serious doubts voiced today against the "materialist" interpretation of evolution, which cannot win the day or the future, because it only is effective in blinding itself to the powers of consciousness, mind and spirit—as contemporary philosophy of mind (and the Mind) will readily admit and rigorously argue:[98] How can we expect a universe that has mind written into

---

    substitute for meaning, equating patterns with events); cf. Egan, ch. 20. Egan is known for his post-religious views; but this ending, instead of instilling the meaninglessness of this search for meaning, purpose and understanding, may also be read to reveal that such meaning, if it is striven after, is not *of* any world, but the Mystery that has *retreated* from all methods of grasping. If one looks in the wrong places and with limited lenses, one will find only subtraction, but no affirmation. In Bahá'u'lláh's insistence on the infinity of worlds always remains a relativism of apophatic "signlessness" of Reality; cf. Bahá'u'lláh, *Gleanings*, 80; *Iqan*, §104. 'Abdu'l-Bahá's infinite cycles of becoming (*nasut*) escape meaninglessness only through the concurrent expression of all of these cycles as unfolding higher spiritual realms (*malakut*) and their unity in the divine mind (*lahut*)—the vertical and horizontal processes of spiritualization; cf. 'Abdu'l-Bahá, *Paris Talks*, #29; *Questions*, ##1, 53; *Selections*, #225; *Promulgation*, ##23, 100, 123, 125;

95. For the refutation on grounds of (1) the complex basis of mathematical divergence and (2) Gödel's incompleteness theorem, as well as (3) other arguments, based on quantum incoherence, cf. Penrose, chs. 1–6.
96. Cf. Harari, chs. 3, 10.
97. In a process context, we could speak of the "purposelessness" of events in their very constitution as aesthetic self-creations that always escape mere functionality; cf. Faber, *God as Poet*, §§21–22. This is also to counter the assumption that the missing meaning/purpose in functionalities (such as algorithms or other material self-repetitive circulations) necessarily indicates not the absence of the right sensitivity for its detection, but its nonexistence; cf. Bataille, chs. 1–2. Purpose is, instead, maybe bound by the sensitivity to the "purposelessness" of becoming, khoric immanence and divine poetics.
98. Cf. Nagel, chs. 1–2; Leslie, *Immortality*, chs. 1–2.

its very foundations (as contemporary panpsychism claims) or follows an evolutionary emerging convergence at the center of its very dynamics to ever repose in algorithmic reduction?

The real question facing this situation may rather be: In what sense can religion, the spiritual awakening of the cosmos, in its transreligious modes of multiplicity (plurality and unity) *creatively* contribute to the future of the driving force of the evolutionary unfolding of spirit, mind and consciousness, as incorporations of the Mystery that always escapes, but loves this process? It may, in this context, be admitted that the traditional functions of religions cannot exhaust themselves in binding humanity to past installments and their outworn shells[99]—which is central to the Bahá'í view of religious "progressiveness" in a spiritually emerging universe.[100] In a transreligious horizon of the future of religions, it will not be enough to retreat either into subjective realms of interiority or into a merely secular world of commonalities that might exhaust themselves in the most common denominator of economic circulations and social pacifications or their elimination in favor of algorithmic elites or enhanced superhumans.[101] The transreligious scenarios envisioned here will have to not only react with reluctant receptions, conserving interpretations, and outraged condemnations of an accelerating realization of this new world around them and their constituencies, they will not be able to be content with merely countering the reductionisms of materiality, algorithmic closedness and unprecedented diversifications of a future post-humanity either.[102] Concurring with Whitehead's bold statement that the "pure conservative is fighting against the essence of the universe,"[103] the transreligious future, I am willing to bet on, will lie in a creative transformation,[104] allowing the polyphilic Mystery to present itself in new embodiments that resist deconstruction by *being* the very manifestations *of* the future of the dynamics of cosmic evolution, wherever it may lead and whatever surprises it may still have in store for us (or "them," the unknown future minds).[105] This is the core of spiritual transformation: to listen to the manifestations of the future where they arise; to develop sensitivities toward their recognition; to become aware

---

99. Cf. Harari, 181–88.
100. Cf. Bahá'u'lláh, *Gleanings*, #31; 'Abdu'l-Bahá, *Promulgation*, #114.
101. Cf. Harari, ch. 10.
102. Cf. Harari, 269–79.
103. Whitehead, *Adventures*, 274.
104. In process thought, John Cobb has made "creative transformation" a central term for the interpretation and activation of the rhythmic transformation of the universe in its diverse societies and environments in relation to, what I have called, the "cycle of love" between Reality and realities in becoming; cf. Cobb, *Christ*, part 1; Faber, *Poet*, §§30, 46.
105. Cf. Haught, *Story*, ch. 8; Faber, *Poet*, §39; *Manifold*, ch. 15; *Becoming of God*, Exploration 16. It is in this contact that Derrida's "indeconstructibility" of "justice" only represents one of the divine attributes that, in the Sufi and Bahá'í view, allow for infinite and inexhaustible manifestations in the "creation" or realization of spiritual worlds in this world (and beyond); cf. Corbin, ch. 1; Savi, *Summit*, chs. 2, 11. As the Manifestations of God are the apex of the unity of these attributes, their appearance is the indication of the future that spiritualization aspires to.

of Reality in them; and to act on this awareness and in ecological, evolutionary and cosmopolitan responsibility.[106]

The future of religions may, then, become the envisagement of a divine manifold.[107] As it unfolds in space-time, it will exhibit a dynamics in which unity and diversity always appear together: in a horizontal, evolutionary, cyclical dynamic, always engaged in movements of transformation from impermanent antagonisms (mutual limiting suppressions) to (liberating and liberated) varieties of unifications, all of them having become, and having been recognized as, horizontal expressions of the nondual unity of difference and unity to the apophatic mystery; *and* in a vertical, oscillating and pulsating dynamics of the mutuality of all of these modes of unity and diversity being stations of the infinitely folding, unfolding and enfolding Sun of Truth/Reality/God.[108] In the spatial (horizontal) enfoldment, this nondual mystery of oneness and difference will proceed through mutual immanence of many folds of the one Mystery beyond any superiority (as it would recreate the illusionary conditions of the subaltern silencing); in its temporal (vertical) unfolding, every religion would represent a different complex of spiritual stations without supersession, as "progress" remains relative to these stations (and multiplicity has vertical niches of diversified speeds).[109] Vertical novelty, in this understanding, would have become the liberating recovery of the lost multiplicity of voices—and its claim of "fulfillment" would have to demonstrate this recovery instead of the repetition of the dialectics of oppression.[110] And as the whole spatiotemporal movement (the coextensive dynamics of horizontal and vertical axes) forms in its own infinite layers the perplexing harmonics of an eternal movement from and into different worlds, the

---

106. Cf. Faber, *Garden*, ch. 9. It is interesting, in this context, to find Shoghi Effendi envisioning a future of humanity that hints at certain elements of post-humanist dynamics, but also at the concurrent spiritualization and intellectual responsibility for this process; cf. Shoghi Effendi, *World Order*, 204: "The enormous energy dissipated and wasted on war, whether economic or political, will be consecrated to such ends as will extend the range of human inventions and technical development, to the increase of the productivity of mankind, to the extermination of disease, to the extension of scientific research, to the raising of the standard of physical health, to the sharpening and refinement of the human brain, to the exploitation of the unused and unsuspected resources of the planet, to the prolongation of human life, and to the furtherance of any other agency that can stimulate the intellectual, the moral, and spiritual life of the entire human race."
107. Cf. Faber, *Manifold*, chs. 9–10, 14–15.
108. Cf. Faber, *Manifold*, ch. 12.
109. Harari's spectral analysis of infinite states of mind beyond current human reach, but also, implicit in unexplored sections of current humanity seems to contradict his myopic vision of the algorithmic disappearance of humanity and mind, but rather imagines the creative inexhaustibility of the mind over the reductive closure of algorithms; cf. Harari, 358–64.
110. Cf. Faber, *Manifold*, ch. 5, Intermezzo 1 and 2, ch. 15; 'Abdu'l-Bahá, *Promulgation*, #41: The dynamics of peace is universal, but expressed through the uniqueness of all religions; and reconciliation must recover such (divine) knowledge without suppressing religious differences in cultural processes of identity and diversification. The unification or reconciliation of religions, then, would be one of liberating their suppressed intentions and identities; cf. P. Smith, *Introduction*, 36; Maneck, "Conversion."

breathing in and out of the Spirit, nothing but mutuality constitutes the different elements of unfolding and enfolding.[111] In light of such an oscillation, religious appearances will never lean themselves to superiority or supersession, denigration or substitution, because it is the *togetherness*, the nondual closeness of all levels of unity and diversity, in which this process enfolds in its two axes that of the Mystery itself.[112] In the "Valley of Unity" of his mystical writing *The Seven Valleys*, Bahá'u'lláh reveals this Mystery to be of such a togetherness of unity and plurality: simultaneously of the unity of religions and of religious pluralism, and differentiated not only by temporal novelty and concurrent pleroma, but by integrated and differentiated layers of unity and multiplicity of spiritual stations by which all spiritual beings may address the Mystery.

> It is clear to thine Eminence that all the variations which the wayfarer in the stages of his journey beholdeth in the realms of being, proceed from his own vision [...] Consider the visible sun; although it shineth with one radiance upon all things, and at the behest of the King of Manifestation bestoweth light on all creation, yet in each place it becometh manifest and sheddeth its bounty according to the potentialities of that place. For instance, in a mirror it reflecteth its own disk and shape, and this is due to the sensitivity of the mirror; in a crystal it maketh fire to appear, and in other things it showeth only the effect of its shining, but not its full disk. And yet, through that effect, by the command of the Creator, it traineth each thing according to the quality of that thing, as thou observest.[113]

The polyphilic pluralism of this passage is different from, and overlays the vertical and horizontal axes of religious pluralism. The "vertical" differentiation, here, is not one of (linear or spiral or cyclical) "temporal" novelty, but of a multiplicity of (parallel) "spatial" layers, horizons and magnitudes of integration and differentiation, of spiritual perceptions and horizons that exist together as the enfolding and unfolding of the Mystery.[114] On a "horizontal" plane (in space-time) these levels are differently realized (enfolded or unfolded) in every spiritual being and differentiated in relation to their power of vision, but also always limited in expression by their diversity capturing this vision: The worshipers of oneness realize the apophatic unity of God/Reality beyond all categories and equally in all religions. The worshipers of the polyphilic appearances of God/Reality enjoy the refractions this unity leaves in different religions. Yet divine *polyphilia* is even more magnanimous than expecting pluralist reactions to answer this diversity. As the image of this text passage reveals, it is always the individual and collective

---

111. Cf. Faber, *Becoming of God*, Sphere 3 and Exploration 16.
112. Cf. Faber, *Garden*, chs. 5, 9 and Epilogue: section 4.
113. Bahá'u'lláh, *Valleys* (Valley of Unity), 29–30.
114. These "vertically" coinherent layers are infinite, but are sometimes in the Bahá'í writings (in utilization of Sufi terminology) presented as two-, three-, five or sevenfold; cf. Momen, "God," 22–31. One influential, classical Sufi differentiation, in allusion also to Shaykhi material, uses five realms: *hahut* (the realm of apophatic Reality), *lahut* (the realm of manifest Reality), *jabarut* (the realm of transhistorical divine realities and activities), *malakut* (the realm of justice and eternal life) and *nasut* (the realm of mercy and physical humanity); cf. Lepain, 43–60.

"character" of the recipient—her capacity to unfurl the enveloped levels of the "transcendence within"—that defines (limits or un-limits) the appearance of the Mystery in its various forms, delineating the spiritual stations or horizons in which one lives and moves. Some of them may only allow for an exclusivist, others for inclusivist or pluralist reflection of the Mystery. Yet *all* of them mirror the unfolding of divine *polyphilia* and should not lead to strife and antagonism. However, the basic insight that would hinder such confrontational reactions to the multiplicity of divine mirrors, in this text, is the "spiritual fact" that not one of these alternatives captures the Mystery "itself," but all such views remain a reflection of one's own horizons, characters and limited realizations of divine attributes and virtues.[115]

---

115. Cf. Bahá'u'lláh, *Gleanings*, ##26, 148; 'Abdu'l-Bahá, *Selections*, #24: all peoples create a creator in their mind; cf. Momen, "God," 14.

Chapter Fifteen

ONE WITH ALL RELIGIONS

Enter the paradise of the spiritual Kingdom, diffuse the lights of the Sun of Truth, cause the waves of this Most Great Ocean to reach all human souls so that this world of earth may be transformed into the world of heaven.[1]

—'Abdu'l-Bahá

The final question to be asked, then, is what, in light of the conversation with religious pluralism, may be the contribution of its polyphilic mode,[2] and its exemplification by the Bahá'í universe of discourse, to the conversation about the future of religions, their reconciliation and unification, in communicating their presupposed divine unity in the ongoing interreligious discourses? What could the pluralism of pluralism look like from a Bahá'í perspective for the general discourse? If we accept, from a polyphilic perspective, that the "superposition" of the vertical and horizontal axes of religious pluralism prohibits simplifications regarding the understanding of the meaning of unity and plurality (the exclusion of one axis by the other or their substitution one for the other), we would neither seek for plurality to generate normative incommensurability between religions (the fallacy of essentialist pluralism)[3] nor try to substitute the discourse on unity with versions that insist on the dissipation of the multiplicity of religions because of their alleged foundational sameness (the fallacy of essentialist unity).[4] And given the complex interferences of the horizontal and vertical axes, as well as the complex intersections of the meaning of unity and multiplicity in the Bahá'í writings, we may also not wish to pursue the path of opposing the fundamental Bahá'í principle of the unity of religions to religious pluralism—as both exhibit the same aim: spiritual peace as the sign of a spiritual maturation of humanity.

Nor should we forget that the oscillating *polyphilia* of the divine Spirit already embraces both axes in a variety of levels of unification and diversification, eternally, as it were, breathing in modes of more or less, wider and smaller, clearer or more blurred, and mirroring itself (its Self) according to the more or less dusted or bright capacities of the mirrors to reflect "its" depth.[5] And while some of these modes of mirroring will be more

---

1. 'Abdu'l-Bahá, *Promulgation*, #128.
2. Cf. Faber and Keller, "Pluralism," passim.
3. Cf. Knitter, *Earth*, ch. 3.
4. Cf. May, 10–12, 27–29.
5. Cf. 'Abdu'l-Bahá, *Selections*, #12; *Paris Talks*, ##28–29, 54; *Promulgation*, ##24, 26, 52, 58, 104; *Questions*, ##17, 21, 24, 67.

inclined toward oneness, others will gleefully appeal to the pleroma of multiplicity, or conversely, in flight from this immensity seek the warmth of a stone in the sunlight rather than the clarity of light in a crystal.[6] However, divine *polyphilia*, here, would also imply that *all* of these reactions *are* unfoldings of the Mystery and that, in another sense, *none* of them is *closer* to the Mystery, as "no sign can indicate His presence or His absence,"[7] and *all* of them are reflections of their own capacities and contingent characters.[8] In fact, Mystery in-sists in *all* of them to the degree of their ability to withstand its presence— and their respective fullness (to capacity) is what counts.[9]

Here the impact of polyphilic pluralism in its apophatic-polyphilic oscillation of spiritual reality, with the assumption and experience of "its" own "subtractive affirmation" of the truth of the multiplicity of religious paths, and with the explication of the manifold of such paths (not only *to*, but) *of* truth as "in-sistence" of this Reality "itself" (with "its" Self), is that it can already on *philosophical* grounds uphold the consequences drawn at this point. And the insight is this: that in order to approximate the apophatic reality *as* spiritual reality (and not as mere imagination or secondary "neutral" truth about truth claims), we need to accept the truth of the manifold appearing in the diverse religious commitments that they commend to their specific paths and their truth *as* the in-sistence of divine or ultimate Reality "itself."[10] Indeed, in this pleroma of truths (irreducible to one another), "it" manifests "itself": as *Divine Manifold*.[11] Here, again, does the polyphilic approach differ from the ambivalence of an apophatic pluralism *and* the simplification of a mystical essentialism.[12] While mystical essentialism will always try to diffuse the differences of the spiritual truth of religious traditions, their uniqueness, as it were, into *one* mystical truth, replacing all prima facie truth of religions with its own *one* truth, apophatic pluralism tries to avoid such simplifications by claiming the truth of apophaticism as secondary critical truth about any prima facie claims of truth primarily confessed to in the diverse traditions.[13] Polyphilic pluralism, however, understands the acceptance of the diverse truth claims of religious traditions neither as a new form of inclusivism (as apophatic pluralism would suggest) nor as mere outer shell of a central truth that would diffuse these differences on a primary level. In fact, it is the specific capacity of *polyphilia* to accept the apophatic-polyphilic oscillation of the divine

---

6. Thereby, as elaborated on Bahá'u'lláh's imagery of *The Seven Valleys* (Valley of Unity) (29–30), referred to in Chapter 14, in fact, *creating* the pluralism of pluralisms (of exclusivism, inclusivism and pluralism), cf. Chapter 7.
7. Bahá'u'lláh, *Iqan*, §104.
8. Cf. Momen, "Relativism: A Basis," 204–6.
9. Cf. Bahá'u'lláh, *Iqan*, §189; *Gleanings*, #124; *Tabernacle*, ##2:20, 2:22; *Days*, #42:9. Yet every new revelation infuses a new capacity into the reality of the becoming universe; cf. Bahá'u'lláh, *Gleanings*, ##36, 109. But novelty can also overburden capacity; cf. Bahá'u'lláh, *Gleanings*, #89.
10. This, again, is the central argument of my rendering of the divine interaction with the process universe of Whitehead in Faber, "God in the Making."
11. This, again, is the central thesis of Faber, *Manifold*.
12. Recall the development of the analysis of pluralism based on mysticism in Chapter 4 and the differentiation between apophatic and polyphilic pluralism in Chapter 5.
13. Cf. K. Rose, *Pluralism*, 7, 56–57.

manifold not as secondary reflective criterion for primary truth claims, but as prima facie truth of all religious traditions *without*, simultaneously, demanding the reduction of the commitments to diverse paths and their unique truths to *one* abstract truth in order to be true.[14] In my view, this can be extracted from process thought (as developed here) on *philosophical* grounds, as I have tried to show throughout this book; and it can be exemplified with the new axial consciousness of the Bahá'í revelation as prima facie truth of a *religious* tradition.

So, in the end, we may try to embrace the complexity of this layered, apophatic-polyphilic principle of unity as one of a (virtually infinite) manifold, that is, as a unity of many folds, permanently enfolding, unfolding and refolding itself in the course of the vast cosmic story of divine reflection in the universe and on this Earth.[15] Diverse religions (and individual capacities and expressions, as well as collective streams within religions) may represent different dynamic stabilizations and stations of the layered emanation of the Mystery, mapped on the spiritual evolution of humanity and maybe other beings (the vertical axis of novelty), which also always aligns itself coextensively onto a landscape of concurrent appearances (the horizontal axis of coexistence)—all of them interpreting and reacting to unique divine manifestations in space-time, localized and evolving at different temporal speeds, intensities and capacities of harmonization. We may heed Bahá'u'lláh's mystical insight of equal cosmic magnitude, namely, "that all these planes and states are folded up and hidden away within [the human being]. 'Dost thou reckon thyself only a puny form / When within thee the universe is folded?' "[16] In avoidance of the poisonous fruits of simplified concepts of unity and by embracing the wonders of a manifold divine harmonics,[17] which is only possible if a multiplicity is sounding together, we might come to the following conclusion: The unity of religions that Bahá'í scriptures, resonant with the philosophical insights of polyphilic pluralism, suggest, as healing elixir,

---

14. On a deeper level, this polyphilic view would also allow to avoid the ambivalence created by the combination of an apophatic withholding from truth claims (equaling a new inclusivism) with the assumption that, therefore, different religions are to be seen as independent phenomena, in no need to be substituted by other religious traditions; cf. K. Rose, *Pluralism*, 34–35, 50, 56–57. In a polyphilic view, as proposed here, religious traditions would *not* be considered "independent" in this sense, even to the point of a new essentialism, as they are involved in a complex transreligious dynamics of coinherence and even coinhabitation; cf. Chapters 11–12. Nor does the polyphilic in-sistence on differentiation need to reduce all communication between religions (or even in establishing criteria for such conversations by diverse religion-specific theologies of religions) to pluralistic engagements, that is, it can embrace a pluralism of pluralisms that embraces religion-specific pluralistic discourses, based on their specific commitments to the symbolisms of their paths, *and* a pluralism of exclusivism, inclusivism and pluralism; cf. Chapter 7.
15. Cf. Deleuze, *Fold*, chs. 6, 9; Faber, *Manifold*, chs. 13, 15; Keller, *Cloud*, ch. 5.
16. Bahá'u'lláh, *Seven Valleys* (Valley of Wonderment), 54–55.
17. Whitehead renders this polyphilic Mystery as "harmony of harmonies"; cf. Whitehead, *Adventures*, 285–86, 295–96; Faber, *Poet*, §§24, 39. This again relates to Deleuze's "polyphony of polyphonies"; cf. Deleuze, *Fold*, 82; Faber, *Manifold*, chs. 1–2, 8, Epilogue (On Chapter 2 and 8).

is to become *one with* (instead of "for" or "instead of") all religions.[18] Two quotations may demonstrate this principle. 'Abdu'l-Bahá observes that the way to reconciliation and unity does not abandon all religions for unity (to be found only in one's own), but, contrarily, proceeds by polyphilically embracing the truth in and of all religions. What is more, 'Abdu'l-Bahá considers it as *essential* to *seek* Truth/Reality in *all* religions.

> How it is necessary for a man to put aside all in the nature of superstition, and every tradition which would blind his eyes to the existence of truth in all religions. He must not, while loving and clinging to one form of religion, permit himself to detest all others. It is essential that he search for truth in all religions, and, if his seeking be in earnest, he will assuredly succeed.[19]

In perhaps the most comprehensive and potent, but concentrated and brief form, Shoghi Effendi has translated this counsel into this memorable expression:

> Let no one, however, mistake my purpose. The Revelation, of which Bahá'u'lláh is the source and center, abrogates none of the religions that have preceded it, nor does it attempt, in the slightest degree, to distort their features or to belittle their value. It disclaims any intention of dwarfing any of the Prophets of the past, or of whittling down the eternal verity of their teachings. It can, in no wise, conflict with the spirit that animates their claims, nor does it seek to undermine the basis of any man's allegiance to their cause. Its declared, its primary purpose is to enable every adherent of these Faiths to obtain a fuller understanding of the religion with which he stands identified, and to acquire a clearer apprehension of its purpose. It is neither eclectic in the presentation of its truths, nor arrogant in the affirmation of its claims. Its teachings revolve around the fundamental principle that religious truth is not absolute but relative, that Divine Revelation is progressive, not final. Unequivocally and without the least reservation it proclaims all established religions to be divine in origin, identical in their aims, complementary in their functions, continuous in their purpose, indispensable in their value to mankind.[20]

Here, this "withness" of the Bahá'í revelation in the concert of religions is spelled out in terms of several negative and affirmative aspects. On the apophatic, subtractive side, the unity of religions that Bahá'ís (should) contemplate does *not* mean the abrogation of other religions; the distortion of their features and the values they emulate; the diminution of their origin and originators; or the denigration of their genuine teachings and the spirit

---

18. Compare this "withness" with Arvind Sharma's claim about Hinduism to be truly pluralistic, because it does not arrogate itself to be the criterion of the truth of other religions, but rather a sample along with them; cf. Sharma, "Can There Be," 60.
19. 'Abdu'l-Bahá, *Paris Talks*, #42. Cf. 'Abdu'l-Bahá, *Promulgation*, #49: "Religions are many, but the reality of religion is one." 'Abdu'l-Bahá, *Paris Talks*, #41: "So shall we see the truth in all religions, for truth is in all, and all are one." 'Abdu'l-Bahá, in *Bahá'í Prayers*, 114: "O Thou kind Lord! Unite all. Let the religions agree and make the nations one, so that they may see each other as one family and the whole earth as one home. May they all live together in perfect harmony."
20. Shoghi Effendi, *World Order*, 57–58. I have quoted from a passage with similar intent and consequence in Chapter 10: *Promised Day*, 108.

that animates them. In other words, the Bahá'í claim to the unity of religions cannot mean the undermining of the allegiances of adherents to them.[21] On the polyphilic, affirmative side, the Bahá'í principle of religious unity must be applied in such a way that any given dialogue with another religion (and by extension between them) should lead to a deeper understanding of the unique contribution of these religions for their adherents and, I would add (especially if this is true), for Bahá'ís, too.[22] By avoiding both eclectic misconceptions of the spirit of other religions and the arrogance of superiority, yet by valuing the unique, "contrasting," that is, irreplaceable and unique, contributions of all of them,[23] "complementary" in their mutual function,[24] we will be able to understand and practice the radical implication of being *with* all religions: the relativity of religious truth in the "superposition" of vertical novelty *and* horizontal diversity in trust of (and being entrusted to us by) the Mystery from which this imperative springs.

In accordance with polyphilic pluralism, I propose that we will follow the Bahá'í principle of unity (of religions) and relativity (of religious truth) if we—meaning the "us" of all positions and identities, that is, wherever we are, in or outside of whatever tradition—are "with" other religions in such a way that by this engagement *all religions*

---

21. We may recognize, here, that Shoghi Effendi does not differentiate "religion" from "revelation," which could be used to imply that only the "revelation" is affirmed, but not the "religion" based on it. While it is true that the Bahá'í writings understand, with regard to the vertical axis, the novelty of its own "revelation" as "fulfillment" and concede the decline and death of religions as a spiritual fact (as explored throughout the book), this "reality" does not empower the alienation of adherence of these religions from their own "revelation" and, hence, the outright denial of the salvific relevance of these "religions" for their adherence.
22. Cf. Faber, "Bahá'u'lláh," 85–88. It would be a grave error to read into this suggestion of the text that this means one has been given the authority to understand the "other" religion better than the deep understanding that immanently to this tradition perpetuates its existence for itself, as it would reintroduce the arrogation of a superiority that the apophatic, subtractive side of the quotation has already excluded. Besides, it would be a regression to the poisonous fruits of unity for the demise of which this book as a whole has tried to argue. But its logical argument is simply that a fundamentally apophatic argument of unity only supports a polyphilic affirmation of multiplicity, not one of exclusivism or superiority (based on the misunderstanding of unity as that of a sedimented, reiterated One). As everything else, it must be understood as means for mutual learning of the inexhaustible depth of the multiplicity of the divine manifold in any limited appearance; cf. Faber, *Manifold*, ch. 5; *Becoming of God*, Exploration 10.
23. Cf. Bahá'u'lláh, *Gleanings*, #22: "[Ea]ch Manifestation of God hath a distinct individuality, a definitely prescribed mission, a predestined revelation, and specially designated limitations. Each one of them is known by a different name, is characterized by a special attribute, fulfills a definite mission, and is entrusted with a particular Revelation."
24. Shoghi Effendi's inclusion of the "complimentary" function of the diverse religions would be seriously undervalued or even contradicted if one would suppose that the "unity" of religions would not allow for profound mutual learning, even as an indication of the divine intention of maturation or "progressive" revelation throughout the infinite cycle of dispensations. It is, in fact, also the contemporary understanding of the attraction of "interreligious theology" to seek out such a complementarity as means of finding compatibility between the diverse traditions without presupposing identity; cf. Schmidt-Leukel, *Pluralism*, 133–36.

are equally elevated in their importance and are pursued by *mutually elevating their unique truths for the unending spiritual process* spiraling over the Earth and through infinite worlds, thereby releasing their innermost spirit to ever more resonate with the divine intention for the education of humankind toward a maturity in which being human would mean to participate in this religious story of cosmic magnitude.[25] This seems to be the meaning of Bahá'u'lláh's original phrase used to be translated into the Bahá'í term "progressive revelation": *'fa-lamma balagha al-amr'*—the "maturation" of religion.[26] The Bahá'í contribution to religious pluralism would, then, mean nothing more, or less, than to (be engaged in contributing to a climate in which all religions can) *become companions* and *consorts* in this spiritual evolution—on the one hand, being aware of its/their own depth of divine manifestation in itself/themselves, as this "bottomless depth" sheds new light on the universal process of spiritualization, and, on the other hand, being of a humble conviviality with others that comes with the expectation of a future beyond themselves.

This seems to be the meaning of Bahá'u'lláh's "glad tidings" (good news, *euangelion*) in the tablet *Bisharat* (which means "glad tidings") and his Book of Laws (*Kitab-i Aqdas*), namely, the imperative for all people and peoples, as well as all religions and their adherents, to "consort" (*'ashiru*) in close proximity and intimacy with one another, not as if, but because all of them (in their universal reality and particularity) *are* members of the same "clan."[27] The word used for "clan" (*'ahirah*), here, must be understood in the context of the Arabic culture surrounding the emergence of Muhammad and the Qur'an, namely, of being nothing without one's clan as one's most defining belonging[28]—so that Muhammad when he was expelled from his clan was basically "dead."[29] Now, if all are part of *one* "clan," there is no "other" anymore against which it can be construed as oppositional identity.[30] All religions belong together: conviviality! 'Abdu'l-Bahá has with great effect used the image of the tree to make the same point, namely, that there is only

---

25. Cf. Shoghi Effendi (*God*, 351–52), relating to the Bahá'í House of Worship in Wilmette, quotes his architect in saying: "'Into this new design,' he, furthermore, has written, '[…] is woven, in symbolic form, the great Bahá'í teaching of unity—the unity of all religions and of all mankind. There are combinations of mathematical lines, symbolizing those of the universe, and in their intricate merging of circle into circle, and circle within circle, we visualize the merging of all the religions into one.'"
26. Cf. Fazel, "Approaches," 43. For the transformation of a more stage-like understanding of "axial ages" to a more pluralistic "axiality" on the basis of the Bahá'í understanding of the cyclicity of the coming of divine Manifestations, cf. Schewel, "Religion," 26–27. This should not, however, upset the idea of a "second" or "new" axial age, as related to the universal, global and cosmic (interstellar) character of the "unity of reality" presupposed in the new axial religious consciousness, as the vertical pluralism in the Bahá'í context highlights the universal impact of the new revelation as precisely expressing and even instigating this character as specific for *this* new axial "age"; cf. Bahá'u'lláh, *Gleanings*, #10; Momen, *Bahá'u'lláh*, 200–1; Stockman, *Bahá'í Faith*, 43.
27. Cf. Bahá'u'lláh, *Tablets* (#3), 22; *Aqdas*, ¶144; Fazel, "Pluralism," 5; "Dialogue," 2.
28. Cf. Aslan, ch. 1; Balyuzi, *Muhammad*, ch. 1; Armstrong, *Muhammad*, ch. 1.
29. Cf. Aslan, ch. 2; Balyuzi, *Muhammad*, chs. 3–8; Armstrong, *Muhammad*, ch. 2.
30. Cf. 'Abdu'l-Bahá, *Selections*, #221; M. W. Khan, chs. 5–6; Aslan, *No god*, ch. 3; Balyuzi, *Muhammad*, ch. 9; Armstrong, *Muhammad*, ch. 3.

one tree of humanity with all of its spiritual streams—there are not two; my tree of salvation, and the tree of damnation for all others.

> The teachings specialized in Bahá'u'lláh are addressed to humanity. He says, "Ye are all the leaves of one tree." He does not say, "Ye are the leaves of two trees: one divine, the other satanic." He has declared that each individual member of the human family is a leaf or branch upon the Adamic tree; that all are sheltered beneath the protecting mercy and providence of God; that all are the children of God, fruit upon the one tree of His love. God is equally compassionate and kind to all the leaves, branches and fruit of this tree. Therefore, there is no satanic tree whatever—Satan being a product of human minds and of instinctive human tendencies toward error. God alone is Creator, and all are creatures of His might. Therefore, we must love mankind as His creatures, realizing that all are growing upon the tree of His mercy, servants of His omnipotent will and manifestations of His good pleasure.[31]

One of the perhaps most potent symbols for the "withness" with and of all religions is the vision of the Bahá'í house of worship, the *mashriq al-adhkar*, the "Dawning Place of the Remembrance" of God/Reality.[32] Bahá'u'lláh devised it to be a place of conviviality of all religions and peoples, indifferent to creed, ethnicity, gender, status and any other differentiation, united as humanity in the remembrance of God/Reality and in the service to all of humanity.[33] It is to be a place of spiritual unity, of the presence of the spiritual worlds in the material, a place of the recitation of scriptures of all religions, of a united meditation and worship beyond any discriminating characteristics (but without erasing their enriching uniqueness).[34] Its heart is not the building, but the transformation issuing from the "heart" of all people and peoples—the spiritual "site" of the revelation of reality/God.[35] Bahá'u'lláh envisioned the construction of the *mashriq al-adhkar* to express all that is best in the world of being, and he mandated its rearing to all peoples of the world.[36] Its space is to be free of any images, in this *emptiness* letting only Reality speak, yielding to the Face of Reality appearing from apophatic hiddenness. It is the architectural equivalent of the movements of the transcending (ascending) apophatic and transcending (descending) polyphilic Mystery.[37] The Dawning Place of Remembrance is, as should our heart be, dedicated "in the name of Him Who is the Lord of all religions."[38]

---

31. 'Abdu'l-Bahá, *Promulgation*, #82.
32. Cf. "Mashriq'l-Adhkár (Arabic: Dawning Place of the Praise of God)," in *The Bahá'í Encyclopedia Project* @ http://www.bahai-encyclopedia-project.org/index.php?option=com_content&view=article&id=70:mashriqul-adhkar&catid=36:administrationinstitutions; Walbridge, *Sacred Acts*, 52. "Remembrance" is the title of the Báb, related to the Primal Will and its Manifestations; cf. Todd Lawson, "Terms," 1–64.
33. Cf. 'Abdu'l-Bahá, *Memorial*, 20; '*Bahá'í World Faith*, 414–419; *Selections*, #60.
34. Cf. Bahá'u'lláh, *Aqdas*, ¶¶115, 150.
35. Cf. 'Abdu'l-Bahá, *Tablets*, 678: "In reality, the radiant, pure hearts are the Mashrak-el-Azcar and from them the voice of supplication and invocation continually reacheth the Supreme Concourse."
36. Cf. Bahá'u'lláh, *Aqdas*, ¶31.
37. Cf. Shoghi Effendi, *God*, 351–52.
38. Bahá'u'lláh, *Aqdas*, ¶31.

Perhaps, then, the "trans" in the conceptual web of the term "transreligious" yields a fifth meaning,[39] inherent in the other four: the "transcendence" of religion(s) into the experience of, and life in, Reality, liberated from, but in polyphilic immanence feely engaged in, and always enlightening, human limitations of the mind's constructions that, if they are not acknowledged in their illusory power, degenerate into a cramped world of antagonistic dualisms into which religions without the practicing of the "trans" will always fall (and have so done in history). Divine manifestations (theophanies, revelations, figures, scriptures) are not of this kind of sedimentation into constructs[40]; they always sunder them, throwing us beyond their self-inflicted exclusivity, thrusting us into radical openness, the space in between and around—infinity flowing through all existents, supporting them as events, not as entities or beings or substances,[41] always becoming in a space of creative freedom and responsiveness,[42] spontaneity (without ulterior motives) and compassionate in-sistence in a world of becoming.[43] If we can reach beyond such constructions that have become prisons, we will, as 'Abdu'l-Bahá suggests, be admitted to Reality like the sun beaming on and in all of them, but not being of them,[44] so that we can live with them in new ways, "in light" of Reality, in which we always already "become," just one moment of recognition and surrender away.[45]

> The bestowals of God which are manifest in all phenomenal life are sometimes hidden by intervening veils of mental and mortal vision which render man spiritually blind and incapable but when those scales are removed and the veils rent asunder, then the great signs of God will become visible and he will witness the eternal light filling the world. The bestowals of God are all and always manifest. The promises of heaven are ever present.[46]

The fifth "trans" in "transreligious," then, may be folding the other four "trans" together: that of a transcending beyond religions (into meta-historical or wider horizons), into their becoming (the transition into new realities and their emergence), within their mutuality (the transformation between and within religions), and deep down to their shared depth (of non-difference beyond divergence). This is the "trans" of "translucency."[47] It relates the potentials of the phenomenal world, expressed in its diverse spiritual and religious facets, as waves of a deeper sea, the Ocean of God.[48] The infinite, unmanifest Reality may let the phenomenal world surface as "its" own manifestation, the world's (or worlds') religions surfing the waves of the ocean on rafts or arcs[49]; or "it"

---

39. Cf. the exposition of the other four meanings of "transreligious" in Chapter 11.
40. Cf. Bahá'u'lláh, *Prayers*, 295; *Gleanings*, #70.
41. Cf. Whitehead, *Concept*, ch. 2.
42. Cf. Whitehead, *Adventures*, 194–97.
43. Cf. Whitehead, *Process*, 342–51; Faber, *Manifold*, chs. 9–10.
44. Cf. 'Abdu'l-Bahá, *Promulgation*, #49; Faber, *Manifold*, ch. 11.
45. Cf. Bahá'u'lláh, *Iqan*, §§44, 74.
46. 'Abdu'l-Bahá, in *Bahá'í World Faith*, 266.
47. Cf. Faber, *Manifold*, 464–69; *Garden*, 210–21.
48. Cf. Bahá'u'lláh, *Tabernacle*, #3; *Tablets*, #17 (247); 'Abdu'l-Bahá, *Promulgation*, #62.
49. Cf. Sours, *Tablet of the Holy Mariner*, 2 (verse 4), 45–47.

may envelop them with "its" depth or as "its" surface surges round them, the islands, archipelagos, lagoons or reefs in "its" midst; or "it" may yield their play as curls and vortices of "its" own face.[50] Religions may be doors or gates to the deeper or higher foldings or unfoldings of Reality,[51] or "its" own expressions within the apophatically "indifferent" and polyphilically immanent mutuality of infinite worlds and realms, indescribably beyond, but already ineffably enfolded within, our "reality."[52]

Images and models abound. The phenomenal reality may become "translucent" as shadow of the *mutual immanence* of all worlds, and in the Mind, Will, Word, Spirit, Manifestation or Body of God.[53] Or we may engage the image of a *holographic encoding* of the manifold of an indefinitely varied dimensionality of spiritual and (differently) physical worlds by which each world may realize itself only in being part of the other, as all worlds would be part of one another—in coinherence.[54] Or we may prefer the *emanation model of cascading worlds* by which each world is enfolded in another horizon of greater mutuality and unification, and unfolded in more constraint horizons of mutual transcendence and diversification, so that in relation to the other worlds each one may relativistically appear as more or less spiritual or physical than the other.[55] Or we speak of *successive unifications* of the multiplicity of cosmic and religious movements of the mind, recovering the immediate life of the diverging past and releasing themselves into a future that is always anticipated as novel fulfillment of this flow.[56]

The process universe supplies the concepts to these images. There is no boundary to the depths and range of universes that the primordial and consequent dimensions of God, the Poet of the world,[57] embrace, envelope, inhere and instigate in ever new creative variations, luring them to ever-new mutuality and manifold diversifications, but, as they are themselves coinhering in a cycle of love with one another and all worlds, uniting

---

50. Cf. Genesis 1:2: "the face of the deep"; Keller, *Face*, ch. 1; Medina, 37, 47.
51. Cf. Bahá'u'lláh, *Gleanings*, #43; 'Abdu'l-Bahá, *Paris Talks*, #45.
52. Cf. Bahá'u'lláh, *Gleanings*, #79; *Aqdas*, ¶116.
53. Cf. 'Abdu'l-Bahá, *Questions*, 69:3; *Promulgation*, #4; *Selections*, ##21, 150:1–2; *Bahá'í World Faith*, 364; McFague, ch. 6; Saiedi, *Gate*, chs. 7–8; Momen, "God," 23–26.
54. The holographic image or model wants to convey, first, that physical reality is the mapping of a deeper, higher-dimensional (quantum) reality implicit in the lower-dimensional image; second, that all locations of physical reality, therefore, mirror in some perspective way all other locations (i.e. its non-locality); third, that the deeper reality is mind-like and, hence, that matter is in some sense a secondary appearance of it; and, fourth, that deeper reality in some sense harbors meaningful constraints, expressed in physical reality as direction, evolution and meaningful coordination of processes. Cf. Bohm, ch. 7; Capra, *Turning Point*; Marshal and Zohar; Talbot, 34–39.
55. Cf. 'Abdu'l-Bahá, *Tablet of the Universe (Lawh-i-Aflákiyyih)*. In this tablet, 'Abdu'l-Bahá understands the multiplicity of physical and spiritual realities as interrelated, as divine emanation allowing for evolution and as mutually immanent. The relativistic picture is even heightened by the fact that every level or plane of reality is in relation to any higher, more spiritually united reality physical, and in relation to lower, more divergent realities, spiritual; cf. Ranjbar; Faber, *Garden*, ch. 5 and Epilogue, section 4.
56. Cf. Haught, *Story*, ch. 1–3.
57. Cf. Whitehead, *Process*, 346; Faber, *Poet*, 14–15.

them all by their apophatic indifference and luring them to new shores by their polyphilic in-sistence in all of them.[58] The four modes of unison in this process universe explicated earlier—the permeating rain of divine in-sistence, the rivers of unending creative flows, the clouds of infinitely diversified potentials, the formless sea of mutuality itself from which all spring and in which all modes end[59]—are just modes of the unison of Process itself, infinitely pulsating in "in/differentiation," simultaneously the divine and mundane differentiation and indifferentiation of one another.[60] The All of diversification is already in unison with all becomings, the minute unifications of the All in all events; and the All of all becomings is the universal mutuality of all realities in the unison of Reality with all realities and their becoming.[61] And the All is always in a movement of overflowing into unprecedented renewal and realization attracted by the future that is the ever-moving harmony of harmonies,[62] "from within" energized and carried by a divine entirely living nexus, the pure life of the Spirit.[63]

The Bahá'í writings concur with all of these images and models without binding themselves to any of them contrary to all others. They can speak of the physical or phenomenal world as shadows, images, surfaces or unfoldings of an infinite and indefinitely many-folded and -folding spiritual reality,[64] unified in, pervaded by and emanating from the Spirit, Word, Mind or Will of God/Reality (not even these images are systematized, but polyphilic expressions of apophatic Reality).[65] They can speak of the mutuality of all physical and spiritual dimensions of this and any world,[66] mediated by the in-sistent presence of the divine Reality in all of them[67] as "innermost Reality of all things" or "Reality of Realities" (*haqiqah-i haqiqat*),[68] the Ocean of which all worlds are waves[69] or

---

58. Cf. Whitehead, *Process*, 350–51; Faber, *Poet*, §§15–16, 24, 30; *Becoming of God*, Explorations 3 and 9; *Garden*, ch. 5; Baier, "Reality," 96–101. The cycle of love *is* the expression of mutual immanence of all realities, which *is* the ultimacy of ultimacy that cannot be reiterated as ultimacy "beyond" non-ultimate reality and, hence, is the circulation of love among them, their mutual ex-sistence, expressed in the in-sistence of Reality/God in the mutuality of all realities: ultimacy is the *medium* of which all isolating dualisms of naming (like God and the world) are abstractions.
59. For their exploration, cf. Chapter 13. Also cf. Whitehead, *Religion*, 88–89; Faber, *Becoming of God*, Exploration, 10.
60. Cf. Whitehead, *Process*, 348; Faber, *Poet*, §§31, 40; *Manifold*, ch. 13; *Becoming of God*, Exploration 11.
61. Cf. Whitehead, *Process*, 340, 345–46, 350.
62. Cf. Whitehead, *Adventure*, 177; Faber, *Poet*, §§16, 24, 43–44; *Manifold*, ch. 15; *Becoming*, Explorations 3 and 13.
63. Cf. Whitehead, *Process*, 105–13; Faber, *Poet*, §39.
64. Cf. Bahá'u'lláh, *Seven Valleys* (Valley of Wonderment), 54–55; 'Abdu'l-Bahá, *Promulgation*, #96; *Questions*, #81; *Selections*, #50; *Medina*, Faith, 42–49.
65. Cf. 'Abdu'l-Bahá, *Questions*, #53; *'Abdu'l-Bahá in London*, 95; *Promulgation*, ##103–104.
66. Cf. 'Abdu'l-Bahá, *Questions*, #67; *Promulgation*, ##4, 93; *Selections*, #137.
67. Cf. Bahá'u'lláh, *Gleanings*, #153; 'Abdu'l-Bahá, *Promulgation*, #96.
68. Bahá'u'lláh, *Iqan*, §§101, 105. The translation of Shoghi Effendi underscores Reality's in-sistence in and indifference from all realities; the original Persian formulation, conversely, highlights the ultimate character of Reality of which all phenomenal realties are only shadows; Savi, *Summit*, 36–37.
69. Cf. 'Abdu'l-Bahá, *Questions*, #82; *Paris Talks*, #28; *Selections*, ##36, 162.

by which they are embraced like swarms of fish in the unfathomable and open sea.[70] They can express the deep implication of the unfolding physical reality with its diversification into the indifference of infinite spiritual unifications approximating Reality, like the beams of the sun becoming indifferentiated in their origin of light, or like drops merging with the sea,[71] until they disappear into nothingness—in the fullness of "its" all-ness besides which there is nothing.[72] And they remind us of the ever new diversifications and unifications, everlastingly pulsating in convivial coinhabitation, in which the All is always indifferentiated in the Ocean of God, but also springs from "it" again as clouds, rain and rivers of spiritual life, ever expressing the unison of a manifold of which religions are only the events, drops, flows and waves.

---

70. Cf. Bahá'u'lláh, *Epistle*, 160; 'Abdu'l-Bahá, *Bahá'í Word Faith*, 339; *Selections*, #218; *Questions*, #10.
71. Cf. 'Abdu'l-Bahá, *Paris Talks*, #17; *Promulgation*, #124; *Questions* #80.
72. Cf. Bahá'u'lláh, *Gleanings*, ##22–23, 125; *Prayers*, #176. Bahá'u'lláh's formulations do not indicate pantheism, as already mentioned, but "indifferentiation" of creation in God such that the All in God is implicated only *as* God and explicated in differentiation *from* God, eminently resonant with Nicolas of Cusa's rhythm of *complicatio* and *explicatio*; cf. Faber, *Poet*, §40; *Manifold*, ch. 12. As there is no merging with the essence (*al-dhat*) of God/Reality (*al-haqq*), the apophatic subtraction remains in all of these enveloping affirmations intact; cf. 'Abdu'l-Bahá, *Questions*, ##53–54.

GLOSSARY

This glossary is not intended to facilitate a complete or sufficient introduction to the complex universe of concepts employed in the discourses on religious pluralism, the unity of religions and the involved matters and methods of the spiritual and academic symbolisms used to express them in this book. It is also not a complete or exhaustive collection of special terms appearing in the corpus of the text. Rather, this glossary wants to allow for a first impression of my own use of specific and unfamiliar terms, names, movements and concepts, so as to simplify the access to their presentation in this book.

'Abdu'l-Bahá (1844–1921) is the eldest son of Bahá'u'lláh and one of only two authentic interpreters of Bábí-Bahá'í texts revered as revelation and scripture. His own writings and talks are considered to be of the same status and relevance as the texts they interpret or to which they add his exploratory voice. He witnessed the tragic events of the imprisonment, torture and successive exiles imposed on his father, the founder of the Bahá'í religion, from a young age on; became an important amanuensis of Bahá'u'lláh and his spokesperson to the authorities for the Bahá'í community in exile; emerged as a most gifted communicator within and without the emerging worldwide Bahá'í community; and was in conversation with many of the leading figures of religious, social and political reform in his time. After his final release from confinement as political prisoner of the Ottoman Empire, effected by the revolution of the Young Turks in 1908, he traveled to Egypt, several European countries, Canada and the United States, between 1911 and 1913, in an effort to promote universal peace and disarmament, racial and religious amity and unity, and the religious principles of the Bahá'í Faith, such as: the unity of Reality/God, of religions and of humanity; equality of the genders; harmony of science and religion; freedom of consciousness and independence of the investigation of truth; deep dialogue between religions; and the overcoming of all prejudices. On the basis of these and other spiritual teachings of Bahá'u'lláh, he called for the ethical, social, economic and political transformation of humanity into a world-embracing civilization of peace. He commissioned the American Bahá'ís with the worldwide expansion of the Faith; invoked the new spirit of the Bahá'í teachings' universal religious reform of human religiosity; and lived exemplarily the characteristics of such a spiritual transformation. When he died in Haifa in 1921, representatives of many religious communities, as diverse as Jewish, Muslim, Christian and Druze, as well as civil authorities whose trust he has won locally and internationally over decades, attended his burial together with scores of the population in the Akko-Haifa area to which he was well known as a humanitarian reformer and spiritual leader of rare appearance. He was interred in the shrine that he built for the Báb on Mount Carmel.

Apophasis is a term that indicates a sense of the inexpressibility of the nature of ultimate reality or God in light of the dialectic of their essential hiddenness in all contingently manifest appearances of their traces in diverse forms, such as nature, mind, self, revelations and religious figures, for instance, founders of religions, and the oral and written expressions of such figures. The term is used in a technical sense in mystical discourses of and on diverse religious traditions worldwide for the methodical way of "unsaying," that is, the untying of consciousness, experience and understanding from the conceptual boundaries by which the mind tries to understand and grasp reality, and as indication of the existential nature of the impossibility to express ultimate reality in any adequate way by whatever medium. It is a process that follows the "word" into the "silence" before it was spoken; an awareness of the "inexpressible stillness" in any "moving expression" of itself; and a way to recognize the immanence of divinity in all reality *as* infinitely transcendent. The use of this term favors cosmological and religious views that are aware of the danger of, and want to perpetually escape, all parochial or limiting claims made on religious or ultimate truth and, hence, is essential for the formulation of religious pluralism. Its related and contrasted term is *polyphilia*.

The Báb (1819–50), Sayyid 'Ali Muhammad of Shiraz, is the prophet-founder of the Bábí religion. He declared himself in 1844 to be the promised eschatological figure expected both by Shi'i and Sunni Islam under the name of the Qa'im or Mahdi, respectively. In the gradual understanding of his revelation, his claim became understood as a self-transignification from the Gate (*báb*) of the twelfth Imam of Shi'ism to the Gate of another figure that the Báb named as the One Whom God Shall Make Manifest, an even greater figure who will be the fulfillment of the desires and expectations of all religions. After forming an initial community of 18 disciples, the Letters of the Living, and their distribution of the Báb's writings, the new religion spread rapidly among diverse sections of the Persian population, and the Báb became recognized as exhibiting an authority that transcends the Prophet Muhammad. As the imperial and religious authorities were intimately aware of the religious and political implications of such a claim, the Báb was incarcerated, condemned to isolation and transported to successively remoter areas of the Persian Empire. Eventually, he was tried and, by the conspiring efforts of the leading authorities of state and religion, committed to martyrium. He was executed by a 750-men strong firing squad in Tabriz in 1850. Bahá'u'lláh defended the status of the Báb as independent universal Manifestation of Reality/God and acclaimed himself as the expected eschatological figure of the Bábí religion, the One Whom God Shall Make Manifest, in the following decades virtually converting the whole remaining Bábí adherence into the nascent Bahá'í community. After hiding the remains of the Báb's body at diverse places for 59 years, known only to a small group of devoted adherents to Bahá'u'lláh, and after Bahá'u'lláh designated a place for the final interment of the Báb on Mount Carmel, 'Abdu'l-Bahá built such a shrine and dedicated it with a ceremonial burial of the Báb in 1909, which became the center of the Bahá'í Gardens in Haifa.

The **Bábí-Bahá'í Religions** are related, successive movements: the first, the Bábí movement, originating in 1844 with the declaration of the Báb in Persia, the Kingdom of Iran, within Shi'i Islam, was in its self-understanding ushering in the fulfillment of the Islamic eschatological expectation of a new figure or figures that will renew or follow the Islamic dispensation, being the sign of the eschatological coming of God on the day of resurrection and judgment; the second, the Bahá'í movement, originating with the declaration of Bahá'u'lláh in 1863, was to be the fulfillment of the expectation of Bábí movement of the coming of a pleromatic eschatological figure that is expected in many religions. Both movements constitute themselves from their inception not as reform movement within their parent religion, but as new religions in their own right. Similar to the relationship between Judaism and Christianity or Hinduism and Buddhism, both religions understand the novelty of their event also to be the fulfillment of their heritage, as all religions become dispensations in one history of religions or one history of divine revelation or engagement of ultimate reality with the world of humanity and the Earth. Despite their successive integration of the world's religions, in a new axial consciousness, as new expressions of the *one* religion of all of humanity, they both understand themselves also as one more dispensation in an unending process of religious renewal beyond themselves.

The **Bahá'í Faith** is the new religion founded by Bahá'u'lláh with his declaration to be the expected eschatological figure of the Bábí religion, first, in 1863, secretly to a few companions, and, from 1866 on, publicly to the Bábí community and the world at large in the form of letters and declarations to religious leaders and kings and heads of state of the time in Asia, Europe and America. Its central figures are the Báb, the Forerunner, Bahá'u'lláh, the Prophet-Founder, and 'Abdu'l-Bahá, the Exemplar and Authorized Interpreter, as well as the great grandson of Bahá'u'lláh, Shoghi Effendi, the Guardian of the Faith, with whom the organization found its greatest expansion to become the second most widely distributed and diversified religious community worldwide after Christianity with currently between five and seven million adherents. Since 1963, the Bahá'í community is governed by the democratically elected Universal House of Justice with the seat in Haifa, Israel, based on the provisions of Bahá'u'lláh, envisioned at the place of his last banishment to Ottoman Syria and Palestine.

The **Bahá'í Writings** name the scriptural, sacred and authoritatively interpretive texts of the Bahá'í Faith. They consist of the writings of the Báb and Bahá'u'lláh, both considered as sacred scripture for Bahá'ís; the writings and talks of 'Abdu'l-Bahá, considered sacred writings and interpretations of these revelations; as well as the authoritative writings of Shoghi Effendi. They comprise roughly about 100,000 documents, reaching from short letters to book-length treaties, and spanning diverse literary forms, such as divine verses, prayers, spiritual reflections, meditations, exhortations, prophesies, instructions, legal ordinances and diagnostic and analytic detections of contemporary situations in cultural, religious, political and social matters. The writings relate often to scriptures and sacred literatures of other religions which, in their own understanding, are to be considered of the same sacred character. The writings of the Bahá'í scriptures are considered the expression of the creative Word of God and, hence, themselves transformative in the spiritual evolution of their readers.

Bahá'u'lláh (1817–92), Mirza Husayn 'Ali of Nur, is the prophet-founder of the Bahá'í religion, the expected eschatological fulfillment of the Bábí religion and of all religions in their envisioning of the coming of such a figure. In his own and the Bahá'í understanding, Bahá'u'lláh is a "Manifestation of God" of the same rank as the founders or revealers of other world-impacting religions, such as Abraham, Moses, Jesus, Muhammad, the Buddha, Zoroaster, Krishna and the Báb. Being from an ancient Persian noble family, he became a prominent Bábí in 1844; survived the pogroms of the religious and imperial leadership of Iran against the Bábí community around and after the martyrdom of the Báb in 1850; was repeatedly imprisoned, tortured and exiled—first to Baghdad in 1853, then to Istanbul and Adrianople in 1863, and, finally, to the prison city of the Ottoman Empire, Akko, in the province Syria in Palestine, near Haifa, in 1868. While his imprisonment in Akko was meant to be final and terminal, his family and companions were released after two years, but remained confined to the city area as political prisoners of the Ottoman government. Bahá'u'lláh's son, 'Abdu'l-Bahá, later arranged for Bahá'u'lláh's movement to properties in the near countryside, Mazrai and Bahji, where he died and was interred. His shrine in Bahji is now the sacred spot (*qiblah*) to which Bahá'ís direct their prayers. In his testament, Bahá'u'lláh installed 'Abdu'l-Bahá as the only authoritative interpreter of his revelation and writings.

Becoming is not intended as a concept opposite "being," but, in terms of process philosophy, names the universal form being takes, namely, to be a process of self-constitution, of coming-to-be. Here, any being is "in becoming" and Being is a mode of Becoming, namely, to-have-become. The implication of this view, in cosmological integration of ontological and epistemological, physical and metaphysical perspectives, is not only that Being is an activity of creative movement, in process philosophy called Creativity, but that every state of things is nothing but a moment within and from the becoming of that state or of that state into another one. Nothing, in this view, has just Being or a state of sameness; not even God or ultimate reality can be understood in static terms of Being or Nothingness. If Becoming is more "original" than Being, in fact, the perpetual, everlasting "origin" of any being, state, continuity and constancy, such as eternity, unchangeability and the like, then nothing can be reduced to "one" origin, but is bound to dissipate into a multiplicity of beginnings and will dissipate in a multiplicity of endings, which are new beginnings. This multiplicity of relatedness is the basis for connectivity and pluralism as natural "habits" of organization, physically, biologically, sociologically and religiously. Related terms are divine manifold, multiplicity, event and process, process thought and Whitehead.

Coinhabitation refers to the three notions of habitation, inherence and correlation. It fuses their meaning in the context of the concept of the unity of religions as well as religious pluralism to indicate that religions are mutually immanent to the extent that they, whether their adherents know it or not, occupy the same spiritual, cosmological and mental open space, defined by the unity of religions in the unity of Reality or God and of humanity. Not only does this term presuppose that no reality or claim to reality can be totally external to any other, such that a relativity of religious truth claims undergirds the inherent self-constitution of any religious identity in differentiation from any other, but this notion conveys that such a mutual immanence is the very basis for the differences to be realized as relational instead of separative. It is an important countermeasure against ideologies that want to understand separation and exclusion, strive and violence, as the natural state of religious communication and, instead, promulgates the common habitat of any differentiation as the spiritually mature aim of all religious development—not as an external aim, but as a presupposed reality to be awakened.

Coinherence refers to the three notions of coherence, inherence and correlation. It fuses their meaning in the context of the concept of the unity of religions as well as religious pluralism to indicate that, on many complex levels, such as the spiritual, communal, doctrinal and cosmological, religions are related in a way that can be demonstrated to be coherent, that is, not haphazardly external, but organically and harmoniously internal; to be inherently related to one another, for instance, by the unity of the ultimate reality to which they are relating; and to be correlative, as their history and deep spiritual roots are understood to be mutually immanent to their origination and development.

Cosmology refers, in this book, to both the physical and the spiritual cosmos of which human beings and their religions are seen as creatively intersectional motors of maturation. Religions harbor always spiritual cosmologies, often explicated in philosophical terms and universes of discourses that embed the immediate religiously driving questions in wider contexts of the origination and meaning of the world as a whole beyond, but inclusive of, humanity. Cosmology also integrates ontology and epistemology, that is, questions of being and of access to knowledge, but, by indicating a "good" or "beautiful" order of things, harmonizes questions of existential nature that seek the relation between necessity and contingency, freedom and grace, nature and culture, mind and matter to one another. Religions are imbedded in cosmologies, and the questions of unity and plurality are always already encoded or justified in cosmological terms. Cosmological universality is also responsible for relativizing any anthropocentric and anthropomorphic tendencies and reductions of religious reflections instead of ecological and interstellar universality by which all religious questions will appear in a new light.

Creativity and God in Process Thought are two mutually related expressions of ultimate reality that are nondually indifferent, yet not identical; but they are also not, in my own understanding, dualistically contrasted to one another. A. N. Whitehead differentiates Creativity and God as activity and actuality, essential acting and purposefully acting. Both are expressions of one another, however, as God is the creative act in which potentials are creatively transformed into values with the purpose to infuse them into all events and processes as means of a seduction to the realization of their best potentials at every given moment—Whitehead calls this the Primordial Nature of God—and the divine reception of the actualizations of these values by all becomings, events and processes, and their cosmic organizations, into God's actuality or self-constitution as creative process—Whitehead calls this the Consequent Nature of God. In both modes of divine activity, Creativity is the very activity of the unification of potentials and actualities (many-becoming-one), and their polyphilic gift to the process of multiplication (one-becomes-many). However, God never exhausts Creativity, as it is the essential activity of all events and processes, which again means that God does not act coercively, but that the power of God, in process thought, is suggestive, receptive and imaginative, creatively instigating more creativity in all acts of becoming. Related terms are becoming, event and process, nondualism, polyphilic pluralism, process thought, A. N. Whitehead and ultimate reality/God.

The **Cycle of Love** indicates the in-sisting, nondual, creative, receptive and suggestive relationship between God and the world, meaning all events and processes comprised by cosmology, as one of mutual immanence. Neither is independent from the other, nor are they identical or definitive expressions of any particular aspect that can be named of this relationship. Rather, they dance in a process of mutuality in which the love of receptive transformation provides the basis for a polyphilic nature of the processuality of the universe. The cycle of love is an apophatic-polyphilic cycle; and it is *of love*, as it identifies itself by the mutual inclusion and transformation of God and the world by a sym-pathy (the feeling of the other in the other), which is driven only by the actualization of divine virtues toward their greatest possible actualizations, as the motif force of mutual relationship and freedom, in the pulsation between unification and multiplication. Related terms are becoming, creativity and God in process thought, divine manifold, multiplicity, *polyphilia*, polyphilic pluralism and ultimate reality/God.

Divine Manifold is a term that indicates an understanding of ultimate reality or God beyond the usual differentiations into their theistic and non-theistic religious renderings, as well as beyond their categorization into pantheistic or panentheistic alternatives to theism. It means to say that divine reality is neither one nor many, but, beyond both of them, accessible only in infinite forms of relational differences and differentiated relations. All such accesses are understood as folds of a manifold, the manifold itself being the folding of unity and difference, one and many, to an origami of theophany, seamlessly infinitely folding, thereby ever escaping any fixations or separations. On this basis, the unity of religions and religious pluralism relate to this manifold as the ultimately apophatic reality that, however, is not an illusion, disappearing in mere relativism, but a divine presence of infinitely manifold, but relationally contained, expressions of ultimate Goodness, Beauty and Truth. Related terms are *apophasis*, *polyphilia* and theopoetics.

Event and Process are not, as often used, opposite terms, indicating singularity and complexity. In the process philosophical perspective, every event is a process, and every process is a series of events. Both event and process are forms of becoming, and both are involved to conceptually understand becoming. The event of becoming is a certain process of identity-forming by which a multiplicity of inherited past events is more or less creatively related, recombined and integrated so as to form a unity that is open to become one of the events of a new multiplicity of events that will form another event in an endless process of self-constitution of events in becoming. The universe, then, is a process of processes, that is, of an infinite multiplicity of events of becoming, forming integrated structures or patterns of repetition in this process of becoming, becoming diversified as organisms, fields, laws, natural realms and *cosmoi*. Religions can also be understood in terms of events and processes, emphasizing their relatedness as a multiplicity in an infinite process of becoming or renewal, indicating the inevitability of religious pluralism and the kind of unity of religions envisioned through the process lens. Related terms are becoming, cosmology and process philosophy.

Horizontal and Vertical Pluralism name a differentiation of religious reality in light of a religious pluralism that relates and unifies the diachronic (temporal) and synchronic (contemporary) dimensions of the plurality of religions, that is, expresses the meaning of the unity of religions as one of a multiplicity in light of the divine manifold. This dual concept is not only descriptive of spatiotemporal facts of human existence, including its religions, but is an analytic instrument creating a basis for the understanding of the shortcomings of religious exclusivism and inclusivism, and suggesting a prescriptive necessity for a way forward beyond any religious strife arising because of claims of truth that leads to mutual denigrations, superiority and supersessionism. It aims at a transreligious peace that is based on a deeper understanding of the field of tensions that vibrates by the relationship of these two dimensions of space and time, of diverse evolution and contemporary alternative identity, and of immanent inheritance and surprising encounter. With this instrument, we can create a field of potential realizations of religious relationships that comprises all possible alternatives and asks how such potentials can lead to or hinder interreligious peace. Related terms are polyphilic pluralism and progressive revelation.

Indifference is a philosophical term that indicates the dialectic of transcendence and immanence, of detachment and compassion, of mystical apophasis and sacred in-sistence in multiplicity of Reality/God. In differentiation from mere indifference, which suggests either ontological separation or emotional lack of care or love or relatedness, here, indifference should be read as "in-difference" or "in/difference." In nondual manner, this means that indifferent Reality that transcends all differentiations "is" only "*in* the differences" of the multiplicity of realities in and on which it in-sists. Related terms are in-sistence, nondualism, *apophasis* and *polyphilia*.

In-sistence is a philosophical term that indicates the "being-in" or "becoming-in" of ultimate reality or God in all reality and experience, on every level of existence. This term means to convey that ultimate reality or God is beyond any definition, even that of "existence" or Being, as these terms are already abstractions from Becoming (or modes of it). While, thereby, Reality/God is beyond being and nothingness, it is not apophatically unavailable or inactive, enwrapped in ancient silence, but is understood as creative activity, active in all phenomenal reality. Ultimate reality or God do not exist, but in-sist. The term has two dimensions: "to insist on" and "to insist in." The latter aspect emphasizes that God or ultimate reality cannot be understood apart from any reality, as they are not identical with, but also not different from, anything; rather they "are" nondually only *in* that which through "it" becomes, or comes into being or existence. The former indicates that Reality/God actively insists *on* this relationality as its polyphilic presence. Through in-sisting "on" and "in" all becoming (all that is), everything ex-sists, that is, becomes "from" or "out of" one another, is relationally mutually immanent in a creative process of becoming. In the context of the unity of religions, this indicates that Reality/God cannot be found beyond the multiplicity of religions relatively related in a mutual constitution of "ex-sistence" from one another. Related terms are coinherence, coinhabitation and indifference.

Interstellar Consciousness/Horizon is, within transreligious discourse, an important corrective against the anthropocentric and anthropomorphic reductions of religious consciousness against which it situates the becoming of religions not only within humanity and contextualizes humanity itself in the wider evolutionary, ecological and cosmological context of a vast universe or multiverse. In this context, not only are parochial views on the exclusive truth of one religion over another, but claims of the universal relevance of these particular views for the whole cosmos, brought in stark relief with the vastness of the multiplicity of the universe in which religious pluralism becomes inevitable, as it is not even clear whether other beings with religious consciousness would be able to communicate in any categories we might have formulated based on the specific evolution of humanity on the planet Earth. Conversely, the unity of this vast multiplicity of cosmic realms also indicates that nothing is merely independent from one another, such that some kind of resonance of characters in the processes of becoming will undergird a relational potential of communication of the religious explorations of these alien beings. Related terms are cosmology, Manifestation of Reality/God, progressive revelation, multiplicity and process thought.

The **Manifestation of Reality/God** is a central concept of the Bahá'í writings indicating the multiplicity and unity of the origination of religious consciousness, formation, identity and history as mediated through human figures by their extraordinary ability to communicate ultimate reality or God. The Báb and Bahá'u'lláh developed this notion from its more unspecific use in Islamic philosophy and wider philosophical considerations of theophanic appearances of divinity in religious history to characterize founders of religions, such as the Buddha, Jesus and Zoroaster, or symbolic representatives of religious renewal, such as Krishna, *beyond* their *own* chosen terminologies of appearances (theophany), incarnations, prophetic or avataric presences of the ultimate or divine with their limited scope and specific indications of oppositional or adversarial content in relation to one another. The inclusive characteristic of "universal Manifestations" is that they manifest ultimate reality or God "in person." Whether this is understood as divinity, prophethood, messengership (messiahship), theophanic appearance (*avatar*) or incarnation becomes secondary, mutually relative and pleromatic as a multiplicity of aspects of this basic event of manifestation. It this function, a Manifestation mediates the apophatic inaccessibility of Reality/God in the multiplicity of "its" polyphilic appearances. All Manifestations are *one* and *equal* in their reality presenting the world with the actualization of all the apophatic divine attributes "in person," and *different* in their specific circumstances of time, place and history, culture and society. Yet they always function as gatherer, instigator and promoter of the spiritualization of human civilization. In the transreligious discussion, the concept of Manifestation can play the role of transformative mediation of the relativity of the seemingly exclusive truths of the diverse religious identities in their own context. Related terms are *apophasis* and *polyphilia*, Bábí-Bahá'í religions, Bahá'í Faith, Bahá'u'lláh, progressive revelation, multiplicity, cosmology and polyphilic pluralism.

Multiplicity is a term alternatively used for manifold, that is, as "*pli*" means "fold," so multiplicity indicates the "foldedness" of reality. In it, unity and difference are addressed simultaneously, as it relates the unbroken continuity of reality in all of its differentiations and the nature of multiplicity as a process of folding, unfolding, enfolding and refolding. As multiplicity is a process of becoming and vice versa, it also indicates events of becoming or processes in which a manifold of events and processes gather together to new events and become part of a new multiplicity of becomings for new events and processes spanning all kinds of organizations and reorganizations that comprise the universe as a cosmos, as a well-tempered order in process. Religious becoming, the becoming of religions from one another, is such a multiplicity. Related terms are divine manifold, progressive revelation, *polyphilia* and process thought.

The **New Axial Age** indicates a diagnosis that signifies a new consciousness of religious connectivity in an age of global communication and the immediate global impact of regional events. While the idea of the axial age, as proposed by the German philosopher Karl Jaspers in the 1950s, intimates the becoming of universal religious consciousness in the middle centuries of the first pre-Christian millennium, the *new* axial age is characterized by religious movements and philosophical considerations that emphasize religious pluralism and the unity of religions, but situate their vision of religious peace and spiritual maturation of humanity in an ecological and cosmic context of the mutual relationality of all phenomenal existence instead of seeking salvation beyond the world. Related terms are transreligious discourse, religious pluralism and the unity of religions.

Nondualism is a term used in philosophy of religion and comparative religious studies to indicate a mode of thought that is mostly associated with the diverse mystical traditions within, between and outside of established religious communities and organizations. Its intention is to facilitate an escape from the mere alternatives of true or false, identity or opposition, unity or multiplicity, one or the other, and being or nothingness. In terms of Aristotelian logic, nondual statements violate the principle of contradiction and the excluded third by affirming solutions that transgress these rules of exclusion. They are structured with a more complex logic of the inclusion of excluded potentials, such as that which is one *and* its opposite (the coincidence of opposites), or *both* relative and absolute *and* neither, or *in* all nothing *of* it. Nondual formulations present us with the apophatic character of ultimate reality or God and the inescapability of the limitation of the human mind to symbolize or articulate reality. Yet they avoid both mere identification (pantheism) and separation (dualism) by including the excluded alternatives as signs of the transcendence of Reality/God. In the transreligious communication of insights of the nondual apophatic character of ultimate reality within any religious symbolism lies the inevitable multiplicity of religious connotations of this ultimate reality or God. Related terms are *apophasis*, multiplicity, becoming, *polyphilia*, polyphilic pluralism and theopoetics.

Polyphilia means the love of multiplicity. It indicates the divine manifold as the apophatic Reality that in-sists in indifference on and in the multiplicity of appearances of reality. It is the activity of Reality/God that loves to generate, infuse, gather and transform reality. It connects with *apophasis* to a *cycle* of transcending *apophasis* and in-sisting immanent love of the manifold. In the transreligious context, however, it specifically counters any non-pluralism as a violation of divine in-sistence, and it contrasts any apophatic pluralism that excludes the active nature of ultimate reality in the constitution of the multiplicity of reality and their recognition in diverse religious accesses. If God loves the manifold, God also loves the manifold *reactions* to the apophatic "indetermination" of any reiteration and sedimentation of wrong over right, true over false conceptualizations of God. Not, then, are these conceptualizations only symbolizations of imagination, but they are also always already revelations and realizations of divine potentials in the actualization of divine attributes, which are infinite, infinitely varied and always newly realizable as events and processes.

Polyphilic Pluralism is the mode the religious pluralism, promoted in this book, that is based on the apophatic-polyphilic cycle of love. On the one hand, it holds to the apophatic nature of Reality/God, which necessitates that there is *no* name and only *many* names, but never the one name, by which "it" can be named or conceptualized; on the other hand, it understands the in-sistence of Reality/God in all reality as "its" *unique* love of the manifold from which springs the necessity for multiple theopoetic symbolizations. Their multiple alternative limitations are not false images, but indications of the pleromatic active, creative and receptive nature of Reality/God to love the manifold reactions to its revelation in a manifold of reality, endlessly tracing the apophatic love in its polyphilic expressions. Diverse religions in their identities become expressions of this divine love for multiple reactions to its in-sistence. Related terms are *apophasis, polyphilia*, the cycle of love, the divine manifold, multiplicity, cosmology and theopoetics.

Process Thought is a generic term comprising process philosophy and process theology, based on the work of A. N. Whitehead, but also applications to areas such as ecology, cosmology, biology, psychology, sociology and physics. While other forms of process philosophy can be found in diverse cultural contexts such as ancient modes of philosophical Daoism (Laozi) and pre-Socratic Greek philosophy (Heraclitus), as well as newer forms of philosophy (Hegel), the term is specifically used for Whiteheadian process philosophy and theology. It is based on his understanding of the world as an organism of processes, consisting of events of becoming and differentiated in diverse organizations based on such processes as they form fields, societies and patterns of structural integrity and repetition, such as physical, biological or social beings, things and events. Related notions, explicatory of the more specific meaning associated with this form of process thought, as used in this book, are becoming, event and process, creativity and God in process thought, theopoetics and A. N. Whitehead.

Progressive Revelation has many meanings in different religious traditions and their specific theological reflections. In the Bahá'í context, it is a profound concept that describes the history of religions as unity and multiplicity such that their dialectic can be decoded as a *process* of unification and multiplication. While linear representations of this notion are of limited value, the complex of becoming of more or less closely related religions in the context of their mutual generation and the ongoing process of such a generation of new religions from old religions can now be understood as an infinite series of novel events of transreligious modes of mutual inheritance, mutual differentiation and complex mutual inclusion. This term is related to the concept of the Manifestations of Reality/God: they signify the driving forces and theophanic appearances of divine reality in the respective religious consciousness and experience of humanity; they are the means of the spiritualization of humanity; and they indicate an infinite cosmic process that far exceeds the planet Earth, as their appearance is a universal cosmic phenomenon and can be understood as the primordial reality of cosmic becoming. Other related terms are multiplicity, polyphilic pluralism, theopoetics and transreligious discourse.

Religious Pluralism has become a concept that universally signifies the need and intention to facilitate peace between religions, given the history of religious violence, but is also a philosophical term that proposes an alternative to religious exclusivism and inclusivism, which both in different degrees live from the superiority of a particular tradition regarding integrity, spiritual power or maturity, and the truth of its claims over and against all others. It can be proposed as parity between religions in their positive and negative impact on human development or with the conviction that all religious imaginations are illusions, leading to naturalism or another form of the dissolution of religious consciousness. Yet it can also foster a new spiritual consciousness of a transreligious nature, leading to, or being explanatory of, deep interreligious dialogues and hybrid religious identities or multiple religious belonging. It can be based on a more apophatic Kantian understanding of the inaccessibility of Reality or a more polyphilic Whiteheadian understanding of the relationality of all imaginations as creative realizations in the process of becoming. Its diachronic and synchronic interferences are the subject matter of this book, and its transreligious nature is among its constructive arguments.

Shoghi Effendi (1897–1957) is the grandson of 'Abdu'l-Bahá and the great grandson of Bahá'u'lláh. Only 24 years of age, he became the Guardian of the Bahá'í Faith per a surprising instruction revealed in the testament of 'Abdu'l-Bahá in 1922, but assumed this function only after a few years of reflection and preparation while Bahiyyih Khanum, the sister of 'Abdu'l-Bahá, led the Bahá'í community. He greatly furthered the organization and expanded the worldwide presence of the Bahá'í Faith; steered its presence in Palestine through the founding of Israel; secured and restored Bahá'í holy places where possible or tried to save them from desacralization and demolition by persecuting state and religious institutions in the countries of the Faith's origination; began the construction of the Bahá'í Gardens and the Bahá'í World Center in Haifa; facilitated the Bahá'í International Community to become part of the earliest United Nations Organization's admission of NGOs; and made all necessary preparations for the first election of the Universal House of Justice, the global governing body of the Bahá'í Faith with the seat at Haifa, in 1963. His extensive writings explore many of the unchartered questions and issues arising at a time of the consolidation of the organization and the exploration of the genuine spirit enshrined in Bahá'í scriptures for the growing global Bahá'í community; and they are the final corpus of authoritative interpretations of the Bahá'í sacred writings. His marriage with the Canadian Mary Sutherland Maxwell, Ruhiyyih

Khanum, herself an important Hands of the Cause of the Faith, who died in 2000 in Haifa, indicated the East-West bonds of the Bahá'í community. Shoghi Effendi passed away unexpectedly in London, in 1957, where he is interred. The understanding and implementation of his vast corpus of advises to individual believers, local, regional and national Bahá'í communities, and other international religious and governate institutions became a legacy that the Bahá'í community still tries to unfold.

Subtractive Affirmation circumscribes the apophatic-polyphilic cycle of love between the divine manifold and the creative becoming of reality as the activity of Reality/God. In this view, *apophasis* is not an effort of mystical unknowing or the surrender to a statement of the impossibility of any knowledge of ultimate reality or God, but an activity of God/Reality itself, namely, of actively subtracting itself from all associations *in* its affirmative in-sistence on and in all of the multiplicity of becoming. This term is an alternative naming of the divine manifold in its activity that is the heart of polyphilic pluralism. Other related terms are Manifestation of Reality/God, progressive revelation, surrationality and theopoetics.

Surrationality names the apophatic dimension in all understanding of ultimate reality insofar as it is generally, in diverse religious traditions, related to a concept of mind, logos, intellect or an intelligible order as representative of divinity or ultimacy, but cannot fathom Reality in its ultimacy itself. Rather, a mystery persists beyond any mind, intellect, rationality and understanding that cannot be rationalized; yet this mystery remains the basis for the intelligibility of the world and the immanent realization of the essential transcendence of Reality/God. In process thought, it correlates with the axiom that becoming is always more fundamental over and against any status, structure, law, being or state of things. All becoming can only be "reduced" to another *becoming*, not any fixed state or law, order or mind. No "origin" can account for the multiplicity of becoming, except the divine manifold, which is per definition beyond categories of unity and plurality, reason and relationality, division and unification. Other related terms include *apophasis, polyphilia*, polyphilic pluralism, theopoetics and process thought.

Theopoetics has a long and diverse history, in one of its origins indicating the Eastern Christianity's concept of "becoming divine" (*theosis*), signifying the sanctification of religious life to lead to the "participation" in divine nature (2 Peter 1:4). In more current theological discussions, this term was more often than not used to indicate the multiplicity of imaginations and images that necessarily flow from the apophatic nature of Reality/God as being beyond any of them, in principle. In my own understanding, the term is related to A. N. Whitehead's differentiation between Creativity and God. While God is as creative as are all beings, even if God is understood (as in the Bábí-Bahá'í religions and with a Qur'anic phrase) as the "best of creators," Whitehead reserves the ability to *save* the world in the transformative memory or reception of its actualization of divine values to God as the Poet of the World. This "theopoetic difference" between God and the world, on the one hand, demonstrates the "ontological difference" between Being and beings *not* to represent (or to be equated to) the divine-mundane difference, rejecting the ontotheological fallacy, and, on the other hand, explicates the apophatic-polyphilic cycle of love as one of the mutuality between divine and mundane imagination, rejecting the one-sided projection thesis of the illusionary application of false images onto apophatic reality.

Transculturalization, as I use it in this and related works, is an analytic category similar in its use of the "trans" to the term "transreligious." In its most basic meanings, this term indicates three related dimensions: the transcendent state of an essence predetermining the meaning of cultures; the transcending movement inherently driving cultures to creative modifications and transitioning into new modes and, eventually, the becoming of a different culture; and a movement of mutual immanence between cultures by which their identity is deconstructed into mutual relativity and interdependent togetherness. The first dimension reminds us of the search for identity, to always desire something, some essence or eternity, beyond the contingency of phenomenal reality, but also warns us that predeterminations might rob the phenomenal cultural realities of their life and vivid changes. The second dimension emphasizes the active movement beyond any fixed identity, relieving us of the search for a transcendent essence, but allowing an adventurous openness of a future or otherness of events and processes not yet realized in current or past instantiations of culture. The third meaning deconstructs identity into a mutuality of movements of cultures into one another as a matter of history and virtual futures. Related terms are becoming, event and process, coinherence, coinhabitation and transreligious discourse.

Transreligious Discourse is a central term to this book, as it not only indicates an analytic category for the understanding of religious history and constitution, but presents a prescriptive theory for the future of religions. Like the "trans" in "transcultural," it harbors multiple dimensions. In the analytic sense it can indicate an essence of religions, as in perennialism; a dynamic of self-transformation without essentialism, as in postmodern theories of religion; and a mutual relation between religious identities engaged in contingent relativities of development, as in religious dialogues and pluralistic theories of religion. "Transreligious" differs from the related adjectives "multireligious" and "interreligious" by emphasizing movement over plurality and becoming over relationship of identities, respectively. In its prescriptive function, as a virtue of the theopoetic cycle of love, however, "transreligious" indicates the vision of a new universal religious community of humanity in the context of ecological "religiosity" inherent in all things, as hinted at by the work of A. N. Whitehead, as I read it; a "religiosity" that facilitates and is the expression of a new civilization of peace in a "civilizing" universe. Related terms are religious pluralism, polyphilic pluralism, horizontal and vertical pluralism, cycle of love, theopoetics, process thought and the unity of religions.

Ultimate Reality/God is a dyad that indicates a non-differentiation between theistic and non-theistic understandings of what is of ultimate existential concern to humanity, but infinitely beyond its grasp. Yet the importance of such a non-differentiation or indifferentiation lies in two other aspects: that ultimate reality is *not* identical with any concept of God in the theistic sense; and that ultimate reality is *not* an ultimate beyond its indifference from and in-sistence in all phenomenal non-ultimate reality, but the ultimate *in* all reality, in its relativity and mutuality. The first implication carries the consequence that the theistic notion of "God" is *secondary* to its own transcendence into the unnamable, ineffable, inaccessible *apophasis* of the nameless Reality that it indicates, but can only polyphilically mediate in any such namings, such as any divine name or attribute. The second implication renders "ultimacy" *irrelevant* if it is not understood as the very *medium* of mutual immanence of all realities, expressing the in-sistence of the divine manifold. It is in this sense that the differentiation, in process thought, between Creativity and God is meant to say that God is *not* ultimate apart from a Creativity, the ultimacy of which is to signify the diffused activity of ex-sistence, of mutual immanence, as the process of all becomings, including, but not confined to, God. It is in this sense that "God" in theistic renderings may not only be compatible with, but expressive of the essential reality of the Manifestation of Reality/God while the nameless Reality beyond its self-manifestations would indicate the self-transcendence of God in "its" Manifestations. And it is in this sense that *the* ultimate in process thought may best be understood as the cycle of love, the process of the becoming as mutual immanence *itself*.

The **Unity of Religions** is a term used as an alternative to that of religious pluralism. It indicates the future of religions as *one* history of human engagement with ultimate reality or God that expresses a new axial age of universal religious consciousness. As used in the Bahá'í universe of discourse, it does not mean uniformity or sameness, but ultimate origin, transformative spirit and ultimate relationality of becoming in the spiritual maturation of humanity and the whole cosmos, as manifested by the interstellar consciousness or horizon of the new axial age. In agreement with polyphilic pluralism, but in contrast to apophatic pluralism, for which unity is only of apophatic unknowability, and perennialism, for which the same mystical apophaticism undergirds all religious experience, alike, the "unity" of the Bahá'í concept is one of multiplicity, like the many folds of a fabric or the many waves of one sea, equally of infinite apophatic depth *and* inexhaustibility of polyphilic realizations. In the apophatic-polyphilic sense of the cycle of love, the unity of religions can convey three related connotations: that there will always be new religions, multiple religions and some mutual relationship in the becoming of religions. The "unity" employed, here, is not a vision or promise of a desire or ideal state in the future, however, but a presumed condition of religious existence to which humanity must be awakened as a form of enlightenment.

Alfred North Whitehead (1861–1947) studied and taught applied mathematics at the University of Cambridge, England, and wrote extensively on mathematics, logic and philosophy of science. After his early work with his student and colleague Bertrand Russell on the logical unification of mathematics could not affirm this premise, which led to the refutation of closed systems by Kurt Gödel and, eventually, the divide between analytic and continental philosophy, his writings in the philosophy of science made relationality and change in form of events and process-patterns the basis of his thought. After his retirement from teaching in London, England, he was called to become a chair in philosophy at the University of Harvard, Cambridge, Massachusetts, where he expanded this process approach to a universal cosmological philosophy of organism, process, creativity and value, which did not dispense of the possibility of including a divine and ultimate dimension to reality. In his late writings, he relativized and included the metaphysical dimension of thought into the development of a human civilization of the future that would be driven by self-transcendence embodied by the values of beauty, truth, art, adventure and peace; and he conceptualized the universe in this civilized form, driven by creative and theopoetic ultimate reality, to realize all desirable potentials of these virtues in an infinite process of becoming of value.

REFERENCES

Abdu'l-Bahá. *'Abdu'l-Bahá in London*. Chicago: Bahá'í Publishing Trust, 1982.
———. *Commentary on the Islamic Tradition "I Was a Hidden Treasure."* Translated by Moojan Momen, in *Bahá'í Studies Bulletin*, no. 3:4 (1995): 4–35.
———. *Divine Philosophy*. New York: Bahá'í Publishing Committee, 1918.
———. *Foundations of World Unity: Compiled from Addresses and Tablets of 'Abdu'l-Bahá*. Wilmette, IL: Bahá'í Publishing, 1971.
———. *Memorial of the Faithful*. Wilmette, IL: Bahá'í Publishing, 1971.
———. *Paris Talks: Addresses Given by 'Abdu'l-Bahá in 1911*. Wilmette, IL: Bahá'í Publishing, 2011.
———. *The Promulgation of Universal Peace*. Wilmette, IL: Bahá'í Publishing, 2012.
———. *The Secrets of Divine Civilization*. Wilmette, IL: Bahá'í Publishing, 2015.
———. *Selections from the Writings of 'Abdu'l-Bahá*. Wilmette, IL: Bahá'í Publishing, 2014.
———. *Some Answered Questions*. Newly translated. Haifa: Bahá'í World Center, 2014.
———. "Tablet of the Universe (Lawh-i-Aflákiyyih)." In *Makátib-i 'Abdu'l-Bahá*. Vol. 1, 13–32, 1997: https://bahai-library.com/abdulbaha_lawh_aflakiyyih.
———. *Tablet to August Forel*. Oxford: George Ronald, 1978.
———. *Tablets of 'Abdu'l-Bahá*. 3 Vols. Chicago: Bahá'í Publishing, 1909–16.
———. *Tablets of the Divine Plan*. Wilmette, IL: Bahá'í Publishing, 1977.
Abdullah, Arif Kemil. *The Qur'an and Normative Religious Pluralism: A Thematic Study of the Qur'an*. London: International Institute of Islamic Thought, 2014.
Abe, Massao. "God and Absolute Nothingness." In *God, Truth and Reality: Essays in Honor of John Hick*. Edited by Arvind Sharma, 33–45. Eugene, OR: Wipf & Stock, 1993.
———. "Kenotic God and Dynamic Sunyata." In *The Emptying God: A Buddhist-Jewish-Christian Conversation*. Edited by John Cobb and Christopher Ives, 3–68. Maryknoll, NY: Orbis Books, 1990.
———. *Zen and Western Thought*. Honolulu: University of Hawaii Press, 1985.
Addison, Donald and Christopher Buck. "Messengers of God in North America: An Exegesis of the 'Abdu'l-Bahá's Tablet to Amír Khán." *Online Journal of Bahá'í Studies* 1 (2007): 180–270.
Akira, Hirakawa. *A History of Indian Buddhism: From Sakyamuni to Early Mahayana*. Delhi: Motilal Banarsidass Publishers, 1993.
Albert, Hans. *Traktat über die kritische Vernunft*. Tübingen: J.C.B. Moor, 1975.
Amanat, Abbas. *Resurrection and Renewal: The Making of the Babi Movement in Iran, 1844–1850*. Los Angeles: Kalimat Press, 2005.
Andrews, Dave. *The Jihad of Jesus: The Sacred Nonviolent Struggle for Justice*. Eugene, OR: Wipf & Stock, 2015.
Arasteh, Reza. *Rumi the Persian, the Sufi*. Abington, Oxon: Routledge, 2008.
Armstrong, Karen. *Fields of Blood: Religion and the History of Violence*. New York: Anchor Books, 2015.
———. *The Great Transformation: The Beginnings of Our Religious Traditions*. New York: Anchor Books, 2007.
———. *A History of God: The 4,000-Year Quest of Judaism, Christianity and Islam*. New York: Random House Publishing, 1993.
———. *Muhammad: A Prophet for Our Time*. New York: HarperCollins, 2006.

Asad, Talal. *Formations of the Secular: Christianity, Islam, Modernity*. Stanford, CA: Stanford University Press, 2003.
———. *Genealogies of Religion: Discipline and Reasons of Power in Christianity and Islam*. Baltimore, MD: Johns Hopkins University Press, 1993.
Ashkenazi, Michael. *What We Know about Extraterrestrial Intelligence: Foundations of Xenology*. Cham: Switzerland: Springer International Publishing, 2017.
Aslan, Resa. *No god but God: The Origins, Evolution, and Future of Islam*. New York: Random House, 2012.
Assmann, Jan. *Moses the Egyptian: The Memory of Egypt in the Western Monotheism*. Harvard: President and Fellows of Harvard College, 1998.
———. *The Price of Monotheism*. Stanford: Stanford University Press, 2010.
———. "Translating Gods: Religion as a Factor of Cultural (Un)Translatability." In *The Translatability of Cultures: Figurations of the Space Between*. Edited by Sanford Budick and Wolfgang Iser, 25–36. Stanford: Stanford University Press, 1996.
The Báb. *Risalah fi's-Suluk (The Way to God)*. Translated by Todd Lawson. In *The Bahá'í Faith and the World's Religions*. Edited by Moojan Momen, 231–47. Oxford: George Ronald, 2003.
———. *Selections from the Writings of the Báb*. Haifa, Israel: Bahá'í World Center, 1976.
Baba, Homi. *The Location of Culture*. London: Routledge, 1994.
Badiou, Alan. *Deleuze: The Clamor of Being*. Minneapolis: University of Minnesota Press, 2000.
Bahá'í Prayers. Wilmette, IL: Bahá'í Publishing, 2009.
Bahá'í World Faith: Selected Writings of Bahá'u'lláh and 'Abdu'l Bahá. Wilmette, IL: Bahá'í Publishing, 1969.
Bahá'u'lláh. *Days of Remembrance: Selections from the Writings of Bahá'u'lláh for the Bahá'í Holy Days*. Haifa: Bahá'í World Center, 2016.
———. *Epistle to the Son of the Wolf*. Wilmette, IL: Bahá'í Publishing, 1988.
———. *Gems of Divine Mysteries*. Aeterna Publishing, 2010.
———. *Gleanings from the Writings of Bahá'u'lláh*. Wilmette, IL: Bahá'í Publishing, 1976.
———. *Hidden Words*. Wilmette, IL: Bahá'í Publishing, 2002.
———. *The Kitab-i Iqan: The Book of Certitude*. Wilmette, IL: Bahá'í Publishing, 1974.
———. "Lawh-i Aqdas (The Most Holy Tablet)." In *Tablets of Bahá'u'lláh, Revealed after the Kitab-i Aqdas*, 7–17. Wilmette, IL: Bahá'í Publishing, 1994.
———. *Lawh Basiṭ al-Haqiqa (Tablet of the Uncompounded Reality)*. Introduced and Translated by Moojan Momen: "Baha'u'lláh's Tablet of the Uncompounded Reality (Lawh Basiṭ al-Haqiqa). In *Lights of Irfan*, 11 (2010): 203–21.
———. "Lawh-i Dunya (Tablet of the World)." In *Tablets of Bahá'u'lláh revealed after the Kitab-i Aqdas*, 81–98. Wilmette, IL: Bahá'í Publishing, 1994.
———. *The Lawh-i Haqq (The Tablet of the Ultimately Real)*. Translated by Stephen Lambden. 2004: http://hurqalya.ucmerced.edu/node/379/.
———. *Prayers and Meditations*. Wilmette, IL: Bahá'í Publishing, 2013.
———. *The Seven Valleys and the Four Valleys*. Translated by Marziah Gail. Wilmette, IL: Bahá'í Publishing, 1991.
———. *The Summons of the Lord of Hosts: Tablets of Bahá'u'lláh*. Haifa: Bahá'í World Center, 2002.
———. *Tabernacle of Unity*. Haifa: Bahá'í World Center, 2006.
———. "Tablet of Ahmad." In *Bahá'í Prayers*. 307–11. Wilmette, IL: Bahá'í Publishing, 2009.
———. *Tablet to Jamal-i-Burujirdi (Lawh-i-Jamál-i-Burujirdí)*. Translated by Khazeh Fananapazir. *Bahá'í Studies Bulletin* 5, no. 1–2 (1991): 4–8: http://bahai-library.com/bahaullah_lawh_jamal_burujirdi.
———. *Tablets of Bahá'u'lláh revealed after the Kitab-i Aqdas*. Wilmette, IL: Bahá'í Publishing, 1994.
Baier, Karl. "Kyoto goes Bultman: Tranreligiőse Studien und existentialle Interpretation." In *polylog* 13 (2005): 85–107.
———. "Transreligiőse Theorie und Existentiale Interpretation." *Interdisciplinary Phenomenology* 2 (2005): 65–86.

———. "Transreligious Studies and Existential Interpretation." In *Samarasia: Studies in Indian Art, Philosphy and Interreligious Dialogue*. Edited by Sadananda Das and Ernst Fűrlinger, 372–92. New Delhi: D.K. Printworld, 2005.

———. "Ultimate Reality in Buddhism and Christianity: A Christian Perspective." In *Buddhism and Christianity in Dialogue: The Gerald Weisfeld Lectures 2004*. Edited by Perry Schmidt-Leukel, 87–116. Norwich, Norfolk: SCM Press, 2005.

Balyuzi, H. M. *Bahá'u'lláh: The King of Glory*. Oxford: George Ronald, 1991.

———. *Muhammad and the Course of Islam*. Oxford: George Ronald, 1976.

Barth, Karl. *The Doctrine of the World of God (Church Dogmatics, Vol. I/1:1)*. Edited by Geoffrey Bromiley and Thomas Torrance. 2nd edition. Edinburgh: T&T Clark, 1975.

Bassuk, Daniel. *Incarnation in Hinduism and Christianity: The Myth of the God-Man*. London: Macmillan Press, 1987.

Bataille, George. *Theory of Religion*. Brooklyn, NY: Zone Books, 1992.

Bauman, Whitney, Richard Bohannon and Kevin O'Brian (eds.). *Grounding Religion: A Field Guide to the Study of Religion and Ecology*. Abington, Oxon: Routledge, 2017.

Becker, Karl, Ilaria Morali and Pheme Perkins (eds.). *Catholic Engagement with World Religions: A Comparative Study*. Maryknoll, NY: Orbis Books, 2010.

Beebe, Stephen. *Between the Menorah and the Cross: Jesus, the Jews, and the Battle for the Early Church*. Bloomington, IN: Xlibris, 2008.

Bellah, Robert and Hans Joas (eds.). *The Axial Age and Its Consequences*. Harvard: President and Fellows of Harvard Colleges, 2012.

Bender, Courtney and Pamela Klassen (eds.). *After Pluralism: Reimagining Religious Engagement*. New York: Columbia University Press, 2010.

Beneke, Chris. *Beyond Toleration: The Religious Origins of American Pluralism*. Oxford: Oxford University Press, 2006.

Berger, Peter. *The Many Altars of Modernity: Toward a Paradigm for Religion in a Pluralistic Age*. Boston: de Gruyter, 2014.

Best, Steven and Douglas Kellner. *Postmodern Theory: Critical Interrogations*. New York: Guilford Press, 1991.

Beverly, John. *Subalternity and Representation: Arguments in Cultural Theory*. Durham: Duke University Press, 2004.

Beyers, Jaco. *Perspectives on Theology of Religions*. Durbanville, South Africa: Aosis, 2017.

Bidwell, Duane. *When One Religion Is Not Enough: The Lives of Spiritually Fluid People*. Boston: Beacon Press, 2018.

Biechler, James and Lawrence Bond. *On Interreligious Harmony: Nicholas of Cusa on Interreligious Harmony: Text Concordance and Translation of De Pace Fidei*. Lewiston, NY: Edwin Mellen Press, 1991.

Boesel, Chris and Wesley Ariarajah (eds.). *Divine Multiplicity: Trinities, Diversities, and the Nature of Relation*. New York: Fordham University Press, 2014.

Boesel, Christian and Catherine. Keller (eds.). *Apophatic Bodies: Negative Theology, Incarnation, and Relationship*. New York: Fordham, 2010.

Bohm, David. *Wholeness and the Implicit Order*. London: Routledge, 1980.

Bond, Laurence (ed.). *Nicolas of Cusa: Selected Spiritual Writings*. Translation and introduction by H. Bond. New York: Paulist Press, 1997.

Bondarenko, Dimitri. "The Second Axial Age and Metamorphoses of Religious Consciousness in the 'Christian World.'" *Journal of Globalization Studies* 2, no. 1 (2011): https://www.socionauki.ru/journal/articles/132657/.

Borg, Marcus (ed.). *Jesus and the Buddha: The Parallel Sayings*. London: Ulysses Press, 2004.

Borsch, Frederick. *The Son of Man in Myth and History*. Philadelphia: Westminster Press, 1967.

Bostrom, Nick. *Superintelligence: Paths, Dangers, Strategies*. Oxford: Oxford University Press, 2014.

Bowers, Keneth. *God Speaks Again: An Introduction to the Bahá'í Faith*. Wilmette, IL: Bahá'í Publishing, 2004.

Bowman, Donna and Clayton Crockett (eds.). *Cosmology, Ecology, and the Energy of God*. New York: Fordham University Press, 2012.

Boyarin, Daniel. *Intertextuality and the Reading of Midrash*. Bloomington: Indiana University Press, 1994.

Boyce, Mary. *Zoroastrians: Their Religious Beliefs and Practices*. London: Routledge, 2003.

Boyer, Pascal. *The Naturalness of Religious Ideas: A Cognitive Theory of Religion*. Berkeley: University of California Press, 1994.

Bracken, Joseph. *The Divine Matrix: Creativity as a Link between East and West*. New York: Orbis Books, 1995.

———. *The One and the Many: A Contemporary Reconstruction of the God-World Relationship*. Grand Rapids, MI: Eerdmans, 2001.

Bracken, Joseph (ed.). *World without End: Christian Eschatology from Process Perspective*. Grand Rapids, MI: Eerdmans, 2005.

Bracken, Joseph and Marjorie Suchocki (eds.). *Trinity in Process: A Relational Theology of God*. New York: Continuum, 1997.

Brainard, Samuel. *Reality and Mystical Experience*. University Park: Pennsylvania University Press, 2000.

Brockman, John (ed.). *What to Think about Machines That Think*. New York: HarperCollins, 2015.

Brodd, Jeffrey. *World Religions: A Voyage of Discovery*. Winona, MN: Saint Mary's Press, 2015.

Brown, Keven. "Abdu'l-Bahá's Response to Darwinism: Its Historical and Philosophical Context." In *Evolution and Bahá'í Belief: 'Abdu'l-Bahá's Response to Nineteenth-Century Darwinism*. Edited by Keven Brown, 1–134. Los Angeles: Kalimat Press, 2001.

———. "'Abdu'l-Bahá's Response to the Doctrine of the Unity of Existence." *The Journal of Bahá'í Studies* 11, no. 3–4 (2001): 1–29.

Brown, Keven (ed.). *Evolution and Bahá'í Belief: 'Abdu'l-Bahá's Response to Nineteenth-Century Darwinism*. Los Angeles: Kalimat Press, 2001.

Brown, Tom. *Awakening Spirits: A Native American Path to Inner Peace, Healing and Spiritual Growth*. New York: Berkeley Publishing, 1994.

Brown, Vahid. "The Beginning That Hath No Beginning: Bahá'í Cosmogony." *Lights of Irfan* 3 (2002): 21–40.

Buck, Christopher. "Bahá'í Universalism and Native Prophets." In *Reason and Revelation: New Detections in Bahá'í Thought*. Edited by Seena Fazel and John Danesh, 173–201. Los Angeles: Kalimat Press, 2002.

———. "Native Messengers of God in Canada? A Test Case for Bahá'í Universalism." *Bahá'í Studies Review* 6 (1996): 97–133.

———. "Ninian Smart (1927–2001)." British Writers, Supplement XXIV. Edited by Jay Parini. Farmington Hills, 269–83. MI: Charles Scribner's Sons/The Gale Group, 2017.

———. *Symbol and Secret: Qur'an Commentary in Bahá'u'lláh's Kitab-i Iqan*. Los Angeles: Kalimat Press, 1995.

———. "A Unique Eschatological Interface: Bahá'u'lláh and Cross-cultural Messianism." In *In Iran: Studies in Bábí and Bahá'í History*. Vol. 3. Edited by Peter Smith, 157–80. Los Angeles: Kalimat Press, 1986.

Budick, Sanford. "Crisis of Alterity: Cultural Untranslatability and the Experience of Secondary Otherness." In *The Translatability of Cultures: Figurations of the Space Between*. Edited by Sanford Budick and Wolfgang Iser, 1–22. Stanford: Stanford University Press, 1996.

Budick, Sanford and Wolfgang Iser (eds.). *The Translatability of Cultures: Figurations of the Space Between*. Stanford: Stanford University Press, 1996.

Buehrens, John and Forrest Church. *An Introduction to Unitarian Universalim*. Boston, MA: Beacon Press, 1989 and 1998.

Buehrens, John and Rebecca Parker. *A House for Hope: The Promise of Progressive Religion for the Twenty-First Century*. Boston: Beacon Press, 2011.

Burton, David. "A Buddhist Perspective." In *The Oxford Handbook of Religious Diversity*. Edited by Chad Meister, 337–50. Oxford: Oxford University Press, 2001.

Butler, Judith. "Critique, Coercion, and Sacred Life in Benjamin's 'Critique of Violence.'" In *Political Theologies: Public Religions in a Post-Secular World*. Edited by Hent de Vries and Lawrence Sullivan, 201–19. New York: Fordham University Press, 2006.

———. *Gender Trouble: Feminism and the Subversion of Identity*. New York: Routledge, 1999.

———. *Giving an Account of Oneself*. New York: Fordham University Press, 2005.

———. "On this Occasion …" In *Butler on Whitehead: On the Occasion*. Edited by Roland Faber, Michael Halewood and Deena Lin, 3–18. Lanham, MD: Lexington Books, 2012.

Cameron, Geoffrey and Benjamin Schewel (eds.). In *Religion and Public Discourse in an Age of Transition: Reflections on Bahá'í Practice and Thought*. Waterloo, Ontario, Canada: Wilfrid Laurier University Press, 2018.

Capra, Fritjof. *The Tao of Physics*. Boston: Shambala, 1991.

———. *The Turning Point: Science, Society, and the Rising Culture*. Toronto: Bantam Books, 1982.

Caputo, John. *Deconstruction in a Nutshell: A Conversation with Jacques Derrida*. New York: Fordham University Press, 1997.

Carter, Robert. *The Nothingness beyond God: An Introduction to the Philosophy of Nishida Kitaro*. St. Paul, MN: Paragon Publishing, 1989.

Catling, David. *Astrobiology: A Very Short Introduction*. Oxford: Oxford University Press, 2013.

Chaitin, Gregory. *Meta Math! The Quest for Omega*. New York: Pantheon Books, 2005.

Chan, Wing-Tsit. *A Sourcebook of Chinese Philosophy*. Princeton: Princeton University Press, 1963.

Chatterjee, Margaret. *Gandhi and the Challenge of Religious Diversity: Religious Pluralism Revisited*. New Delhi: Promilla and Co., 2005.

Chen, Ellen. *The Tao De Ching: A New Translation with Commentary*. St. Paul, MN: Paragon House, 1989.

Cheng, Chung-ying. "A Chinese Religious Perspective." In *The Oxford Handbook of Religious Diversity*. Edited by Chad Meiste, 351–64. Oxford: Oxford University Press, 2001.

Cheung, Albert. "The Common Teachings from Chinese Culture and the Bahá'í Faith: From Material Civilization to Spiritual Civilization." *Lights of Irfan* 1 (2000): 39–40.

Chew, Phyllis. *The Chinese Religion and the Bahá'í Faith*. Oxford: George Ronald, 1993.

———. "The Great Tao." *The Journal of Bahá'í Studies* 4, no. 2 (1991): 11–39.

———. "Religious Pluralism in the Chinese Religion and the Bahá'í Faith." *Word Order* 34, no. 1 (2002): 27–44.

Chiang, Ted. "Story of Your Life." In *Stories of Your Life and Others*. 91–145. New York: Vintage Books, 2016.

Chittick, William. *Imaginal Worlds: Ibn 'Arabi and the Problem of Religious Diversity*. Albany: State University of New York Press, 1994.

Chopra, Deepak. *Life after Death: The Book of Answers*. London: Rider, 2008.

Chryssides, George. *Exploring New Religions*. New York: Continuum, 2001.

Chryssides, George and Ron Geaves. *The Study of Religion: An Introduction to Key Ideas and Methods*. London: Bloomsbury, 2007.

Clarke, J. J. *The Tao of the West: Western Transformation of Taoist Thought*. New York: Routledge, 2000.

Clooney, Francis X. *Comparative Theology: Deep Learning across Religious Borders*. Malden, MA: Wiley-Blackwell, 2010.

Clooney, Francis X. (ed.). *The New Comparative Theology: Interreligious Insights from the Next Generation*. New York: T&T Clarke, 2010.

Cobb, John. "Some Whiteheadian Assumptions about Religious Pluralism and Pluralism." In *Deep Religious Pluralism*. Edited by David Griffin, 243–64. Louisville, KY: Westminster John Knox, 2005.

———. *Beyond Dialog: Toward a Mutual Transformation of Christianity and Buddhism*. Philadelphia: Fortress Press 1982.

———. "Can a Buddhist Be a Christian, Too?" *Japanese Religions* 11, no. 2–3 (1980): 35–55.
———. *Christ in a Pluralistic Age*. Philadelphia: Westminster Press, 1975.
———. *A Christian Natural Theology: Based on the Thought of Alfred North Whitehead*. Louisville: Westminster John Knox, 1974 and 2007.
———. "The Relativization of the Trinity." In *Trinity in Process: A Relational Theology of God*. Edited by Joseph Bracken and Marjorie Suchocki, 1–22. New York: Continuum, 1997.
———. "Trajectories, and Historic Routes." In *Semeia* 24 (1982): 89–98.
———. *Transforming Christianity and the World: A Way beyond Absolutism and Relativism*. Edited by Paul Knitter. Maryknoll, NY: Orbis Books, 1999.
Cobb, John (ed.). *Back to Darwin: A Richer Account of Evolution*. Grand Rapids, MI: Eerdmans, 2008.
———. *Religions in the Making: Whitehead and the Wisdom Traditions of the World*. Eugene, OR: Cascade Books, 2012.
Cobb, John and David Griffin. *Process Theology: An Introductory Exposition*. Louisville: Westminster John Knox, 1976.
Cobb, John and Christopher Ives (eds.). *The Emptying God: A Buddhist-Jewish-Christian Conversation*. Maryknoll, NY: Orbis Books, 1990.
Cole, Juan. "The Concept of Manifestation in the Bahá'í Writings." *Bahá'í Studies* 9 (1982): http://bahai-library.com/cole_concept_manifestation.
———. "'I am all the Prophets': The Poetics of Pluralism in Bahá'í Texts." *Poetics Today* 14, no. 3 (Fall 1993): 447–76.
———. Introduction to the Translation of the Bahá'u'lláh's *Tablet to Mirza Abu'l-Fadl Concerning the Questions of Manakji Limji Hataria*: *Baha'u'llah on Hinduism and Zoroastrianism*. In https://bahai-library.com/bahaullah_cole_questions_manakji.
———. "The World as Text: Cosmologies of Shaykh Ahmad al-Ahsa'i." In *Studia Islamica* 80 (1994): 145–63.
Cole-Turner, Ronald (ed.). *Transhumanism and Transcendence: Christian Hope in an Age of Technological Enhancement*. Washington: Georgetown University Press, 2011.
Collins, Adele and John Collins. *King and Messiah as the Son of God: Divine, Human, and Angelic Messianic Figures in the Biblical and Related Literatures*. Grand Rapids, MI: Eerdmans Publishing, 2008.
Connolly, William. *Pluralism*. Durham: Duke University Press, 2005.
Conway Morris, Simon. *Life's Solution: Inevitable Humans in a Lonely Universe*. Cambridge: Cambridge University Press, 2003.
———. *The Runes of Evolution: How the Universe Became Self-Aware*. West Conshohocken, PA: Templeton Press, 2015.
Corbin, Henry. *Alone with the Alone: Creative Imagination in the Sufism of Ibn 'Arabi*. Princeton, NJ: Princeton University Press, 1997.
Cornille, Catherine. "The Dynamics of Multiple Belongings." In *Many Mansions? Multiple Religious Belonging and Christian Identity*. Edited by Catherine Cornille, 1–6. Maryknoll, NY: Orbis Books, 2010.
———. *The Im-Possibility of Interreligious Dialogue*. New York: Crossroad, 2008.
Cornille, Catherine (ed.). *Many Mansions? Multiple Religious Belonging and Christian Identity*. Maryknoll, NY: Orbis Books, 2010.
Cousins, Ewert. *Christ of the 21st Century*. New York, NY: Continuum, 1992.
Coward, Harold. *Pluralism: Challenge to World Religions*. Maryknoll, NY: Orbis Books, 1985.
Coward, Harold (ed.). *Modern Indian Responses to Religious Pluralism*. Albany: State University of New York, 1987.
Cracknell, Kenneth. *In Good and Generous Faith: Christian Responses to Religious Pluralism*. Peterborough: Epworth, 2005.
Crockett, Clayton (ed.). *Secular Theology: American Radical Theological Thought*. New York: Routledge, 2001.

Crow, Michael. *The Extraterrestrial Life Debate, 1750–1900: The Idea of a Plurality of Worlds from Kant to Lowell.* Mineola, NY: Dover Publications, 1999.

Cruikshank, Julie. "Claiming Legitimacy: Prophecy Narratives from Northern Aboriginal Women." *American Indian Quarterly* 18, no. 2 (1994): 147–67.

Daene-Drummond, Celia. *EcoTheology*. Darton: Longman and Todd, 2008.

———. *A Primer in Ecotheology: Theology for a Fragile Earth.* Eugene, OR: Wipf & Stock, 2017.

The Dalai Lama. *Toward a True Kinship of Faiths: Hoe the World's Religions Can Come Together.* London: Abacus, 2010.

Dalela, Ashish. *Mystic Universe: An Introduction to Vedic Cosmology.* Pasadena, CA: Shabda Press, 2016.

Das, Sadananda and Ernst Fűrlinger (eds.). *Samarasia: Studies in Indian Art, Philosophy and Interreligious Dialogue.* New Delhi: D.K.Printworld, 2005.

Daschke, Derek and Michael Ashcraft (eds.). *New Religious Movements: A Documentary Reader.* New York: New York University Press, 2005.

Daoud, Yousef. *The Rose and the Lotus: Sufism and Buddhism.* Bloomington, IN: Xlibris, 2009.

Davies, Paul. *The Goldilocks Enigma: Why Is the Universe Just Right for Life?* Boston, MA: A Mariner Book, 2006.

———. *The Last Three Minutes: Conjectures about the Ultimate Fate of the Universe.* New York: BasicBooks, 1994.

Davis, Colin. *Levinas: An Introduction.* Cambridge: Polity Press, 1996.

D'Costa, Gavin. "The Impossibility of a Pluralist View of Religions." *Religious Studies* 32, no. 2 (1996): 223–32.

———. "Preface." In *Christian Uniqueness Reconsidered: The Myth of a Pluralistic Theology of Religions.* Edited by Gavin D'Costa, viii–xxii. Maryknoll, NY: Orbis Books, 1990

D'Costa, Gavin (ed.). *Christian Uniqueness Reconsidered: The Myth of a Pluralistic Theology of Religions.* Maryknoll, NY: Orbis Books, 1990.

Dean, Thomas (ed.). *Religious Pluralism and Truth: Essays on Cross-Cultural Philosophy of Religion.* Albany: State University of New York Press, 1995.

Deleuze, Gilles. *Difference and Repetition.* New York: Columbia University Press, 1994.

———. *The Fold: Leibniz and the Baroque.* Minneapolis: University of Minnesota Press, 1992

Deleuze, Gilles and Felix Guattari. *A Thousand Plateaus.* Minneapolis: University of Minnesota Press, 1987.

Derrida, Jacques. "Différance." In *Margins in Philosophy.* 1–28. Chicago: University of Chicago Press, 1984.

———. *Margins in Philosophy.* Chicago: University of Chicago Press, 1984.

Desal, Gaurav and Supria Nair (eds.). *Postcolonialism: An Anthology of Cultural Theory and Criticism.* Rutgers State University, 2005.

Sister Devamata. *Sri Ramakrishna and His Disciples.* La Crescenta, CA: Ananda Ashrama, 1928.

Dick, Steven. *The Biological Universe: The 20th Century Extraterrestrial Life Debate and the Limits of Science.* Cambridge: Cambridge University Press, 1996.

———. "Cosmotheology: Theological Implications of the New Universe." In *Many Worlds: The New Universe, Extraterrestrial Life, and the Theological Implications.* Edited by Stephen Dick, 191–210. Philadelphia: Templeton Foundation Press, 2000.

———. *Life on Other Worlds: The 20th Century Extraterrestrial Life Debate.* Cambridge: Cambridge University Press, 1998.

———. *Plurality of Worlds: The Origins of the Extraterrestrial Life Debate from Democritus to Kant.* Cambridge: Cambridge University Press, 1982.

Dick, Steven (ed.). *The Impact of Discovering Life beyond Earth.* Cambridge: Cambridge University Press, 2015.

———.*Many Worlds: The New Universe, Extraterrestrial Life, and the Theological Implications.* Philadelphia: Templeton Foundation Press, 2000.

Dienberg, Thomas and Michael Plattig (eds.). *"Leben in Fülle": Skizzen zur christlichen Spiritualität.* Münster: LIT, 2001.

Diessner, Rhett. *Psyche and Eros: Bahá'í Studies in a Spiritual Psychology*. Oxford: George Ronald, 2007.
Dombrowski, Daniel. *A Platonic Philosophy of Religion: A Process Perspective*. Albany: State University of New York Press, 2005.
Drees, William. *Religion, Science and Naturalism*. Cambridge: Cambridge University Press, 1996.
D'Sa, Francis. *Gott, der Dreieine und der All-Ganze: Vorwort zur Begegnung zwischen Christentum und Hinduismus*. Düsseldorf: Patmos, 1987.
Duhem, Pierre. *Medieval Cosmology: Theories of Infinity, Place, Time, Void, and the Plurality of Worlds*. Chicago: University of Chicago Press, 1987.
Dumoulin, Heinrich. *The History of Zen Buddhism*. Toronto: Random House, 1963.
Dunbar, Hooper. *A Companion to the Study of the Kitáb-i-Íqán*. Oxford: George Ronald, 2000.
Dupuis, Jacques. *Christianity and the Religions: From Confrontation to Dialogue*. Maryknoll, NY: Orbis Books, 2002.
———. *Toward a Christian Theology of Religious Pluralism*. Maryknoll, MA: Orbis Books, 2001.
Durkheim, Emile. *The Elementary Forms of Religious Life*. Translated by Karen E. Fields. New York: The Free Press, 1995.
Dyson, Freeman. *Infinite in All Directions*. New York: HarperCollins Publishers, 2004.
Eck, Diana. *India: A Sacred Geography*. New York: Harmony Books, 2012.
———. *A New Religious America: How a "Christian Country" Has Become the World's Most Religious Diverse Nation*. New York: HarperCollins, 2001.
Edwards, Denis. *Ecology at the Heart of Faith*. Maryknoll, NY: Orbis Books, 2006.
Egan, Greg. *Diaspora: A Novel*. New York: HarperPrism, 1998.
Ehrman, Bart. *How Jesus Became God: The Exaltation of a Jewish Preacher from Galilee*. New York: HarperOne, 2014.
Ekbal, Kamran. "Daéna-Dén-Dín: The Zoroastrian Heritage of the 'Maid of Heaven' in the Tablets of Bahá'u'lláh." In *Scripture and Revelation: Papers presented at the First Irfan Colloquium*. Edited by Moojan Momen, 125–70. Oxford: George Ronald, 1997.
Ellwood, Robert. *Mysticism and Religion*. New York: Seven Bridges Press, 1999.
Elverskog, Johan. *Buddhism and Islam on the Silk Road*. Philadelphia: University of Philadelphia Press, 2010.
Esack, Farid. *Qur'an, Liberation and Pluralism: An Islamic Perspective of Interreligious Solidarity against Oppression*. Oxford: Oneworld, 1996.
Esslemont, J. E. *Bahá'u'lláh and the New Ear: An Introduction to the Bahá'í Faith*. Wilmette, IL: Bahá'í Publishing Trust, 2006.
Faber, Roland. "Apocalypse in God: On the Power of God in Process Eschatology." *Process Studies* 31, no. 2 (2002): 64–96.
———. "Baha'u'llah and the Luminous Mind: Baha'i Gloss on a Buddhist Puzzle." *Lights of Irfan* 18 (2017): 53–106.
———. "Becoming Intermezzo: Eco-Theopoetics after the Anthropic Principle." In *Theopoetic Folds: Philosophizing Multifariousness*. Edited by Roland Faber and Jeremy Fackenthal, 212–38. New York: Fordham University Press, 2013.
———. *The Becoming of God: Process Theology, Philosophy and Multireligious Engagement*. Portland, OR: Wipf & Stock, 2017.
———. "Bodies of the Void: Polyphilia and Theoplicity." In *Apophatic Bodies, Apophatic Bodies: Negative Theology, Incarnation, and Relationship*. Edited by Christian Boesel and Catherine Keller, 200–26. New York: Fordham, 2010.
———. "De-ontologizing God: Levinas, Deleuze and Whitehead." In *Process and Difference: Between Cosmological and Poststructuralist Postmodernism*. Edited by Catherine Keller and Anne Daniell, 209–34. New York: State University of New York Press, 2002.
———. "Der transreligiöse Diskurs: Zu einer Theologie transformativer Prozesse." *polylog* 9 (2002): 65–94.

———. *The Divine Manifold*. Lanham, MD: Lexington Books, 2014.

———. "Ecotheology, Ecoprocess, and *Ecotheosis*: A Theopoetical Intervention." *Salzburger Zeitschrift für Theologie* 12 (2008): 75–115.

———. *Freiheit, Theologie und Lehramt. Trinitätstheologische Grundlegung und wissenschaftstheoretischer Ausblick*. Innsbruck: Tyrolia, 1992.

———. *The Garden of Reality: Transreligious Relativity in a World of Becoming*. Lanham, MD: Lexington, 2018.

———. *God as Poet of the World: Exploring Process Theologies*. Louisville: WJK, 2008.

———. "God in the Making. Religious Experience and Cosmology in Whitehead's *Religion in the Making* in Theological Perspective." In *L'experience de Dieu: Lectures de Religion in the Making d'Alfred N. Whitehead (=Aletheia)*. Edited by Michel Weber and Samuel Rouvillois, 179–200. Janvier: Ecole Saint-Jean, 2005.

———. "God's Advent/ure: The End of Evil and the Origin of Time." In *World Without End: Christian Eschatology from Process Perspective*. Edited by Joseph Bracken, 91–112. Grand Rapids, MI: Eerdmans, 2005.

———. "Gottesmeer—Versuch über die Ununterschiedenheit Gottes." In *"Leben in Fülle": Skizzen zur christlichen Spiritualität*. Edited by Thomas Dienberg and Michael Plattig, 64–95. Münster: LIT, 2001.

———. "Immanence and Incompleteness: Whitehead's Late Metaphysics." In *Beyond Metaphysics? Conversations on A. N. Whitehead's Late Thought*. Edited by Roland Faber, Brian Henning and Clinton Combs, 91–110. Amsterdam: Rodopi, 2010.

———. "In the Wake of False Unifications: Whitehead's Creative Resistance against Imperialist Theologies." Claremont, 2005: http://faber.whiteheadresearch.org/files/FaberR-In_the_Wake_of_False_Unifications.pdf.

———. "'The Infinite Movement of Evanescence'—The Pythagorean Puzzle in Plato, Deleuze, and Whitehead." *American Journal of Theology and Philosophy* 21, no. 1 (2000): 171–99.

———. "Introduction: Negotiating Becoming." In *Secrets of Becoming: Negotiating Whitehead, Deleuze, and Butler*. Edited by Roland Faber and Andrea Stephenson, 1–50. New York: Fordham University Press, 2010.

———. "Khora and Violence: Revisiting Butler with Whitehead." In *Butler on Whitehead: On the Occasion*. Edited by Roland Faber, Michael Halewood and Deena Lin, 105–26. Lanham, MD: Lexington Books, 2012.

———. "Laozi, a Lost Prophet? The Challenge of the Dao De Jing for the Bahá'í Universe of Discourse." *Lights of Irfan* 19 (2018): 34–110.

———. "Messianische Zeit. Walter Benjamins 'mystische Geschichtsauffassung' in zeittheologischer Perspektive." *Münchner Theologische Zeitschrift* 54 (2003): 68–78.

———. "Multiplicity and Mysticism: Toward a New Mystagogy of Becoming." In *The Lure of Whitehead*. Edited by Nicholas Gaskill and A. J. Nozek, 187–206. Minneapolis: University of Minnesota Press, 2014.

———. "Must 'Religion' Always Remain as a Synonym for 'Hatred?': Whiteheadian Meditations on the Future of Togetherness." In *Living Traditions and Universal Conviviality: Prospects and Challenges for Peace in Multireligious Communities*. Edited by Roland Faber and Santiago Slabodsky, 167–82. Lanham, MD: Lexington Books, 2016.

———. "The Mystical Whitehead." In *Seeking Common Ground: Evaluation and Critique of Joseph Bracken's Comprehensive Worldview*. Edited by Marc Pugliese and Gloria Schaab, 213–334. Milwaukee, WI: Marquette University Press, 2012.

———. "Nicht-Ich und Nicht-Wiedergeburt. Zur Entmythologisierung des Reinkarnationsgedankens in Buddhadasas Dhamma-Sprache und A. N. Whiteheads Ereignissprache." *Ursache und Wirkung* 10, no.1 (2000): 42–48.

———. "On the Unique Origin of Revelation, Religious Intuition and Theology." *Process Studies* 28, no. 3–4 (1999): 273–89.

———. "Organic or Orgiastic Metaphysics? Reflections on Whitehead's Reception in Contemporary Poststructuralism." *Japanese Journal of Process Thought* 14 (2010): 203–22.

———. "Personsein am Ort der Leere." *NZSTh* 44 (2002): 189–98.

———. "Process, Progress, Excess: Whitehead and the Peace of Society." In *Recent Advances in the Creation of a Process-Based Worldview: Human Life in Process*. Edited by Łukasz Lamża and Jakub Dziadkowiec, 6–20. Newcastle upon Tyne: Cambridge Scholars Publishing, 2016.

———. *Prozeßtheologie. Zu ihrer Würdigung und kritischen Erneuerung*. Mainz: Matthias Grünewald Verlag, 2000.

———. "The Sense of Peace: A Para-doxology of Divine Multiplicity." In *Polydoxy: Theology of Multiplicity and Relation*. Edited by Catherine Keller and Laurel Schneider, 36–56. London: Routledge, 2011.

———. "Surrationality and Chaosmos: A More Deleuzean Whitehead (and a Butlerian Intervention)." In *Secrets of Becoming: Negotiating Whitehead, Deleuze, and Butler*. Edited by Roland Faber and Andrea Stephenson, 157–77. New York: Fordham University Press, 2010.

———. "Theopoetic Justice: Towards an Ecology of Living Together." In *Beyond Superlatives: Regenerating Whitehead's Philosophy of Experience*. Edited by Roland Faber, J. R. Hustwit and Hollis Phelps, 160–78. Newcastle upon Tyne: Cambridge Scholars Press, 2014.

———. "Touch: A Philosophic Meditation." In *The Allure of Things*. Edited by Roland Faber and Andrew Goffey, 47–67. Lanham, MD: Bloomsbury Academic, 2014.

———. "Transkulturaltion. Dogmatische Überlegungen zum 'Wesen des Christentums' im Fluss." In *Inkulturation. Historische Beispiele und theologische Reflexionen zur Flexibilität und Widerständigkeit des Christlichen*. Edited by Rupert Klieber and Martin Stowasser, 160–87. Vienna: LIT Verlag, 2006.

———. "Trinity, Analogy and Coherence." In *Trinity in Process: A Relational Theology of God*. Edited by Joseph Bracken and Marjorie Suchocki, 147–72. New York: Continuum, 1997.

———. "Uniting Earth to the Blue of Heaven Above: Strange Attractors in Whitehead's Symbolism." In *Rethinking Whitehead's Symbolism: Thought, Language, Culture*. Edited by Roland Faber, Jeffrey Bell and Joseph Petek, , 56–78. Edinburgh: Edinburgh University Press, 2017.

———. "Zeitumkehr. Versuch über einen eschatologischen Schöpfungsbegriff." *Theologie und Philosophie* 75, no. 2 (2000): 180–205.

Faber, Roland and Jeremy Fackenthal (eds.). *Theopoetic Folds: Philosophizing Multifariousness*. New York: Fordham University Press, 2013.

Faber, Roland and Andrew Goffey (eds.). *The Allure of Things*. Lanham, MD: Bloomsbury Academic, 2014.

Faber, Roland and Catherine Keller. "Polyphilic Pluralism: Becoming Religious Multiplicities." In *Divine Multiplicity: Trinities, Diversities, and the Nature of Relation*. Edited by Chris Boesel and Wesley Ariarajah, 58–81. New York: Fordham University Press, 2014.

———. "A Taste for Multiplicity: The Skillful Means of Religious Pluralism." In *Religions in the Making: Whitehead and the Wisdom Traditions of the World*. Edited by John Cobb, 180–207. Eugene, OR: Cascade Books, 2012.

Faber, Roland and Santiago Slabodsky (eds.). *Living Traditions and Universal Conviviality: Prospects and Challenges for Peace in Multireligious Communities*. Lanham, MD: Lexington Books, 2016.

Faber, Roland and Andrea Stephenson (eds.). *Secrets of Becoming: Negotiating Whitehead, Deleuze, and Butler*. New York: Fordham University Press, 2010.

Faber, Roland, Jeffrey Bell and Joseph Petek (eds.). *Rethinking Whitehead's Symbolism: Thought, Language, Culture*. Edinburgh: Edinburgh University Press, 2017.

Faber, Roland, Michael Halewood and Deena Lin (eds.). *Butler on Whitehead: On the Occasion*. Lanham, MD: Lexington Books, 2012.

Faber, Roland, Brian Henning and Clinton Combs (eds.). *Beyond Metaphysics? Conversations on A. N. Whitehead's Late Thought*. Amsterdam: Rodopi, 2010.

Faber, Roland, J. R. Hustwit and Hollis Phelps (eds.). *Beyond Superlatives: Regenerating Whitehead's Philosophy of Experience*. Newcastle upon Tyne: Cambridge Scholars Press, 2014.

Fananapazir, Khazeh. "Day of God (*Yawmu'llah*) and the Days of God (*Ayyamu'llah*)." In *Scripture and Revelation: Papers presented at the First Irfan Colloquium.* Edited by Moojan Momen, 217–38. Oxford: George Ronald, 1997.

———. *Islam at the Crossroads.* Oxford: George Ronald, 2015.

Farmer, Ronald. *Beyond the Impasse: The Promise of a Process Hermeneutic.* Macon, GA: Mercer University Press, 1997.

Fazel, Seena. "Bahá'í Approaches to Christianity and Islam: Further Thoughts on Developing an Inter-religious Dialogue." *Bahá'í Studies Review* 14 (2008): 41–53.

———. "Interreligious Dialogue and the Bahá'í Faith: Some Preliminary Observations." In *Revisioning the Sacred: New Perspectives on a Bahá'í Theology.* Edited by Jack McLean, 127–52. Los Angeles: Kalimat Press, 1997.

———. "Is the Bahá'í Faith a World Religion." *Journal of Bahá'í Studies* 6, no. 1 (1994): 1–16.

———. "Religious Pluralism and the Bahá'í Faith." *Interreligious Insight* 1, no. 3 (2003): 42–49.

———. "Understanding Exclusivist Texts." In *Scripture and Revelation: Papers presented at the First Irfan Colloquium.* Edited by Moojan Momen, 239–82. Oxford: George Ronald, 1997.

Fazel, Seena and John Danesh (eds.). *Reason and Revelation: New Detections in Bahá'í Thought.* Los Angeles: Kalimat Press, 2002.

Ferrer, Jorge. "The Future of World Religion: Four Scenarios, One Dream." *Tikkun* (Winter 2012): 14–16, 63–64.

———. *Participation and the Mystery: Transpersonal Essays in Psychology, Education, and Religion.* Albany: State University of New York Press, 2017.

———. *Revisioning Transpersonal Theory: A Participatory Vision of Human Spirituality.* Albany: State University of New York Press, 2002.

Ferrer, Jorge and Jacob Sherman. "The Participatory Turn: Spirituality, Mysticism, Religious Studies." In *The Participatory Turn: Spirituality, Mysticism, Religious Studies.* Edited by Jorge Ferrer and Jacob Sherman, 1–78. Albany: State University of New York Press, 2007.

Ferrer, Jorge and Jacob Sherman (eds.). *The Participatory Turn: Spirituality, Mysticism, Religious Studies.* Albany: State University of New York Press, 2007.

Fitzgerald, Timothy. "Hinduism and the World Religion Fallacy." *Religion* 20, no.1 (1990): 1–16.

Flasch, Kurt. *Metaphysik des Einen bei Nikolaus von Kues.* Leiden: Brill, 1973.

Fletcher, Jannine Hill. *Monopoly on Salvation? A Feminist Approach to Religious Pluralism.* New York. Continuum, 2005.

Foltz, Richard. *Religions of the Silk Road: Premodern Patterns of Globalization.* New York: Palgrave Macmillan, 2010.

Ford, Lewis. "Neville on the One and the Many." *Southern Journal of Philosophy* 10 (1972): 79–84.

Forman, Robert. "Mystical Knowledge: Knowledge by Identity." *Journal of the American Academy of Religion* 61, no. 4 (1993): 705–38.

Foucault, Michel. *Power/Knowledge: Selected Interviews and Other Writings, 1972–1977.* New York: Harvester House, 1989.

Fox, Matthew. *Meister Eckhart: Mystic-Warrior for our Time.* Novato, CA: New World Library, 2014.

Franke, William. *On What Cannot Be Said: Apophatic Discourses in Philosophy, Religion, Literature, and the Arts.* Notre Dame, IN: University of Notre Dame 2007.

Fredericks, James. *Buddhists and Christians: Through Comparative Theology to Solidarity.* Maryknoll, NY: Orbis Books, 2004.

Friberg, Stephen. "Evolution and Bahá'í Belief, by Keven Brown and Eberhart von Kitzing: Commentary." *Bahá'í Studies Review* 8 (1998): https://bahai-library.com/friberg_brown_kitzing_commentary.

Garfield, Jay. *The Fundamental Wisdom of the Middle Way: Nāgārjuna's Mūlamadhyamakakārikā.* Oxford: Oxford University Press, 1995.

Gaskill, Nicholas and A. J. Nozek (eds.). *The Lure of Whitehead.* Minneapolis: University of Minnesota Press, 2014.

Geaves, Ron. "The Danger of Essentialism: South Asian Communities in England and the 'World Religions' Approach in the Study of Religion." *Contemporary South Asia* 14, no.1 (2005): 75–90.
Genta, Giancarlo. *Lonely Minds in the Universe*. Springer Praxis Publishing, 2010.
Geraci, Robert. *Apocalyptic AI: Visions of Heaven in Robotics, Artificial Intelligence, and Virtual Reality*. Oxford: Oxford University Press, 2010.
Gill, Sam. *Native American Religions: An Introduction*. Belmont, CA: Wadsworth Books, 2005.
von Glasenapp, Helmuth. *Jainism: The Indian Religion of Salvation*. Delhi: Motilal Banarsidass, 1999.
Godfrey-Smith, Peter. *Other Minds: The Octopus, the Sea, and the Deep Origins of Consciousness*. New York: Farrar, Straus and Giraux, 2016.
Golitzin, Alexander. "'Suddenly, Christ': The Place of Negative Theology in the Mystagogy of Dionysius Areopagites." In *Mystics: Presence and Aporia*. Edited by Michael Kessler and Christian Sheppard, 8–37. Chicago: Chicago University Press, 2003.
Goodenough, Ursula. *The Sacred Depths of Nature*. Oxford: Oxford University Press, 1998.
Goodman, Lenn. *Religious Pluralism and Values in the Public Sphere*. New York: Cambridge University Press, 2014.
Gowans, Christopher. *Philosophy of the Buddha*. London: Routledge, 2003.
Gregorios, Paulos Mar (ed.). *Neoplatonism and Indian Philosophy*. Albany: State University of New York Press, 2002.
Griffin, David. "John Cobb's Whiteheadian Complementary Pluralism." In *Deep Religious Pluralism*. Edited by David Griffin, 39–66. Louisville: Westminster John Knox, 2005.
———. *Pantheism and Scientific Naturalism: Rethinking Evil, Morality, Religious Experience, Religious Pluralism, and the Academic Study of Religion*. Claremont, CA: Process Century Press, 2014.
———. *Process Theology: On Postmodernism, Morality, Pluralism, Eschatology and Demonic Evil*. Claremont, CA: Process Century Press, 2017.
———. *Reenchantment without Supernaturalism: A Process Philosophy of Religion*. Ithaca, NY: Cornell University Press, 2001.
———. "Religious Pluralism: Generic, Identist, and Deep." In *Deep Religious Pluralism*. Edited by David Griffin, 3–38. Louisville: Westminster John Knox, 2005.
Griffin, David (ed.). *Deep Religious Pluralism*. Louisville: Westminster John Knox, 2005.
Grigg, Ray. *The Tao of Zen*. Edison, NJ: Alva Press, 1994.
Grimm, John. "Native North American Worldviews and Ecology." In *Worldviews and Ecology: Religion, Philosophy, and the Environment*. Edited by Mary Evelyn Tucker and John Grimm, 41–54. Maryknoll, NY: Orbis Books, 1994.
Grimm, John and Mary Evelyn Tucker. *Ecology and Religion*. Washington, DC: Island Press, 2014.
Grumett, David. *Teilhard de Chardin: Theology, Humanity and Cosmos*. Leuven: Peeters, 2005.
Grung, Anne Hege. *Gender Justice in Muslim Christian Readings: Christian and Muslim Woman Making Meaning of Texts from the Bible, the Koran and the* Hadith. Leiden: Brill, 2015.
Gura, Philip F. *American Transcendentalism: A History*. New York: Hill and Wang, 2007.
Guthke, Karl. *The Last Frontier: Imagining Other Worlds from the Copernican Revolution to Modern Science Fiction*. Ithaca, NY: Cornell University Press, 1990.
Gutting, Gary. *French Philosophy in the Twentieth Century*. Cambridge: Cambridge University Press, 2001.
Haight, Roger. *The Future of Christology*. New York: Continuum, 2005.
———. *Jesus: Symbol of God*. Maryknoll, NY: Orbis Books, 1999.
Hallamish, Moshe. *An Introduction to the Kabbalah*. Albany: State of New York University Press, 1999.
Hamid, Idris Samawi. *The Metaphysics and Cosmology of Process According to Shaykh Ahmad al-Ahsa'i: Critical Edition, Translation and Analysis of* Observations in Wisdom. Ann Arbor, MI: UMI, 1998.
Hanegraaff, Wouter. *New Age Religion and Western Culture: Esotericism in the Mirror of Secular Thought*. Albany: State University of New York Press, 1998.
Hansen, Chad. *A Daoist Theory of Chinese Thought: A Philosophical Interpretation*. Oxford: Oxford University Press, 1992.

Happold, Frank. *Mysticism: A Study and an Anthology.* Harmondsworth: Penguin Books, 1990.
Harari, Yuval. *Homo Deus: A Brief History of Tomorrow.* New York: HarperCollins, 2017.
Harkin, Michael and David Lewis (eds.). *Native Americans and the Environment: Perspectives on the Ecological Indian.* Lincoln: University of Nebraska Press, 2007.
Harris, Elisabeth, Paul Hedges and Shanthikumar Hettiarachchi (eds.). *Twenty-First Century Theologies of Religions: Retrospective and Future Prospects.* Leiden: Brill, 2016.
Hartshorne, Charles. "Whitehead's Revolutionary Concept of Prehension." In *Creativity in American Philosophy.* Edited by Charles Hartshorne, 103–13. Albany: State University of New York Press, 1984.
Hartshorne, Charles (ed.). *Creativity in American Philosophy.* Albany: State University of New York Press, 1984.
Harvey, Peter. *Buddhism.* New York: Continuum, 2001.
Hatcher, John. *Close Connections: The Bridge between Spiritual and Physical Reality.* Wilmette, IL: Bahá'í Publishing, 2005.
———. *The Face of God Among Us: How the Creator Educates Humanity.* Wilmette: Bahá'í Publishing, 2010.
———. *The Purpose of Physical Reality.* Wilmette, IL: Bahá'í Publishing, 2005.
Hatcher, William and Douglas Martin. *The Bahá'í Faith: The Emergent Global Religion.* Wilmette, IL: Bahá'í Publishing, 2002.
Hatchison, William. *Religious Pluralism in America: The Contentious History of a Founding Ideal.* Ann Arbor, MI: Sheridan Books, 2003.
Haught, John. *Deeper Than Darwin: The Prospect for Religion in the Age of Evolution.* Philadelphia, PA: Westview Press, 2004.
———. *God after Darwin: A Theology of Evolution.* Philadelphia, PA: Westview Press, 2001.
———. *The New Cosmic Story: Inside Our Awakening Universe.* New Haven: Yale University Press, 2017.
Hayes, Terrill, et al. *Peace: More Than the End of War.* Wilmette, IL: Bahá'í Publishing, 2007.
Hazini, Nima. "Neoplatonism: Framework for a Bahá'í Metaphysics." 1995: https://bahai-library.com/hazini_neoplatonism_framework_metaphysics.
Heim, Mark. *The Depth of the Riches: A Trinitarian Theology of Religious Ends.* Grand Rapids, MI: Eerdmanns, 2001.
———. *Salvations: Truth and Difference in Religion.* Maryknoll, NY: Orbis Books, 1995.
Heim, Mark (ed.). *Grounds for Understanding: Ecumenical Resources for Responses to Religious Pluralism.* Cambridge: Eerdmans, 1998.
Hengel, Martin. *Judaism and Hellenism: Studies in their Encounter in Palestine during the Early Hellenistic Period.* Eugene, OR: Wipf & Stock, 1974.
Henrici, Peter. "The Concept of Religion from Cicero top Schleiermacher: Origins, History, and Problems with the Term." In *Catholic Engagement with World Religions: A Comparative Study.* Edited by Karl Becker, Ilaria Morali and Pheme Perkins, 1–22. Maryknoll, NY: Orbis Books, 2010.
Herrick, James. *The Making of the New Spirituality: The Eclipse of the Western Religious Tradition.* Downers Grove, IL: InterVarsity Press, 2003.
———. *Scientific Mythologies: How Science and Science Fiction Forge New Religious Beliefs.* Downers Grove, IL: IVP Academics 2008.
Hetherington, Norris (ed.). *Cosmology: Historical, Literary, Philosophical, Religious and Scientific Perspectives.* New York: Routledge, 2008.
Hewitt, Harold (ed.). *Problems in the Philosophy of Religion: Critical Studies of the Work of John Hick.* New York: St. Martin's Press, 1991.
Hick, John. "Can There Be Only One True Religion? Invited Commentary." *Bahá'í Studies Review* 10 (2001): 1–6.
———. "Infallibility." *Religious Studies* 36, no. 1 (2000): 35–46.
———. *An Interpretation of Religion: Human Responses to the Transcendent.* New Haven: Yale University Press, 2005.

———. *The Metaphor of God Incarnate: Christology in a Pluralistic Age*. Louisville: Westminster John Knox, 2005.

———. *Problems of Religious Pluralism*. Basingstoke: Macmillan, 1985.

Hick, John and Paul Knitter (eds.). *The Myth of Christian Uniqueness: Toward a Pluralistic Theology of Religions*. Maryknoll, NY: Orbis Books, 1987.

Hines, Brian. *Return to the One: Plotinus's Guide to God-Realization*. Salem: Adrasteia, 2004.

Hiti, Philip. *The Origins of the Druze People and Religion*. New York: BiblioBaazar, 2007.

Horgan, John. *The End of War*. San Francisco: McSweeney's, 2012.

Horton, Chelsea. *"As ye have faith so shall your powers and blessings be": The Aboriginal-Bahá'í Encounter in British Columbia*. Simon Fraser University (MA Thesis), 2003.

Hosinski, Thomas. *Stubborn Fact and Creative Advance: An Introduction to the Metaphysics of Alfred North Whitehead*. Lanham, MD: Rowman and Littlefield, 1993.

Hughey, Mathew. "Race and Racism: Perspectives from Bahá'í Theology and Critical Sociology." *Journal of Baha'i Studies* 27, no. 3 (2017): 7–56.

Hurtado, Larry. *Lord Jesus Christ: Devotion to Jesus in Earliest Christianity*. Grand Rapids, MI: Eerdmans, 2003.

Huxley, Aldous. *The Perennial Philosophy*. New York: HarperPerennial, 2009.

van Huyssteen, J. Wentzel. *Alone in the World? Human Uniqueness in Science and Theology*. Grand Rapids, MI: Eerdmans, 2006.

———. *Essays in Postfoundationalist Theology*. Grand Rapids, MI: Eerdmans Publishing, 1997.

Hyman, Gavin. *The Predicament of Postmodern Theology: Radical Orthodoxy or Nihilist Textualism?* Louisville: Westminster John Knox, 2001.

Ingram, Paul. *Buddhist-Christian Dialogue in an Age of Science*. Tokyo: Kosei Publishing, 1997.

Islam, Sirajul. *Sufism and Bhakti: A Comparative Study*. Washington, DC: The Council for Research in Values and Philosophy, 2004.

Izutsu, Toshihiko. *Sufism and Taoism: A Comparative Study of Key Philosophical Concepts*. Berkeley: University of California Press, 1984.

James, E. O. *The Ancient Gods: The History and Diffusion of Religion in the Ancient Near East and the Eastern Mediterranean*. Edison, NJ: Castle Books, 2004.

Janzten, Grace. *Power, Gender and Christian Mysticism*. Cambridge: Cambridge University Press, 2000.

Jaspers, Karl. *The Great Philosophers*. Vols. 1–2. New York: Harcourt, Brace and World, Inc., 1962, 1966.

———. *The Origin and Goal of History*. Zürich: Artemis, 1949.

Johnson, Keith. *Rethinking the Trinity and Religious Pluralism: An Augustinian Assessment*. IVP Academic, 2011.

Johnson, Rick. "The Active Force and That Which Is Its Recipient: A Bahá'í View of Creativity." *Journal of Bahá'í Studies* 27, no. 4 (2017): 29–60.

Jones, Richard. *Mysticism Examined: Philosophical Enquiries into Mysticism*. Albany: State University of New York Press, 1993.

———. *Nagarjuna: Buddhism's Most Important Philosopher*. Scotts Valley, CA: CreateSpace, 2014.

Jones, Serena. *Feminist Theory and Christian Theology: Cartographies of Grace*. Minneapolis: Fortress Press, 2000.

Josephson, Jason. *The Invention of Religion in Japan*. Chicago: University of Chicago Press, 2012.

Kaplan, Stephen. *Different Paths, Different Summits: A Model for Religious Pluralism*. Lanham, MD: Rowman and Littlefield, 2002.

Karlberg, Michael. *Beyond the Culture of Contest: From Adversarialism to Mutualism in an Age of Interdependence*. Oxford: George Ronald, 2004.

Katz, Steven. *Mysticism and Philosophical Analysis*. New York: Oxford University Press, 1978.

Kaufman, Gordon. *God–Mystery–Diversity: Christian Theology in a Pluralistic World*. Minneapolis: Fortress Press, 1996.

Keel, Othmar. *The Symbolism of the Biblical World: Ancient Near Eastern Iconography and the Book of Psalms.* San Francisco: Seabury Press, 1978.
Keller, Catherine. *Cloud of the Impossible: Negative Theology and Planetary Engagement.* New York: Columbia University Press, 2015.
———. *Face of the Deep: A Theology of Becoming.* New York: Routledge, 2003.
———. *God and Power: Counter-Apocalyptic Journeys.* Minneapolis: Fortress Press, 2005.
———. *Intercarnations: Exercises in Theological Possibilities.* New York: Fordham University Press, 2017.
———. "Introduction: The Process of Difference, the Difference of Process." In *Process and Difference: Between Cosmological and Poststructuralist Postmodernism.* Edited by Catherine Keller and Anne Daniell, 1–30. New York: State University of New York Press, 2002.
———. *On Mystery: Discerning God in Process.* Minneapolis: MN: Fortress Press, 2008.
———. "Process and Chaosmos: A Whiteheadian Fold in the Discourse of Difference." In *Process and Difference: Between Cosmological and Poststructuralist Postmodernism.* Edited by Catherine Keller and Anne Daniell, 55–72. New York: State University of New York Press, 2002.
———. "Theopoetics and the Pluriverse: Notes on a Process." In *Theopoetic Folds: Philosophizing Multifariousness.* Edited by Roland Faber and Jeremy Fackenthal, 179–94. New York: Fordham University Press, 2013.
———. "The Unspeakable Conviviality of Becoming." In *Living Traditions and Universal Conviviality: Prospects and Challenges for Peace in Multireligious Communities.* Edited by Roland Faber and Santiago Slabodsky, 141–64. Lanham, MD: Lexington Books, 2016.
Keller, Catherine and Anne Daniell (eds.). *Process and Difference: Between Cosmological and Poststructuralist Postmodernism.* New York: State University of New York Press, 2002.
Keller, Catherine, Michael Nausner and Mayra Rivera (eds.). *Postcolonial Theologies: Diversity and Empire.* St. Louis: Chalice Press, 2004.
Keller, Catherine and Laurel Schneider (eds.). *Polydoxy: Theology of Multiplicity and Relation.* London: Routledge, 2011.
Kessler, Michael and Christian Sheppard (eds.). *Mystics: Presence and Aporia.* Chicago: Chicago University Press, 2003.
Khan, Inayat. *The Soul's Journey.* New Lebanon: Omega Publications, 2001.
Khan, Maulana Wahiduddin. *The Prophet of Peace: Teachings of the Prophet Mohammad.* New Delhi: Penguin Books, 2009.
Kiblinger, Kristin. *Buddhist Inclusivism: Attitudes toward Religious Others.* New York: Routledge, 2017.
Kinsley, David. *Ecology and Religion: Ecological Spirituality in Cross-Cultural Perspective.* London: Pearson, 1998.
Kirkham, Richard. *Theories of Truth: A Critical Introduction.* Cambridge: MIT Press, 1995.
Kisak, Paul (ed.). *Religious Cosmology: Religious Explanations for the Origin of the Universe.* Scotts Valley, CA: CreateSpace, 2016.
Kitagawa, Joseph Mitsuo. *The Quest for Human Unity: A Religious History.* Minneapolis: Fortress Press, 1990.
Klieber, Rupert and Martin Stowasser (eds.). *Inkulturation. Historische Beispiele und theologische Reflexionen zur Flexibilität und Widerständigkeit des Christlichen.* Vienna: LIT Verlag, 2006.
Kloetzli, Randolph. "Nous and Nirvana: Conversations with Plotinus—An Essay in Buddhist Cosmology." *Philosophy East and West* 57, no. 2 (2007): 140–77.
Kluge, Ian. "The Aristotelian Substratum of the Bahá'í Writings." *Lights of Irfan* 4 (2003): 17–68.
———. "The Bahá'í Faith and Conviviality." In *Living Traditions and Universal Conviviality: Prospects and Challenges for Peace in Multireligious Communities.* Edited by Roland Faber and Santiago Slabodsky, 37–46. Lanham, MD: Lexington Books, 2016.
———. "Further Explorations in Baha'i Ontology: Ontologies of Self and Change." *Lights of Irfan* 7 (2006): 163–200.
———. "Neoplatonism and the Bahá'í Writings I." *Lights of Irfan* 11 (2010): 149–202.
———. "Neoplatonism and the Bahá'í Writings II." *Lights of Irfan* 12 (2011): 105–93.

———. "Postmodernism and the Bahá'í Writings." *Lights of Irfan* 9 (2008): 61–178.
———. "Relativism and the Bahá'í Writings." *Lights of Irfan* 9 (2008): 179–238.
Knepper, Timothy. *Negating Negation: Against the Apophatic Abandonment of the Dionysian Corpus*. Eugene, OR: Wipf & Stock, 2014.
Knitter, Paul. *Without Buddha I Could Not Be a Christian*. Oxford: Oneworld, 2009.
———. "Can Christian Theology Be Only Christian? A Dialogical Theology for the Third Millennium." In *Theology toward the Third Millennium: Theological Issues for the Twenty-First Century*. Edited by David Schultover, 83–102. Lewiston, NY: Edwin Mellen Press, 1991.
———. "My God Is Bigger Than Your God: Time for Another Axial Shift in the History of Religion." *Studies in Interreligious Dialogue* 17, no. 1 (2007): 100–18.
———. *No Other Name? A Critical Survey of Christian Attitudes toward the World Religions*. Maryknoll, NY: Orbis Books, 1986.
———. *One Earth, Many Religions: Multifaith Dialogue and Global Responsibility*. Maryknoll, NY: Orbis Books, 1995.
———. *Introducing Theologies of Religion*. Maryknoll, NY: Orbis Books, 2007.
Knitter, Paul (ed.). *The Myth of Religious Superiority: Multifaith Explorations of Religious Pluralism*. Maryknoll, NY: Orbis Books, 2015.
Knitter, Paul and Roger Haight. *Jesus and Buddha: Friends in Conversation*. Maryknoll: NY: Orbis Books, 2015.
Kohn, Livia. *The God of Dao: Lord Lao in History and Myth*. Ann Arbor: The University of Michigan, 1998.
Kondrath, William. *God's Tapestry: Understanding and Celebrating Difference*. Herndon, VA: The Alban Institute, 1989.
Kourosh, Sohrab. *Self-Study Notes for the Kitáb-i-Íqán: The Book of Certitude*. Vol. I. South Lake, TX: Kourosh Publishing, 2016.
Kraay, Klaas (ed.). *God and the Multiverse: Scientific, Philosophical and Theological Perspectives*. New York: Routledge, 2015.
Kraidy, Marvan. *Hybridity: The Cultural Logic of Globalization*. Philadelphia, PA: Temple University Press, 2005.
Kraus, Elisabeth. *The Metaphysics of Experience: A Companion to Whitehead's Process and Reality*. New York: Fordham University Press, 1998.
Krishan, Y. "The Origin and Development of the Bodhisattva Doctrine." *East and West* 34, no. 1/3 (1984): 199–232.
Krishna, Sankaran. *Globalization and Postcolonialism: Hegemony and Resistance in the Twenty-First Century*. Lanham, MD: Rowman and Littlefield Publishers, 2009.
Küng, Hans. *Global Responsibility: In Search for a New World Ethics*. Portland, OR: Wipf & Stock, 2004.
Küng, Hans and Karl-Josef Kuschel. *A Global Ethic: A Declaration of the Parliament of the World's Religions*. New York: Continuum Publishing Company, 1995.
Kurtz, Lester. *Gods in the Global Village: The World's Religions in Sociological Perspective*. Los Angeles: Sage, 2012.
Kurzweil, Ray. *The Age of Spiritual Machines: When Computers Exceed Human Intelligence*. New York: Penguin Books, 2000.
———. *The Singularity Is Near: When Humans Transcend Biology*. New York: Penguin Books, 2005.
Lai, Whalen and Michael von Brück, *Christianity and Buddhism: A Multicultural History of Their Dialogue*. Maryknoll, NY: Orbis Books, 2001.
Lambden, Stephen. "The Background and Centrality of Apophatic Theology in Bábi and Bahá'í Scripture." In *Revisioning the Sacred: New Perspectives in Bahá'í Theology*. Edited by Jack McLean, 37–78. Los Angeles: Kalimat Press, 1997.
———. "Dimensions of Abrahamic and Babi-Bahā'ī Soteriology: Some Notes on the Bahā'ī Theology of the Salvific and Redemptive role of Bahā'-Allāh." University of California Merced: http://hurqalya.ucmerced.edu/node/345.

———. "The Mysteries of the Call to Moses: Translation and Notes on a Tablet of Bahá'u'lláh addressed to Jinab-i Khalil." *Bahā'ī Studies Bulletin* 4, no. 1 (1986): 33–78.

———. "The Sinaitic Mysteries: Notes on Moses/Sinai Motifs in Bábi and Bahá'í Scripture." In *Studies in Honor of the Late Hasan M. Balyuzi*. Edited by Moojan Momen, 65–184. Los Angeles: Kalimat Press, 1988.

———. *Some Aspects of Isrā'īliyyāt and the Emergence of the Bābī-Bahā'ī Interpretation of the Bible*. Newcastle University, dissertation, 2002.

———. "The Word Bahá: Quintessence of the Greatest Name." *Bahá'í Studies Review* 3, no. 1 (1993): 19–42.

Lambert, Yves. "Religion in Modernity as a New Axial Age: Secularization or New Religious Forms." *Sociology of Religion* 60, no. 3 (1999): 303–33.

Lample, Paul. *Revelation and Social Reality: Learning to Translate What Is Written into Reality*. West Palm Beach, FL: Palabra Publications, 2009.

Lamża, Łukasz and Jakub Dziadkowiec (eds.). *Recent Advances in the Creation of a Process-Based Worldview: Human Life in Process*. Newcastle upon Tyne: Cambridge Scholars Publishing, 2016

Lanzetta, Beverly. *Emerging Heart: Global Spirituality and the Sacred*. Minneapolis, MN: Fortress Press, 2007.

———. *Radical Wisdom: A Feminist Mystical Theology*. Minneapolis: Fortress Press, 2005.

Laszlo, Erwin. *Science and the Akashic Field: An Integral Theory of Everything*. Rochester, VT: Inner Traditions, 2007.

———. *The Self-Actualizing Universe: The Akasha Revolution in Science and Human Consciousness*. Rochester, VT: Inner Traditions, 2014.

Latour, Bruno. *Politics of Nature: How to Bring Sciences into Democracy*. Cambridge: Harvard University Press, 2004.

Lavoie, Jeffrey. *The Theosophical Society: The History of a Spiritualist Movement*. Boca Raton, FL: BrownWalker Press, 2012

Lawson, Todd. "The Báb's Epistle on the Spiritual Journey toward God." In *The Bahá'í Faith and the World's Religions*. Edited by Moojan Momen, 231–47. Oxford: George Ronald, 2003.

———. "Globalization and the *Hidden Words*." In *Baha'i and Globalization*. Edited by Margit Warburg, Annika Hvithamar and Moojan Momen, 35–54. Aarhus: Aarhus University Press, 2005.

———. "The Terms 'Remembrance' (*dhikr*) and 'Gate' (*báb*) in the Báb's Commentary on the Sura of Joseph." In *Studies in Honor of the Late Hasan M. Balyuzi*. Edited by Moojan Momen, 1–64. Los Angeles: Kalimat Press, 1988.

Lee, Anthony (ed.). *Circle of Unity: Bahá'í Approaches to Current Social Issues*. Los Angeles: Kalimat Press, 1984.

Lee, Hyo-Dong. *Spirit, Qi, and the Multitude: A Comparative Theology for the Democracy of Creation*. New York: Fordham Press, 2014.

Leirvik, Odbjorn. "Interreligious Studies: A New Academic Discipline." In *Contested Spaces, Common Ground: Space and Power Structures in Contemporary Multireligious Societies*. Leiden: Brill, 2017.

Leopold, Anita Maria and Jeppe Sinding Jensen (eds.). *Syncretism in Religion: A Reader*. New York: Routledge, 2005.

Lepain, Jean-Marc. "The Tablet of All Food: The Hierarchy of the Spiritual Worlds and the Metaphoric Nature of Physical Reality." Translated by Peter Terry. *Baha'i Studies Review* 16 (2010): 43–60.

Lepard, Brian. *Hope: For a Global Ethics*. Wilmette, IL: Bahá'í Publishing, 2005.

———. *In the Glory of the Father: The Bahá'í Faith and Christianity*. Wilmette, IL: Bahá'í Publishing, 2008.

Leslie, John. *Immortality Defended*. Malden, MA: Blackwell Publishing, 2007.

———. *Universes*. London: Routledge, 1996.

Leue, William. *Metaphysical Foundations of a Theory of Value in the Philosophy of Alfred North Whitehead*. Ashfield: Down-to-Earth Books, 2005.

Lewels, Joe. *The God Hypothesis: Extraterrestrial Life and its Implications for Science and Religion.* Leland, NC: WildFlower Press, 2005.

Lings, Martin and Clinton Minnaar (eds.). *The Underlying Religion: An Introduction to the Perennial Philosophy.* Bloomington, IN: World Wisdom, 2008.

Long, Jeffrey. "Anekanta Vedanta: Toward a Deep Hindu Religious Pluralism." In *Deep Religious Pluralism.* Edited by David Griffin, 130–45. Louisville, KY: Westminster John Knox, 2005.

———. "Tentatively Putting the Pieces Together: Comparative Theology in the Tradition of Sri Ramakrishna." In *The New Comparative Theology: Interreligious Insights from the Next Generation.* Edited by Francis X. Clooney, 151–70. New York: T&T Clarke, 2010.

———. "Truth, Diversity, and the Incomplete Project of Modern Hinduism." In *Hermeneutics and Hindu Thought: Toward a Fusion of Horizons.* Edited by Rita Sherma and Arvind Sharma, 179–210. Berlin/Heidelberg, Germany: Springer Science, 2008.

———. *A Vision of Hinduism: Beyond Hindu Nationalism.* London: I.B.Tauris & Co. Ltd., 2007.

Loomba, Ania. *Colonialism/Postcolonialism.* Abington, Oxon: Routledge, 2015.

Lopez, Donald. *The Story of Buddhism: A Concise Guide to Its History and Teachings.* New York: Harper SanFrancisco, 2001.

Lundberg, Zain. "The Bedrock of Bahá'í Belief: The Doctrine of Progressive Revelation." *Lights of Irfan* 1 (2000): 53–67.

———. "From Adam to Bahá'u'lláh: The Idea of a Chain of Prophets." *Lights of Irfan* 3 (2002): 59–82.

———. "The New Age Phenomenon and the Bahá'í Faith." *Lights of Irfan* 1 (2000): 69–80.

Lutyens, Mary. *Krishnamurti: The Years of Awakening.* New York: Farrar Straus and Giroux, 1975.

Lyotard, Jean-Francois. *The Postmodern Condition: A Report on Knowledge.* Minneapolis: University of Minnesota Press, 1984.

Macquarrie, John. *Mediators between Human and Divine: From Moses to Muhammad.* London: Bloomsbury, 1999.

Majumdar, Deepa. *Plotinus on the Appearance of Time and the World of Sense: A Pantomime.* New York: Routledge, 2016.

The Mandukya Upanishad, in *The Upanishads.* Introduction and translation by Eknath Aeswaran. Tomales, CA: The Blue Mountain Center of Meditation, 2007, 203–5.

Maneck, Susan. "Conversion of Religious Minorities to the Bahá'í Faith in Iran: Some Preliminary Observations." *Journal of Bahá'í Studies* 3, no. 3 (1990): https://bahai-library.com/maneck_conversion_minorities_iran.

———. "Women in the Bahá'í Faith." In *Religion and Women.* Edited by Arvind Sharma, 211–28. Albany: State University of New York Press, 1994.

Maor, Eli. *To Infinity and Beyond: A Cultural History of the Infinite.* Princeton: Princeton University Press, 1991.

Margolis, Joseph. *The Truth about Relativism.* Oxford: Blackwell, 1991.

Marshal, Ian and Daniel Zohar. *Who's Afraid of Schrödinger's Cat? An A-to-Z guide to the All in New Science Ideas You Need to Keep with the New Thinking.* New York: William Morrow, 1997.

Martin, Alfred. *Comparative Religion and the Religion of the Future.* New York: D. Appleton and Company, 1926.

Martin, Grant. "Why the Bahá'í Faith Is Not Pluralist." *Lights of Irfan* 8 (2007): 179–202.

Martin, Jerry (ed.). *Open Theology: Is Transreligious Theology Possible? Open Theology* 2 (2016): 261–302: https://www.degruyter.com/dg/page/is-transreligious-theology-possible/open-theology-is-transreligious-theology-possible.

Massumi, Brian. *Parables for the Virtual: Movement, Affect, Sensation.* Durham & London: Duke University Press, 2002.

Ma'sumian, Bijan. "Mysticism and the Bahá'í Faith." *Deepen* 6, no. 3 (1995): 12–17.

———. "Realms of Divine Existence as described in the Tablet of All Food." *Deepen* 3, no. 2.2 (1994): 11–17.

Masuzawa, Tomoko. *The Invention of World Religions: Or, How European Universalism Was Preserved in the Language of Pluralism*. Chicago: University of Chicago Press, 2005.
Matt, Daniel. *The Essential Kabbalah: The Heart of Jewish Mysticism*. San Francisco: HarperCollins, 1996.
May, Dann. "The Bahá'í Principle of Religious Unity." In *Revisioning the Sacred: New Perspectives in Bahá'í Theology*. Edited by Jack McLean, 1–36. Los Angeles: Kalimat Press, 1997.
Mbiti, John. *African Religions and Philosophy*. Portsmouth, NH: Heinemann International, 1969.
McCagney, Nancy. *Nagarjuna and the Philosophy of Oneness*. Lanham, MD: Rowman and Littlefield, 1997.
McDaniel, Jay. *Gandhi's Hope: Learning from Other Religions as a Path to Peace*. Maryknoll, NY: Orbis Books, 2005.
———. *Of God and Pelicans: A Theology of Reverence for Life*. Louisville: Westminster John Knox, 1989.
McFague, Sallie. *The Body of God: An Ecological Theology*. Minneapolis: Fortress Press, 1993.
McGinn, Bernard. "The God beyond God: Theology and Mysticism in the Thought of Meister Eckhart." *The Journal of Religion* 61, no. 1 (1981): 1–19.
———. *The Mystical Thought of Meister Eckhart: The Man from Whom God Hid Nothing*. New York: Crossroads Publishing, 2001.
McIntosh, Mark. *Mystical Theology*. Malden, MA: Blackwell, 1998.
McLean, Jack. "Prolegomena to a Bahá'í Theology." *The Journal of Bahá'í Studies* 5, no. 1 (1992): 37–44.
McLean, Jack (ed.). *Revisioning the Sacred: New Perspectives on a Bahá'í Theology*. Los Angeles: Kalimat Press, 1997.
McLeod, W. H. "The Influence of Islam on the Thought of Guru Nanak." *History of Religions* 7, no. 4 (1968): 302–16.
McKim, Robert. *On Religious Diversity*. Oxford: Oxford University Press, 2005.
Medina, John. *Faith, Physics and Psychology: Rethinking Society and the Human Spirit*. Wilmette, IL: Baha'i Publishing Trust, 2006.
Mehanian, Courosh and Stephen Friberg. "Religion and Evolution Reconciled: 'Abdu'l Bahá's Comments on Evolution." *The Journal of Bahá'í Studies* 13, no. 1–4 (2003): 55–93.
Meister, Chad. *Introducing Philosophy of Religion*. London: Routledge, 2009.
Meister, Chad (ed.). *The Oxford Handbook of Religious Diversity*. Oxford: Oxford University Press, 2001.
Mellert, Robert. *What Is Process Theology?* New York: Paulist Press, 1975.
Metz, Johan Baptist. *Faith in History and Society: Toward a Practical Fundamental Theology*. New York, NY: Crossroads Publishing, 2007.
Midgley, Mary. *Evolution as a Religion: Strange Hopes and Stranger Fears*. New York: Routledge, 1992.
Milbank, John, Catherine Pickstock and Graham Ward. *Radical Orthodoxy: A New Theology*. London: Routledge, 1999.
Mislin, David. *Saving Faith: Making Religious Pluralism an American Value at the Dawn of the Secular Age*. Ithaca, NY: Cornell University Press, 2015.
Mollenkott, Virginia Ramsey. *Omnigender: A Trans-Religious Approach*. Cleveland: Pilgrim Press, 2001.
Momen, Moojan. "Apocalyptic Thinking and Process Thinking: A Baha'i Contribution to Religious Thought." *Lights of Irfan* 13 (2012): 243–70.
———. *Bahá'u'lláh: A Short Biography*. Oxford: Oneworld, 2007.
———. *Buddhism and the Bahá'í Faith*. Oxford: George Ronald, 1995.
———. "The God of Bahá'u'lláh." In *The Bahá'í Faith and the World's Religions*. Edited by Moojan Momen, 1–38. Oxford: George Ronald, 2003.
———. *Islam and the Bahá'í Faith*. Oxford: George Ronald, 2000.
———. *Hinduism and the Bahá'í Faith*. Oxford: George Ronald, 1990.
———. "Learning from History." *Journal of Bahá'í Studies* 2, no. 2 (1989): http://bahai-library.com/momen_learning_from_history.
———. "Mysticism and the Bahá'í Community." *Lights of Irfan* 3 (2002): 107–20.

———. "Persecution and Resilience: A History of the Baha'i Religion in Qajar Isfahan." *Journal of Religious History* 36, no. 4 (2012): 471–85.
———. "Relativism: A Basis for Bahá'í Metaphysics." In *Studies in Honor of the Late Hasan M. Balyuzi*. Edited by Moojan Momen, 185–218. Los Angeles: Kalimat Press, 1988.
———. "Relativism: A Theological and Cognitive Basis for Bahá'í Ideas." *Lights of Irfan* 12 (2010): 367–97.
———. *Understanding Religion: A Thematic Approach*. Oxford: Oneworld, 2009.
Momen, Moojan (ed.). *The Bábí and Bahá'í Religions, 1844–1944: Some Contemporary Western Accounts*. Oxford: George Ronald, 1981.
———. *The Bahá'í Faith and the World's Religions*. Oxford: George Ronald, 2003.
———. *Scripture and Revelation: Papers presented at the First Irfan Colloquium*. Oxford: George Ronald, 1997.
———. *Selections of the Writings of E. G. Browne on the Bábi and Bahá'í Religions*. Oxford: George Ronald, 1987.
———. *Studies in Bábí and Bahá'í History*. Los Angeles: Kalimat Press, 1982.
———. *Studies in Honor of the Late Hasan M. Balyuzi*. Los Angeles: Kalimat Press, 1988.
Morris, Rosalind (ed.). *Can the Subaltern Speak? Reflections on the History of an Idea*. New York: Columbia University Press, 2010.
Mortensen, Viggo (ed.). *Theology and the Religious Dialogue*. Grand Rapids, MI: Eerdmans Publishing, 2003.
Mullan, David. *Religious Pluralism in the West: An Anthology*. Hoboken, NJ: Wiley-Blackwell, 1998.
Nagel, Thomas. *Mind and Cosmos: Why the Materialist Neo-Darwinian Conception of Nature Is Almost Certainly False*. Oxford: Oxford University Press, 2012.
Naghdy, Fazel. *A Tutorial on the Kitab-i-Iqan: A Journey through the Book of Certitude*. 2012.
Nah, David. *Christian Theology and Religious Pluralism: A Critical Evaluation of John Hick*. Eugene: OR: Pickwick Publications, 2012.
Nah, Robert. *Religious Pluralism in the Academy: Opening the Dialogue*. New York: Peter Lang, 2001.
Nash, Ronald. *Is Jesus the Only Savior?* Grand Rapids, MI: Zondervan, 1994.
Nayar, Pramod. *Postcolonialism: A Guide for the Perplexed*. London: Continuum, 2010.
Neely's History of the Parliament of Religions and Religious Congresses of the World's Columbian Exposition. Edited by Walter Houghton et al. Chicago: F. Tennyson Neely, 1894.
Netland, Harold. *Dissident Voices: Religious Pluralism and the Question of Truth*. Vancouver, BC: Regent College Publishing, 1999.
———. *Encountering Religious Pluralism: The Challenge to Christian Faith and Mission*. Downers Grove, IL: InterVarsity Press, 2001.
Neufeld, R. W. "The Response of the Ramakrishna Mission." In *Modern Indian Responses to Religious Pluralism*. Edited by Harold Coward, 65–84. Albany: State University of New York, 1987.
Neville, Robert. *Creativity and God: A Challenge to Process Theology*. Albany: State of New York University Press, 1995.
———. *Ultimates: Philosophical Theology One*. Albany: State University of New York Press, 2013.
Neville, Robert (ed.). *Ultimate Realities: A Volume in Comparative Religious Ideas Project*. New York: State University of New York Press, 2001.
Neville, Robert and Wesley Wildman, "On Comparing Religious Ideas." In *Ultimate Realities: A Volume in Comparative Religious Ideas Project*. Edited by Robert Neville, 187–210. New York: State University of New York Press, 2001.
Newland, Guy. *Appearance and Reality: The Two Truths in the Four Buddhist Tenet Systems*. Ithaka, NY: Two Lion Publications, 1999.
Nhat Hanh, Thich. *Interbeing: Commentaries on the Tiep Hien Precepts*. Berkeley: Parallax Press, 1987.
———. *Living Buddha, Living Christ*. New York: Riverhead Books, 1995.
Nicolescu, Basarab. *From Modernity to Cosmomodernity: Science, Culture and Spirituality*. Albany: State University of New York Press, 2014.

Nishida, Kitaro. *An Inquiry into the Good*. Translated by Masao Abe and Christopher Ives. New Haven: Yale University Press, 1990.

———. *Logik des Orts. Der Anfang der modernen Philosophie*. Darmstadt: Wissenschaftliche Buchgesellschaft, 1999.

Nongbri, Brent. *Before Religion: A History of a Modern Concept*. New Haven, CT: Yale University Press, 2012.

Novak, Philip. *The World's Wisdom: Sacred Texts of the World's Religions*. San Francisco: HarperCollins Publishers, 1995.

Odin, Steve. *Process Metaphysics and Hua-Yen Buddhism: A Critical Study of Cumulative Penetration vs. Interpenetration*. Albany: State University of New York Press, 1982.

O'Meara, Thomas. *Vast Universes: Extraterrestrials and Christian Revelation*. Collegeville, MN: Liturgical Press, 2012.

Overzee, Anne Hunt. *The Body Divine: The Symbol of the Body in the Works of Teilhard de Chardin and Ramanuja*. Cambridge: Cambridge University Press, 1992.

Owen, Suzanne. "The World Religions Paradigm: Time for a Change." *Arts and Humanities in Higher Education* 10, no. 3 (2011): 253–68.

Owen, Thomas. "Religious Plurality and Contemporary Philosophy: A Critical Surve." *Harvard Theological Review* 87, no. 2 (1994): 197–213.

Pals, Daniel. *Seven Theories of Religion*. New York: Oxford University Press, 1996.

Panikkar, Raimon. *The Experience of God: Icons of the Mystery*. Minneapolis, MN: Augsburg Fortress, 2006.

———. *The Intra-religious Dialogue*. New York: Paulist Press, 1999.

———. "The Pluralism of Truth." *World Faiths Insight* 26 (1990): 7–16.

———. *The Silence of God: The Answer of the Buddha*. Maryknoll, NY: Orbis, 1989.

Parrinder, Geoffrey. *Avatar and Incarnation: The Divine in Human Form in the World's Religions*. Oxford: Oneworld, 1997.

Parsons, Terrence. "The Traditional Square of Opposition." In *Stanford Encyclopedia of Philosophy*. 2017: https://plato.stanford.edu/entries/square/.

Paul, Eric Robert. *Science, Religion, and Mormon Cosmology*. Urbana: University of Illinois Press, 1992.

Penrose, Roger. *The Emperor's New Mind: Concerning Computers, Minds, and the Laws of Physics*. New York: Penguin Books, 1989.

Penrose, Roger, et al. *The Large, the Small and the Human Mind*. Cambridge: Cambridge University Press, 1999.

Perry, Ann Gordon. *Unseen Witnesses: Sarah Farmer and Portsmouth Peace Treaty*. Duncanville, TX: Nine Petal Press, 2017.

Perry, M. L. *The Last War: Racism, Spirituality and the Future of Civilization*. Oxford: George Ronald, 2005.

Peters, Ted. *God as Trinity: Relationality and Temporality in Divine Life*. Louisville, KY: Westminster John Knox, 1993.

———. *Science, Theology, and Ethics*. Farnham, UK: Ashgate, 2003.

Phan, Peter and Jonathan Ray (eds.). *Understanding Religious Pluralism: Perspectives from Religious Studies and Theology*. Eugene, OR: Pickwick Publications, 2014.

Pinker, Steven. *The Better Angels of Our Nature: Why Violence Has Declined*. New York: Viking, 2012.

Plate, S. Brent. *A History of Religion in 5½ Objects: Bringing the Spiritual to Its Senses*. Boston: Beacon Press, 2004.

Prabhu, Joseph. Talks on the Emergent Second Axial Age: https://berkleycenter.georgetown.edu/events/religious-identity-in-an-emergent-second-axial-age.

Prabhu, Joseph (ed.). *The Intercultural Challenge of Raimon Panikkar*. Maryknoll, NY: Orbis Books, 1996.

Prothero, Stephen. *God Is Not One: The Eight Rival Religions That Run the World*. New York: HarperCollins, 2010.

Prothero, Stephen (ed.). *A Nation of Religions: The Politics of Pluralism in Multireligious America*. Chapel Hill: University of North Carolina Press, 2006.

Pugliese, Marc and Gloria Schaab (eds.). *Seeking Common Ground: Evaluation and Critique of Joseph Bracken's Comprehensive Worldview*. Milwaukee, WI: Marquette University Press, 2012.

Pui-lan, Kwok. *Postcolonial Imagination and Feminist Theology*. Louisville, KY: WJK, 2005.

Quinn, Philipp and Kevin Meeker (eds.). *The Philosophical Challenge of Religious Diversity*. New York: Oxford University Press, 2000.

Quinn, Sholeh. "The End of History?" In *Reason and Revelation: New Detections in Bahá'í Thought*. Edited by Seena Fazel and John Danesh, 157–72. Los Angeles: Kalimat Press, 2002.

Race, Alan. *Christians and Religious Pluralism: Patterns in the Christian Theology of Religions*. London: SCM Press, 1983.

———. *Thinking about Religious Pluralism. Shaping Theology of Religions for Our Time*. Minneapolis: Fortress Press, 2015.

Radhakrishnan, Sarvepalli. *East and West in Religion*. London: George Allen & Unwit Ltd., 1933.

Rahner, Karl. *Foundations of Christian Faith: An Introduction to the Idea of Christianity*. New York: Crossroad, 2005.

Ramadan, Tariq. *The Quest for Meaning: Developing a Philosophy of Pluralism*. London: Penguin Books, 2010.

Ranjbar, Vahid Houston. "One Physicist's First Look at 'Abdu'l-Bahá's Tablet of the Universe": https://medium.com/@vahidhoustonranjbar/one-physicists-first-look-at-abdu-l-baha-s-tablet-of-the-universe-db541a951348.

Reat, Ross and Edmund F. Perry. *A World Theology: The Central Spiritual Reality of Humankind*. Cambridge: Cambridge University Press, 2010.

Red Star, Nancy. *Star Ancestors: Extraterrestrial Contact in the Native American Tradition*. Rochester, VT: Bear and Co., 2012.

Renard, John (ed.). *Fighting Words: Religion, Violence, and the Interpretation of Sacred Texts*. Berkeley: University of California Press, 2011.

Rigopoulos, Antonio. *Dattatreya: The Immortal Guru, Yogin, and Avatara: A Study of the Transformative and Inclusive Character of a Multi-faceted Hindu Deity*. Albany: State University of New York Press, 1998.

Riley, Gregory. *One Jesus, Many Christs: How Jesus Inspired Not One True Christianity But Many*. Minneapolis: Fortress Press, 2000.

———. *The River of God: A New History of Christian Origins*. New York: HarperCollins, 2003.

Roemischer, Jessica. "A New Axial Age: Karen Armstrong on the History—and the Future—of God": www.enlightennext.org/magazine/j31/armstrong.asp?page=1

Rose, Kenneth. *Knowing the Real: John Hick on the Cognitivity of Religions and Religious Pluralism*. New York: Peter Lang Publishing, 1996.

———. *Pluralism: The Future of Religion*. New York: Bloomsbury, 2013.

Rose, Philip. *On Whitehead*. Belmont: Wadsworth, 2002.

Rothblatt, Martine. *Virtually Human: The Promise—and the Peril—of Digital Immortality*. New York: St. Martin's Press, 2014.

Roy, Louis. *Mystical Consciousness: Western Perspectives and Dialogue with Japanese Thinkers*. Albany: State University of New York Press, 2003.

Rubinstein, Mary-Jane. *Worlds without End: The Many Lives of the Multiverse*. New York: Columbia University Press, 2014.

Rudolph, Kurt. "Syncretism—From Theological Invective to a Concept in the Study of Religion." In *Syncretism in Religion: A Reader*. Edited by Anita Maria Leopold and Jeppe Sinding Jensen, 68–85. New York: Routledge, 2005.

Rue, Loyal. *Religion Is Not About God: How Spiritual Traditions Nurture Our Biological Nature and What to Expect If They Fail*. New Brunswick, NJ: Rutgers University Press, 2005.

Runzo, Joseph. *Global Philosophy of Religion: A Short Introduction*. Oxford: Oneworld Publishing, 2012.

———. *Reason, Relativism and God*. New York: Palgrave Macmillan, 1986.

Rüpke, Jörg (ed.). *A Companion to Roman Religion*. Malden, MA: Blackwell Publishing, 2007.

Sadakata, Akira and Hajime Nakamura. *Buddhist Cosmology: Philosophy and Origins*. Tokyo: Kosei Publishing, 1999.
Seager, Richard. *Dawn of Religious Pluralism: Voices from the World's Parliament of Religions 1893*. LaSalle, IL: Open Court, 1994.
———. *The World's Parliament of Religions: The East/West Encounter, Chicago, 1893*. Bloomington: Indiana University Press, 2009.
Seager, Richard and Diana Eck. *Dawn of Religious Pluralism: Voices from the World's Parliament of Religions, 1893*. Chicago, IL: Open Court Publishing, 1994.
Saiedi, Nader. *Gate of the Heart: Understanding the Writings of the Báb*. Waterloo, ON: Wilfrid Laurier University Press, 2010.
———. *Logos and Civilization: Spirit, History, and Order in the Writings of Bahá'u'lláh*. Baltimore: University Press of Maryland, 2000.
Savi, Julio. "The Baha'i Faith and the Perennial Mystical Quest: A Western Perspective." *Baha'i Studies Review* 14 (2007): 5–22.
———. "Religious Pluralism: A Bahá'í Perspective." *World Order* 31, no. 2 (1999/2000): 25–41.
———. *Towards the Summit of Reality: An Introduction to the Study of Baha'u'llah's Seven Valleys and Four Valley*. Oxford: George Ronald, 2008.
Schaefer, Udo. "Bahá'u'lláh's Unity Paradigm—a Contribution to Interfaith Dialogue on a Global Ethics." Lecture given on September 30, University of Erlangen, 1994.
———. *Beyond the Clash of Religions: The Emergence of a New Paradigm*. Stockholm: Zero Palm Press, 1998.
Schewel, Benjamin. "Religion in an Age of Transition." In *Religion and Public Discourse in an Age of Transition: Reflections on Bahá'í Practice and Thought*. Edited by Geoffrey Cameron and Benjamin Schewel, 1–12. Waterloo, Ontario, Canada: Wilfrid Laurier University Press, 2018.
Schilpp, Paul (ed.). *The Philosophy of Alfred North Whitehead*. La Salle, IL: Open Court, 1991.
Schimmel, Annemarie. *As Through a Veil: Mystical Poems in Islam*. Oxford: Oneworld, 2001.
———. *The Empire of the Great Mughals: History and Culture*. London: Reaktion Books, 2017.
———. *Mystical Dimensions of Islam*. Chapel Hill: University of North Carolina Press, 2001.
Schmidt, Leigh. *Restless Souls: The Making of American Spirituality*. New York: HarperCollins, 2005.
Schmidt-Leukel, Perry. *Buddhism, Christianity and the Question of Creation: Karmic or Divine?* Burlington, VT: Ashgate, 2006.
———. "Exclusivism, Inclusivism, Pluralism: The Tripolar Typology—Clarified and Reaffirmed." In *The Myth of Religious Superiority: Multifaith Explorations of Religious Pluralism*. Edited by Paul Knitter, 13–27. Maryknoll, NY: Orbis Books, 2015.
———. *Religious Pluralism and Interreligious Theology: The Gifford Lectures—an Extended Version*. New York: Orbis Books, 2016.
Schmidt-Leukel, Perry (ed.). *Buddhism and Christianity in Dialogue: The Gerald Weisfeld Lectures 2004*. Norwich, Norfolk: SCM Press, 2005.
Schneider, Laurel. *Beyond Monotheism: A Theology of Multiplicity*. New York: Routledge, 2008.
Scholem, Gershom. *Major Trends in Jewish Mysticism*. New York: Schocken Books, 1995.
Schuon, Frithjof. *The Transcendent Unity of Religions*. Wheaton, IL: Quest Books, 2005.
Selin, Helaine (ed.). *Nature across Cultures: Views of Nature and the Environment in Non-Western Cultures*. Dortrecht: Springer, 2003.
Sells, Michael. "Apophasis in Plotinus: A Critical Approach." *Harvard Theological Review* 87, no. 3–4 (1985): 47–65.
———. *Mystical Languages of Unsaying*. Chicago: University of Chicago Press, 1994.
Senzaki, Nyogen. "Sufism and Zen." *On Zen Mediation*. 1936: https://wahiduddin.net/hik/hik_senzaki.htm.
Shah-Kazemi, Reza. *Common Ground between Islam and Buddhism*. Louisville: Fons Vitae, 2010.
Sharma, Arvind. "Along a Path Less Traveled: A Plurality of Religious Ultimates." In *The World's Religions: A Contemporary Reader*. Edited by Arvind Sharma, 198–202. Minneapolis: Fortress Press, 2011.

———. "Buddhism Meets Hinduism: Interaction and Influence in India." In *The World's Religions: A Contemporary Reader*. Edited by Arvind Sharma, 234–40. Minneapolis: Fortress Press, 2011.

———. "Can There Be More Than One Kind of Pluralism." In *The Myth of Religious Superiority: Multifaith Explorations of Religious Pluralism*. Edited by Paul Knitter, 56–61. Maryknoll, NY: Orbis Books, 2015

———. *The Philosophy of Religion and Advaita Vedanta: A Comparative Study in Religion and Reason*. University Park: Pennsylvania State University Press, 1995.

———. *A Primal Perspective on the Philosophy of Religion*. Dordrecht, NL: Springer 2006.

Sharma, Arvind (ed.). *God, Truth and Reality: Essays in Honor of John Hick*. Eugene, OR: Wipf & Stock, 1993.

———. *Religion and Women*. Albany: State University of New York Press, 1994.

———. *The World's Religions: A Contemporary Reader*. Minneapolis: Fortress Press, 2011.

Sharma, Arvind and Kathleen Margaret Dugan. *A Dome of Many Colors: Studies in Religious Pluralism, Identity, and Unity*. Harrisburg, PA: Trinity Press International, 1999.

Shaviro, Steven. *Without Criteria: Kant, Whitehead, Deleuze, and Aesthetics*. Cambridge: MIT Press, 2009.

Shaw, Rosalind and Charles Steward (eds.). *Syncretism/Anti-Syncretism: The Politics of Religious Synthesis*. New York: Routledge, 1994.

Sherma, Rita and Arvind Sharma (eds.). *Hermeneutics and Hindu Thought: Toward a Fusion of Horizons*. Berlin/Heidelberg, Germany: Springer, 2008.

Shoghi Effendi. *The Advent of Divine Justice*. Wilmette, IL: Bahá'í Publishing, 1990.

———. *Directives from the Guardian*. Scotts Valley, CA: CreateSpace, 2015.

———. *God Passes By*. Wilmette, IL: Bahá'í Publishing, 1970.

———. *The Light of Divine Guidance*. Vol. 2. Germany: Bahá'í Publishing, 1985.

———. *The Promised Day Is Come*. Wilmette, IL: Bahá'í Publishing, 1996.

———. *The World Order of Bahá'u'lláh*. Wilmette, IL: Bahá'í Publishing, 1993.

Smart, Ninian. *Dimensions of the Sacred: An Anatomy of the World's Beliefs*. Berkeley: University of California Press, 1996.

———. *The Phenomenon of Religion*. New York: Macmillan, 1973.

———. *World Philosophies*. Edited by Oliver Leaman. New York: Routledge, 2008.

———. *The World's Religions*. 2nd edition. Cambridge: Cambridge University Press, 1998.

Smith, Huston. *Forgotten Truth: The Common Vision of the World's Religions*. San Francisco: HarperSanFrancisco, 1992.

———. *The World's Religions*. New York: HarperCollins, 1991.

Smith, Jonathan Z. "A Matter of Class: Taxonomies of Religions." In *Relating Religion: Essays in the Study of Religion*. 160–78. Chicago: University of Chicago Press, 2004.

———. *Relating Religion: Essays in the Study of Religion*. Chicago: University of Chicago Press, 2004.

Smith, Peter. "The American Bahá'í Community, 1894–1917." In *Studies in Bábí and Bahá'í History*. Edited by Moojan Momen, 85–224. Los Angeles: Kalimat Press, 1982.

———. *An Introduction to the Bahá'í Faith*. Cambridge: Cambridge University Press, 2008.

———. *The Bábí and Bahá'í Religions: From Messianic Shi'ism to a World Religion*. Cambridge: Cambridge University Press (George Ronald), 1987.

———. *A Concise Encyclopedia of the Bahá'í Faith*. Oxford, Oneworld, 2008.

Smith, Peter (ed.). *In Iran: Studies in Bábí and Bahá'í History*. Vol. 3. Los Angeles: Kalimat Press, 1986.

Smith, Phillip. "Bahá'í Faith and Religious Diversity." *Bahá'í Studies Review* 1, no.1 (1991): https://bahai-library.com/smith_religious_diversity.

Smith, William C. *The Meaning and End of Religion*. Minneapolis: Fortress, 1991.

Snodgrass, Judith. *Presenting Japanese Buddhism to the West: Orientalism, Occidentalism, and the Columbian Exposition*. Chapel Hill: University of North Carolina Press, 2003.

Soulen, R. Kendall. *The Divine Name(s) and the Holy Trinity. Volume I: Distinguishing the Voices*. Louisville, KY: Westminster John Knox, 2011.

Sours, Michael. *The Station and Claims of Bahá'u'lláh*. Wilmette, IL: Bahá'í Publishing, 1997.

———. *The Tablet of the Holy Mariner: An Illustrated Guide the Bahá'u'lláh's Mystical Writing in the Sufi Tradition*. Los Angeles: Kalimat Press, 2002.
———. *Without Syllable and Sound: The Worlds Sacred Scriptures in the Bahá'í Faith*. Los Angeles: Kalimat Press, 2000.
Spivak, Gayatri. *A Critique of Postcolonial Reason: Toward a History of the Vanishing Present*. Harvard: President and Fellows of Harvard College, 1999.
———. *Death of a Discipline*. New York: Columbia University Press, 2003.
Spong, John. *Eternal Life: A New Vision: Beyond Religion, beyond Theism, beyond Heaven and Hell*. New York: HarperOne, 2009.
Srinivas, Tulasi. *Winged Faith: Rethinking Globalization and Religious Pluralism Through the Sathya Sai Baba Movement*. New York: Columbia University Press, 2010.
Stace, Walter. *Mysticism and Philosophy*. London: Macmillan, 1951.
Stcherbatsky, Theodore. *Buddhist Logic*. 2 Vols. Dover Publishing, 1984.
———. *The Conception of Buddhist Nirvana*. Delhi: Motilal Barnasidass, 2003.
Stein, Roberts. *Jesus, the Temple and the Coming of the Son of Man: A Commentary on Mark 13*. Downers Grove, IL: InterVarsity Press, 2015.
Steinhart, Eric. *Your Digital Afterlives: Computational Theories of Life after Death*. New York: Palgrave Macmillan, 2014.
Stenger, Victor. *God and the Multiverse: Humanity's Expanding View of the Cosmos*. Amherst, NY: Prometheus Books, 2014.
———. *The New Atheism: Taking a Stance for Science and Reason*. Amherst, NY: Prometheus Books, 2009.
Steward, Charles. "Relocating Syncretism in Social Science Discourse." In *Syncretism/Anti-Syncretism: The Politics of Religious Synthesis*. Edited by Rosalind Shaw and Charles Steward, 264–85. New York: Routledge, 1994.
Steward, Robert. *Can Only One Religion Be True? Paul Knitter and Harold Netland in Dialogue*. Minneapolis: Fortress Press, 2013.
Stockman, Robert. *'Abdu'l-Bahá in America*. Wilmette, IL: Bahá'í Publishing, 2012.
———. *The Bahá'í Faith: A Guide for the Perplexed*. New York: Bloomsbury Academic, 2013.
———. *The Bahá'í Faith in America: Early Expansion, 1900–1912*. Oxford: George Ronald, 1995.
———. "Progressive Revelation": https://bahai-library.com/stockman_encyclopedia_progressive_revelation.
Stonier, Tom. *Beyond Information: The Natural History of Intelligence*. London: Springer, 1992.
———. "Machine Intelligence and the Long-Term Future of the Human Species." *AI & Society* 2 (1988): 133–39.
Stroumsa, Guy. *A New Science: The Discovery of Religion in the Age of Reason*. Cambridge, MA: Harvard University Press, 2010.
Suchocki, Marjorie. *Divinity and Diversity: A Christian Affirmation of Religious Pluralism*. Nashville, FL: Abington Press, 2003.
———. *God–Christ–Church: A Practical Guide to Process Theology*. New York: Crossroads Publishing, 1995.
Sundermann, Werner. "MANI." *Encyclopædia Iranica*, online edition. 2009: http://www.iranicaonline.org/articles/mani-founder-manicheism.
Susskind, Leonard. *The Cosmic Landscape: String Theory and the Illusion of Intelligent Design*. New York: Back Bay Books, 2006.
Sutcliffe, Steven. "New Age, World Religions and Elementary Forms." In *New Age Spirituality: Rethinking Religion*. Edited by Steven Sutcliffe and Ingvild Saelid Gilhus, 17–34. Abington, Oxon: Routledge, 2013.
Sutcliffe, Steven and Ingvild Saelid Gilhus (eds.). *New Age Spirituality: Rethinking Religion*. Abington, Oxon: Routledge, 2013.
Swidler Leonard, et al. *Death or Dialogue: From the Age of Monologue to the Age of Dialogue*. London: SCM Press, 1990.
Taherzadeh, Adib. *The Revelation of Bahá'u'lláh*. Vol. 1. Oxford: George Ronald, 2001.

Tai-Seal, Tom. *Thy Kingdom Come: A Biblical Introduction to the Bahá'í Faith*. Los Angeles: Kalimat Press, 1992.

Teasdale, Wayne. *The Mystic Heart: Discovering the Universal Spirituality in the World's Religions*. Novato, CA: New World Library, 1999.

Talbot, Michael. *The Holographic Universe*. New York: HarperPerennial, 1991.

Taylor, Bonnie. *One Reality: The Harmony of Science and Religion*. Wilmette, IL: Bahá'í Publishing, 2013.

Teilhard de Chardin, Pierre. *The Phenomenon of Man*. New York: HarperCollins, 2002.

Theissen, Gerd. *The Religion of the Earliest Churches: Creating a Symbolic World*. Minneapolis, MN: Fortress Press, 1999.

Thiel, John. *Nonfoundationalism*. Minneapolis: Fortress Press, 1994.

Tipler, Frank. *The Physics of Immortality: Modern Cosmology, God, and the Resurrection of the Dead*. New York: Anchor Press, 1997.

Toffler, Alvin. *Future Shock*. New York: Random House, 1970.

Toynbee, Arnold. *An Historian's Approach to Religion*. London: Oxford University Press, 1956.

Tracy, David. *The Analogical Imagination: Christian Theology and the Culture of Pluralism*. New York: Crossroads Publishing, 1998.

Traphagan, John. *Science, Culture and the Search for Life on Other Worlds*. Dordrecht: Springer, 2016.

Troxel, Duane. "Extraterrestrial Life": http://Bahá'í-library.com/compilation_extraterrestrial_life.

———. "Intelligent Life in the Universe and Exotheology in Christianity and the Bahá'í Writings": http://bahai-library.com/troxel_extraterrestrials_exotheology.

Trungpa, Chögyam. *Cutting through Spiritual Materialism*. Boulder, CO: Shambala, 2002.

Tucker, Mary Evelyn and John Grimm (eds.). *Worldviews and Ecology: Religion, Philosophy, and the Environment*. Maryknoll, NY: Orbis Books, 1994.

Tweed, Thomas A. "American Occultism and Japanese Buddhism: Albert J. Edmunds, D. T. Suzuki, and Translocative History." *Japanese Journal of Religious Studies* 32, no. 2 (2005): 249–81.

Underhill, Evelyn. *Mysticism: A Study in the Nature and Development of Spiritual Consciousness*. Mineola, NY: Dover Publishing, 2002.

Unger, Roberto. *The Religion of the Future*. Harvard: President and Fellows of Harvard Colleges, 2014.

The Universal House of Justice. *To the World's Religious Leaders*. Haifa: 2002, https://www.bahai.org/library/authoritative-texts/the-universal-house-of-justice/messages/20020401_001/1#392291398.

The Upanishads. Introduction and translation by Eknath Aeswaran. Tomales, CA: The Blue Mountain Center of Meditation, 2007.

Vakoch, Douglas (ed.). *Astrobiology, History, and Society: Life beyond Earth and the Impact of Discovery*. Dordrecht: Springer, 2013.

Vanhoozer, Kevin (ed.). *The Cambridge Companion to Postmodern Theology*. Cambridge: Cambridge University Press, 2003.

Vasquez, Manual. *More Than Belief: A Materialist Theory of Religion*. Oxford: Oxford University Press, 2011.

Velasco, Ismael. "Achieving Reconciliation in a Conflicting World." *The Journal of Bahá'í Studies* 18, no. 1–4 (2010): 95–134.

Versluis, Arthur. *Perennial Philosophy*. Minneapolis, MN: New Cultures Press, 2015.

Swami Vivekananda. *Complete Works*. Vol. I. Hollywood: Vedanta Press, 2003.

———. *Complete Works*. Vol. VII. Hollywood: Vedanta Press, 1972.

———. *Complete Works*. Vol. VIII. Hollywood: Vedanta Press, 1947.

———. *Sisters & Brothers of America: Swami Vivekananda's Speech at World's Parliament of Religions, Chicago, 1893*. Edited by Sankar Srinivasan. India: LeoPard Books, 2017.

Vrajaprana, Pravrajika. *Living Wisdom: Vedanta in the West*. Hollywood: Vedanta Press, 2014.

de Vries, Hent and Lawrence Sullivan (eds.). *Political Theologies: Public Religions in a Post-secular World*. New York: Fordham University Press, 2006.

de Waal, Francis. "Primates, Monks, and the Mind: A Case for Empathy." *Journal of Consciousness Studies* 12, no. 7 (2005): 38–54.
Walbridge, John. "The Bábi Uprising in Zanjan: Causes and Issues." *Iranian Studies* 29, no. 3/4 (1996): 339–62.
———. *Sacred Acts, Sacred Spaces, Sacred Time*. Oxford: George Ronald, 1996.
———. *The Wisdom of the Mystic East: Suhrawardi and Platonic Orientalism*. Albany, NY: State University of New York Press, 2001.
Waldenfels, Hans. *Absolute Nothingness: Foundations for a Buddhist-Christian Dialogue*. New York: Paulist Press, 1980.
Walker, Theodore and Chandra Wickramasinghe. *The Big Bang and God: An Astro-Theology*. New York: Palgrave Macmillan, 2015.
Warburg, Margit, Annika Hvithamar and Moojan Momen (eds.). *Baha'i and Globalization*. Aarhus: Aarhus University Press, 2005.
Ward, Keith. *In Defense of the Soul*. Oxford: Oneworld, 1998.
———. *God, Chance and Necessity*. Oxford: Oneworld, 2009.
———. *Pascal's Fire: Scientific Faith and Religious Understanding*. Oxford: Oneworld, 2007.
Wargo, Robert. *The Logic of Nothingness: A Study of Nishida Kitaro*. Honolulu: University of Hawaii Press, 2005.
Warren, Marianne. *Unraveling the Enigma: Shirdi Sai Baba in the Light of Sufism*. New Delhi: Sterling Publishers, 2004.
Weintraub, David. *Religions and Extraterrestrial Life: How Will We Deal with It?* Basingstoke, UK: Springer Praxis Books, 2014.
Weisse, Wolfram, et al. (eds.). *Religions and Dialogue: International Approaches*. Muenster: Waxman, 2014.
Welsch, Wolfgang. *Vernunft. Die zeitgenössische Vernunftkritik und das Konzept der transversalen Vernunft*. Frankfurt: Suhrkamp, 1995.
White, Robert. "A Bahá'í Perspective on an Ecologically Sustainable Society." In *Worldviews and Ecology: Religion, Philosophy, and the Environment*. Edited by Mary Evelyn Tucker and John Grimm, 96–112. Maryknoll, NY: Orbis Books, 1994.
Whitehead, Alfred North. *Adventures of Ideas*. New York: Free Press, 1967.
———. *The Concept of Nature*. Cambridge: Cambridge University Press, 1993.
———. *The Function of Reason*. Boston: Beacon Press, 1929.
———. Immortality." In *The Philosophy of Alfred North Whitehead*. Edited by Paul Schilpp, 682–700. La Salle, IL: Open Court, 1991.
———. "Mathematics and the Good." In *The Philosophy of Alfred North Whitehead*. Edited by Paul Schilpp, 666–81. La Salle, IL: Open Court, 1991.
———. *Modes of Thought*. New York: Free Press, 1968.
———. *Process and Reality: An Essay in Cosmology*. Edited by D. R. Griffin and D. W. Sherburne. New York: Free Press, 1978.
———. *Religion in the Making*. New York: Fordham University Press, 1996.
———. *Science and the Modern World*. New York: Free Press, 1967.
———. *Symbolism: Its Meaning and Effect*. New York: Fordham University Press, 1985.
Wilber, Ken. *The Spectrum of Consciousness*. Wheaton, IL: Quest Books, 1993.
Wilber, Ken (ed.). *Quantum Questions: Mystical Writings of the World's Greatest Physicists*. Boston, MA: Shambala, 2001.
Wildman, Wesley. *In Our Own Image: Anthropomorphism, Apophaticism, and Ultimacy*. Oxford: Oxford University Press, 2017.
Wilkinson, David. *Science, Religion, and the Search for Extraterrestrial Intelligence*. Oxford: Oxford University Press, 2013.
Williams, Paul and Anthony Tribe. *Buddhist Thought: A Complete Introduction to the Indian Tradition*. New York: Routledge, 2000.
Willis, Jon. *All These Worlds Are Yours: The Scientific Search for Alien Life*. Yale: Yale University Press, 2016.

Witherington, III, Ben. *Jesus the Sage: The Pilgrimage of Wisdom*. Minneapolis: Fortress Press, 1994.
Wittenveen, H. J. *Universal Sufism*. Arcata, CA: Wild Earth Press, 2013.
Wong, Eva. *Taoism: An Essential Guide*. Boston, MA: Shambala, 1997.
Woodman, Ross. "Metaphor and Language of Revelation." *The Journal of Bahá'í Studies* 8, no. 1 (1997): 1–27.
Woods, Richard. *Meister Eckhart: Master of Mystics*. London: Continuum, 2011.
Woolley, Benjamin. *Virtual Worlds: A Journey in Hype and Hyperreality*. London: Penguin Books, 1994.
Xing, Guang. *The Concept of the Buddha: Its Evolution from Early Buddhism to the Trikāya Theory*. New York: Routledge, 2010.
Yagi, Saiichi and Leonard Swidler. *A Bridge to Buddhist-Christian Dialogue*. New York: Paulist Press, 1988.
Young, Garry and Monica Whitty. *Transcending Taboos: A Moral and Psychological Examination of Cyberspace*. London: Routledge, 2012.
Young, Robert. *Colonial Desire: Hybridity in Theory, Culture, and Race*. London: Routledge, 1995.
———. *Postcolonialism: A Very Short Introduction*. Oxford: Oxford University Press, 2003.
Ziolkowski, Eric (ed.). *A Museum of Faiths: Histories and Legacies of the 1893 World's Parliament of Religions*. Oxford: Oxford University Press, 1993.
Zohar, Danah and Ian Marshall. *The Quantum Society: Mind, Physics, and the New Social Vision*. New York: Quill, 1994.

INDEX

'Abdu'l-Bahá 21, 24n27, 99, 101–103, 107–110, 115n35, 129n30
Abe, Masao 130
Advaita Vedanta 22, 38–39, 100
'ahad 114
'ahirah 194
AI(s) (artificial intelligence) 1n2, 19, 173, 181
Akko (Acre) 23n27, 105, 107, 201, 204
al-bada' 100, 161
algorithm 19, 182–83
al-haqq 74, 147
Allah 22, 35, 39, 114, 145–46
al-rahim 22
al-rahman 22
Amida Buddha 39
apophasis 56, 62, 116, 202, 206–10, 212, 214
apophatic subtraction 117
apophaticism 44, 61, 79, 130, 190
'aql 54
Aristotle 31n16, 128n20
'ashiru 194
atman 71n14, 101, 147
Aurobindo, Sri 15n21, 139
avatar(s) 96, 139, 147, 147n65, 150n82, 180, 208
axial age 15, 15n20, 18, 18n44, 43, 137–38, 194n26
  new 15, 15n22, 16, 19, 43, 89n60, 112, 112n10, 137, 139–40, 160, 194n26, 209, 214
axis/axes of pluralism 103, 110, 112–13, 115–18, 120, 142, 179
  horizontal 172
  vertical 97, 109, 114

Bábi-Bahá'í religions 15, 15n21, 140n30
Báb, the 39n73, 105
Bahá'í Faith 15, 23n27, 48n56, 54n13, 69, 70, 75n47, 88, 89n60, 95, 98–100, 105–6, 139, 162, 171, 173–74, 201, 203
Bahá'í religion 3, 14, 77–78, 106, 109, 111, 139–42
Bahá'í scripture 21, 24, 112, 112n13, 112n14, 113, 143–44, 159n46, 191, 203, 211

Bahá'í writings 5, 8, 8n36, 22, 24–26, 30, 44–46, 53–54, 54n13, 60n59, 69–76, 85, 89, 94n13, 95, 99n43, 100n49, 102n60, 114–15, 117–19, 147, 151, 158n40, 160–61, 163–65, 171, 174–75, 175n39, 178, 186n114, 189, 193n21, 198, 203, 208
Bahá'u'lláh 8, 45, 65n90, 71
batin 119, 119n56, 147
becoming, the 17n22, 18, 121n68, 129n30, 132, 135, 141, 146, 204, 208–9, 213–14
beings 62, 129n30, 145, 149n76, 154, 156, 160, 162, 164, 166, 177, 191, 196, 205, 208, 210, 212
  spiritual 46, 118, 158–59, 162–65, 167, 170–71, 173, 175, 178, 186
Besant, Annie 106, 108n26, 109
bifurcation 77–78, 93, 102
Big Five, the 3, 23n27
Bisharat 194
bodhisattva 55n18, 158, 176
Book of Laws (*Kitab-i Aqdas*) 194
Bracken, Joseph 111n6
brahman 33, 35, 38–39, 48, 57n27, 71n14, 74n39, 101, 120n58, 143, 147
Browne, E. G. 78, 79n69
Buddha(s) 5n17, 15, 25n39, 33, 35, 39, 55n18, 65n90, 72, 96, 114, 120n58, 138, 144–47, 148n69, 148n73, 149n77, 150n83, 158, 180, 204, 208
Buddha-nature 138, 145–46, 176
Buddha-land 158
Buddhism 3, 22, 46, 54, 57n27, 64n86, 96–97, 103–4, 130, 138, 143, 145, 145n55, 146, 158, 176, 180, 203
Byzantine Empire 104

Camus, Albert 158
caruna 22
Chan (Buddhism) 138
chaosmos 86n44
Chinese religions 5

Christ 5n17, 39, 96, 96n26, 99n46, 105, 114, 120n58, 141, 145–47, 148n73, 150n86, 151n86, 157, 167n106
Christianity 3–4, 6, 32, 33n30, 34, 45, 48, 63n77, 89n57, 96–98, 104, 115n35, 130, 139, 141n33, 143–45, 145n55, 148n69, 149n77, 157, 203
Christology 57n26, 147n65
civilization 6, 15–16, 93–94, 99, 105, 156, 170, 175, 175n38, 201, 208, 213
cleaving of the heaven 97
Cobb Jr., John B. 37–38, 78n65, 111n5, 130, 145n55, 148n69, 167n106, 184n104
coercion 59, 178
coherence 4, 37, 49, 54, 54n13, 56, 82, 133n59, 144, 205
coincidentia oppositorum 148
coinhabitation 58, 135, 142–44, 149–52, 170, 175–76, 191, 199, 204
coinherence 63, 120, 133, 133n59, 138, 142–44, 147, 148n69, 149n76, 151, 170, 181, 191n14, 197, 205
community 16–17, 19–20, 27, 29, 33, 70, 96, 105, 107, 109, 149n77
compassion 22, 55, 58–60, 63, 65, 74, 85, 121, 146, 151, 158, 162, 207
composition 30, 43–44, 128, 144n52
Confucianism 89n57, 103, 138, 180
Confucius 15, 149n77
consciousness 2, 6, 8, 13, 15, 18, 44, 55–56, 63, 65, 72, 76, 79, 151, 162–66, 170, 181–84, 191
  interstellar 137, 157, 159, 208, 214
  new axial 16, 22, 89, 111–12, 139, 166, 191, 203
  religious 15n20, 16, 79, 152, 162, 170, 194n26, 208–9, 211, 214
  transreligious 137, 140
  universal 8, 15–16, 34n38, 94, 171
Consequent Nature (of God) 39n73, 58, 71, 120, 154, 205
continuity 7n27, 27, 54, 106, 113, 115, 117, 141, 204, 209
contrasting 60, 63, 70, 73n33, 101, 133, 193
convergence(s) 14, 119–20, 146, 151, 156, 163–65, 167, 171n15, 184
conviviality 16, 20, 59, 79, 93, 103, 105, 107, 109, 115, 121, 135, 142, 152, 159, 163–64, 173, 194–5
Copernican turn 155
cosmic epoch 154, 176

cosmos 1, 18–19, 49, 129n30, 153, 155, 157, 161, 164, 172–73, 175, 184, 205, 208–9, 214
cosmology 6, 16, 137, 154, 160, 160n52, 205
creative transformation 2, 26, 59, 71, 120, 133, 167n106, 184, 184n104
creativity 38, 54, 58–59, 61, 63–64, 71, 84, 91
cycle of love 59–60, 86, 145n55, 170n13, 184n104, 197, 198n58, 206

daena 5
dao 5, 35, 74, 120, 143
dao jiao 5, 96
Daoism 89n57, 96, 103–4, 138, 158, 161, 180, 210
Dawning place of Remembrance 195
De Pace Fidei 50n66, 103
deconstruction 3n7, 27n58, 82, 84, 86, 88, 90, 184
Deleuze, Gilles 7n30, 84, 111n3, 135
denigration 22, 27–28, 65–66, 95, 186, 192, 207
devas 145
dharma 5, 35, 40, 55, 138, 146, 150
dharmakaya 33, 38, 74n39, 143, 145–47, 148n69
dhat 39n73, 71, 71n14, 146
Din-al Ilahi 104, 139
discourse 2–4, 6–9, 27, 30, 32, 48, 50, 53–54, 56, 69, 75, 77, 82–84, 86–89, 103, 111–12, 119, 143–44, 147, 153, 170, 180, 182, 189
  transreligious 7–9, 125–35, 137, 159, 167, 181, 208–9, 211, 213
dispensation 72n26, 96n26, 97, 99, 115, 141n33, 172n19, 203
divergence(s) 16, 25, 34, 60, 69–79, 83–5, 87, 89, 105, 120–21, 148, 151, 159, 174, 182, 183n95, 196
divine attribute(s) 22, 90n63, 113n17, 143, 161, 166, 177, 184n105, 187, 208, 210
Divine Manifold 63, 74, 74n39, 185, 190, 193n22, 204, 206–7, 209–10, 212, 214
Dresser, Horatio 108
Dualism 73, 84, 173n25, 209
Du Bois, W. E. B. 106

Earth, the 1, 9, 14, 16, 18–19, 83, 111, 131, 135, 153, 155, 156n34, 157, 159, 160n52, 162, 164, 165n87, 166, 169, 171, 171n15, 173, 175–76, 181, 191, 194, 203, 208, 211

Einstein, Albert 155
emanation 22, 26, 44, 93, 170, 191, 197
emergence 6, 13, 18, 98, 121, 161, 164–65, 170, 194, 196
emptiness 38, 85, 148, 195
enfolding 185–86, 191, 209
enlightenment 2, 4, 25n39, 46, 46n36, 54, 60n59, 72, 76, 138, 214
entanglement 18
environment 113, 153, 165n92, 166, 176, 181
equality 16, 22–24, 26–28, 73, 97, 99, 106, 108, 110, 113, 115, 117, 143, 201
eschatology 157
essentialism 24, 40, 79, 84n24, 127, 130, 190, 191n14, 213
euangelion 194
Eurocentrism 4, 6, 82
event 1, 18, 60, 72–73, 90, 94–95, 97, 100n51, 108n26, 110, 114–15, 121, 139–44, 149–50, 153, 179, 203–4, 206
Everett III, Hugh 34
evolution 13, 18, 22–23, 26, 28, 38, 44, 56, 70, 117, 153, 155–56, 159, 161–62, 163, 165–67, 170, 175, 181, 183–84, 191, 194, 203
exclusivism 30–31, 34n39, 35, 40, 62, 69–70, 83n22, 84n24, 86–87, 87n50, 88, 88n56, 89, 89n58, 101, 121, 140, 159, 177n53, 207, 211
exobiology 156
exotheology 157
experimentation 128, 131–32, 134, 157

fa-lamma balagha al-amr 194
fallacy 3, 189, 212
  of essentialist pluralism 189
  of misplaced concreteness 3
fanaticism 1, 14, 109
Farmer, Sarah 103, 106–8
feeling(s) 2, 5n13, 6, 8, 13, 53, 99, 128n20, 129n30, 175n38, 181, 206
Ferrer, Jorge 48, 48n56, 49, 55n21, 56, 57n30, 70n8, 98n35, 111n5, 172n20
field(s) 3–5, 7, 9, 17, 30–32, 40, 46, 55, 69–70, 77, 94–95, 97–98, 113, 121, 126, 155, 167, 179–80
  of a divine matrix 135n78, 142, 159, 167, 174, 178
  of energy or consciousness 55
  of exclusivism, inclusivism and pluralism 30–31, 86, 88–89, 89n58, 121, 140, 172, 191n14

  of existence 85
  non-personal 55
finality 27–28, 33, 70, 95, 163
flow(s) 6–7, 44, 100, 104, 128, 131, 138, 140, 162, 176, 197–98, 212
  multireligious 7
fold, the 84, 180
fourfold dilemma 114, 117–18
fractal(s) 47n48, 127
fragmentation 18, 26, 84n24, 127n14, 133
fulfillment 19, 33, 55n18, 56, 60, 95–96, 100, 141, 141n35, 142, 142n36, 143, 149, 149n75, 149n76, 161, 163, 172, 174, 179, 179n73, 185, 193n21, 197, 202
future
  of humanity 2, 8, 16, 107n26, 169, 175, 180, 185n106
  of religion(s) 4, 5n13, 8, 8n34, 9, 30, 48–49, 98n35, 169–87, 189, 213

Gibran, Khalil v
glory of God 105
God
  creative nature of 58
  transpersonal image of 73
Godhead 39, 39n73, 45, 50n67, 71n14, 103, 145
Good, the 22, 44, 61, 93
Green Acre 103, 106–10
Griffin, David Ray 37
Guru Nanak 112n10, 139

Hafez 45
hahut 71n14, 147–48, 186n114
haqiqah-i haqiqat 198
harmony 20, 22, 37, 64, 117–18, 138–39, 148, 165n90, 171n14, 176, 179, 198, 201
heart 6, 55, 72, 79, 96, 96n26, 170, 195, 195n35, 212
Hebrew Bible 97, 113n19, 151
Heidegger, Martin 39
Heim, Mark 32n25, 33
Hellenism 98, 158
hen 35
Herron, George 106
Hick, John 33n28, 35–36, 36n51, 38, 56, 70n9, 72n23, 75n47, 78n65, 85, 111n4
Hinduism 3, 48, 57n27, 88, 96, 103–5, 105n15, 112n10, 130, 139, 192n18, 203
ho logos tou theou 147
homo deus 182

horizon(s) 9, 18, 41, 53–54, 63, 94, 97, 99, 121, 125, 130, 137–39, 143, 153, 156, 158, 160–62, 169, 178, 197, 208
   transreligious 7, 139, 144, 184
Huxley, Aldous 47
hybridity 17n38, 34, 82, 96n26
hypostases 44

ibadat khana 104
Ibn ʿArabi, Muhammad 45–46, 113n17, 146
identity(s) 1, 24, 27, 29–31, 46, 48, 75, 83, 88, 96, 127, 129, 133, 145, 160, 177, 194, 204, 206–8, 213
   hybrid 139
   minority 83
   pantheistic 47
   religious 9, 49, 66, 74, 132–33, 177
   spiritual 96
idolatry 22, 64, 146
image(s) 8, 13, 46, 55, 73, 78, 97, 115, 117, 165, 175, 186, 194–95, 197–98
   of God 46
   transpersonal 73
imagination 1n2, 16, 17n38, 25, 45–46, 57, 62–63, 72–73, 78, 88, 91, 104, 144, 167, 177, 190, 210–11
immanence 7n30, 21, 37n55, 46, 49, 132, 161, 183n97, 196, 202, 207
   mutual 40, 58, 61, 63, 64n86, 74, 84n24, 85n32, 88, 118–19, 127n12, 142, 145n55, 153, 161, 171, 185, 197, 198n58, 205–6, 213–14
immortality 176
impersona(e) 36
impermanence 18, 73n31, 85, 86n44, 90, 94, 95n23, 102, 133–34, 161, 170, 175–76
Inayat Khan 50n65, 109
incarnation(s) 96, 146, 150n82, 157, 180, 208
inclusivism 5n13, 30–31, 35, 37n55, 40, 56, 62, 69–70, 78n63, 79, 86–89, 89n58, 105n15, 107n26, 110, 121, 140, 171n17, 176n48, 177n53, 190, 191n14, 207
incompatibility 83, 113n16
indeterminacy 39n73, 155
indetermination 39n73, 63, 114, 210
   apophatic 57n28
India 48, 88, 104, 109, 139
indifference 53, 61, 63–64, 66, 85n32, 102, 110, 117, 119, 125, 145, 148, 195, 197–99, 207–9, 213
in/differentiation 195
indistinction 73, 96, 119

infinity 21, 119, 158, 161, 173, 196
initial aim 166
insistence 40, 61–64, 66, 72, 74–75, 79, 85, 90, 115, 139–40, 143, 163, 167, 190, 196, 198, 207
integration 28, 96–97, 131, 138, 169, 178, 181, 186, 203
intensification 6, 129
intensity 46, 64, 77, 100, 117, 179
intercommunication 85, 87n50, 154
intermezzo 84
ʿirfan 54, 102n60
Ishvara 39
Islam 3, 22, 96, 104, 130, 139, 143–44, 146
Islamic Caliphate 104

Jainism 103, 176
Jamal-i Burujirdi 90, 110
Jaspers, Karl 15, 209
Jessup, Henry 105–6
Jesus 72, 144–46, 152, 159n46, 160n48, 167n106, 208
Judaism 3, 3n7, 96, 98, 104, 158, 203
juncture 78, 93, 102, 125

Kabbalah 45
Kabir 139
Kali 139
Kant, Immanuel 36
khora 85, 85n32, 127, 154
kiblah 107
Kitāb-i Aqdas 194
Knitter, Paul 33, 33n28, 56, 72n23, 93, 111n7, 130
Krishna 65n90, 83n22, 96, 99, 99n46, 101, 120n58, 147, 149n77, 204, 208
Krishnamurti, Jiddu 109

lahut 71n14, 147, 148n69, 148n73, 178n64, 183n64, 186n114
landscape 3, 14, 47, 94–95, 97, 121, 137, 157, 160, 171, 191
   mystical 48
   noetic 58
   polyphilic 132
Laozi 76n53, 96, 149, 180
level(s) 17–19, 25, 31, 43–44, 49, 59, 78, 81–82
   of apophatic indifferentiation 119
   of existence 46
   of unification and diversification 60, 189
   of worlds 19
Lewis, David 34

INDEX   249

life
  divine 102
  immortal 115
  nonorganic 174
  ocean of 108
  spiritual 17, 47, 54, 127, 129, 185n106, 199
liqa' Allah 171
logos 89n59, 143, 147
Lord Lao 96, 148, 180
love of the manifold 61, 210

Madhyamika 46
magnitude 18, 73, 144, 153, 186
  cosmic 154, 169, 177, 191, 194
Mahayana 55n18, 138, 145–46, 176
Mani (Prophet) 5n17, 96
Manichaeism 5, 104
Manifestation(s) 4, 25, 25n39, 61, 64, 72, 74–75, 114–15, 119–120, 138n8, 141n33, 142n37, 147, 147n65, 148, 149, 149n76, 149n77, 150–51, 151n88, 166, 166n99, 167n105, 172, 179n73, 180, 194n26, 197, 208
mashriq al-adhkar 195
materialism 18, 155
  scientific 173n25
matrix 32, 69, 87n48, 88, 88n53, 89n56, 97, 164–65
  divine 135n78, 142, 159, 167, 174–75, 178
mazhar-i ilahi 147, 151
medium of intercommunication 85, 154
Mehar Baba 139
Meister Eckhart 39, 45, 50n65, 50n67, 71n14, 127n12, 134n61
metaphysics 36, 158
mind (*nous*) 44, 48, 143
minority 3–4, 71, 83, 88, 118n49, 135
mirror 21, 25, 48, 59, 71, 74, 77n61, 85, 94, 145n55, 148, 151, 166, 187, 189
  of the apophatic God 45, 147–48
  of the divine Spirit 57n26, 166, 189
mixture 39, 70, 97, 143
monism 22, 37n35, 71n14, 73, 81, 84, 101n55, 138
monocentrism 39
monotheism 24, 138
Moses 65n90, 72n26, 96
movement
  cosmic 19, 161
  of cosmic evolution 18
  creative-responsive 59
  interspiritual 98, 173–74
  mystical 54

pluralistic 126
polyphilic 119
  of subtractive affirmation 64, 118
  transreligious 44, 119, 121, 140, 151, 180
Muhammad (prophet) 72, 144–45, 147, 194, 202, 204
Muhammad Akbar 104, 139
Muhammad Reality 146
Muhammadan light 147
Mulla Sadra 45
Mulamadhyamikakarika 46
Multiplicity 1
  polyphilic 119, 163
  transreligious 135
multiverse 34, 148, 154–59, 182, 209
mutuality 1, 16, 18, 33–34, 39, 58–59, 63, 65–66, 83, 88, 102, 108, 112–13, 116, 170, 181, 185–86, 196–98, 206, 213–14
Mystery of Distinction and Unity 111–21, 125, 137
Mystery 50, 53, 63, 66, 72, 75, 89, 143, 182, 190–91
  Apophatic 56, 64, 120n58, 176, 185
  of consciousness 6, 163, 164, 165, 182, 183
  divine 25, 63, 116
  insisting 65
  non-dual 185
  polyphilic 134, 184, 191n17, 195
  of Reality/God 25, 50, 147, 198
  transreligious 153
mysticism 43–51, 53–57, 71, 116n19, 190n12

NAACP 106
Nabi 2, 76, 83, 86, 144, 172, 175, 178
nafs 71
Nagarjuna 46, 47n41, 64n86, 71
Native peoples of America 179
nature(s)
  apophatic 24, 35, 47n48, 118, 162, 172
  apophatic-polyphilic 138
  brahman-atman 101, 147
  Buddha 33, 35, 138, 145–46, 176
  Theophanic 162
negotiation(s) 53, 93, 98, 102, 112, 118
Neoplatonism 45n26
Nestorianism 104, 147n65
Nexus 94, 198
  entirely living 198
New Age 7, 49, 108n26
New Testament 105, 141n33, 177n53
Nicolas of Cusa 45, 46n36, 64n86, 103, 159n46, 199n72

Nikaya tradition 138, 145
Nirmanakaya 145
nirvana 33–34, 91n65, 145, 158
Nishida, Kitaro 85n32, 130
non-difference 45, 49, 50, 61, 102, 120, 132, 196
nondualism 22, 45–46
nothingness 44, 58, 127n12, 199
nous 44, 45n17, 48, 143
novelty 27, 58, 61, 73–74, 94–98, 100, 105–10, 113–15, 117, 121, 130–32, 140–41, 169, 174, 176–80, 185–86, 193
  diachrony of 114
  vertical 98, 106, 110, 172n18, 177, 185, 193
  vertical axis of 108, 191
nur muhammadiyyah 147

ocean of God 1–199
Old Testament 97
Omega Point 19
One (*hen*), the 35
Oneness 29, 41, 45, 47, 53, 71, 79, 81n2, 82, 86, 106, 114, 118, 120, 134, 140, 149, 177, 185–86, 190
  apophatic 119, 127n12
  of (all) religions 81n2, 106
  of truth 118
open whole 133
openness 9, 56, 110, 170, 196
  radical 9
organism(s) 21, 58–59, 84, 94, 120–21, 153, 156, 166, 172–73, 176–77, 181
origami 84
oscillation 60, 129, 134, 145, 153–54, 178, 181, 186
  apophatic-cataphatic 32
  apophatic-polyphilic 135, 190
otherness 33, 71, 84
  new dualism of 84
  of religions 33

Panikkar, Raymond 48
Pantheism 45, 73
paradigm(s) 17–19, 131, 138, 156, 158–60
  of unity and plurality 9, 111
paradox(es) 2, 19, 41, 115, 155, 161, 177
Parliament of Religions 99n42, 103, 109
participation 48–49, 57, 61, 98n35, 175n38
St. Paul (Apostle) 96
Peace 8, 14–16, 20, 22–23, 30, 48, 59, 63, 65, 75–76, 78, 86, 93, 99, 103, 105–8, 110, 134, 138, 141, 162, 169, 170, 172, 175, 180, 189

perennialism 47
persona(e) 36
persuasion 17, 59, 82, 104, 125, 138
Philosophy 40, 43–44, 46, 57, 100, 111, 153, 154, 159, 180, 183
Plenitude 23, 113, 154–55
pleroma 56, 93, 174, 186, 190
Plotinus 44–45, 48, 71, 116
Pluralism 29–92
  apophatic 53–66, 70, 71, 74, 79, 85, 89, 90, 116, 125, 167, 169, 172, 186, 190–91, 193
  horizontal 95–97, 105–6, 141
  of pluralisms 81–91, 93, 97, 99, 158–60, 163, 172–73
  polyphilic 53–66, 71, 74, 79, 85, 89–90, 116, 125, 167, 171–72, 186, 190–91, 193
  religious 2–7, 9, 16–17, 19–20, 29–41, 43, 48–49, 53, 61, 63, 65, 69–70, 73, 75–79, 81, 83, 90, 94, 99, 109, 112, 115–16, 121, 125–26, 130, 135, 137, 158–59, 162, 164, 167, 169, 175, 179, 181–82, 186, 189, 194
  transreligious 119, 139
  vertical 44, 93–102, 105, 140–41, 167
plurality 9, 11, 13–20, 23–24, 26, 29, 41, 43, 49, 50–51, 54, 56, 69–70, 77, 83, 84, 86, 88, 94–95, 97–98, 111, 116, 127, 135, 141, 154, 174, 177, 184, 186, 189
pluralization 32, 56
  differential-relational 32
  monocentric-polycentric 32
Poet of the World 59, 197
Polycentrism 34, 39
polyphilia 57, 61, 64, 65, 66, 72, 85, 111, 116, 121, 186, 187, 189, 190
postcolonialism 81, 82, 181
poststructuralism 3, 81, 82, 84
pratitya-samutpada 158
pratyekabudha 138
Primordial Nature (of God) 58, 120, 154, 166
process(es) 3–4, 9, 18, 21, 23–24, 26–27, 37–39, 44, 54–66, 72, 74–79, 82, 84, 88, 94, 102, 114, 116, 121, 132–33, 135, 141, 153–54, 156, 161–64, 167, 169, 178, 194, 197
  transreligious 60, 83, 127, 130, 132–33, 135, 138, 143, 167
process thought 4, 9, 37, 38, 40, 48, 57–58, 62, 82, 84, 121, 161, 163, 191
progression 7, 9, 16, 26–27, 70–1, 76, 113, 173, 178–79

prophet(s) 6, 16, 96, 112, 144–46, 192
Pseudo–Dionysius the Areopagite 45
Psyche 44

Qur'an 22, 90, 114, 120, 145, 150, 194

Rahner, Karl 45n18
raj'a 143
Ramakrishna 8, 15, 32, 106, 109, 139
Rasul 144
rationalism 54
Real, the 35, 105
reality 5, 8, 15, 20, 21–23, 35–38, 45–47, 55, 61–62, 64–66, 71, 73, 82, 85, 90, 101, 117, 120, 126, 130, 133–35, 144–48, 150, 152, 154, 161–62, 175–76, 183, 190, 195–99
  ultimate 8, 15, 20–23, 35, 36–38, 43–47, 49, 53, 55, 57, 62, 65, 70–71, 73, 85, 91, 98, 102, 126, 139, 145–48, 154, 158, 163, 167, 180, 190
realm(s) 4, 16, 18–19, 44, 49, 104, 154, 157, 165, 176, 184, 197
reconciliation 84, 91, 93–94, 98–99, 102–3, 114, 119, 120, 134, 185, 189, 192
reductionism 7, 56, 79, 84, 179, 184
relationality 2, 19, 34, 38–39, 40–41, 58–61, 63, 66, 83, 86, 88, 117, 128–29, 132, 138, 155, 157–59
relativism 25, 30, 35, 40, 46, 49, 53–54, 56, 64, 71–74, 79, 82–83, 85, 87, 90, 97–98, 102, 116, 118, 161, 183, 190
relativity 30, 34, 43, 45–46, 48–49, 53, 64, 73, 75, 85, 112–13, 116, 118, 130, 155, 157, 183, 193
  of religious truth 30, 43, 45, 113, 116, 193
religio 5
religion(s) 4–8, 14–15, 18, 23, 25n39, 27–37, 43, 45, 48–49, 65, 76, 94–96, 100, 104–6, 111, 121, 139, 140–42, 157–59, 162–63, 167, 169–87, 193
religiosity 2, 4, 8, 19, 96, 163, 165–67, 169–70, 172–74, 176–78
Religionswissenschaft 4, 125
Remembrance 28, 58, 61, 65, 72, 179, 195
resonance 15, 49, 53, 129, 130, 133–34, 137, 143, 145–46, 153, 159, 171, 177
revelation 9, 14, 21, 24–25, 27, 46, 48–49, 62, 64–65, 70, 72–73, 75–77, 93–97, 100, 106–10, 112–15, 119–20, 131, 134, 139–42, 144, 146–51, 166, 172, 177–78, 180–81, 190–96

revolution 155, 182
  transhuman 50, 53, 63, 66, 72, 75, 89, 143, 182, 190–91
rhizome 84
Rose, Kenneth 5n13, 31n16, 56, 57n27–28, 61n66, 63n78, 70n8, 72n23, 87n49, 88n56, 98n35, 131n45, 171n15, 172n21
Rumi, Jalal ad–Din 45, 165

sage(s) 106
salvation 18, 22, 30–36, 39, 48–49, 57–58, 100, 138–39, 146, 149, 151, 157–58, 161, 195
sambhogakaya 39, 146
samsara 46, 91, 146, 158
sanatana dharma 100, 106
satchitananda 9
Sathya Sai Baba 139
Schmidt-Leukel, Perry 87, 99, 126–28, 130, 143, 146, 149
Schuon, Frithjof 47
science 176
scripture(s) 79, 112, 114, 150
Second Vatican Council 48
self, the 25
self-centeredness 35, 85
self-communication 164
self-identity 14, 121
self-manifestation 21, 116
self-realization 166
self-reference 30, 39
self-transcendence 94
Seven Valleys 8, 44, 64, 120, 186
Shakyamuni Buddha 145, 147
Sharma, Arvind 88
Shaykh Ahmad al-Ahsa'I 24
Shirdi Sai Baba 15, 112, 139
Shiva 35
Shoghi Effendi 65n90, 79, 102, 106, 112–13, 135, 140, 151, 161–62, 171–72, 174, 178, 185, 192–95, 198
Siddhartha Gautama 146
Sikhism 3, 96, 139, 149
silence 46, 49, 53–55, 61, 64, 73, 130–32, 158
singularity 19, 78, 111, 181
scepticism 55, 98
skillful means 119, 138
Smith, Huston 47
Smith, Wilfred Cantwell 5n14, 16n27, 24n32, 84n24, 138n8
Son (of God) 144
soul 44, 120, 139, 142, 178

speed 26, 75, 125, 165, 178, 185, 191
  spiritual 26, 165, 178n68
spirit 14, 18, 25–27, 57, 65, 74, 89, 103–6, 109, 143–44, 49, 152, 159, 161–62, 165–66, 173–76, 178, 183, 186, 189, 192–94, 197–98
spiritual station 26, 185–87
spirituality 4, 49, 69, 98, 110, 121, 125, 160, 172, 180
strategies 50, 83, 130, 133, 143, 170, 174, 175
  transreligious 130, 133
substantialization 34
sub-stare 83
substitution 28, 65, 95–96, 141, 186, 189
succession 142
Sufism 23, 45
Suhrawardi, Yahya 45
sukham sukham kal 176
sunyata 38, 57, 120, 134, 145
superiority 5, 27–28, 35–37, 65, 95, 104, 110, 113–14, 117–18, 147, 151, 185–86, 193
superposition 115–16, 119, 139, 179, 189, 193
supersession 27, 28, 65, 95, 100, 185–86
surah 114
surrationality 54, 86, 116, 129
survival 20, 135, 142, 157, 169–70
Suzuki, T. D. 106, 109
Symbolism (book) 94, 153, 178, 181
syncretism 5, 121, 129
synthesis 5, 7, 18, 58, 60, 69, 73, 94, 98, 100, 111, 119, 132, 140, 147, 149–50, 166, 169, 179
Syria 23, 105, 107

tat tvam asi 71
Teilhard de Chardin, Pierre 13, 19, 163
Thatagatagarbha 138
Theism 45, 49, 71, 73, 90, 96, 101
theology
  mystical 45
theophany 114, 119, 147, 170
theopoetics 61, 135
Theosophy 24, 103, 108
Tillich, Paul 39
togetherness 59–60, 79, 84–85, 110, 116–17, 133, 143, 176, 186
trans (in transreligious), the 125
transcendence 8, 18, 49, 94–95, 130, 158, 161, 167, 176, 187, 196–97
transcendentalism 24, 108
transculturalization 127
transhumanism 173, 181

transformation 2, 4, 7, 14–22, 26, 35, 49, 55, 59–61, 70, 72, 90–91, 96, 99, 106–7, 120, 128–29, 130–31, 133–34, 143–44, 151–52, 158–59, 167, 171, 174–76, 181, 184–85, 194
transgression 33, 173, 180
transition 84–85, 87, 121, 131–32, 167, 196
translucency 60, 175, 196
transmigration 139
transmutation 133–35, 145–46, 152, 159, 180
transreligiosity 169
trinity 38–39, 96, 98, 133, 157
Truth (Reality/God) 48, 185

ultimacy 38, 39
ultimate, the 18, 36, 38–40, 44, 62, 85, 143, 147–48, 170, 180, 198
ultimates, the 38–39
unification 8, 15, 19–20, 26, 32–33, 35, 38, 60, 75, 77, 82–86, 88–89, 94, 97–98, 114, 117, 133–34, 154, 159, 161, 169, 172, 175–76, 179, 180, 182, 185, 189, 197–99
unio mystica 47
union 99, 116, 174
uniqueness 26, 35, 47, 64–65, 78, 89, 94, 100, 113–15, 118, 121, 129, 134, 167, 174, 177–78, 185, 190, 195
unison 61, 65–66, 83, 93, 113–15, 148, 163, 167, 174–76, 178, 198, 199
unity 154, 156–57, 159, 162–64, 167, 169–75, 178, 180–81, 183–86, 189–95
unity of reality 81, 85, 126, 144, 159, 178, 194
unity in diversity 70, 71, 117
universe(s)
  of discourse 3, 86, 112, 143–44, 153, 180
universality
  interstellar 137
unknowability 36, 39, 46, 53, 61
unknowing 54, 132, 134
unsaying 47, 63

valuation 16, 25, 38, 53, 58, 60, 64, 77, 120, 141, 167, 171
value 18, 30, 32, 48, 53, 56, 59, 60, 76, 88, 95, 111, 113, 115, 132, 134–35, 141, 155, 157, 161, 172, 175, 177, 180–81, 192–93
variation 8, 19, 31, 50, 61, 82, 89, 116, 119, 120, 163, 178, 186, 197
variety 15, 25, 48, 82, 104, 139, 156, 189
Vedanta 32, 56, 99–101, 105, 109, 111, 139
Vedas 8, 23, 35, 96, 105, 109, 133–34, 145, 177

Vedic religion 97, 158
verticality 100
violence 13, 14, 20, 23, 27–30, 55–56, 59, 69, 89, 93, 171, 178
virtuality 19
virtue 22, 25, 27, 85, 90, 96, 99, 105, 138, 143, 166, 177, 187
Vishnu 96, 101
vision 4, 15, 16, 19, 32, 34–35, 37, 39, 48–49, 58–59, 61, 76–78, 98–100, 104, 109, 118, 120–21, 129, 131, 139, 144, 150, 155, 159, 165, 169–70, 172–74, 176, 179, 181–82, 184–86, 195–96
Vivekananda, Swami 32, 99–101, 103, 105–6, 109, 111, 139

wahdat al-wujud 45
warfare 1, 69
Whitehead, Alfred North 3, 4n10, 6, 9, 14, 24, 37–40, 46, 47n42, 57–59, 62n76, 64, 71

wholeness 9, 18, 133–34, 180–81
Will (of God) 39, 198
Wisdom (divine) 161–62
Word (of God) 39, 74, 118, 137, 141, 145–46, 148, 151
world(s) 1–2, 8–9, 14–15, 18–24, 26–27, 36, 38–39, 44–45, 49–50, 55, 60, 63, 65, 69, 73, 94, 120, 125, 131, 157, 181, 184, 195–98
world-consciousness 56
World Soul (*psyche*) 44

xenology 156

Yahweh 35, 39

zahir 115, 119
Zen 47, 50, 64, 130, 138
Zoroaster 5, 72, 96, 114, 138, 149–50
Zoroastrianism 3, 5